Privilege
and
Scandal

ALSO BY JANET GLEESON

NONFICTION

The Arcanum

The Moneymaker

FICTION

The Grenadillo Box

The Serpent in the Garden

The Thief Taker

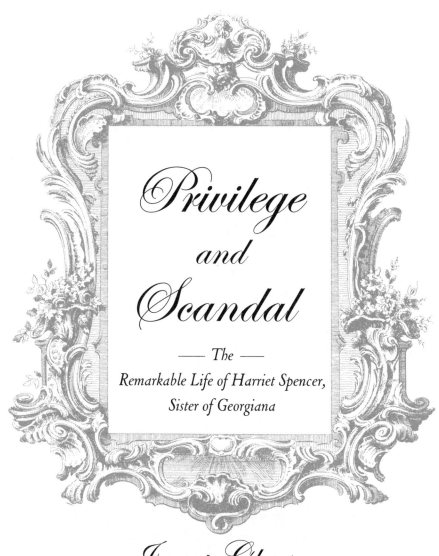

Privilege
and
Scandal

—— The ——
Remarkable Life of Harriet Spencer,
Sister of Georgiana

Janet Gleeson

CROWN PUBLISHERS

NEW YORK

Published in the United States by Crown Publishers, an imprint of the
Crown Publishing Group, a division of Random House, Inc., New York.
www.crownpublishing.com

CROWN is a trademark and the Crown colophon is a registered trademark
of Random House, Inc.

Originally published as *An Aristocratic Affair: The Life of Georgiana's Sister, Harriet Spencer,
Countess of Bessborough,* by Bantam Press, a division of Transworld Publishers,
a division of Random House Group Limited, London, in 2006.

Library of Congress Cataloging-in-Publication Data
Gleeson, Janet.
Privilege and scandal: the remarkable life of Harriet Spencer, sister of
Georgiana / Janet Gleeson. — 1st ed.
p. cm.
Includes bibliographical references and index.
1. Bessborough, Henrietta Frances Spencer Ponsonby, Countess of,
1761–1821. 2. Granville, Granville Leveson Gower, Earl, 1773–1846.
3. Great Britain — Social life and customs — 19th century. 4. Great Britain —
Social life and customs — 18th century. 5. Nobility — England — Biography.
6. Gower family. I. Title. II. Title. Remarkable life of Harriet
Spencer, sister of Georgiana.
DA522.B4G54 2007
942.07'3092 — dc22 2006039186

ISBN 978-0-307-38197-2

Printed in the United States of America

Design by Lauren Dong

10 9 8 7 6 5 4 3 2 1

First U.S. Edition

For Paul and my children
Lucy, Bee, and James

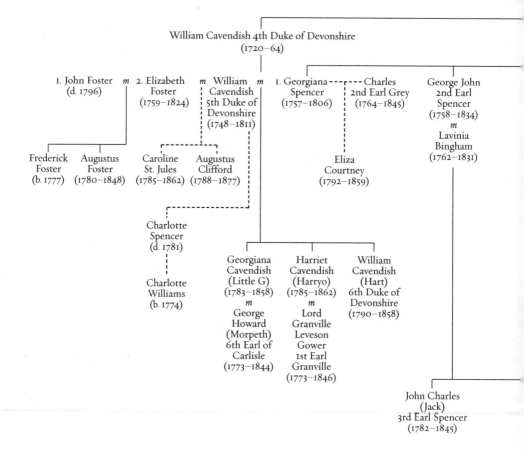

William Cavendish 4th Duke of Devonshire
(1720–64)

1. John Foster (d. 1796)	*m* 2. Elizabeth Foster (1759–1824)	*m* William Cavendish 5th Duke of Devonshire (1748–1811)	*m* 1. Georgiana Spencer (1757–1806) - - - Charles 2nd Earl Grey (1764–1845)	George John 2nd Earl Spencer (1758–1834) *m* Lavinia Bingham (1762–1831)

Frederick Foster (b. 1777)   Augustus Foster (1780–1848)   Caroline St. Jules (1785–1862)   Augustus Clifford (1788–1877)

Eliza Courtney (1792–1859)

Charlotte Spencer (d. 1781)

Charlotte Williams (b. 1774)

Georgiana Cavendish (Little G) (1783–1858) *m* George Howard (Morpeth) 6th Earl of Carlisle (1773–1844)

Harriet Cavendish (Harryo) (1785–1862) *m* Lord Granville Leveson Gower 1st Earl Granville (1773–1846)

William Cavendish (Hart) 6th Duke of Devonshire (1790–1858)

John Charles (Jack) 3rd Earl Spencer (1782–1845)

A SIMPLIFIED FAMILY TREE

SHOWING HARRIET'S PLACE IN

THE SPENCER, CAVENDISH, AND

PONSONBY FAMILIES

NOTE: DOTTED LINES DENOTE EXTRAMARITAL
AFFAIRS AND THEIR ISSUE.

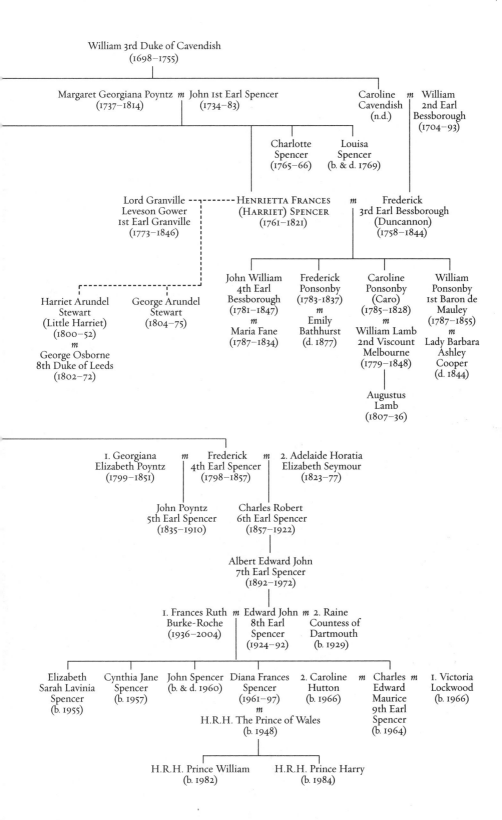

Contents

Author's Note: Families and Titles

Harriet's story involves three aristocratic families: the Spencers (Earls and Countesses Spencer), the Ponsonbys (Earls and Countesses of Bessborough), and the Cavendishes (Dukes and Duchesses of Devonshire). Their various titles, coupled with their habit of using the same name for various family members, can be highly confusing. In order to simplify matters I have often called family members by their nicknames. Nevertheless, the following may be helpful to those unused to the complexities of the peerage:

- Earls and countesses (as in the Spencer and Bessborough families), along with most peers and peeresses apart from dukes and duchesses, are also called Lord X and Lady X.

- Eldest sons of dukes and earls take their father's subsidiary title as a courtesy title (so-called because they are not entitled to sit in the House of Lords). Thus Earl Spencer's eldest son is Viscount Althorp (or Lord Althorp); the Earl of Bessborough's eldest son is Viscount Duncannon (or Lord Duncannon); and the Duke of Devonshire's eldest son is Marquess of Hartington (or Lord Hartington).

- Daughters and younger sons of dukes are termed Lord X or Lady X (as in Lady Harriet Cavendish); daughters of earls are titled Lady X (as in Lady Caroline Ponsonby), while younger sons are titled the Honorable X (as in the Hon. Frederick Ponsonby).

INTRODUCTION

ONE MORNING in late December, 1821, at 2 Cavendish Square, London, Sally, lady's maid to the late Countess of Bessborough, was called unexpectedly to her mistress's bedchamber. She answered the summons with a heavy heart, wondering who had called her and for what purpose. Her mistress had died in tragic circumstances in Italy a month earlier. Sally had served her for nearly thirty years; she had tended her in the last painful hours of her life, closed her eyes when she died, and accompanied her body on the long journey from Florence across wintry Europe to Derbyshire. The funeral had taken place only a week before, and she had yet to reconcile herself to the loss.

But when Sally entered the room the scene that greeted her pushed all such melancholy thoughts from her mind. A large fire had been lit and two of her mistress's sons stood waiting for her. Both seemed agitated and expectant as they confronted their final unwelcome duty—the task of sorting through their mother's correspondence. Harriet, as Lady Bessborough was known by everyone, had always kept her letters in her bedroom, crammed in drawers and her writing desk, some unsorted, others endorsed to be burned unread in the event of her death. They included potentially scandalous documents: letters from Harriet's mother, Lady Spencer, and sister Georgiana, Duchess of Devonshire, discussing intimate matters—affairs, pregnancies, illegitimate children—and letters from lovers. What should her devoted sons do? Understandably, but sadly for later historians, they decided to repair the façade of respectability surrounding their mother's life. Having lit a large fire in the grate, they ordered the terrified Sally to "say who [the letters] were from." Sally was reluctant, feeling this was a grave betrayal of the trust between herself and her mistress, but since she relied on the goodwill of the family for her pension she did as she was ordered. Thus as she identified each letter the vast majority were burned. The significance of this action was not lost upon the younger of the brothers, and tears poured down his cheeks. "Thus was many valuable letters destroyed: the Dowager Lady Spencer and [Georgiana,] late Duchess of Devonshire with many other clever people." Georgiana's only son was distraught when he discovered that his mother's letters had been burned rather than being returned to him, but Harriet's eldest son was unrepentant in defense of his actions. "There were so many painful subjects in that correspondence and so much that I knew it was wished to have destroyed,"[1] he declared.

Even when the desk was bare and all its contents reduced to ashes, the ordeal was not ended. Certain crucial letters were missing: Harriet's most personal correspondence from the man who had been her lover and friend for almost half her life, a dashing diplomat twelve years her junior, Lord Granville Leveson Gower. Harriet had stored these intimate letters separately in a locked cedarwood box, which she took with her wherever she traveled. She had always promised Granville that they would be returned to him when she died, and presumably at some stage during her last illness she had had the presence of mind to give the box to Sally to hand on to Granville. As yet Sally had not carried out this request.

If such compromising material should fall into the wrong hands, her sons feared, the family's name might become a source of ridicule and gossip. Reputations and promising political careers might be jeopardized. The box had not been discovered among the possessions in Harriet's room. Where was it? Fearing what was coming, Sally shook her head and refused to cooperate. Undeterred, the brothers called for the housemaid and repeated the question. The girl admitted that she had seen the box in Sally's room. Sally later recorded:

> The poor box was brought forward; I had the key. The letters and all
> it contained was burned; I happened to have a few stray letters of
> hers to the duchess in my desk; looked them up and gave them to the
> Duke of Devonshire and the poor cedar box that has never lost its

sweet perfume is still mine . . . alas how many hours, days, months of misery would the contents of that box have told, some of happiness no doubt but ended in bitter grief and enervating regrets for the days that was gone for ever.[2]

A fate that was only slightly more fortunate awaited the other half of this correspondence—the letters that Harriet had written to Granville. As a sparkling testimony to the life of one of the most fascinating women of the Regency age, as well as a record of enduring love, Granville had always treasured Harriet's correspondence, and even after his marriage he had kept her letters carefully. A century later, when Granville's daughter-in-law, Castalia, began deciphering Harriet's notoriously difficult scrawl, she too was gripped by the letters. But, like the prudish brothers, she was also deeply embarrassed by the record of sexual indiscretion they contained.

Torn between terror of plunging the family into scandal and realization of the letters' historical significance, Castalia edited out the most sensitive references to the affair and published them, intending to then burn the originals. According to a half-burned note still in the Leveson Gower family, she was dissuaded from following this drastic course and decided instead to deposit the letters in a bank. What course of action she actually followed remains uncertain; ever since Castalia's publication of the Granville letters in 1914, the originals have been lost.*

As it turned out, the frantic efforts of the families to suppress the story of Harriet's life and romantic entanglements were in vain. Thousands more letters that Harriet and her family, friends, and lovers wrote to one another had been squirreled away in royal palaces, ancestral mansions, and modest family archives throughout the country. Pieced together, they reveal one of the most poignant love affairs of the Regency age.

The span of Harriet's life (1761–1821) coincides almost exactly with one of the longest reigns in history, that of George III. The king's marriage and coronation took place in September 1761. Harriet's

---

* I am grateful to Dr. Amanda Foreman for this information. Despite her tip, a search of the family safety deposit box yielded nothing of relevance.

mother, Lady Spencer, emerged from her "lying-in" and resumed her social engagements to find London thronging with crowds waiting expectantly to see the king's bride, Princess Charlotte of Mecklenburg-Strelitz, descend from her carriage to kneel at the feet of her future husband. The pair had never met until that moment, but within hours Charlotte had donned a gown of silver and white, an ermine-trimmed train of purple velvet, and a tiara that was so heavy she could barely stand, and the pair were married.

In Harriet's socially elite world, marriage was a woman's only career option, and nineteen years later she too would bow to convention and select a husband from a close-knit circle. "Girls are often married, hardly knowing their husbands or what marriage is," Harriet would later write ruefully; nor did she expect that marriage would go hand in hand with love. "Where love does not introduce itself," wrote Harriet's friend Lady Melbourne to Lord Byron, "there can be no jealousies, torments, and quarrels."[3] Yet once wives had produced the requisite heirs to ensure the family line continued, they were granted surprising freedom. Fashionable women saw little of their husbands, attending separate social events and frequently spending long periods apart from them. With so much time at their disposal, it is hardly surprising that flirtations and extramarital affairs reached epidemic proportions. Harriet was not alone in embroiling herself in numerous sexual liaisons, but appearance was all. Affairs were tolerated only if they were conducted discreetly. Should a married woman's affair become overt, and cause her husband to seek divorce, rarely was even the wealthiest aristocratic wife spared the fall from grace.

The six decades that Harriet's story spans open a window on aristocratic life at its most intimate and louche. It is a tale intertwined with public scandal, royal intrigue, and high political and literary drama. Petted and spoiled by Marie Antoinette, Harriet lived through the French Revolution and George III's madness; she dodged the Prince Regent's clumsy amorous advances; and she traveled through war-torn Europe during the rise and fall of Napoleon. She juggled the demands of lovers and family, submitting to the dangers of childbirth and the rigors of eighteenth-century medical treatments, meanwhile fretting over children and servants, as well as her lover's constancy and her own reputation. All this and more is vibrantly expounded in her letters. Illuminating one of history's most colorful periods, her correspondence remains a key source of information about the times and is quoted in countless studies of the period. Given her historical significance, not to mention the myriad colorful dramas of her journey through life, it seems odd that no full biography of Harriet has ever been written. This book is an attempt to redress that imbalance; I hope I have done her remarkable story justice.

Harriet's bookplate by Giovanni Battista Cipriani

Privilege
and
Scandal

ONE

The Eligible Match
1761 – 1780

"I MUST PUT DOWN what I dare tell nobody. I should be ashamed were it not so ridiculous," wrote Harriet to her lover. ". . . In my fifty-first year I am courted, followed, flattered, and made love to . . . thirty-six years, a pretty long life, I have heard and spoken that language, for seventeen years . . ."[1]

Love of one form or another was always to be the force that fashioned Harriet's existence. Tall of stature, yet voluptuous in her figure, she was a woman of haunting allure. Her high-cheekboned narrow face was dominated by features that seemed over-large in their fragile surroundings—a slender aristocratic nose, a provocative full-lipped mouth, and huge dark almond-shaped eyes that could grow warm, amused, intelligent, or dreamy according to whim. The portraitist John Hoppner, famous for his portrayals of glamorous aristocrats, painted Harriet in her mid-twenties, just as fashions in portraiture became less formal and more revealing. She is shown in profile, arms stretched protectively around her two eldest sons, delicately chiseled features and slender neck emerging from the froth of a deep collar. Her hair dark, unpowdered, adorned only with a simple band, tumbles naturally about her delicate face, giving her the air of a glamorous latter-day Venus rather than a Madonna—the usual allusion for mother-and-child portraits. Slanting eyes gaze at one of her sons, but focus in the distance, and something in this come-hither look exudes the intellect, artlessness, and allure that made Harriet so compelling to friends and lovers alike.

The admiration that Harriet received at an early age sprang from her social standing as much as from her unusual looks. She was born Lady Henrietta Frances Spencer,* in Wimbledon, on June 16, 1761, into one of the wealthiest and most venerable dynasties in England. As she was the third of John and Margaret Georgiana Spencer's children,† her birth received less attention than did her older siblings'. Fair-haired, blue-eyed Georgiana, who would achieve future fame as the fashionable Duchess of Devonshire, had been born in 1757 and was doted on by her mother as her favorite and firstborn child. George John (who would become Viscount Althorp) had arrived a year later, six weeks prematurely, and was celebrated as much for surviving as for being the only male heir. But Harriet failed to rouse the same passionate affection and, despite the fact that her mother claimed to have "uncommon tenderness . . . for my children," the only surviving reference she made to Harriet in her early days is one of coolness rather than warmth:

> The child (who by the bye is a little ugly girl) and myself are thank god as well as our situations will permit us to be. I cannot say she is quite so small or so frightful as George was, though she has not much less of either of those commodities she has . . . no one beauty to brag of but an abundance of fine brown hair.[2]

Harriet may have taken third place in her mother's affections, but Lady Spencer had strong views on how she wanted Harriet to be raised, even from the earliest days of infancy. Producing legitimate children had always been key to an eighteenth-century aristocratic wife's existence, although many mothers relinquished their responsibilities with the baby's safe delivery, leaving breast-feeding, care, and education to others. But by the time of Harriet's birth, ideas about motherhood and child-rearing were changing. The writings of John Locke and Jean-Jacques Rousseau taught that the expression of passion and emotion was something to be desired. Bound up with this was the fact that children were to be viewed as individuals who were entitled to kindness,

---

* Harriet was hardly ever called Henrietta Frances, and for the purpose of continuity I have called her by the name by which she is most commonly termed.
† John Spencer became the First Earl Spencer in 1765 when Harriet was four; the present Lord Spencer (brother of Diana, Princess of Wales) is the Ninth Earl.

and the bond between a mother and her children was something to nurture and encourage. Mothers should enjoy treating their offspring with affection and play an active role in their care and education.

On a more practical level, changes were also under way. Conventional thought had always deemed babies to be hungry from the moment of delivery. In addition to breast milk, infants were often fed "pap," a confection of bread and water, or of flour, sugar oil of almonds, butter, and sugar. Alcohol was also regarded as being beneficial. A letter from Jonathon Binns, a medical expert, written in 1772, advised the mother of a baby to "give him a little red or white wine every day. He may at different times take about one glass; but be very cautious of it if his eyes be somewhat sore and inflamed. Red port is preferable to white, provided he is sufficiently open in his belly."[3] Babies' clothes were similarly outlandish: swaddling bands of cotton ten or twenty feet long were often wrapped tightly from the armpit to below the hips to keep the spine straight and protect the legs from damage caused by kicking. Cleanliness was also viewed warily—infants were seldom washed or changed, for it was believed clean linen sucked the strength from a body.

New theorists now began to advocate kinder and more natural methods. Dr. William Cadogan, an eminent physician of the day, championed the benefits of fresh air and loose clothing and cleanliness. Rousseau echoed these notions, calling upon aristocratic women to abandon swaddling and return to breast-feeding themselves rather than employing others. But the shift did not happen overnight and, in the Spencer nursery, tradition was modified with the new, rather than wholeheartedly embraced. Like most aristocratic mothers Lady Spencer had a wet nurse to feed Harriet, but the child was not given pap. Neither was she swaddled in dirty rags; she was washed regularly—often with cold baths, which her mother thought advantageous to good health—and dressed in exquisite baby clothes: caps and gowns of fine cambric and lawn trimmed with lace and delicately embroidered, as befitting her rank and status.

It was not only with exquisite clothes and a coterie of nursemaids that Harriet was pampered from her earliest days. Luxury surrounded her. Her father, John Spencer, the great-grandson of the Duke of Marlborough and the intrepid Sarah Jennings, was the possessor of

100,000 acres of land, a string of noble residences—including Althorp, the three-centuries-old family seat in Northampton—and an income said to be worth more than £17,000 a year (over £1 million today).*⁴ With so much wealth at his disposal, John Spencer had made a career out of spending his fortune on every conceivable luxury. Wimbledon Park,† the house in which Harriet was born, was designed by Lord Burlington as a Palladian temple to pleasure and good taste. Interiors were extravagantly embellished with carved and gilded woodwork. Walls were lined in silk, damask, or hand-painted papers from China, and every room used by the family was bedecked with the most sumptuous furnishings and works of art available.

Set upon high ground, overlooking the grounds where the tennis championships now take place, Wimbledon Park, with its columned portico, loomed over the surrounding 1,200 acres, much as the Spencers themselves held sway over the world they inhabited. In the parkland more vast sums were lavished on improvements to conform to the Spencers' desire for a pleasingly picturesque and "untamed" wilderness. This was an age in which the educated and wealthy elite had begun to react against the formalities of civilization, to appreciate natural and sublime landscapes and to see the countryside and country pursuits— whether farming, walking, fishing, gardening, hunting, or riding—as being healthy and spiritually beneficial antidotes to the artificiality and excesses of life in town. Thus a serpentine drive was cut and coverts were installed to encourage partridge, pheasants, and hares, so that Lord Spencer and his guests might amuse themselves shooting.

Lady Spencer was a firm advocate of the pleasures of country living, claiming to detest city life: "a sink of sin and sea coal,"⁵ she would call it. Wimbledon was only an hour's easy drive from London, yet it provided a sanctuary from the bustle, and clean air in which to bring up a young family. "I did not think there could have been so beautiful a place within seven miles of London. The park has as much variety of ground,

---

* Modern monetary equivalents are approximately sixty times those of the eighteenth/early nineteenth century.
† The house was demolished after a fire in 1785 and a new, smaller one was built by Henry Holland. This house was later sold and demolished; the building housing the artesian well that supplied the house with water, some subterranean passages, and old garden walls are all that now remain.

as if it were an hundred miles out,"[6] wrote Hannah More, one of Lady Spencer's friends, admiringly after a visit to the house. As a small child Harriet, standing at the large sash windows, could gaze down upon grassland and copses that had been "improved" by "Capability" Brown; she could amuse herself with visits to the family's menagerie, which contained an assortment of exotic birds and animals, including two pet monkeys; or she could go boating and fishing on the lake—which the family termed a "pond."

However much the Spencers loved country living, city life was an inevitable part of rich aristocratic life and one that they also whole-heartedly embraced. During the earliest years of Harriet's childhood, the Spencers occupied themselves with the finishing touches to the family's new London residence. The palatial Spencer House in St. James's* was intended to exalt its owners and overawe visitors fortunate enough to be invited to enter its massive doors. Designed by John Vardy and James "Athenian" Stuart, who had just returned from Greece, the house's interiors were the first to incorporate Greek architectural detail accurately, thus introducing to London the fashion for neoclassical styles. The house had a library thirty feet long, a saloon that was almost twice that size, and public and private interiors adorned with finery. Exquisite antique treasures were amassed from Europe and arranged in the hall. Vast collections of rare books filled the library; cupids, celebrating the theme of love, cavorted around the looking glasses in the Great Room, magnifying and multiplying the Spencers' opulence, grandeur, and good taste. Even the walls of Lady Spencer's dressing room—a room not intended for public display—were hung with masterpieces by Titian, Leonardo, Rubens, Poussin, and Veronese. "I do not apprehend there is a house in Europe of its size, better worth the view of the curious in architecture, and the fitting up and furnishing [of] great houses, than Lord Spencer's in St. James's Place,"[7] wrote one overawed visitor.

---

* The house was used by the Spencer family until the end of the nineteenth century. The original contents have subsequently been removed—some of the furnishings are at Kenwood, most at Althorp. In the 1980s the lease was taken over by Lord Rothschild's company RIT Capital Partners and the house was restored under the direction of David Mlinaric at a cost of £18 million; it is the only eighteenth-century house on such a scale to survive intact and is open to the public at specified times.

But for all his vast wealth and the opulence with which he surrounded himself, Harriet's father was not a man at ease with life, and his unhappiness was often to cloud the Spencer family's existence. Gainsborough's portrait of him, painted when Harriet was two, shows a young man with a wide forehead, large dark eyes, and a hawkish nose, who bears more than a passing resemblance to his youngest surviving daughter. There is a diffident set to his thin-lipped mouth, and a certain brooding gleam in his eyes that hints at a melancholic side to his character rooted in a childhood blighted by ill health, an excess of wealth, and little parental supervision.

Born a sickly baby, John Spencer had surprised everyone by surviving childhood, and was only eleven when his alcoholic father died and he came into his vast fortune. His mother remarried soon after, leaving her son's upbringing largely to the haphazard care of servants and tutors, and paying little attention to his education or moral upbringing. The interest in art that was to feature so prominently in his later life manifested itself when he joined the Dilettante Society, a dining club based in St. James's Street; founded in the interests of promoting classical connoisseurship, in reality it was notorious for drunken excesses and embellishing memories of foreign amorous conquests over copious glasses of port. "The nominal qualification for membership is having been in Italy, and the real one, being drunk,"[8] sneered Horace Walpole, who never joined the select band.

As he grew up, John Spencer was afflicted by a variety of troublesome maladies. He suffered from gallstones, gout, and difficulties in breathing, as well as from deafness, which made him withdrawn and impaired his relationship not only with his friends and peers but also with his family. Lady Spencer would later write movingly of how his deafness prevented him from attempting to talk to his grandson John for fear he would not understand the reply.[9] Added to this, his life was obstructed by an unusual limitation of his inheritance* that forbade him from taking an active role in government. Thus the only way he could exert influence was indirectly, by spending large sums of money

---

* Amanda Foreman, in *Georgiana, Duchess of Devonshire*, p. 6, explains that Sarah, the widowed Duchess of Marlborough (John's grandmother), left him her fortune on the condition that he should never take a position in government.

to assist the candidates he supported—often members of his family—
or in lavish hospitality to encourage political debate and so promote his
interests. Otherwise he filled his days traveling about his various
houses or abroad, and in self-indulgence—eating and drinking to excess, which further damaged his health, or sitting up till dawn over
hands of faro or whist.

But Harriet's father was much more than a moody libertine; beneath his profligate and prickly exterior lay an affectionate heart that
found fulfillment in his blissfully happy marriage. He had married for
love in what became one of the most romantic unions of his day. Harriet's mother, Margaret Georgiana Poyntz, was seventeen when he, a
young man of twenty, was first captivated by her. She was the daughter
of Stephen Poyntz of Midgham in Berkshire, a successful career diplomat and courtier who had risen to become ambassador to Sweden and
a Privy Counselor to George II. Margaret Georgiana was attractive
rather than beautiful, with coppery brown hair that she wore swept
back from her face, and large thoughtful dark eyes. Her warm outgoing
character, lively intelligence, and ease swiftly melted John Spencer's
reticence. "I do not wonder at your liking Lady Spencer," wrote Lady
Stafford to her son years later; "all men formerly liked her and she was
most captivating and pleasing. But the beauty of it was that she managed them *all* without their knowing it . . . she some how or another has
the art of leading, drawing, or seducing people into right ways."[10]

The Spencer marriage represented a coup of the first order for Lady
Spencer's socially ambitious mother, Mrs. Poyntz. Determined that her
daughter should marry as well as possible, she had used any means at
her disposal to propel her into the right social spheres. Travel on the
Continent was one way in which she gained entrée to high society and
mingled with the elite without going to the trouble and expense of entertaining, and it may have been through their travels that the Poyntzes
gained an introduction that brought them to one of John Spencer's entertainments at Althorp. "'Tis her way to beg letters to the most considerable people wherever she comes, and she always stays to dine or sup
with them, that she may talk of it in the place she goes to,"[11] said the diarist Lady Mary Coke, describing Mrs. Poyntz's shameless modus
operandi.

However the introduction came about, Margaret Georgiana's charm and obvious intelligence captivated the awkward John Spencer, while she thought him "handsomer than an angel." But the couple could not marry before John's twenty-first birthday without his family's approval. Uncertain whether this would be forthcoming, John Spencer decided to wait, traveling abroad for a "tour" while the months passed. Before he left he presented his bride-to-be with a token of his love — a ruby surrounded by diamonds engraved with the motto *Mon coeur est tout à toi/gardez le bien pour moi.** As he left, "the last glimpse I had of him in his utmost perfection . . . was on a very prancing grey horse with a long tail and mane his saddle etc. green and gold at the head of a large cavalcade,"[12] wrote Margaret Georgiana, overcome with misery at her parting with the man she referred to in letters as "Recneps" (Spencer spelled backward).

When he returned, shortly before his birthday, the pair were as besotted with each other as ever. "O Thea you would love him if you saw him he is vastly tanned but everything adds to his beauty,"[13] wrote the adoring Margaret Georgiana to her friend Thea Cowper. Weeks later, during a lavish series of celebrations at Althorp for his birthday, the pair were secretly married.

> As soon as dinner was over today Spencer begged he might show me something — it was the license and he smiling asked me if I would marry him now. I told him with all my heart, in short what we both said in joke looked in earnest for Lady Cowper [John Spencer's mother] overheard us and said it would be the best scheme in the world but to take off all suspicion she made us begin the ball . . . and then one by one we met in her bed chamber . . . we both behaved very well spoke loud and distinct but I trembled so much I could hardly stand. We are now come out again, nobody seems to suspect us.[14]

Superficially the Spencers' attraction to each other seemed to be one of opposites. Lady Spencer's easygoing gregariousness was balanced by her husband's diffidence; his penchant for flamboyant dress and wanton extravagance was countered by her preference for simplicity and plainness. But the two had more in common than first ap-

---

* My heart belongs to you/keep it carefully for me.

peared. Lord Spencer's passion for books—he acquired a vast collection of some five thousand rare volumes for the library at Spencer House in London—was shared by Lady Spencer. Both loved riding and horses and other outdoor pursuits, including gardening and fishing. Lady Spencer could also, when circumstances demanded, turn her hand to spending money on clothes and jewels and works of art on a scale appropriate to the wife of one of the richest men in England. Naturally sociable, she loved putting on extravagant entertainments, and her husband's wealth and social standing gave her the chance to sponsor and befriend fashionable artists, writers, musicians, and philosophers; to take up countless philanthropic causes; and, most important, to support Spencer interests by cultivating many leading politicians of the day.

Within the sumptuous walls of the three main Spencer residences Harriet and her siblings grew up witnessing their parents hold balls, garden parties, assemblies, and concerts at which politicians mingled with members of the royal family and distinguished practitioners of the arts. Harriet described a typical evening at Wimbledon Park as "several people disjointing about politics and horses just by me . . . with a whole band of music rambling away as loud as they can in the next room, and to complete the whole Mama making billiard bets and the dogs fighting."[15]

Harriet's description also points to Lady Spencer's enthusiasm for the pastime that she shared with her husband and would later prove the undoing of both her daughters. Gaming was an exciting and dangerous antidote to the strictures of protocol, and an aristocratic obsession; it also gave the socially ambitious easy entrée to elite circles. Lady Spencer, like many wellborn girls of her day, had been brought up to regard card-playing as part of everyday existence. "I have known the Poyntzes in the nursery, the Bible on the table, the cards in the drawer,"[16] remarked Lord Lansdowne. After her marriage, with such huge wealth at her disposal, the passion for play became an addiction she could never conquer. She and Lord Spencer passed long hours at the tables, and from childhood both Harriet and her sister came to regard the playing of games of chance as part of the daily routine.

In her heart Lady Spencer knew gambling "deep" was a destructive vice. In later years, she would frequently warn her daughters of the perils of faro and whist. "Play, with all its accompaniment of waste of time, agitation of mind, fatigue from late hours, and distress of circumstances you have been sufficiently warned against by precept though not by example. It is a painful subject for me to write upon, I will therefore only say that you will wound my heart a thousand ways if you ever engage in it,"[17] she exhorted Harriet on the eve of her marriage. But the warnings, though often repeated, were fruitless, never erasing Harriet's childhood impressions any more than her mother's own attraction toward play.

The love the Spencers had felt for each other at their marriage grew and deepened as each year passed. Lady Spencer adored her husband, and the letters she wrote to him on the rare occasions when they were apart convey deep affection and compatibility. "I am ashamed at this long scrawl, but it is not easy my dearest Spencer to stop when I am talking with you,"[18] she would write in letters crammed with gossip, political news, and her latest good causes. The Spencers' open mutual tenderness mirrored the altering tenets of the age. Alongside the kinder approach to child-rearing and an appreciation of nature, the upper echelons embraced the cult of sensibility—a more liberal view of the world, in which increasing importance was attached to the declaration of emotion and love. As part of the shift, men as well as women felt impelled to display—and on occasion to enhance—their emotions in every area of their life. This trend even extended to parliament, where members often burst into tears when debates became particularly heated. "There was not a dry eye in the house,"[19] wrote the diarist Creevey after a debate in 1815 in which both Burke and Fox sobbed loudly as they spoke.

Being the focus of such constant and openly displayed love transformed John Spencer. On grand social occasions he might put on a mask of haughtiness, but at home, lavished with attention, he was happier than anywhere. When Harriet was six, the Earl of March joined a Spencer house party and was struck by the harmony of the family's existence. Althorp boasted "an excellent library, a good parson, the best English and French cookery you ever tasted, strong coffee and half-crown whist," while Harriet's parents were "the happiest people I think I ever saw in the marriage system."[20]

The loyalty and tenderness, even in moments of difficulty and unhappiness, that Harriet witnessed between her parents was to color her view of how a husband should behave and what an ideal partnership should entail. John Spencer could be distant, or short-tempered and stern, especially if he was unwell. Day-to-day supervision of Harriet's upbringing and education was left to Lady Spencer and the train of nursery staff the couple employed, but Harriet never doubted her parents' affection for each other or for her, and however difficult her father was during his low points he provided a constant anchor in her life. "Papa bid us observe how much persecution increased zeal for the religion so oppressed, which he said was a lesson against oppression, and for toleration . . . "[21] wrote Harriet after witnessing a communion service in Montpellier. Years after her father's death, she would still remember him fondly:

> I took a beautiful ride tonight to Kingsgate, with the moon shining on the sea, and wandered about the great house there . . . to me it must always be a melancholy spot, for the reason that makes it so makes me also like to go there. It was the last place I saw my poor father in, and though so many years are past since I lost him, whenever he is strongly recalled to my mind, it leaves a deep impression of sorrow on me, which however painful it may be sometimes, I should be very sorry to lose . . . [22]

From her earliest childhood Harriet became accustomed to constant change. The Spencers divided their time between their various houses, drifting from Wimbledon and London, where they spent most of the spring and summer, to their country seat, Althorp, in Northamptonshire, for the autumn and winter months, often stopping en route at Holywell House, a gothic mansion in St. Albans that had once belonged to Harriet's great-grandmother Sarah, Duchess of Marlborough. During the hunting season Lord Spencer, in order to indulge his passion for chasing with the hounds, took up residence in the family hunting lodge at Pytchley, near Kettering. When they were not in one of their own homes, the couple passed much time journeying about the country to visit friends, or, when Lord Spencer's health took a turn for the worse, lodging in fashionable health resorts such as Buxton, Cheltenham, Bristol, or Bath, to consult medical experts, bathe, and take the waters. They also made extended journeys abroad, to see the sights, or to sample the cures in foreign health resorts, or to forge new and useful connections—and above all to spend money. On one visit abroad they bought so much that they had to charter an additional vessel especially to transport their acquisitions back to England.

During these travels Harriet, as the youngest child, was often left behind, and much of her early childhood was passed in the nursery, well cared for, but distanced from her parents for days, weeks, or months on end. When Harriet was two her father's health deteriorated so badly that the Spencers decided to travel to the fashionable spas of Europe in search of a cure. Lady Spencer could not bear the idea of leaving all her children behind, and took Georgiana, who was then six, with her, leaving Harriet and her brother in the care of nurses and governesses. Two years passed before the younger children saw their parents again.

Harriet's lessons began at an early age. When she was five years old she was reading and writing and learning to ride, draw, speak French, and play the piano and harpsichord. Aristocratic daughters did not traditionally receive much more than this in the way of formal education: few attended school; the majority were taught by governesses at home. Intellectually, morally, and socially, however, the Spencers' expectations of their children were higher than most. Lady Spencer wanted her daughters to be proficient in traditional feminine accomplishments; but, being highly educated herself, she was keen too that they should be versed in more masculine subjects such as classics, religion, geography, and history.

In her eyes moral education and manners were as important as academic knowledge. Harriet was instilled with the importance of family loyalty, duty, and etiquette, although in keeping with Rousseau's theories that nothing should be done to break the natural spirit, and that children were innocent and entitled to freedom and happiness, Harriet's outbursts of childish temper—or, as her grandmother put it, her "little depressions"—were usually discouraged with the promise of approval, rather than with the threat of punishment. "I shall be much pleased if I find she has ever got the better of herself and made herself good humoured when she was inclined to be of humour and naughty,"[23] Lady Spencer wrote to Georgiana about her younger sister's tantrums.

Even when she was away Lady Spencer carefully monitored her

children's education. She wrote constantly to them and the staff entrusted with their care, and her letters brim with details of the places she visited and the events she attended, often with histories of towns as well as biographies of the people she met. Her letters to her children are openly warm and loving; she told them how much she longed to see them, as well as suggesting ways they might improve themselves. Sometimes when she was away it was not only to the governess that she gave instructions, but to Georgiana, regarding her younger sister. "Has Harriet got a tune yet to practise on the harpsichord?"[24] she demanded when Harriet was eight. Georgiana was naturally affectionate and easily fell into the maternal role; Harriet in her turn began to regard her older siblings with adoration, turning to them for the attention and advice she might otherwise have received from her parents.

The gulf between Harriet and her mother was to widen when, in 1765, Lady Spencer gave birth to a third daughter, Charlotte, "a sweet little poppet."[25] Even among the well-to-do, the eighteenth century was a period in which babies were ravaged by diseases such as smallpox and typhus. Mothers lived in constant dread that their children might die but were expected to take such tragedy in their stride. Charlotte was less robust than her older siblings and perished a year after she was born, when Harriet was five. Another daughter, Louise, was born three years later, but she too died at a few weeks old. The deaths destroyed the hopes of Lady Spencer for more children, but she could not reconcile herself to their loss. She grew profoundly depressed—"I eat very little yet and can seldom sleep without laudanum,"[26] she confessed to her friend several months after Charlotte's death—and she became obsessed with the health of the remaining members of her family, terrified that any tiny complaint might augur further tragedy.

By now Harriet already showed signs of a formidable memory and a way with words unusual for her years. But she was a frail child, small for her age and painfully thin. Partly because she was unable to bear the thought of losing another child, and in the belief that a milder climate would help her grow strong, Lady Spencer decided to send Harriet away to school. The decision was not unusual; a sound knowledge of foreign languages was a prerequisite of any cultured aristocratic lady, and many wellborn girls were partly schooled abroad. In any case, never having felt the same passionate attachment for Harriet that she had for Georgiana, her mother did not find the thought of separation hard to bear. Thus, while Georgiana and George were tutored at home, from the age of seven onward, Harriet spent much of the next three years dispatched to a succession of convent boarding schools in France and Belgium.

On these long foreign stays it was her maternal grandmother, the bumptious, travel-loving Mrs. Poyntz, who accompanied Harriet, taking lodgings near the various establishments Harriet attended to supervise her settling in. The sudden jolt from private tuition in the most lavish surroundings to schooling in a foreign country, away from all that was familiar, did not impair Harriet's development. The abbé teaching her in Brussels reported he had never known a child of such a young age to show such an aptitude. Her grandmother was equally impressed: "She has really a most amazing understanding and by way of conversation out does any child I ever knew,"[27] Mrs. Poyntz proudly wrote of her young charge.

But the wrench from home, the long separations from her brother, sister, and parents, and the deaths of her younger siblings had a profound effect upon Harriet in other ways. She grew nervous and insecure. She began to crave reassurance, and her neediness became manifest in emotional outbursts and occasional willfulness on the one hand, and a desperate desire for love on the other. Yearning for love also spurred her to form strong and long-lasting attachments with those who cared for her while she was abroad. She was delighted when after an absence of four years she returned to the school she had attended at Tours. "I was very glad to see l'abbé, La Bonelle my old bonne, and Mlle. and the abbess of the pension who all knew me again and said '*a voilà* Lady Henriette.' "[28] The affection she felt for those who cared for her was obvious too in the sensitivity of her behavior toward them. At Christmas, a Belgian custom was to hand over the keys of the house to a child and allow her to take on the role of mistress. Harriet, delighted to be thus honored, after much deliberation ordered boiled beef and suet for her grandmother's dinner and turkey for everyone else. She asked for her lessons to take place in the morning rather than the afternoon so that her tutors might join her, and invited several poor children to share the meal.

While Harriet's lessons in French and reading and writing took place under the eye of the abbé, Mrs. Poyntz ensured she was also schooled in the social graces. Harriet was tutored by an eminent dancing master in dancing and the equally crucial matters of etiquette and deportment—how to enter a room, curtsy, walk, and sit down in an elegant, ladylike manner. The lessons were put into practice when she joined her grandmother on her social excursions. She was dressed in Grecian costume for the ridotto, when she looked so enchanting that "Mr. A.—gave her 20 louis and the Prince called her little angel."[29]

These diversions came to an abrupt end three months later when Harriet developed measles. The disease was potentially a life-threatening one, and Mrs. Poyntz dreaded having to report her granddaughter's condition to Lady Spencer, when she was already grieving for her dead baby. She tried to make Harriet's symptoms sound less serious than they were—not easy when Harriet was coughing, her neck was sore, and "her face very full . . . her eyes much affected." The doctor was summoned, bled her, and provided physic; several weeks later the worst was over, although Mrs. Poyntz was still uneasy. Harriet was pale and, having lost her appetite, had grown thinner than ever. "I was in hopes to have returned her to you plumper and looking better than ever you saw her but now I fear for some time she will not get her good looks,"[30] Mrs. Poyntz wrote. She was also distraught because, since her illness, Harriet held her head at an awkward angle. The doctor had reassured Mrs. Poyntz the problem would rectify itself in a few days, but she remained concerned. "It makes her hold herself awry, which vexes me to see, for her famous dancing master had made her the gentlest figure of every dance which I hope she will be again."[31]

The diarist Lady Mary Coke met Harriet and her grandmother in Aix; they had been joined by George Spencer and were due to be reunited with Lord and Lady Spencer the next day, after a year's separation. Lady Mary thought both the children looked thin but that Mrs. Poyntz was ebullient as ever and relishing her role as guardian. "She has talked me to death," wrote Lady Mary; "tis prodigious the civilities she says she receives wherever she goes; she dined with the Archbishop of Lyons, and his fondness for the children would have surprised me." She concluded rather waspishly, "Tis a good woman but she loves bragging."[32]

By the time Harriet was ten, frequent partings from her mother and siblings, and constantly moving from one school to another, had turned her into an observer of life rather than a participant in it. Watching others had become a habit that enabled her to draw her own conclusions about all she saw. "The Dauphiness [Marie Antoinette] is so fair and so handsome, it is impossible not to admire her, but Mad[ame] de Provence is quite black and ugly,"[33] she wrote with beady-eyed honesty of an encounter with the French royal family.

Harriet had also acquired a poise and maturity beyond her years. When she was ten and staying in Nice her nurse died suddenly. William Jones, her brother's tutor, was amazed at her composure. "Lady Harriet behaved upon the occasion with a presence of mind and a steadiness that are very unusual at her age."[34] But beneath the façade of maturity she remained sensitive, fearful of disapproval, and still prone to emotional outbursts. Unsurprisingly, death terrified her, and when her party passed by the bodies of miscreants recently broken on the wheel and hanging on gallows she was horrified at the spectacle and the awful crime for which they had been punished. "It was for a shocking murder of a young woman who was going to have a child, and whom they cut to pieces,"[35] she recorded.

Lord Spencer's response to Harriet's fears was always to force her to confront them. To conquer her terror of death he insisted on taking her to see some corpses preserved in a church crypt. Harriet was openly apprehensive, but her father told her, "It is foolish and superstitious to be afraid of seeing dead bodies." As her eyes adjusted to the gloom she was overcome by terror. "On every side there were horrid black ghastly figures, some grinning, some pointing at us, or seeming in pain . . . I could hardly help screaming and I thought they all moved."[36] According to Harriet, her father's reaction to her fear "was not angry but very kind," but then he told her that to conquer her feelings she must touch one of the corpses. More petrified than ever, Harriet begged to be allowed to touch a child, but her father still insisted that she examine in close detail some of the other bodies. "Their skin was all dark brown and quite dried up on the bones . . . and felt like marble,"[37] she wrote afterward.

There were other perils that Lord Spencer encouraged Harriet to face—hailstones so large the servants were knocked over; drunken postilions who fell off their horses; the rustles of robbers on dark nights. "We heard a terrible whistling all round us, but papa said it was only poachers." Not to mention the discomforts of uncomfortable and unhygienic accommodation. "The sitting room of our inn opened into the stables, there was no room in the inn so my sister and I were wrapped up in a blanket and lay on the floor. Papa says girls of our age should learn not to make a fuss."[38]

The diary Harriet kept of this journey was written for her father. It reveals not only her fears and the keen eye that would characterize her adult correspondence, but the exalted circles to which she was exposed from childhood. During a play by Voltaire, Harriet remarked that Louis XV seemed to sleep most of the time, and that his mistress Madame du Barry sat in a box on the other side of the theater from the rest of the royal party. The family attended a hunting party on St. Hubert's day in which the royal family alone had fifteen hundred horses taking part. Harriet was spellbound: " . . . such numbers of people in red, blue, and green gold glittering in the sun with their piqueurs, servants, horses, and carriages made it a fine sight,"[39] she remembered.

In Versailles the surroundings were memorable in a different way. The Spencer family attended high mass and took dinner with Marie Antoinette, who kissed Georgiana and Harriet and gave them flowers. Harriet thought the dauphine "not regularly handsome, but her complexion and countenance are beautiful and she has so much grace and dignity . . ."[40] Clearly Marie Antoinette was much taken with Harriet, for even when her parents were elsewhere and she stayed in her "pension" (boardinghouse) she was often invited to join the dauphine in her boudoir. Years later she would tell the diarist Thomas Moore how during one visit Marie Antoinette was to give an audience to ambassadors seated at the foot of her bed: "The child [Harriet], anxious to see this ceremony hid herself in the bed-curtains and was so astonished and even terrified by the change that took place in the Queen's countenance on the entrance of the Ambassadors that the feeling has never been forgotten by her to this hour."[41]

Everywhere they went it was fifteen-year-old Georgiana who was fêted and admired. Harriet, by now well drilled in how to behave at grand social occasions, relished the spectacle. But compared with Georgiana she was still scrawny and childish and less assured in polite company. As her glamorous older sister donned new gowns, danced and chatted easily, charming everyone she met, Harriet stepped back into the shadows to observe and admire from the sidelines. "My sister was dressed in her new white lutestring Polonaise, trimmed with blue and white gauze. She looked very pretty and did not seem at all uncomfortable, though it is the first time she has worn gauze,"[42] she recorded after a visit to her mother's friend Lady Clermont. In Paris Georgiana socialized with her parents, while Harriet attended school every day, returning home at night, often to find her parents otherwise engaged. She accepted her lot uncomplainingly, relieved to escape the ordeal of society and find a friend of hers, Caroline Townshend, among the other pupils at the school.

The rigors of travel and the constant round of social engagements did little to help Lord Spencer's fragile health, which deteriorated steadily throughout the journey. By the time the family reached Montpellier, he was so ill that he needed two operations. Harriet and Georgiana were distraught, but the surgeon assured them he was recovering and told them to show the same fortitude as their father. *"Les filles d'un hero ne doivent pas pleurer."** Soon afterward the trip was curtailed and the family returned home.[43]

Among those who had been beguiled by Georgiana along the way was one of the most eligible bachelors in England, the twenty-four-year-old William Cavendish, the Fifth Duke of Devonshire. A year later, Harriet's life was irrevocably altered when Georgiana left the family to marry the duke and metamorphose into London's most alluring society hostess.

LEFT ALONE WITH her parents, Harriet found herself becoming the focus of their attentions. She did not always find the adjustment easy. On trips abroad she was happy to converse in English, French, or Italian, but certain social occasions seemed utterly terrifying. *"Je voudrai bien vous avoir pour une de notre partie,"*†[44] she wrote to her sister of one particularly complicated dance she was expected to perform. Georgiana was not the only person Harriet missed. George was by now a student at Trinity College, Cambridge. When a ball had to be canceled owing to

---

* The daughters of a hero must not cry.
† I wish you were in our party.

their grandmother's illness, one of Harriet's chief regrets was that she would not see her brother.

Back on British soil, Lady Spencer set about exactingly putting the finishing touches to Harriet's education. She was disturbed by reports of Georgiana, who by now had made Devonshire House,* the duke's vast London residence, a hub for Whig society. Night after night Georgiana organized dazzling soirées, at which leading politicians not only mingled, played cards, talked, and flirted, but indulged in worrying dissipation and excess. Thus she redoubled her efforts to instill Harriet with the moral and religious strength to resist temptation when her turn came to marry. At Althorp she read with Harriet every morning, and at Bath, while Lord Spencer immersed himself in the waters, or was pushed around town in his wheelchair, she and Harriet attended assemblies, went riding or fishing, or took excursions together. Hungry for love and attention, Harriet quickly recognized that, by agreeing with her mother, the affection she received grew. She learned to tailor her behavior, to control her emotions and profess opinions that she knew her mother wanted to hear, and, on occasion, to dissemble. Clearly her strategy worked. Lady Spencer would never feel as passionately or spontaneously affectionate toward Harriet as she did toward Georgiana, but during these years a quiet fondness grew between them, and when Harriet was sixteen her mother thought her "very much improved of late, she is grown vastly more serious and seems really in earnest in trying to correct some of those defects which every lady may find in their characters."[45]

Harriet was by now almost as tall as her sister, and her unusual looks met with differing reactions. The rakish Richard Fitzpatrick, one of the habitués of Georgiana's Devonshire House assemblies, thought her "delicious,"[46] but Frederick Robinson saw Harriet at her presentation at court and told his brother that she was not exactly handsome, although he allowed her figure was good and she was well dressed,[47] while her grandmother, the Countess of Cowper, thought she had

---

* The house, designed by William Kent and situated in Piccadilly, was demolished in the 1920s to make way for a block still known as Devonshire House. The original gates can still be seen at the Piccadilly entrance to Green Park.

"both handsome and ugly days."[48] On one thing everyone agreed: Harriet's looks improved when she was away from Georgiana and could not be directly, and unfavorably, compared.

Both in appearance and temperament Harriet had inherited much from her father; her long, rather narrow face, pale coloring, and aristocratic nose were all Spencer features. So too was her thoughtful nature, and her occasionally nervous disposition. The long periods she had spent away from her family had served to make her less dizzy and impulsive than her sister and had perhaps contributed to her love of reading. She devoured books on everything from classical mythology, history, and philosophy to travelogues, letters, novels, and poetry, gleaning a level of sophistication unusual for her age. She was still inclined to reticence, but when she forgot her shyness there was another side to Harriet, a side that relished company and craved compliments and became drawn, irresistibly, to the heady, frivolous, dangerously exciting world in which her sister played such a prominent role.

BY NOW THE Spencers' thoughts had inevitably begun to turn to finding a suitable partner for their youngest daughter. Her attractiveness and accomplishments, the promise of a generous marriage settlement, and a social position that might help any aspiring politician's career all combined to make Harriet a highly eligible marriage proposition. But, whatever her parents hoped, she was in no hurry to take the plunge. Part of her reluctance was rooted in her devotion to Georgiana, which had deepened in her teenage years. In preparation for entering the marriage market, she had spent much time at Devonshire House with Georgiana as her chaperone. The fun of joining in her sister's lavish entertainments, and the intimacy of staying alone with her, sometimes sharing her bed when the party was over, was something Harriet treasured and had no desire to relinquish. Her apprehension was compounded by having witnessed the difficulties of Georgiana's transformation from daughter to wife. Georgiana had attracted much public criticism for falling prey to dissipation and vice, added to which her husband was often distant with her. Marriage offered independence and status, but these to Harriet seemed poor compensation for separation from her devoted sister and family and for the pitfalls that awaited.

Harriet's hesitancy to choose a partner did not stop the subject from becoming a source of speculation. "I had a letter yesterday from Lady Essex who . . . says she saw you and my sister at the play, that my sister look'd very handsome, and that she hears she is going to be marry'd directly to the Duke of Roxburgh,"[49] wrote Georgiana to her mother, when Harriet was seventeen. There were also rumors that Lord Trentham had proposed and Harriet had turned him down. When Georgiana fell ill in February 1778, Lady Spencer rushed to Chiswick House* to nurse her, sending Harriet to stay in London on her own. Harriet, heavily reliant on her sister and mother, found the separation hard to bear. "She is quite alone poor soul and very miserable,"[50] reported Lady Spencer. Harriet had slept in Georgiana's bed the night before her symptoms emerged and Lady Spencer was terrified she might contract the same illness. Even when Georgiana was recovered enough to eat "asparagus with appetite,"[51] Harriet was kept away because several servants had caught the same infection. But Lady Spencer consoled herself with the thought that she seemed to be enjoying herself at last; "she does not lead a very solitary life as Mrs. Howe, Mrs. Graham, Miss Lloyd, and several others take it by turns to dine or sup with her and half London will call upon her to enquire after [her] sister."[52]

In her heart of hearts Harriet knew she could not delay the choice of a husband indefinitely. In eighteenth-century society, a son's marriage was seen as important in securing a family line, but the marriage of a daughter was equally significant—a means of consolidating family fortune, strengthening bonds of friendship, improving a career or status. The Spencers, in common with every aristocratic family, regarded their youngest daughter's choice of a husband as a matter of the utmost seriousness. They wanted Harriet to make her own choice and marry for love, as they had done, but they were anxious too that she should marry well to secure her own future and that of her children. Inevitably this involved choosing a husband from the small and select circle in which they moved.

---

* Another of the Duke of Devonshire's properties—an elegant Palladian villa some six miles from central London overlooking the Thames. The house was designed by Lord Burlington in an adaptation of Palladio's Villa Rotunda in Vicenza. The house survives and is now administered by English Heritage.

Early the following year, Harriet was presented at court, and the hunt for a partner began in earnest. Mothers played a key role in this delicate game, chaperoning their daughters to the right functions, introducing them to the right people. By day Harriet might promenade in Hyde Park, or parade down Bond Street for fittings with makers of dresses, stays, hats, shoes, and gloves, and to show off her charms to any eligible gentlemen who happened to pass by. Afternoons were filled with dinners or tea parties at which a hand or two of whist might be played, after which came a rigorous evening round of visits to operas, plays, and dances.

The exhausting routine paid swift dividends. Harriet impressed the Prince of Wales, who was a year younger than she, before he fell passionately for Mary Hamilton, one of his siblings' governesses. Georgiana's letters to her brother mention that other men were also ardent in their pursuit of Harriet; "a friend of mine...lurched his head against the carriage,"[53] she reported, although tantalizingly she fails to say who this was. Richard Sheridan, the witty, handsome, hard-drinking, and duplicitous son of an Irish actor, who had already achieved fame as the author of *The Rivals* and *The School for Scandal,* was a friend of Georgiana's, and was instantly drawn to her attractive, clever younger sister. But Sheridan was married to the talented and beautiful singer Elizabeth Linley. Her reputation had given him an entreé to Devonshire House and fashionable society, and, for the time being at least, he was too eager for Georgiana's help in securing a seat in parliament to risk alienating himself by seducing her sister.

The man who ultimately captured Harriet's attention was a first cousin of Georgiana's husband, the Duke of Devonshire.* The soft-spoken, affable Frederick Ponsonby, Viscount Duncannon, had recently returned to London after completing his education in the traditional manner with a grand tour abroad. Three years Harriet's senior, he seemed to everyone a perfect choice. Tall and pleasant-looking, with an angular face, a rather small mouth, and a heavy chin, he was heir to William, the Second Earl of Bessborough, who owned vast estates in Ireland, including 27,000 acres and a classical mansion

---

* The Duke of Devonshire's aunt had married Viscount Duncannon's father, the Second Earl of Bessborough.

in County Kilkenny. In England there was further wealth—an elegant country villa and farmland in Roehampton; estates in Cambridgeshire, Leicestershire, and Nottinghamshire; and a grand London house in Cavendish Square.

And yet Duncannon was very different in temperament from many of the flirtatious self-assured men Harriet met at Devonshire House. His mother, Caroline Cavendish, had died when he was only two, and his father had not remarried. Never having known a mother's affection, he was awkward with members of the opposite sex, socializing when he had to, but preferring a hand of cards in his club or solitary pursuits such as drawing and painting and collecting prints and cartoons.

But he was also a dutiful and adoring son to his father, and knew that as eldest son he was expected to marry well. With so many family connections in common, to him Harriet seemed the ideal wife. Thus, spurred on by his father and Cavendish relatives, Duncannon began to pay diffident court to Harriet, calling frequently at Devonshire House when she was staying with her sister, or at Spencer House or Wimbledon Park. Harriet, no doubt reassured by the Cavendish connection, which would ease the dreaded separation from her sister, read his reticence as a sign of a benevolent, mature, and sensitive character and gave him every encouragement.

The burgeoning romance was interrupted in the summer of 1780, when London fell into the grip of anti-Catholic violence during the Gordon Riots. Harriet and her parents did not witness the rampaging mob, since they had earlier traveled to Bath. (Lord Spencer was suffering from gout and it was hoped the waters would prove beneficial.) From London Georgiana wrote describing the frightening scenes: "The King's bench is burnt down, and I suppose you know that Ld. Mansfield's was burnt this morning; the mob is a strange set, and some of it composed of mere boys,"[54] she reported.

The disruption in the capital spread outward like a stain. In the elegant streets of Bath a mob surrounded the new Roman Catholic chapel and set it alight, and coaches arriving from London had NO POPERY chalked on their sides. The writer Fanny Burney was staying in the city at the same time and deplored the effect of the disruption on Catholic residents and ailing visitors. "Alas! To what have we all lived!—the poor invalids here will probably lose all chance of life from

terror. The Catholics throughout the place are all threatened with destruction, and we met several porters, between ten and eleven at night,
privately removing goods, walking on tiptoe, and scarcely breathing."[55]
By then Duncannon's pursuit of Harriet had reached an advanced
stage, and although there were still other contestants for her hand,
Georgiana predicted that his suit would end successfully.

> I think Lord Duncannon seems to be the first of lovers . . . the most
> affectionate one I ever saw. I believe Lord Frederick* will be in de-
> spair if he does not get them married before November for he longs
> to have the wedding.[56]

We do not know whether Duncannon followed Harriet to Bath, or
whether he continued his suit by letter; no correspondence from this date
survives. What is certain is that as soon as the Spencers returned to
Wimbledon in July the affair gathered pace. Lady Spencer knew it was
merely a matter of waiting for the proposal. "The lovers go on mighty
well," she wrote to George Spencer; ". . . he [Duncannon] stayed late yesterday morning and upon my saying he was at liberty to come when he
pleased he came again in the evening [and] stayed all night—ordered his
horses to go away this morning, but asked leave to stay [to] dinner
which he did and is here still at 9 o'clock at night."[57] By the end of the
following month Duncannon had made a formal proposal, speaking to
Lord Spencer as well as to Harriet. Lady Spencer was in no doubt that
the attraction between them was powerful. "Lord Duncannon seems
very much in earnest indeed and Harriet, if I can judge of anything, almost as far gone as himself,"[58] she gleefully reported.

Georgiana was ecstatic, pressing her mother for further details, apparently also convinced that this was a love match and oblivious to the
fact that, consciously or not, she had put pressure on her sister to marry
within the Cavendish fold. "I am so happy I don't know how to express
all I feel about it. It is the most charming thing that ever was, in all respects it is the marriage one should have wished,"[59] she wrote, brimming with emotion.

---

* Frederick Cavendish, Viscount Duncannon and the Duke of Devonshire's uncle.

Unlike Georgiana, Harriet did not delude herself that she was deeply in love. Writing to her friend Miss Shipley shortly after the engagement was announced, she openly confessed her lukewarm feelings:

I have a very high opinion of Lord Duncannon . . . There are many people whose manners and conversation I should like better, as flirts only . . . but when one is to choose a companion for life (what a dreadful sound that has) the inside and not the out is what one ought to look at, and I think from what I have heard of him, and the great attachment he professes to have for me, I have a better chance of being reasonably happy with him than with most people I know.[60]

There are two ways to interpret this curiously detached reasoning: Harriet may have been trying to think maturely, to look beneath the surface and eschew the glitz and glamour of Devonshire House, in favor of something more enduring. Alternatively, what had won her over was the wish to reinforce the relationship with Georgiana by marriage within the Cavendish clan; she had persuaded herself this was all she needed to be happy. As Miss Lloyd, a friend of Lady Spencer, put it, "By marrying him she made no new connections, for now her sister's and hers would be the same."[61] Either way, Harriet's expectations of marriage were greatly underpinned by what she had observed of her parents' and sister's relationships. She had not been privy to the passion of the Spencers' whirlwind courtship, or the secret drama with which they married. Nor had she seen passion in Georgiana's marriage; romantic love was something she had encountered only in the pages of novels. She recognized her father was difficult, yet she believed the love between her parents had blossomed because it had been reinforced by intellectual respect and the sharing of social pursuits. So, Harriet persuaded herself, affection would transform Duncannon as her mother's devotion had softened her father, and with him she would find the security and love she had always craved.

Both Lord Bessborough and the Spencers at first proclaimed delight at the match. But as soon as the detailed negotiations of the marriage settlement got under way the Spencers discovered cause for grave concern. Despite the vast Bessborough estates and the connection to the wealthy Cavendishes, the match was not as financially advantageous as they had believed it would be. Lord Bessborough was a heavy gambler as well as a connoisseur of antiquities and sculpture, and the costs of pursuing a political career and the extravagant purchases he had made had left the family heavily indebted. He could offer only £2,000 a year for the couple to live on and £400 a year pin money (the only money an aristocratic woman had to spend as she wished—thus her only financial independence) for Harriet.[62] In modern terms this equates roughly to an income of £120,000 and spending money for Harriet of £24,000, but this was less than a tenth of what Georgiana had to live on, and far less than Harriet had been used to enjoying.

Lady Spencer foresaw trouble ahead and although Georgiana did her best to reassure her—"to be sure, what you tell me of the circumstances is very small indeed, however should my sister like him, with her charming way of thinking I daresay she would be very happy"[63]—her mother remained unconvinced and felt duty-bound to point out the dangers to Harriet. "I have thought it my duty to represent strongly to her the inconveniences of so small a fortune compared to what she has hitherto seen and experienced in life."[64] Having seen the temptations of fashionable London life to which Georgiana had fallen prey, and knowing the closeness of the sisters, she was terrified of what might befall her second daughter should she be drawn into extravagance.

But she believed that Duncannon's prudent character and affection for Harriet would overcome this drawback. "I really think his character will give her a better chance of happiness than a much larger fortune if they like each other as much as I suspect they do."[65] By now the relationship had reached a stage where it would be impossible to extricate Harriet from the proposed marriage without causing a scandal and insulting the powerful Cavendish family. Lady Spencer could not bring herself to be the cause of such upset. Instead she wrote a long letter to Harriet on the eve of her wedding, impressing upon her the pitfalls to be avoided.

> . . . examine your own conduct continually and if you find in the smallest degree that you give a preference to one man rather than another, or are more flattered with his notice or approbation than with other people, resolve from that moment, however unnecessary the doing it may seem to you, to avoid him . . .

The next great object, and which is to be a most essential one, because I foresee how much your comfort and happiness will depend upon it, is your expenses. I made a little calculation of them some time ago, which I hope you will make a trial of. Alter it if by experience you find it necessary, but lay down some rule and abide by it; never allow yourself to borrow of anybody, and determine at all events not to run in debt to tradesmen etc. . . .[66]

Few among the Spencers' friends and acquaintances realized their concerns. The diarist and socialite Mrs. Delany reflected the general view in thinking the match must give "great satisfaction; as besides rank and fortune this is a most worthy amiable man, and I believe by all accounts she is a very valuable young woman, and I hope will have the good sense not to fall into those giddy errors, which have hurt her sister."[67]

One man looked harder and expressed doubts. "I confess I was surprised at his choice," wrote Horace Walpole in September. "I know nothing to the prejudice of the young lady—but I should not have selected for so gentle and very amiable a man, a sister of the empress of fashion, nor a daughter of the goddess of wisdom."[68] In other words, in his view Duncannon was hopelessly outclassed.

Throughout their three-month engagement, while the complexities of the marriage settlement were thrashed out, the trousseau bought, and wedding preparations made, Harriet's feelings vacillated wildly. "I wish I could have known him a little better first," she wrote; "there are some things which frighten me sadly, he is so grave and I am so giddy." Then, as if trying to convince herself, she reasoned, "it is impossible one should be very well acquainted with anybody in the intercourse of the world."[69]

But there was no one to whom she could turn for advice. England was under threat from France and, throughout the country, aristocrats were forming groups of militia to fight against impending invasion. Georgiana had gone to Portsmouth, accompanying the duke, whose troops were camped nearby. Her brother, newly engaged to Lavinia Bingham, the daughter of the Earl of Lucan, was also at camp, and further preoccupied with illness. Lord Spencer too was once again ill, and her mother so distraught there was no opportunity for proper discussion of such a delicate subject. "I am forced to make light of everything to keep up mama's spirits,"[70] she confessed sadly.

The wedding took place by special license at Spencer House in London, on November 27, 1780. Lady Spencer watched Duncannon slip the ring on Harriet's finger, her heart swollen with doubt as well as pride. She had tried to convince herself that the marriage was for love and that all would be well, but as Harriet bade her farewell after the wedding breakfast and mounted into her carriage with Viscount Duncannon, she was overcome with a rush of emotion that she could not contain. Tears poured down her cheeks.

The next day she wrote to Harriet to apologize. "I was foolish at feeling so much as I did yesterday, but whenever I have time to reflect on the comfortable prospect you have before you, it makes me reproach myself for repining one moment at the loss of you, such sensations are all selfish and I will have done with them."[71] But even after she sealed and dispatched the letter to Harriet, a sense of foreboding remained.

Two

Marriage and Motherhood
1780–1782

I MMEDIATELY AFTER THE WEDDING Harriet and Duncannon left town and traveled north to spend a month calling on various friends and relations. Lady Spencer followed their progress, uneasily imploring Harriet to keep in constant touch: "nothing could be more welcome than your abominable scrawl from Biggleswade," she wrote, bombarding her daughter with questions and practical advice. "Pray send me an exact account of how you pass your time and whether you like Milton better than London. I am rather anxious to know whether you took your diamonds with you, it was an idle thing if you did and I am half afraid if Lucy did not remember to put cotton over them that they are by this time reduced to powder—pray send me a full account of all this."[1]

On their return, six weeks after the wedding, Harriet and Duncannon took up residence with Lord Bessborough, sharing their time between the family's country seat in Roehampton, conveniently situated only a few short miles from the Spencers' Wimbledon Park, and a house in Cavendish Square. Bessborough House* was an elegant Palladian villa, designed for Lord Bessborough by William Chambers—for whom it was his first private commission. The house had a grand external horseshoe staircase sweeping up to a great columned portico and was set amid formal parterres and a romantic parkland dotted with

---

* The house was subsequently sold by the family and became a Catholic seminary. It was renamed Parkstead House and then Manresa House and now belongs to Roehampton University.

temples and rotundas. Bessborough was a noted connoisseur of antiq-uities and an avid collector of paintings and Harriet found elegantly stuccoed interiors adorned with paintings by Salvator Rosa, Nicolas Poussin, Jan van Eyck, and Rubens, and expensive furniture by Ince and Mayhew. Sculpture was another of Bessborough's passions. So keen a patron of the sculptor Nollekens was he that it was claimed that even the sculptor's dog recognized him and stopped barking when he came to call—because he always had a bread roll in his pocket.

Much about Bessborough must have reminded Harriet of her own father. Like John Spencer, he was a prominent member of the Dilet-tante Society. He had traveled widely and was one of the first aristo-crats to tour Greece and Constantinople, which he visited with his artist friend Jean Etienne Liotard. A portrait of Bessborough painted by Liotard in Constantinople shows him dressed in opulent oriental garb, complete with turban, brocade sash, and ermine-trimmed coat. But, as Harriet soon discovered on moving in with her father-in-law, in other respects Bessborough was very different in temperament from the distant and delicate John Spencer. Blessed with robust good health, Bessborough could be brusque and unsympathetic when other family members were ill. A famous extrovert and raconteur, he was also well known for being exasperatingly garrulous, and on occasion overbear-ing. "[He] can never grow better or worse or *other* than *he is*. It is in-credible what nonsense he talks. People listen and laugh; *cela lui suffit*,* he puts it all down to his credit, and stands like a mountebank with a circle around him, which he entertains with marvellous thing much in the same style,"[2] wrote one of his contemporaries, Mrs. Hervey, after an encounter.

As daughter-in-law, Harriet was expected to defer to Bessborough in all matters; to keep him company and act as hostess when he re-quired it; to disappear when he did not. These were duties that she em-braced wholeheartedly. Accustomed to the closeness of the Spencer household, she found that Bessborough's presence offered a reassuring bridge to full independence. However, for Lady Spencer, who had been accustomed to bossing her daughter with little interference, the new strictures on Harriet's conduct were to prove more problematic.

---

* That's enough for him.

Lady Spencer wanted to guide her daughter through the maze of convention that surrounded her newlywed status. Before the couple were observed by the king and queen in public at the opera, it was important, she reminded Harriet, to attend a "drawing room," one of the queen's twice-weekly audiences at St. James Palace. Above all she was frantic to find out whether Harriet was pregnant. Georgiana had been married for six years yet had still failed to produce a child, and Lady Spencer longed to become a grandmother. "I want so much to know how you do and whether the prince has paid his respects to you yet." (The "prince" was an eighteenth-century euphemism for menstruation.) Harriet infuriated her mother by omitting to reply to these inquiries. "I conclude there is no prince by your not mentioning it,"[3] Lady Spencer pressed.

When Harriet eventually let slip that she was feeling queasy, her mother needed no more evidence to confirm her suspicions. "Harriet is I really believe breeding—it is beginning very early, poor thing, and she is miserably sick and uncomfortable but she seems much in earnest in wishing to act prudently and I have great hopes she will behave vastly well,"[4] she excitedly told George Spencer. Lady Spencer advised Harriet to retreat to the quiet of Roehampton for the early stages of her pregnancy, when the risk of a miscarriage was highest. But Duncannon and his father thought such precautions unnecessary and, since they had the final word, Harriet remained at Cavendish Square, to carry on with the round of making and receiving visits that was expected of newlyweds.

At first all seemed to go well. Duncannon would later remember these weeks as some of the most frenetic and exhausting of his life, but he seemed a devoted lover, attentive and affectionate toward Harriet. Lord Bessborough too was clearly growing fond of his young daughter-in-law. Lady Spencer was delighted after dropping in at Cavendish Square one evening with Georgiana and Harriet's friend Miss Shipley. "[Duncannon] read some adventures to us as we worked—Lord Bessborough came home about eleven, seemed quite delighted with seeing us all in such a snug way and insisted upon cramming us with mutton broth, roasted apples, and toasted cheese. He was in fine spirits and it finished our evening very comfortably. I hope these little parties will be very much the fashion among us . . ."[5]

A month later, everyone still thought the ménage blissfully content. "Harriet's closet is becoming a *vrai bijou*," Lady Spencer reported confidently to Georgiana; "she and her husband pass many comfortable hours in it. I trust indeed that all will go on very well in that quarter . . ."[6] Harriet actively encouraged this impression. When Duncannon presented her with a bouquet of roses in February, she sent some to Georgiana as proof of his affection.

In fact, behind the facade the relationship was already under strain. Duncannon had not easily adapted to marriage and his solitary nature found the constant social engagements demanded of a newly married aristocrat an ordeal. It is uncertain what precisely lay at the root of the friction between them, but several factors probably played a part. Harriet, unlike Duncannon, was accustomed to leading an outgoing life. She had been well schooled in social graces; perhaps her gregariousness, added to her intellect and glamour, made him feel gauche when they were out together. Perhaps too her expectations of openly displayed affection and sentiment—so readily forthcoming in her own family—jarred with his natural reserve. Motherless from the age of two, Duncannon had no recollection of seeing his parents together and no notion of domestic harmony against which to match his behavior. The sexual relationship and novelty of having a woman at his disposal may also have caused him to grow possessive and resentful of other demands upon Harriet's time and attention, and overly suspicious of other men's gazes.

What is certain, however, is that his affability could quickly disappear, and he would turn offensive and domineering, to the extent of losing control of himself in public. Georgiana already had an inkling of his ill temper when Harriet sent her a sample of the roses Duncannon had given her. "Whilst he behaves well I am his *très* humble servant and I am going to write to him with great punctuality and *doux comme miel*,"[7] she told her mother—the obvious implication being that he did not always behave well.

In the small gossipy world that made up Whig society Duncannon's less pleasant side did not long remain a secret. Whispers began to circulate; Duncannon had taken to flying into rages with Harriet and humiliating her in public. Lord Bessborough knew what was happening, but although he recoiled at his son's behavior and doubtless felt sympathetic toward Harriet, he was unable or unwilling to restrain him.

Harriet had never been subjected to openly harsh treatment in her life, and although she told herself she must act discreetly at all costs she struggled to do so. Her emotions, which had always been close to the surface, were particularly high in the early stages of her pregnancy. Furthermore, in the eyes of society, marital breakdown represented an indelible stain on a woman's reputation; thus, at the age of nineteen, she stared failure in the face. Harriet said nothing of her agonies to her family, but when Duncannon berated her in public she was unable to stop herself from becoming tearful and agitated, and the predicament was plain for all to see. The Spencers learned of the situation but, fearing that to intervene would only worsen matters, instead conspired in collective denial and tried to carry on as if nothing untoward were happening.

Matters came to a head when a senior member of the Cavendish family stepped in. The Duke of Devonshire's sister, the Duchess of Portland, witnessed several scenes in which Duncannon criticized Harriet so unkindly in public that her distress was embarrassing for everyone present. Feeling his behavior had begun to reflect badly on the entire Cavendish family, she called Duncannon aside one evening and discreetly but firmly cautioned him. He should improve his manners toward his wife if he did not wish to plunge the family into scandal and ruin his own good reputation. Shocked by her tone, Duncannon muttered a reply that convinced the duchess he would do as she asked and all would be well. Instead, only a few days later, at a ball at the Duchess of Portland's house, the crisis escalated.

Duncannon had been playing cards happily with his friends when Harriet entered the room dressed glamorously and wearing her diamonds. Immediately, he grew irritated by the attention she attracted and began to bombard her with criticism. It was inappropriate to have worn her diamonds, he claimed, shouting at Harriet in such an unpleasant manner that she grew distressed and faint and there were fears she might miscarry. Unable to contain herself, the Duchess of Portland flew to Harriet's defense, chastising Duncannon roundly in front of her guests. He, boiling with rage, accused the duchess of unjustly attacking him and meddling in matters that were no concern of hers. He had done nothing wrong, Harriet was his wife and thus under his control; in his view, therefore, *he* rather than Harriet was due an apology. When none was forthcoming from the duchess he stormed from the room.

In the days that followed there was a standoff. Duncannon refused to back down in his assertion that it was *he* who had been publicly wronged rather than Harriet and *he*, therefore, who deserved to be placated. Meanwhile the Duchess of Portland remained so outraged at his behavior that she wrote, reminding him in the strongest terms of the reason for her fury.

> I was hurt and disappointed beyond measure to think that the very serious conversation I had with you some few mornings before would have been so totally disregarded and forgotten—indeed the very first evening that you came to me after that conversation *the night of the Ridotto* I never felt more ashamed or hurt than I did for you and I must tell you that your behaviour did not escape the notice of the company who heard it as well as myself with astonishment. The cards were going to your mind, nothing had happened to put you out of humour, but upon Lady Duncannon's coming into the room, as I thought very properly dressed, your temper was immediately ruffled because she had put on her diamonds . . . such sort of behaviour in a man is so perfectly new that I do not know how to account for it or reason upon it . . . recollect the most respectable characters in this country—have you perceived or ever heard of such conduct in them? . . . Indeed, my dear Lord . . . you have not one moment to lose, I look upon it that your character is as much at stake as ever man's was—you may possibly think that this letter is dictated by resentment or some remains of my anger the other night, but whatever warmth I might have shown at that or any other time, it could only have been occasioned by a desire of saving you from impending ruin . . . in short if you do not examine yourself and take a resolution to make a total change in your actions the consequence must be that you will be hated and detested by those who naturally and otherwise would have loved you, and despised and laughed at by the rest of the world . . .[8]

Realizing that if he were to bully his wife into submission the feisty duchess would only fight back, Duncannon now backed down and wrote her a fawning apology: "If I can appease you I will fall upon my knees, I will kiss your foot."[9] But his excuse—that he was tired after a long committee meeting and fearful that Harriet might miscarry—did not allay the duchess's fears one jot. She replied unbendingly that if anyone were to blame should Harriet miscarry it would be him. "I certainly do not mean to aggravate your misfortune, but as your sincere friend and well wisher I must disclose to you in the utmost confidence my apprehensions that the frequent agitations that I have perceived your conduct to occasion her may have been the cause of this unhappy event. I trust in God she will recover this, and that it will hereafter be uppermost in your mind to reward her affection for you with that confidence which she so well deserves."[10]

The fact that in Harriet's correspondence with her mother there are no direct references to this very public argument speaks volumes. In late-eighteenth-century society, aristocratic wives were in certain senses extremely liberated, but they were still regarded as their husbands' possessions. Provided they did not actually imprison their wives or endanger their lives, husbands were by and large free to act as badly toward them as they pleased. They could chastise them with impunity or resort to corporal punishment as well as verbal abuse if they felt so inclined. Harriet understood this and was adamant that her place was with Duncannon. For their part, the Spencers, knowing there was very little either she or they could do, apart from pray that by ignoring the problem it would improve, must have been thankful for her resolve. "May God almighty bless her and support [her] in the difficult part I fear she has to act through life," wrote Lady Spencer with uncharacteristic openness to Georgiana. "Though I trust all is for the best her persevering in the right path is the likeliest way to make her happy here and must make her so hereafter."[11]

In the immediate aftermath of the row Harriet and Duncannon left town and went to Roehampton. Lady Spencer bombarded Harriet with inquiries after her health: "If you have any pain in your back or any illness beside sickness I will come to you."[12] The stress of the situation made Harriet develop a worrying cough. When the couple dropped in at Wimbledon Park a few days later, Lady Spencer reported that Harriet "seems better and coughs up,"[13] though, mindful of family solidarity, she did not allow herself to comment further on the relationship.

Three days later Harriet rushed back to London, leaving Duncannon in the country. Lady Spencer worriedly asked her friend Mrs. Howe to call in on her, and her concern mounted when Harriet refused to see Mrs. Howe on two occasions. Meanwhile, responding to the family disquiet, Georgiana reduced her social engagements and kept her sister company as often as she could.[14] But the dilemma remained: Georgiana could not keep perpetual watch over Harriet once Duncannon returned or demanded that Harriet rejoin him. In any case, too much intervention would exacerbate an already delicate situation, giving Duncannon the impression that the Spencers were in league against him. Yet if they did nothing he might feel exonerated and thus subject Harriet to further upset and cause her to lose her unborn child.

Fraught with uncertainty, Lady Spencer could not help herself from further intervention. She pressed Harriet to come and stay with her, suggesting that if she asked her doctor to advise the visit Duncannon could not refuse the request. Harriet followed this counsel and was allowed a fleeting visit. Not surprisingly, however, her mother's continual meddling had the very effect everyone had hoped to avoid. Duncannon became increasingly resentful of the Spencer influence and demands on his wife. Lady Spencer realized too late and tried to smooth matters by self-consciously including flattering messages to Duncannon in many of her letters to Harriet. But the frequent references to correspondence going astray and being misdirected imply that she had reached the unpalatable conclusion that Duncannon's jealousy of Harriet's family, and of her mother in particular, was now leading him to tamper with and intercept their mail.

By July, with only a month until the baby was due, uneasy peace descended as everyone put aside their differences and rallied around Harriet in preparation for the birth. The Duncannons, together with Lady Spencer, Georgiana, and several other friends, crammed themselves into a single coach to travel together to Lady Aylesford's ball — no easy matter given Georgiana's and her mother's vast hooped skirts "and Harriet's encumbrance."[15] Afterward, Duncannon decided Harriet should pass the last uncomfortable weeks of pregnancy away from the heat of the city, in the rural tranquillity of Roehampton. Always a firm devotee of the benefits of country living, Lady Spencer was temporarily placated, but as the time for delivery drew nearer she grew uneasy and once again could not prevent herself from interfering.

Although recent research[16] has shown that during the eighteenth century maternal mortality occurred in only 2 percent of cases, and that 98 percent of births took place successfully with no intervention, in those days childbirth was something all women regarded with dread and trepidation. Perinatal complications were widely regarded as one of the most common reasons for a young woman to die—and before the advent of modern anesthesia, everyone knew that even straightforward labors and deliveries were often painful and prolonged. Most aristocrats favored delivery in London, where the best medical assistance was readily on hand. Lady Spencer was thus adamant that Harriet should be ensconced in Cavendish Square in good time for the delivery, but once again Duncannon stood in her way, refusing to allow Harriet to leave Roehampton. Harriet was still in the country, feeling "fidgety and uncomfortable," at the end of the first week of August. Lady Spencer now decided that medical advice was the most tactful way to achieve her aim of moving her daughter back to London. Even Duncannon could not argue with a doctor.

From the first days of her pregnancy Harriet had been looked after by Dr. Denman, a leading male midwife or *accoucheur,* the eighteenth-century equivalent of an obstetrician. Lady Spencer heartily approved of his natural noninterventional approach to labor, which departed from tradition in advocating fresh air and cleanliness rather than the hot and stuffy unhygienic rooms that had previously been the norm. Having enlisted Denman's support, Lady Spencer arrived unannounced at Roehampton one Saturday morning. She found Duncannon absent, and Harriet (as Lady Spencer later attested) suffering from severe pains, and "so complaining that it was thought proper to remove her immediately to town, which was not effected without difficulty from so much increase of pain in the carriage that I grew quite terrified about her."[17] No sooner was Harriet settled into Cavendish Square than her pains miraculously subsided. We do not know how her husband responded to the discovery that once again his mother-in-law had made her presence felt and whisked his wife to town against his express wishes.

In an agony of suspense Lady Spencer returned to Wimbledon to await a summons from Duncannon. Aristocratic women were usually assisted in their labor by a close female relative, and Lady Spencer was determined that she would fulfill this role and be present at the birth of her first grandchild. In Plympton, Georgiana could not help ruefully comparing her sister's impending motherhood with her own childless state, and was deeply moved by "some beautiful children in the village, *almost* as I expect the little brat to be." She, like every other woman of her day, was terrified by the thought of Harriet's labor. "I am sure every pain in her body will be answered by the ideal pain of my mind."[18]

Meanwhile, Harriet passed the next twelve interminable days growing increasingly uncomfortable and restless, writing letters to Georgiana and playing games with Charlotte Williams, the Duke of Devonshire's seven-year-old illegitimate daughter. The doctors treated her symptoms in the usual eighteenth-century manner, by bleeding, which Lady Spencer believed made her more comfortable.

Her labor began at three o'clock in the morning of Friday, August 31. Duncannon's messenger arrived at Wimbledon just as Lady Spencer was about to have breakfast. She rushed to Cavendish Square, arriving to find Dr. Denman and attendants on hand with clean linen and water. "And in two hours after I arrived she produced a fine bouncing boy. She is vastly well and so is the child,"[19] wrote Lady Spencer proudly to George, adding what she dared not confess to poor childless Georgiana: "I feel so well pleased with my new acquired title of grandmother that I care not how often it may become my due." The delighted Lady Spencer could not bring herself to leave Harriet until midafternoon, when she went home in time to eat the second course of dinner, before dashing back to Cavendish Square to sit with Harriet until ten, "nursing them both and writing letters . . . when I returned to Wimbledon supped, played at commerce and Macao, lost my money, sat up late, and went to bed quite tired."[20]

Despite her own childless predicament, Georgiana greeted the news of the birth of John William Ponsonby with unstinting good wishes. "I cannot express my joy, my happiness at my dearest dearest dear sister's being so well . . . I can scarce stay where I am, I am so impatient to see her and the dear little boy. Pray send me an exact account of him, are his eyes black or blue? What would I give to see her suckling him . . ."[21] A few days later she wrote again, dismayed that reports of French ships being sighted in the Channel meant that she and the duke must stay with his regiment, and longing for a baby of her own: "How much more than words can express should I be obliged to dear demure Dr. Denman would he enable me to give little Ponsonby a playfellow or a wife . . ."[22]

NEW MOTHERS HAD a month in which all their usual household duties were suspended and they were not expected to do anything except receive the occasional visitor—usually close female family members—and recover from the birth. Denman, no doubt urged on by Lady Spencer, was tyrannical in impressing on Harriet the importance of observing this tradition, warning that her health "for months if not years depends upon the care she takes now."[23] Harriet was not allowed to move from her bed, or even to have her sheets changed for several days. Meanwhile Lady Spencer bustled back and forth, nursing Harriet and showering her with advice, while privately admitting that becoming a grandmother had not lived up to her expectations. "Instead of the quiet calm thankfulness I hoped to have experienced I felt nothing but an agitation and hurry of spirits that prevented reflection and made me dash into everything that was purposed like any who was drunk,"[24] she confessed in her journal.

It is little wonder she felt agitated. Over the following days, she sometimes called in on Harriet as many as six times a day, then wrote detailed reports to an anxious Georgiana. "The boy has sucked slept and done everything else he ought to do with the most brilliant success," she recorded, before going on to describe his appearance: "He looks very red and very brown—he has no eyebrows and an enormous wide mouth but in revenge he has beautiful blue eyes, a head of dark brown hair and every circumstance that denotes health about him."[25] Harriet's recovery was steady; she ate a special diet of boiled chicken and rabbit, and was treated with a glister,* only venturing up to eat in her dressing room and receive visitors there ten days after John's birth.

In keeping with the latest thinking, Harriet was determined to breast-feed John herself, rather than employ a wet nurse as her mother

---

* A type of enema.

had done. Lady Spencer was supportive of her desire. "I hope [she] will make an excellent nurse, which I am more desirous of as she is so very anxious about it herself."[26] Harriet did not take to breast-feeding as easily as she expected—she complained of soreness "occasioned by [John's] biting too hard, which puts her to a good deal of pain"[27]—but nevertheless John seemed to thrive, and Duncannon, brimming with pride at his new son, seemed a changed man, affectionate and considerate toward Harriet. "[He] behaves vastly well and with unaffected tenderness to [Harriet] and they both seem happy beyond description in the little boy,"[28] reported a delighted Lady Spencer, praying that the earlier difficulties between Harriet and Duncannon were now over.

But Harriet's lying-in did not continue as smoothly as it began. A fortnight after John's birth, Duncannon developed a cold that turned into an autumn fever. The family doctor, Dr. Warren, was summoned and assured Duncannon his condition was not serious. Nevertheless, he grew melancholic, wanting Harriet to nurse him instead of staying in her room. Harriet was terrified that she or the baby might catch Duncannon's infection, but his recent kindness toward her, coupled with fear of rekindling his temper, eclipsed everything else. She passed the next days rushing from nursing John to sit by Duncannon's side, read to him, write letters for him, instruct his servants, and perform any other service he asked.

The demands of her baby, together with looking after the ailing Duncannon, took a predictable toll. Harriet developed a pain in her side, possibly the onset of the tuberculosis that was to plague her later in life. Lady Spencer recommended rubbing the affected area briskly with a flannel. Significantly, she did not attempt to dissuade Harriet from looking after Duncannon: she understood Harriet's predicament too well.

Lord Spencer's health had also taken a turn for the worse, and this coupled with social commitments meant that Lady Spencer now had to travel to Althorp. While she was away, she monitored Harriet through her friend Mrs. Howe, who dropped in daily to Cavendish Square. On her first visit both Dr. Denman and Dr. Warren were at the house. Warren said that Duncannon was not seriously ill and had ordered the exhausted Harriet to rest. But Harriet, still fearful of her husband's displeasure, refused to return to bed even when drooping with tiredness. "[She] never leaves Lord Duncannon when she can help it,"[29] said Mrs. Howe sympathetically. Two days later she again reported, "Lady Duncannon is so much with her lord . . . that I could but just see her today." A few days later, Duncannon's health suddenly improved and his melancholy disappeared; with this, Harriet's strength seemed to return. "His lowness too is gone off, with this has taken such a load off Lady Duncannon's mind; she is in charming spirits."[30] Harriet's appearance had also begun to bloom. "[She] looks in high beauty today, her complexion has a little glow, her hair is dressed, and she has a handsome cap on."

Despite the improvement Harriet was exhausted, which affected her milk, and John failed to thrive, which in turn made Harriet downcast and fretful. Lady Spencer ordered rest. "I think you do not keep yourself quiet enough which fatigues your spirits. Lady Weymouth, who is very strong and certainly very well accustomed to these things, does not get off chair above twice in the day."[31] There were also problems with the nursery staff. John's head nurse had to be dismissed, according to Lady Spencer, because of "some defect very possibly in her teeth which makes her unfit for such an office." In fact Lady Spencer had discovered the nurse feeding him pap to settle him because she doubted her mistress had enough milk. "I do not think this sounds natural or reasonable as you are able and willing to suckle him all day long if he wants it," she advised her overwrought daughter. A fortnight later Dr. Warren suggested Harriet should employ a wet nurse or supplement the child's feed, while Lady Spencer, blaming Duncannon for the difficulties, urged her to do nothing but remain calm. "I am firmly convinced that if they will *vous laissez faire* you will make one of the best nurses in the world . . . indeed I have very little doubt that Lord Duncannon's illness has prevented the child thriving."[32]

By now the month of Harriet's lying-in had passed and Lord Bessborough was impatient to organize the christening as soon as possible. To celebrate the birth of their first grandchild the Spencers presented Harriet with a new gown—a sign not only of generosity, but perhaps too of continuing concern at their daughter's financial predicament. The detailed instructions Lady Spencer gave Harriet for her "mantua maker," as female dressmakers were known, highlight the intricacies of fashions of the age. For much of the eighteenth century the appearance of female dress had been dominated by the hooped petticoat, a garment made from linen and whalebone, which held out the skirts in graduated circles. But by the 1780s the hoop was used mainly for court dress and formal balls; otherwise the bustle—a large roll made from cork or cushion stuffing—was tied around the waist to hold out the dress. Since flimsy materials were favored and no drawers were worn beneath petticoats, the hems of gowns were often weighted down to avoid the embarrassment of accidental exposure. Lady Spencer suggested such a measure to Harriet: "There must be no wadding in the gown, only the sarcenet lined with Persian and the border must be thinly wadded and quilted in a pattern in the same shape and same as your printed linen borders, which you had better show her. The petticoat likewise should have only a deep border of quilting and no diamonds at top or very large ones, which ever you like best."[33]

John's christening took place in the late afternoon of October 8, 1781. In the event, Harriet did not wear the dress her mother had given her, instead donning an even grander gown "of striped gauze ermined with blond upon a pale pink lutestring,"[34] that Georgiana had sent her. Georgiana's extravagant presents also included "a whole set of things for the child to lie upon the couch made exactly after the Queen of France's," which, Lady Spencer declared, "were altogether both beautiful and magnificent."[35] She was delighted to see her daughter so well attired; yet the extravagance of the gifts made her wince. Ever since Harriet's engagement she had fretted that Georgiana's immoderateness might lure Harriet into an addictive world of consumption, and that this would present Duncannon with further cause for grievance. "Be assured you will ever find more happiness in a reasonable than in a dissipated life. I am sure we both know an example of this in she who is equally dear to us,"[36] she warned Harriet.

A month later Georgiana returned from Devon and the sisters were reunited. "She and Harriet cried pretty plentifully at the pleasure of seeing each other," reported Lady Spencer, delighted to see her favorite child again, yet still terrified that Georgiana's return would tempt Harriet into excess. When a new play was about to open at Ham, Lady Spencer advised Harriet not to attend. "You have acquired already a reputation as a mother, do not go and lose it for the first little temptation that comes in . . . you risk heating yourself with a crowd of people shut up in a small room and catching cold going out of it." Then, as if to add further weight to her argument, she added, "I beg you will be guided by Lord Duncannon, who I am sure cannot quite approve of it."[37]

At first Harriet concurred with her mother's suggestion, but Duncannon disagreed. He often attended social events without his wife, but he determined that on this occasion Harriet should accompany him to the play. Lady Spencer's constant interference since the birth of the baby had severely riled him—whatever his faults, with six visits a day from his bossy mother-in-law we can hardly blame him. Matters grew increasingly strained, so much so that Lady Spencer became terrified that Duncannon would forbid all communication between Harriet and her family. Yet even this fear did not halt her interference; instead she told Harriet to write to her in secret. "Fix your time for writing to me to be as soon as ever Lord Duncannon goes out to take his morning ride, because I do not choose your correspondence with me should ever be in his way . . . seal up your letters directly—direct it to me and initialise it to your father with two lines under the word *Althorp,* which will save Lord Duncannon the trouble of franking and give it immediately to Mr. Caulson desiring it may go by the first opportunity."[38]

HAPPILY FOR HARRIET and her mother, as the old year ended and a new one began, Duncannon's attentions were diverted from family jealousies by political events. The Ponsonbys, Spencers, and Cavendishes were all members of the Whig oligarchy, a privileged cluster of families who had supported the Glorious Revolution of 1688 that brought William of Orange to the throne, and they saw their duty as keeping the powers of the constitutional monarchy in check. Within the parliament of the day there were no firmly defined political parties, but a network of loyalties that changed and shifted according to prevailing issues. The Devonshire House Whigs, and Georgiana in particular,[39] had fallen under the spell of Charles James Fox, the charismatic thirty-three-year-old son of Henry Fox, Baron Holland. Fox was not a handsome man—with his crow-black bushy eyebrows, swarthy complexion, and squat muscular build he resembled a gypsy rather than a gentleman—but he had boundless energy and was one of the most brilliant orators of his day. He also had a talent for clarifying even the most complex of subjects and thought women were as important and influential to his political cause as were men. "His conversation is like a brilliant player at billiards," Georgiana wrote of him; "the strokes follow one another piff puff."[40] Duncannon was another firm follower of Fox's. The two mingled often not only at Georgiana's grand soirées but in the less refined surroundings of Brooks's—a fashionable gentlemen's gaming club in St. James's, much frequented by the Whigs—where both loved to drink and play cards late into the night.

Fox and the Whigs were supporters of the American colonists, who had severed all allegiance with the British crown, and vehemently opposed the stance of the current administration headed by Lord North. When North's government collapsed following the decisive defeat and surrender of the British under Cornwallis at Yorktown in November 1781, a new administration, headed by Lord Rockingham, was formed. In this government the senior position of secretary of state was shared between Fox and Lord Shelburne, a sympathizer with the king. Fox ensured that his loyal supporters within the Devonshire House circle were well rewarded for their assistance. The young playwright Richard Sheridan, after only two years in parliament, was granted office as undersecretary of state for the northern office. Harriet's brother, George Spencer, was given a place in the Treasury; Duncannon was appointed to the Admiralty.

Georgiana's reward for hosting soirées for Fox and his acolytes was to continue at the heart of political discussion—to be privy to Fox's thoughts, to be able to question, discuss, learn from the most dynamic politician of the day. To Georgiana, and to Harriet, who would enjoy similar privilege, this was a cherished prize. Politics had always been part of the lives of Spencer females; Harriet and Georgiana, like many daughters in Whig households,[41] had grown up hearing political discussion, and even though their father had been prevented from playing a direct political role they had often watched their mother and other family members actively support family interests in elections. Politics was as much part of the fiber of their being as social skills, indeed, as recent research has shown,[42] in the rarified world of the "ton" successful politics depended much upon female sociability—a quality both Georgiana and Harriet possessed in abundance. Females not only canvassed in elections, they played hostess to established and aspiring politicians and joined in the political debate without embarrassment. Thus for Harriet, as well as for Georgiana, the door that had always been ajar now opened wider, revealing a world that had never seemed so fascinating.

At this stage Harriet's life alternated between two extremes. There were periods of solitude at Roehampton, where she was often left for days on end to her own devices. Here, unafraid of Duncannon's temper, she spent her time writing long letters to her mother, in which every detail of John's progress was recorded. She threw herself into the life of a country chatelaine, mimicking her mother's interest in gardening and in charitable pursuits, feeding the poor and giving gifts to the needy, reminding herself of a fact she found increasingly difficult to believe—the privilege and good fortune of her own existence.

Harriet loved the quiet life and was devoted to John, but only up to a point. A life of protracted solitude in the knowledge that her sister was at the heart of so much excitement was not something she could wholeheartedly embrace. When Roehampton could no longer hold her, she turned to London and immersed herself in a hectic world of power, fashion, and indulgence. "Harriet came there very late and afterwards, between one and two, came here by way of supping, that is eating an orange with me," wrote Lady Spencer worriedly to Georgiana after an entertainment at Ranelagh Gardens at which the Prince of Wales was present. "She looks pretty well, but they keep terrible hours, which will destroy her health and her nerves in time."[43]

Whenever Harriet called on Georgiana at Devonshire House she found her sister preoccupied by politics. Two years earlier Georgiana had helped in canvassing support for Fox in the 1780 election, and he now begged Georgiana's help in again representing himself to the electorate.[44] Harriet watched Georgiana dress herself in the Whig colors of blue and buff and take the platform with other wellborn ladies. Here, she realized, was an exciting alternative to mindless frivolity or stultifying isolation—a means to satisfy her love of gossip and society, and stretch her intellect. At her sister's house, conversing with the dazzling and brilliant Fox, flirting with the libidinous yet cultivated Prince of Wales, discussing the latest debates with Sheridan, Harriet began to discover a purpose that filled a void and reinforced her beleaguered sense of identity.

But before political interests could properly stir Harriet, unexpected events intervened. In July, only three months after he had come to power, Rockingham died and Shelburne was appointed in his stead. Shelburne was notorious for his treacherous nature; Walpole described him as "a fictitious violin, which is hung out of a music shop to indicate in what goods the tradesman deals; not to be of service, nor to be depended on for playing a true note. He was so well known that he could only deceive by speaking truth."[45] Unable to do business with someone so untrustworthy and violently opposed to his views, Fox resigned his position. To demonstrate their solidarity, Duncannon, along with George Spencer and several other leading Whigs, followed suit.

As parliament and politics wound down for the summer, Harriet and Duncannon joined the Devonshires at Plympton in Devon. Lady Spencer promised to keep watch over John, but bade Harriet farewell with an anxious heart. Duncannon, she suspected, was once again tampering with Harriet's correspondence and giving the wrong forwarding instructions to prevent her from keeping in touch. "I do not like going against Lord D's instructions. I should be uneasy . . . as you are going so far if I did not know you were in good hands, but I depend much upon Lord Duncannon's care."[46] Again and again her letters to Harriet are larded with conciliatory remarks designed to appease her difficult husband. "Pray tell Lord Duncannon the fine magnolia he gave me did not flower till yesterday . . . I have just been to look at it and the flower is . . . very magnificent indeed."[47]

Harriet had been suffering from a troublesome cough when she left town, and Lady Spencer hoped that in Devon she would pass her days in what she regarded as healthy pursuits—sea bathing, riding and walking, and quiet evenings. Georgiana did her best to reassure her mother. "Lord Duncannon, my sister and I took a short walk around our little fort, which by the bye is vastly pretty . . . we stayed at home all the evening, we drew and the Duke . . . read. How much more one enjoys oneself than in the hurry of a town."[48] In fact, many days were spent far less circumspectly, staying in bed till late, then dressing up to inspect the Duke of Devonshire's regiment and enjoy a frenzy of dinners and dances. "We dawdled this morning away and then set out to dine at General Grey's and go to the Long room. My sister and I were dressed in white nightgowns and hats and feathers . . . and we were more admired than you can conceive; they said we looked and danced like twins," wrote Georgiana.[49]

Lady Spencer took her promise to keep watch over John seriously. Throughout Harriet's absence she made regular visits to Roehampton at different times of day to surprise the servants and make sure he was properly cared for. Harriet was still in Devon on John's first birthday and Lady Spencer marked the occasion by conscientiously ordering his nurse to bring him to her for the afternoon, then writing to Harriet to remind her of her maternal duty. "He looked most delightfully . . . I never saw a healthier, sweeter tempered, or more sensible child in my life."[50] By contrast Georgiana let slip that she and Harriet had passed the day in a more extravagant manner. "We put on some new riding habits called the Plympton uniform, and I had a surprise for my sister of a new pink gown, which she knew nothing of till she put it on. In the evening the servants danced and we danced with them."[51]

The Devonshire party also included Lady Elizabeth Foster— Bess—a new friend who would play a pivotal role in the lives of both sisters. Georgiana had first come across Bess with her sister Lady Erne in Bath, where the pair were taking the waters. "I never knew people who have more wit and good nature,"[52] wrote Georgiana soon after meeting them. Bess had recently separated from her husband, John Thomas Foster, ostensibly on account of his "selfish brutal passion,"[53] but in part because she detested living in Ireland, estranged from the bustle of society. Since then she had been forced into a life of penury; her father, the Earl of Bristol, begrudgingly supplemented the pittance her husband paid her with £300 a year (£18,000), despite an income of £20,000 a year.* Even worse, she had been forced to relinquish the care of her two sons, without any rights to see or even to write to them. The marriage had disintegrated when Bess was pregnant with her youngest child, Augustus, and she had been forced to give him up as soon as he was weaned. Since divorce required an act of parliament, and was thus available only to the very wealthy, the Fosters, like most unhappy eighteenth-century couples, had agreed on a private separation and Bess had consigned herself to what her brother, Frederick Hervey, termed "a gloomy dismal fate," unable to remarry, with no rights over her children and no means of supporting herself.[54]

If Harriet had ever considered leaving Duncannon, meeting Bess

---

* These figures are based on those published by Chapman & Dormer.

provided a salutary example of what life would hold in store if she did. Instead of distrusting Bess or resenting Georgiana's growing affection for her, as both Lady Spencer and George Spencer did, Harriet took warmly to her and during the time they spent together at Plympton formed the foundation of a friendship that would last all their lives.

Harriet returned to London in the autumn and settled herself dutifully in Roehampton to look after John. During these months she saw her mother infrequently. Lady Spencer claimed this was because she found it difficult to find a convenient time or mode of transport to visit her. "I have my cabriolet but the postillion is ill just now, and I have my horses, but no groom except your father's whom I dare trust myself with, so that I can only ride early, which would not suit your sister's hours as well as I could wish.[55] Behind such excuses we sense something more—a cover for Duncannon's reluctance to receive her. Harriet's forays to town and appearances in society now also became less frequent. "Harriet came here last night from the play with her eyes swelled out of her head at Mrs. Siddons' acting,"[56] recorded Lady Spencer of a rare evening at the Covent Garden Theatre, at which Harriet and Duncannon joined a party of Cavendishes in the family box. Harriet had not looked her best and had hinted something was wrong. "I wish you would learn to speak out, as mystery only destroys confidence—if you are breeding say so—or if you have a pain in your head or in your side or a cold—but I do not love doubtful expressions on interesting subjects . . . I do beg you will comply with my earnest request—of letting me know at the very first moment anything that distresses vexes or ails you . . . I speak strongly my dearest Harriet but it is to assist you in getting rid of what I think is a defect . . . a want of frankness."[57]

Harriet only confirmed her mother's suspicion that she was pregnant after Georgiana, much to the delight of the Spencers and Cavendishes, made a similar announcement. From Bristol Lady Spencer wrote wistfully, "I begin myself to long for a granddaughter."[58] Harriet was again suffering from violent nausea; this, Lady Spencer believed, was mainly because she was drinking too much and eating unwisely. "The chief fault I myself know in your management is your swallowing without chewing large mouthfuls of meat . . . besides this cut drink."[59] Georgiana, more sympathetic to her sister's malaise, reassured her: "I am very sorry you are so sick . . . I will nurse you very well when I come."[60]

Harriet treated her sickness with traditional remedies: the popular eighteenth-century cure-all, powdered bark—made from the bark of chinchona tree, from which the alkaloid quinine is nowadays extracted—and asses' milk, which was widely believed to have health-giving properties. When the sickness subsided, she threw herself into motherhood and household duties, doting on John and fretting over every minor ailment. Lady Spencer, equally eager to believe in the myth of domestic harmony, told herself that the marriage had at last settled down, and that Harriet's wholesome life and the new baby on the way meant that love between her daughter and Duncannon had really begun to grow. On the anniversary of their wedding she regarded their future together with optimism. "You give a very comfortable account of your way of living, God grant to you and dear Lord Duncannon continuation of the rational happiness you seem so well calculated to enjoy."[61]

THREE

Birth and Bereavement
1783

WHILE HARRIET WAS LIVING QUIETLY at Roehampton during the early months of her second pregnancy, Georgiana showed no such restraint, exhausting herself in London by continuing to entertain frequently and on a lavish scale. Reports of her eldest daughter's excesses soon reached Lady Spencer. Despite her preoccupation with Lord Spencer's ailments she grew terrified Georgiana's immoderateness would end in her miscarrying the child it had taken nine years to conceive, and she begged Harriet to impress upon her sister the need for rest. "I am afraid [Georgiana] worries her spirits and she does not know the harm that may do her, do try what you can to make her keep quiet a little while—I have so often miscarried I have good reason to believe from mere agitation of mind that I dread it for her."[1] Harriet replied consolingly, promising to do as her mother asked, but a few weeks later, when the nausea that had beset her vanished, the appeal of Roehampton paled and she too was drawn back to the excitements of London.

Pregnancy had hitherto been regarded as an ungainly state to be hidden rather than vaunted. Yet the sisters had no inhibition in throwing themselves into a whirl of breakfasts, dinners, assemblies, suppers, and visits to the theater. The frenetic socializing of two of London's most famous beauties, their expectant condition plain for all to see, invested the condition with a new modishness, so much so that Horace Walpole remarked on the latest way of wearing a bustle. "On prétend," he wrote to the Countess of Ossory in January 1783, "that certain invisible machines, of which one heard much a year or two ago, and which were said to [be] constructed of cork, and to be worn somewhere or other behind, are now to be transplanted somewhere or other before, in imitation of the Duchess of Devonshire's pregnancy . . ."[2]

Georgiana, with Harriet by her side, played hostess to French aristocrats and diplomats, and held a grand breakfast at Chiswick, at which the trees, shrubs, and sculptures in the garden were festooned with garlands of flowers. Guests included Louis XIV's cousin the Duc de Chartres, who wore a coat with pornographic buttons; these he showed off to Harriet, who innocently exclaimed, " '*quelle étrange boutons*,' not knowing what they were."[3] Both Harriet and Georgiana knew such escapades were at odds with their mother's view of how respectable ladies should behave. But Lady Spencer was conveniently distant, at the Derbyshire spa of Buxton, and it was all too easy for them to tailor the reports they sent and neglect to mention anything remotely contentious. Nevertheless, word of her daughters' dizzy lives soon reached Lady Spencer, and her sense of propriety was deeply offended. "The three Frenchmen I hear by everybody are detestable—I shall be glad if Monsieur d'Adhemar [the French ambassador] takes up the ton of being pleased and wishing to please, as I believe it is the only way to succeed here,"[4] she wrote, bristling with disapproval, from Buxton.

Torn between an ailing husband and wayward daughters, Lady Spencer was to find that her nerves grew increasingly frayed in the weeks that followed. When word reached her that Harriet had taken to gambling imprudently and had attended the opera, despite being troubled with nosebleeds and a persistent cough, she could take no more and expressed her disapproval unsparingly:

The hours and life you lead are certainly too irregular and I do not by any means approve of the hurry and fidget the fire scene at the opera would have given you . . . I hope with you when your little child is born it will be a reason for your leading a much quieter life . . . the inclination you have for play makes me still more uneasy than anything else. All the argument I can make use of on that subject with any efficacy is to remind you that you can no way wound my peace of mind more deeply than by running into that particular vice and believe me it is much easier to stop it now than it will be hereafter.[5]

Yet Harriet's penchant for gambling that so worried her mother was far from unusual: given her background, it would have been more surprising had she not been addicted to play. Gaming was a national obsession that infected every echelon of society, none more than the moneyed classes. While one critic may have exaggerated when he wrote, "Conversation among people of fashion is almost annihilated by universal card-playing . . . the people of quality scarce ever meet but to game,"[6] it was certainly true that in the circles in which Harriet and Lord Duncannon mingled men thought nothing of passing all night at the fashionable gaming clubs of London. "The gaming at Almack's, which has taken the *pas* of Whites, is worthy of the decline of our Empire, or Commonwealth, which you please. The young men of the age lose five, ten, fifteen thousand pounds in an evening there. Lord Stavordale, not one and twenty, lost eleven thousand there, last Tuesday, but recovered it by one great hand at hazard; he swore a great oath, — 'now if I had been playing *deep,* I might have won millions,'"[7] Horace Walpole observed wryly.

He was not alone in declaiming the destructive effects of the aristocratic passion for gambling. Newspapers of the age reflect public fascination and horror at the excessive losses and wins of aristocrats, and abound with tales of the suicides, duels, and ruin wrought by games of hazard, casino, faro, macao, and whist. The details were recounted not only to satisfy the appetites of readers for such salacious stories but also to illustrate the prevailing view that the aristocratic addiction to gambling was exerting a damaging effect on those of the lower echelons, drawing them to similar temptations that might lead to the ruination of the country. *The Times* declared:

The number of new gaming houses, established at the West-end of town, is, indeed, a matter of very serious evil, but they are not likely to decrease while examples of the same nature are held forth in the higher circles of life. It is needless to point out any one of these houses in particular: it is sufficient for us to expose the tricks that are practised at many of them to swindle the unsuspecting young men of fortune, who are entrapped into these whirlpools of destruction. The first thing necessary is, to give the guest a good dinner and plenty of wine, which most of these houses do gratis. When they are sufficiently intoxicated, and having lost all the money about them, their acceptance is obtained to Bills of Exchange to a considerable amount, which are frequently paid, to avoid the disagreeable circumstance of a public exposition in a Court of Justice.[8]

Wellborn women gambled just as recklessly as men, as much to alleviate the boredom of their lives as in the futile hope of growing richer. Lady Spencer had been brought up around gaming tables, and even in later years, although her fondness for cards distressed her, she could never resist a hand of whist. Georgiana had already caused herself and her family acute anxiety and embarrassment with gambling debts that exceeded her generous allowance, yet she too was unable to dampen her passion for play. But it was not only through her sister that Harriet was exposed to temptation, but through her husband too. Duncannon had witnessed his father's fondness for gaming since early childhood, and despite his financial limitations he too struggled to control his passion for play.

Gambling was also intertwined with the political world, for which Harriet's fascination was rekindled. Chief among those who captivated her attention was the man who already held sway over Georgiana—Charles James Fox. Since his resignation from the government over the appointment of Shelburne, Fox had returned to the drawing rooms and gaming tables of fashionable Whig society, where his charisma ensured that he was always surrounded by a coterie of followers and admirers. Harriet was not alone among those he held spellbound. After all-night sessions of cards at Brooks's, the Prince of Wales became equally enthralled when Fox held forth on his ideals and ambitions. Horace Walpole observed this unusual method of morning-after-the-night-before tutoring: "[Fox's] bristly black person, and shagged breast quite open, and rarely purified by any ablutions, was wrapped in a foul linen night-gown, and his bushy hair dishevelled. In these cynic weeds, and with epicurean good humor, did he dictate politics—and in this school did the heir of the Crown attend his lessons and imbibe them."[9]

In parliament, meanwhile, the unpopular Shelburne did not have enough support to maintain a majority. In February 1783, William Pitt, Shelburne's recently appointed Chancellor of the Exchequer and hitherto a friend of Fox's, was dispatched to invite Fox to join forces with the government and thus bolster his support. Fox's reply was uncompromising: he was happy to join Pitt but could not join any administration headed by Shelburne. "Then we need discuss the matter no further," replied Pitt. "I did not come here to betray Lord Shelburne."

Burning with indignation, Fox airily declared, "My friendships are perpetual, my enmities are not so,"[10] then he astonished everyone by joining forces with Lord North, whose handling of the war in America throughout the previous decade he had so bitterly criticized. One contemporary described the unlikely alliance as resembling a union between Herod and Pontius Pilate.[11]

Faced with the combined supporters of North and Fox, Shelburne could no longer command a majority and resigned on February 24, 1783. George III had detested Fox ever since his violent opposition to government policy in America. "That young man has so thoroughly cast off every principle of common honor and honesty, that he must become as contemptible as he is odious,"[12] he had written to Lord North in 1774. Fox's growing closeness to the Prince of Wales, with whom George III had a fraught relationship, had only increased the king's distrust. Anxious to avoid the unpalatable eventuality of a government that included Fox, the king thus invited Pitt to lead his administration. But Pitt, knowing he could not yet carry enough support, refused. Increasingly desperate, the king then tried Lord Weymouth, Lord Temple, and Lord Gower, and when they too turned down the offer on the grounds of insufficient backing he threatened abdication. Meanwhile, at Brooks's, Fox and his friends passed the time laying wagers on how long his reign would last. Eventually the king ceded to the inevitable. A new government with the Duke of Portland at its nominal head was installed; Fox was Foreign Secretary and Lord North in charge of Home affairs. The king was so livid that when Fox kissed his hand, Lord Townshend observed that he "turned back his ears and eyes just like the horse at Astley's when the tailor he had determined to throw was getting on him."[13]

With the new administration came a new office for Duncannon. He was appointed a Lord of the Admiralty and the duties of office, combined with the draw of the gaming tables of Brooks's, meant that Harriet was left largely to her own devices. She passed much of the final stages of pregnancy at Devonshire House, with Georgiana, waiting to see who would be first to begin her labor. In the event, on July 6, 1783, at Cavendish Square, after a labor that was "both sharper and more tedious than we had flattered ourselves it would have been after so many previous pains," Harriet's second son, Frederick, "a remarkably fine boy,"[14] was safely delivered. He was a large, thriving baby who suckled easily, and unlike her first lying-in there were no interruptions from Duncannon.

Six days after Frederick's birth, following a lengthy and painful labor, also supervised by Dr. Denman, Georgiana's first child, a daughter, whom she named Georgiana, or Little G, was born. A month later, the Spencer, Cavendish, and Ponsonby families congregated in the hall of Wimbledon Park, which had been bedecked with flowers and fruit, for the christenings of both children. Georgiana was dressed all in white, in a dress trimmed with Brussels lace, which matched that of Little G's christening gown. Harriet and Frederick were equally lavishly clad, while young John wore an elaborate costume given to him by the Duke of Devonshire.

It was the last time the three families would be united in such happy circumstances. Lord Spencer's health had not improved; he was suffering from a multitude of ailments, including gout, breathlessness, and, worst of all, deafness, "which I fear has increased, it is a most uncomfortable thing—I think I could bear it much easier myself than see him suffer by it,"[15] confessed Lady Spencer. As soon as the christening was over the Spencers set out for Kingsgate, near Margate, in Kent. Everyone hoped the sea air would revive Lord Spencer in a way the waters of Buxton had failed to do, but in a fever of worry Lady Spencer left without a proper goodbye to Harriet, excusing herself on the grounds that she could not "venture to stay for Harriet whose sensibility was too great for me to venture to meet in the miserable situation my poor harassed mind was in—I therefore thought the making my escape was the best thing for us all."[16] Only to George could she confide her worst fears:

The parting with you all was too much for me now and you who have as much sensibility as anybody I know will not I trust think me quite unreasonable—I should not quit you without a heart rending idea of what our next meeting might be—God grant than these melancholy imaginations may be groundless.[17]

Alone at Roehampton, Harriet had already reached the distressing realization that her father was fighting for his life. She fell into low spirits, which, combined with the demands of feeding the voracious Frederick, made her grow weak, and once again her troublesome cough returned. "I think I never saw [Harriet] look so ill—she has a dreadful cough and she is sick every instant—I confess I think her giant [Frederick] is too much for her—but she will not hear anybody who says this," pronounced George Spencer's wife, Lavinia, a week after the christening.[18] Harriet begged her mother to let her join her by the sea, but Lady Spencer dissuaded her. "Our stay is too short and if the weather grows worse too uncertain to let you take such a long tedious journey . . . another reason is that there is no means of bathing at this place."[19] The truth, that the sea air had failed to stem Lord Spencer's deterioration, was something she did not wish to admit to herself, let alone to Harriet.

Instead, she tried to help Harriet by filling her letters with practical advice. "If you find [that] suckling Frederick weakens [you,] you ought for both your sakes . . . to leave off or lessen the quantity of your milk by suckling him less often and feeding him oftener, which as he is so large and stout a child will possibly agree with him better, than living quite upon milk,"[20] she told Harriet on the day of John's second birthday, deliberately not mentioning Lord Spencer's worsening condition.

Harriet, Duncannon, and the children went to stay with Cavendish cousins in East Sussex just as Lord and Lady Spencer, despairing that sea air would effect any improvement, moved to Bath. "I like your way of life at Compton Place. It is healthy, sociable and reasonable,"[21] wrote Lady Spencer wistfully. However, Harriet did not find the visit as restful as she had hoped. Lady George Cavendish "teased her cruelly," Georgiana wrote, with rumors concerning Georgiana's friendship with "the eyebrow [Fox] and Bess's friendship with the Duke of Dorset, and the Duke's affair with Lady Jersey, 'the infernal,' " and "so blended with truth that my sister was quite hurt."[22]

As Harriet dodged awkward questions in Sussex, in Bath a train of the city's finest medical experts ministered to her father, who had now lost all appetite and struggled to swallow even the smallest glass of curative waters. In these unhappy circumstances the city had lost its former appeal for Lady Spencer, and she could not help reminiscing nostalgically about the last time Harriet had been with her, before her marriage. "I have been down to the pump room and parade since I arrived and taken a look at the old house—I do not want these remembrances of you, my heart reminds me of you often enough without them—however I miss you some how or other more here than anywhere." As Lord Spencer grew ever more weak, Harriet's mother was overwhelmed by a torrent of emotion that wiped everything else from her mind. "My whole thought and attention are so taken up with your father's health that I feel stupefied to almost everything else."[23]

She sat helplessly as a succession of eminent doctors prodded and poked Lord Spencer, dosed him on cordials and emetics and draughts of medicinal waters, doused him in the baths, and then pronounced their judgments. "Your father . . . certainly has some gout in his stomach, which he keeps off by laudanum, it is hoped the small quantity of Bath waters he takes will by degrees drive it into his feet,"[24] she reported. Days later Lord Spencer was so weak and stupefied by laudanum that he spent most of his time dozing. Walking the three or four steps from the roadside to the pump room had proved too much; he had nearly fainted on one occasion. But all the various doctors still claimed "that the waters are the best remedy" and that he was stronger than he was. A week later Lord Spencer was dead.

The stalwart Lady Spencer was shattered by the loss. She took laudanum to help her through the first days and nights following his death, and when her son George, now the Second Earl Spencer, arrived and tried to persuade her to leave, she could hardly bring herself to follow his advice. "I own I wish much to remain here till my dear, dear husband is removed—there is something inexpressibly painful to me in the thoughts of abandoning him to servants and so soon avoiding and flying from what I have long and so ardently loved,"[25] she wrote poignantly in her diary. Having agreed to leave when George and her brother came to fetch her, she was overcome by emotion. "I was half frantic and wanted to go into his room—I had not power to pass by his door and my brother and George were forced to drag me downstairs and lift me into the coach."[26]

At Althorp, the devastated dowager Lady Spencer awaited her husband's coffin.[27] The richly ornamented hearse first passed through the town of Northampton, where the staff from Althorp joined a procession numbering three thousand people, including charity boys, tenants, local gentlemen and tradesmen, mourning carriages, a rider carrying the coronet on a crimson velvet cushion, and liveried, plumed footmen. The procession wound its way at a stately pace through the cobbled streets and thence to the house. Here the body was laid out in state in the grand drawing room, where estate workers could pass by and pay their respects. "I believe it was the most solemn, the most numerous, and most respectful procession that has ever been seen in this kingdom,"[28] wrote Robert Hawdon, the Spencers' understeward.

Imprisoned by a maelstrom of grief, Lady Spencer was unable to witness this with her own eyes. For the past forty years she had been a constant companion to her husband; she had loved him above all else. Now, without him, she became a shadow of her former self, devoid of appetite and unable to sleep without a sedative. "I have had two tolerable nights . . . as I had four hours' good sleep without laudanum," she confessed to Harriet, to whom she turned for solace. "I long to . . . talk with you on the many subjects we have to derive consolation from . . . we shall by this means strengthen each other's resignation."[29] Harriet made brief, frequent visits to her mother during the weeks after her father's death, "and we are both the better for having met,"[30] although, according to Georgiana, Duncannon's distrust of his mother-in-law had not diminished and despite her bereavement he would not permit Harriet to "be with her [mother] above three days at a time."[31]

Lady Spencer was the sole executor of her husband's will—a duty that entailed long meetings and the unraveling of a lifetime's expenditure. Examination of the Spencer accounts revealed that the years of reckless spending on building and art, not to mention political expenses and gambling, had seriously depleted the family's wealth. The Spencers no longer possessed the princely fortune they had always assumed would be theirs. Among the debts, it also now emerged that half of Harriet's settlement of £20,000 had never been paid; £10,000 was still owed to Lord Bessborough. The entire family would have to make economies to pay this and other outstanding sums.

The excesses of her married life had often made Lady Spencer uneasy—although she would never have said so to her adored husband. But now that he was gone, and circumstances were altered, she decided to adopt the simple existence to which she had always aspired. She would retire to Holywell House, the relatively modest Spencer residence near St. Albans that had previously been used only as a stopping-off point between London and Northampton, and devote herself to farming and charitable pursuits. The rest of the estate she would hand over to George, who in return agreed he would pay off the debts and increase her annual allowance from £3,000 to £4,000. The complexities of the estate took George months to unravel. The following autumn the delicate question of how to find the £10,000 to pay Lord Bessborough was still unresolved and Lady Spencer drafted the following proposal for her son's approval:

> I had hoped by this time to have fulfilled my trust by paying your lordship the £10,000 due as the remainder of Lady Duncannon's fortune. My son has been disappointed by a person who had engaged to supply him with the money and your lordship need not be told how difficult it is at this time to raise any—we hope however to succeed by the beginning of the summer when your lordship shall receive both the interest and the principal due upon it to that tune unless your lordship would rather choose to have the whole £10,000 secured by a mortgage in which case it shall be made out immediately.[32]

Part of the reason for their prevarication may have been the Spencers' ongoing concerns regarding the Bessborough finances. Their offer of an immediate mortgage was aimed to tempt Lord Bessborough to accept a measure that effectively protected the principal sum from gambling debts, and thus safeguarded the settlement money for Harriet's children.

Georgiana had been at Chatsworth when news of her father's death reached her, and was so upset that she developed a fever that then spread to the duke and Little G.[33] By the time she visited her mother in December, Lady Spencer had turned a corner and she was "dining at table and eating like other people," and taking an interest in her family, and, above all, in the gripping events unfolding in the world at large. George and Harriet had roused her from the lassitude of grief by feeding her snippets of political and social news. "I am sure your whole mind is taken up with politicks, which touch me little more than as a curious unpleasant transaction,"[34] Lady Spencer wrote to Harriet at the year's end, with more prescience than she knew.

FOUR

Politics and Play
1784

HARRIET BEGAN WEANING her baby as the new year dawned. Frederick had been so continually hungry that feeding him had left her feeling drained and low. "I sincerely hope it will be some time before you are breeding again and that you will eat a great deal of blancmange, calves' foot, and hartshorn jelly, issinglass boiled in milk, and other things of that sort,"[1] Lady Spencer advised. Harriet had asked her to come and stay at Roehampton, but Lady Spencer refused the invitation on the grounds that it might offend her brother—perhaps a tactful way of avoiding Duncannon. Instead she begged Harriet to persuade her husband to let her come and stay at St. Albans. "I would take the greatest care of your diet, hours, etc., and am sure I should do you good."[2] In fact, Harriet had no desire to live a life of early nights and regular hours. Even as she nursed Frederick in her boudoir in the quiet of Roehampton, she had been well aware that the subject of politics dominated everyone's thoughts and conversation, and once she was free she rushed to London and plunged herself eagerly into the political fray.

No sooner had Parliament reopened following the summer recess than Fox embarked on a dangerous and controversial course of action that was to have widespread repercussions among the Whigs. Ever the gambler, he decided to take a grand risk and put forward a bill aimed at reorganizing the East India Company. The business was vast—with a revenue of £7 million and control of a population of thirty million people—yet for years it had been maladministered by directors who had grown fabulously rich on its resources. Everyone knew that something needed to be done, but the problem of what and how was one that politicians had been too frightened to address.

Fox audaciously stepped in where others feared to tread. His new bill proposed that the company should be governed by a commission of seven men to be selected by parliament—in other words, Fox's friends. Not surprisingly, the king and Fox's opponents regarded such measures as a further infringement of royal power, compounding Fox's earlier sin of forcing himself upon an unwilling monarch. Pitt accused Fox of "absolute despotism" but failed to convince the majority of MPs to follow him, and when the bill was presented to the Commons for the vote Fox's magnetism and brilliant oratory were enough to win the day. But elsewhere support for "the man of the people" began to waver. City merchants fretted that if Fox were allowed to reform the East India Company, he might next turn his attentions elsewhere—perhaps to their own institutions. The press added further fuel to the whispers; spurred by financial incentives from Pittite supporters, newspapers proclaimed that Fox was cashing in on the wealth of the Indies for his own benefit, flouting the wishes of the king, and thus threatening the very existence of the monarchy upon which national stability depended. Lampoonists took up the baton, portraying a monstrous oversized Fox, exotically dressed as "Carlo Khan," charging the company headquarters astride an elephant with Lord North's face.

The swing against Fox brought the chance for which the king had prayed: a means to rid himself of his enemy. Capitalizing on the new mood of distrust, George III made it clear to his peers that he would regard anyone who voted for the bill as his personal enemy. George Spencer wrote to his mother of "the extraordinary events of last night," and described the bill's demolition in the House of Lords. "The whole bedchamber and all the household court voted against us and decided the question, and it is known from very good authority that many of them had direct intimations from the king that such conduct would be agreeable to him ... I think the immediate consequence must be a total change of administration and an immediate dissolution of parliament."[3]

Having already secured Pitt's agreement that he would take on the role of first minister, the king immediately sent word to North that the seals of his department and Fox's were to be submitted via their undersecretaries. He would not receive them personally, "as audiences on such occasions must be unpleasant."[4] A day later, on December 19, 1783, the twenty-four-year-old William Pitt was announced in the House of Commons as Britain's youngest ever first minister.*

There was little the embattled Whigs could do to stem the tide against them, yet at first they did not comprehend the gravity of their predicament. Georgiana, writing to her friend Lady Elizabeth Foster, reported that by early January 1784 "the Duke of Portland and all his party, all and one have resigned, and Mr. Pitt and Lords Gower and Thurlow are in, but we have the majority still in the House of Commons, which, it is supposed, must rout them."[5] In fact, although Pitt was defeated sixteen times over the next three months, his position at the head of government was one he would occupy, with only short interruption, for the remainder of his life. By contrast, Fox would not return to office for more than twenty-two years.

Over the next three months Pitt rallied support for his ministry. The press campaign championing him had wrought its influence: demonstrations showing support for the king were held throughout the country. Lady Spencer, outraged to learn that the town of St. Albans was one of the first to join the "political bustle" and address — thanks to George III — for dispensing with Fox's administration, did her utmost to prevent it. "I sent immediately to some of our principal friends to say how disagreeable such a step would be to your brother and me but they are all like mad men and assure me there is no stopping it for that there are not six people in the town who are not eagerly for it . . ."[6] she grumbled.

Causes have long been grasped by those with empty or unhappy lives. Harriet loved her children passionately, yet politics drew her on many levels, providing a sense of purpose, companionship, something to stretch her intellect, and an addictive taste of masculine power and excitement. Eighteenth-century society, and Fox in particular, acknowledged that women could play a useful role in supporting political causes. Both Harriet and Georgiana had been brought up to believe it was important for women to be well informed and to support family

---

* The term *prime minister* was not yet in current use, although this is, in effect, what Pitt was.

interests. Despite dismissing politics as "an odious subject," Lady Spencer had often joined the hustings in Northampton, and her activities were far from unusual. The presence of aristocratic women was widely acknowledged to help a candidate's campaign, bringing a touch of exalted glamour.[7] The Duchess of Portland (the Duke of Devonshire's sister), Mrs. Crewe, Lady Archer, Lady Jersey, and Mrs. Damer were among other celebrated women to offer political support when necessary.

But there was an invisible line that women were expected not to cross. It was one thing to wave from a carriage window or shake hands or wear rosettes and sashes and stand decorously on a platform; it was quite another to lead political discussion and express opinion forcefully. As Harriet returned to society, Georgiana was in Bath, accompanying the Duke of Devonshire, who was sipping the waters in an attempt to treat his gout. In her sister's absence, Harriet cultivated company of influence, and having listened assiduously began to dazzle them with her grasp of political subjects. She attended assemblies, dinners, and debates at parliament to hear Fox and his opponents put forward their views; she wrangled with supporters of Pitt and the king. Reports of her holding forth, expounding pro-Fox ideals, and entering into vociferous arguments swiftly reached her mother, who felt she was in danger of compromising her reputation.

> Never mind what other people are saying, dearest Harriet, but I entreat you to avoid entering into disputes on that odious subject—it is easy to excuse yourself by saying you fear to hurt the cause you wish well to, by trying to support it, or that you are not sufficiently informed to talk upon the matter, with fifty other ways you have ingenuity enough to find out—for connected as you are I do not wish you to appear or to be uninterested upon it—but in the situation as things now are trust me—if you dare allow yourself to argue upon it you will nine times out of ten say things you will afterwards wish unsaid.[8]

Harriet disingenuously gave the appearance of deferring to her mother's warning. But Pitt's call for a dissolution of parliament and a general election only added to her determination to delve deeper into politics, and when Georgiana returned from Bath the sisters swiftly traveled to Northampton and then on to St. Albans to campaign for the Whig candidates who would be helpful to their brother. They failed in Northampton but succeeded in St. Albans. Even Lady Spencer could not deny their effectiveness—it was she who had summoned them when she feared the Spencer candidate might lose. "So last night I sent for your two sisters," she told George, "who set out an hour ago with Mr. Sloper and a very large body of friends to make a regular canvass. It is amazing what this has already done."[9]

Flushed with excitement, the sisters hurtled back to London.[10] They had determined to help Fox in his battle for a seat in the borough of Westminster, a battle they knew would be fraught with risk. Although many borough constituencies were controlled by a single patron or a handful of powerful voters—the so-called pocket boroughs—Westminster was unusual in that every male "inhabitant householder" had the right to vote. With an electorate of eighteen thousand it was the largest and arguably one of the most "democratic" constituencies in the land. Fox was one of three candidates battling against two Pittites—Lord Hood, a naval hero, and Sir Cecil Wray, a wealthy landowner—for one of the two seats available.

Georgiana and Harriet had witnessed enough elections to know they were riotous affairs. Opposing factions were unafraid to resort to intimidation, and all too often a pushing crowd turned to a rampaging mob and heckling spilled over into open violence. Then as now the press were partisan and delighted in stories that gave color and glamour to the debate and that portrayed their chosen candidates favorably while denigrating the opposition. As A-list celebrities of the day, Harriet and Georgiana had always attracted attention. They offered everything of which gossip journalists dream: looks, status, money, sparkling characters—and flaws. Both knew that in joining the election battleground they would attract attention—this, after all, was the raison d'être of female canvassers. Recent research[11] has further suggested that Fox wanted glamorous female support to enhance his own manliness, and thus to highlight Pitt's famous indifference to women. In fact his adversaries tried to use his female support as a weapon against him—attacking their actions and, by implication, their morality. Even before polling opened, the *Morning Post*—the mouthpiece of Pitt and the king—began to cast slurs upon Georgiana. "We hear that the Duchess of Devonshire grants favours to those who promise their votes and interest to Mr. Fox,"[12] it proclaimed, implying that the favors in question were sexual. Buoyed up by the mood of political fervor, Georgiana and Harriet were undeterred. When the polling began, on April 1, they boldly joined Fox on his platform. Fox was dressed in a buff-and-blue uniform, inspired by the colors of Washington's army— a costume he had first donned during the American War of Independence. Georgiana and Harriet and a clutch of other society ladies, including Mrs. Crewe, the Duchess of Portland, and Mrs. Damer, trawled the streets, sporting hats decorated with foxtails, to shake hands, stroke babies' cheeks, and distribute medals to encourage Fox's supporters to vote.

From the beginning the atmosphere in the streets was tense. Fights erupted between groups of sailors and chairmen; at least two people lost their lives and many were seriously hurt, including a boy whose fingers were severed. Harriet and Georgiana were undaunted by the bustle, and to begin with it seemed as if their presence was working. After the first day's polling, Fox narrowly led with nine votes more than Hood and over a hundred more than Wray. Infuriated by his early lead, and what it deemed the unfair advantage of glamorous canvassers, the *Morning Post* furiously attacked "the ladies who interest themselves so much in case of elections ... perhaps [they are] too ignorant to know that they meddle with what does not concern them, but they ought at least to know that it is usual, even in these days of degeneracy, to expect common decency in a married woman, and something of dignity in a woman of quality."[13]

Over the days that followed, such comments became increasingly vitriolic and focused on Georgiana rather than the other women who took part. Georgiana was accused of paying excessive sums for modestly priced goods in order to win votes. Five guineas were rumored to have been paid for a bundle of broccoli and twenty pounds for a loaf of bread, all in the hope of influencing the electorate; even worse, it was said that Georgiana had traded kisses for votes. As her closest ally, Harriet too came in for a share of criticism and sexual innuendo. "It was observed of the Duchess of Devonshire and Lady Duncannon while they were soliciting votes in favour of Mr. Fox on Saturday last, that they were the most *perfect pieces* that ever appeared upon a canvass," sneered the *Morning Post*.

Harriet could keep her nerve during the bustles and heckling in the street, but the criticisms in the papers were a different matter—she had never experienced public censure before. "How dreadfully ill all our elections go," she wrote to her brother the evening after the polling had opened. "My sister and I . . . attempted canvassing for Westminster but it has not succeeded. You see how sadly we have been termed for it. Indeed we had no idea of its being talked of in the way it is."[14] To judge from her later actions, the disarming surprise she expressed was feigned—she was embellishing her misgivings and defending herself against slurs in the papers, in the hope that George would pass the comments on to their mother and that this would forestall further chastisement. Certainly, despite the despair she professed in her letter, Harriet showed no inclination to withdraw from the fray. Even when Georgiana faltered from exhaustion and distress at the criticisms she attracted, Harriet remained steadfast. "As I felt tired and heated I don't go out, but my sister is gone to the Opera quite well to sport her cockade," Georgiana reported.[15]

The initial advantage that the allure of beautiful and celebrated women brought to Fox's campaign did not last. A week into the polling he had dropped to third place. Anti-Fox cartoonists reflected the general mood, depicting Harriet and Georgiana in ever more unflattering guises.

In St. Albans, with increasing gloom Lady Spencer tracked her daughters' activities, hardly knowing what to believe and what to discount but certain that they must be causing irreparable damage to their health as well as their reputations. "It is impossible," she wrote furiously to Georgiana, ". . . that you and your sister should not be ill with such a continued agitation and exertion of mind as well as body."[16] Georgiana defended herself against the accusations, especially the one that she had kissed a butcher for his vote, claiming that they were entirely unjustified—it was Harriet and another female supporter who had been compromised and thus given rise to the accusation of trading kisses. "I don't see how I could have done otherways. My sister and Lady —— [name illegible] were both kissed, so it's very hard I who was not should have the reputation of it."[17]

We do not know what Duncannon thought of all the fuss; there are no mentions of him throughout the weeks of the election, so presumably he was busy in Knaresborough, canvassing for his own seat. Given the quantity of criticism in the press—hardly a day passed without some mention of Georgiana, and Harriet was always her accomplice—it seems impossible that he was ignorant of her activities. Moreover, given the fact that women of Harriet's standing were frequently highly political, and that in his print collection there are images featuring his wife—several of them far from flattering—we can assume he not only turned a blind eye to the slurs in the press, but also supported her activities. There was good reason for his magnanimity. Fox was an ally of his as well as Harriet's; remaining on good terms with him was essential to his career. And since the Duke and Duchess of Portland and Lord John Cavendish, all high-ranking members of the Cavendish family, openly encouraged female support for the Whig cause, he could hardly disagree.

By contrast, Lady Spencer suffered torment and agony with each new report that arrived from London. Her doom-laden prophecies were soon partly realized. Georgiana became so exhausted from the physical exertions and worn down by the accusations in the press that she left London for a few days to join her mother. Harriet, however, was undaunted. She refused to give up, instead making fleeting visits to Roehampton to see John, who was ill, then returning to town to continue with what her mother believed was the path to ruin. Certain now that she had lost control of her wayward daughter, Lady Spencer turned to her only available weapon. She wrote increasingly forthright letters, preying upon Harriet's conscience and her feelings for her sister to make her give up her cause.

I have fretted my self abominably, I must own, my dearest Harriet, both about you and your sister. My first wish is that you may never, either of you, deserve blame; the next that you may never suffer it. If you knew what pain the scandalous lies and abuse of you, or rather of your sister, gives me, you would neither of you, I am sure, venture again upon a conduct that subjects you to such insults. There is a degree of dignity and delicacy which a woman should never depart from. I know it has been from the best intention you have both been led to take the part you have done, but let this be a lesson to you, my dearest Harriet, never to go in any matter beyond the strictest rules of propriety.[18]

Before Harriet could cede to such coercion, the Foxites intervened. By the end of April all the householders of Westminster who were eligible to vote had done so and Fox lagged a hundred votes behind Wray, with Hood leading the field. "This general election will rout us *de fond en comble*,"* predicted George Spencer, who thought the Whigs would be lucky to retain thirty seats and that Fox would certainly fail in Westminster. Fox's dwindling fortune was pounced upon by the cartoonists. Rowlandson's engraving titled *The Departure* is one of the kinder ones, showing Fox, seated on an ass outside Carlton House, taking leave of Georgiana and Harriet, one of whom looks at her sister and says:

> *Ah! Sister, Sister, must he then depart*
> *To lose poor Reynard: almost breaks my heart.*

Despite the innuendos and inauspicious signs, the Foxites were not yet ready to give up. Many others made crude references to the manner of their soliciting votes and relationship with Fox. They realized that the only way of boosting Fox's count now was to bring voters from outlying villages to the polls. Meanwhile, knowing that Georgiana was their strongest weapon, the Duke and Duchess of Portland, together with Lord John Townshend, begged her to return, promising her mother that she and Harriet would be better chaperoned by male supporters of the party during their canvassing. Faced with such a powerful lobby, Lady Spencer crumbled.

On Georgiana's return to London, she and Harriet rode about in the Duke of Devonshire's carriage and ferried voters to and from Covent Garden. "Neither entreaties nor promises were spared," wrote the diarist Nathaniel Wraxall in his journal. "In some instances even personal caresses were said to have been permitted, in order to prevail on the surly or inflexible; and there can be no doubt of common mechanics having been conveyed to the hustings on more than one occasion . . ."[19]

---

* From top to bottom.

Realizing Fox might still turn the election around and seeing the effect of female glamour upon the voters the opposition followed suit, enlisting the aid of Countess Salisbury, wife of the newly appointed Lord Chamberlain, to canvass support. But the haughty thirtysomething Lady Salisbury was little match for the youthful allure of Georgiana, aged twenty-six, and twenty-two-year-old Harriet riding about town in a coach emblazoned with the ducal coat of arms.

Throughout the first fortnight in May the sisters canvassed hard and, fearful of arousing their mother's wrath again, avoided writing to her. Lady Spencer had by now decided to spare herself worry and not read the papers. "I have no comfort in writing to you while your abominable bustles last," she told Harriet, "nor you I fancy in writing to me, at least I guess so by hearing so seldom from you . . . I look upon you now as under the influence of a strong delerium."[20]

When the polls finally closed on May 17, almost seven weeks after their opening, the final count showed Hood the winner with 6,694 votes, Fox second with 6,234, and Wray third with 5,998. Thanks in no small part to the efforts of Georgiana and Harriet, Fox had won his place in parliament. The mood, once the result was known, was euphoric. Fox, hoisted onto a laurel-wreathed ceremonial throne, led a procession of Whigs, with two dozen blue-and-buff-uniformed horsemen, marching down the Strand. A banner above his head proclaimed the motto SACRED TO FEMALE PATRIOTISM—acknowledging the importance of Georgiana and Harriet and other female supporters to his success. The triumphal column of Whigs passed Carlton House, the Prince of Wales's residence, and then swept on to Devonshire House in Piccadilly, where Georgiana stood on the balcony and Fox raised his glass in her honor.

The prince had done surprisingly little to assist Fox during his campaign—he had been seriously ill after a prolonged drinking session—but now he suddenly rallied and threw a series of lavish balls and dinners to celebrate Fox's triumph. Meanwhile, in the coffee shops of St. James's, a print was posted that portrayed Harriet and Georgiana as icons of female patriotism. *Wisdom led by Virtue and Prudence to the Temple of Fame* portrayed Georgiana as Virtue and Harriet in the guise of Prudence; together they lead a triumphant Fox (Wisdom) toward the Temple of Fame, while Harriet announces:

Triumph and Fame shall every step attend
His king's best subject and his country's friend.

At last Lady Spencer was appeased.

Elsewhere in the country, Fox's supporters had not been so fortunate. A hundred and twenty Whig followers—Fox's martyrs, as they became known—lost their seats. William Pitt was returned with a majority of over two hundred. Duncannon was one of the lucky ones to remain, not because of his political prowess but because his seat was a safe one controlled by the Cavendish family. He returned victoriously to London to reclaim his now illustrious wife. We have no way of knowing Harriet's frame of mind as she welcomed him back to her bed; nevertheless, by the following month she was again pregnant.

FIVE

Ungovernable Passions
1784 - 1786

THAT SUMMER THE DUNCANNONS planned to leave London and spend the summer in the Dorset town of Weymouth with Harriet's brother, George, and his family, who were visiting the town. Among the three Spencer children George held the moral high ground. He was kind and intelligent, but more staid than either of his sisters, frequently acting as arbiter between Harriet and Georgiana and the sanctimonious Lady Spencer, who usually deferred to his judgment when calamities arose. Since his father's death, George, now the Second Earl Spencer, increasingly shouldered the responsibility of overseeing his sisters' well-being, safeguarding their reputations, and providing a sympathetic ear and, later, a helpful purse when necessary. He was devoted to both sisters, but Harriet, with whom he had spent much time alone as a child, and whose vulnerabilities he recognized, held a special place in his affections.

A shadow in their closeness was cast by his wife, Lavinia. The eldest daughter of the Earl of Lucan, Lavinia was strong-willed, moody, and prone to superciliousness. "[She] seemed to raise herself three feet in order to look down with contempt on me," Georgiana's friend Bess Foster complained after a meeting with Lavinia in Naples the following summer; "she . . . almost turned her back to poor me, and after a decent time went away without ever enquiring about my health, or saying a common civil thing to me."[1] Lavinia had given birth to a son, John (usually called Jack), a year after Harriet's John was born, but would suffer a string of miscarriages for the next five years—the time when Harriet and Georgiana were producing their children. The disappointments can have done little to help her short temper and perhaps partly explain her resentment of George's attentions to his mother and sisters. Lady Spencer, ever conciliatory and fearful of causing a lasting rift, tried to impress upon her daughters the need for tolerance: "She [Lavinia] has great inequalities of temper but if you can overlook them or at least appear not to see them, you will find she has a great deal of real warmth and goodness of heart at the bottom,"[2] she reminded Harriet sternly during the holiday.

That summer, however, both families looked with optimism to the days ahead. George and Duncannon were already friends; George greatly admired Duncannon's talent for drawing, and the two enjoyed shooting and playing cards together. Like Harriet, Lavinia was expecting a child and George was certain that adults and children would live "as in one house and shall I have no doubt be very comfortable."[3]

The Spencers settled into their lodgings two weeks before Harriet, but in late July, just as the Duncannons were due to arrive, Lady Spencer wrote with the sad news that Harriet had suffered a miscarriage. She had tried to persuade Harriet to stay in Roehampton and rest, but Harriet could not resist the thought of a holiday with her brother and reasoned the sea air would help her to get better. By early August she and the family had arrived at Weymouth. "She looks pale of course and seems nervous and weak but upon the whole is I think better than I expected to see her . . ."[4] reported George in answer to his mother's anxious inquiry.

Harriet's confidence in the benefits of a seaside holiday reflected a vogue that had gathered steady pace throughout the century. For fashionable society, passing a few weeks in resorts such as Margate, Southampton, Brighthelmstone (as Brighton was known), or Weymouth was by now a well-established routine. A change of scenery was considered beneficial to the spirits and stimulating to the mind, a contrast from unhealthy city life, while drinking sea water and bathing in it was thought to bring medicinal benefits—curing complaints ranging from gonorrhea and gout to melancholy, scrofula, constipation, and infertility.

Health aside, Weymouth offered all discerning aristocrats such as Lords Spencer and Duncannon and their young families could desire. There were fine sheltered sandy beaches for bathing, a harbor and sheltered waters suitable for fishing and sailing, and exquisite country-side for exploring. The Duke of Gloucester, the king's youngest brother, had sparked the town's popularity by building himself a grand residence, Gloucester Lodge. Four years after Harriet's visit with her brother, the king would give the resort his seal of approval by visiting his brother and venturing into the sea, accompanied by the music of a massed band and surrounded by bathing machines and attendants emblazoned with "God Save the King." Knowing of the town's fashionable reputation, Lady Spencer worried that evening entertainments might lead her daughter astray. And when George let slip that the day after the Duncannons' arrival they had attended a ball where they played whist and "Lavinia and my sister sat like two grave gentlewomen,"[5] her anxieties over Harriet's fondness for cards were instantly resurrected. "Gentle exercises are good for both you and the children but the less violent exercise or fatigue you undergo the better, and no gambling, I beg,"[6] she exhorted Harriet by return of post.

Four days later Harriet ventured into the sea and found it revived her. At Weymouth, as at most fashionable resorts, men and women were supposed to bathe at different parts of the beach. On the fore-shore Harriet would have entered a bathing room—a sort of waiting room where refreshments and newspapers were available. Here she wrote her name on a slate and waited to be summoned once a bathing machine—a sort of horse-drawn wooden beach hut raised on wheels—became available. Inside, with the help of a female assistant (as often as not a drunken one), stays and bodices were unlaced and petticoats discarded. Harriet may then have donned a voluminous shift or, more probably, prepared herself for bathing in the nude. When her assistant signaled Harriet was ready, the vehicle lurched across the beach into waist- or chest-deep water. A telescopic awning was released and, with the attendant's aid, Harriet could then gingerly descend the steps into the water, safe in the knowledge that she was protected from prying eyes. The assistant was also there to ensure Harriet thoroughly submerged every part of herself—including her head.

Not everyone observed such prudish methods of bathing. Lavinia was outraged by "the number of naked people constantly paddling before the windows—I was astonished yesterday to see seven girls about fourteen or fifteen years old standing in the water with their cloths tucked up above their waists* and boys stark naked of the same age romping with them—if such sights continue to adorn our view I shall certainly borrow our horse's blinkers and put them on cousin and sister."[7]

If Harriet witnessed such spectacles they did not deter her from bathing and she and the children went in the sea several times during the holiday. Meanwhile, the two families settled into an easy routine. Most mornings Duncannon and George, accompanied by various friends, went riding or sailing or fishing, returning with baskets filled with fish and oysters, while the children played and Harriet and Lavinia received visitors, walked, and bathed. There were also frequent picnics, and visits to neighbors and to assemblies. "You cannot imagine my dearest Harriet how much pleasure it gives me to hear that Lavinia and you are upon such cordial terms,"[8] declared Lady Spencer, delighted at the happy reports that reached her.

Even at Weymouth, the status of the Spencers and Duncannons ensured that Harriet and her party were treated as celebrities. When the frigate *Hebe* anchored there, George and Duncannon were invited aboard and, having sailed about for several hours and admired a demonstration of tacking, were given an eleven-gun salute on their departure. From earliest childhood Harriet had witnessed her parents receiving public attention, and had been groomed in how to comport herself with appropriate decorum. But the restrictions on her behavior that public scrutiny imposed did not always sit easily and there were times when she paid little heed to the impression she was making. "Your scrape at the ball was very distressing but was an effect as all your scrapes are—not of a want of common sense but of a want of making use of it—was it not easy to suppose that being the first woman there they would show some attention to you—and should you not therefore naturally have told the master of the ceremonies you would come towards the end of the ball but could not be there at the beginning . . . the way you murmur an excuse I am afraid the company still think you was all that time dressing,"[9] rebuked Lady Spencer after an embarrassing incident when Harriet was expected to open a dance and appeared several hours late.

---

* The fashion for wearing drawers had not yet taken hold.

The holiday signaled a new phase in the Duncannons' marriage. With few of London's distractions to draw them apart and their children thriving, the couple grew close, seemingly more content than they had ever been, and the harmony appeared set to continue when they returned to London that autumn. Lady Spencer heard that "Lord D's behaviour to [Harriet] was the most affectionate, complaisant, and attentive that can be imagined and carried with it an air of perfect concord and content."[10] Duncannon's kindness had helped Harriet to recover her looks and confidence, and to enjoy her role as mother and chatelaine of Roehampton. George also noticed that she looked better and seemed happier than she had for some time. One day when he was shooting at Wimbledon—where he saw more pheasants and game than on any estate in Norfolk—he met Harriet and Duncannon. "They were riding out and I suppose heard I was there, she looks very well and the brats are too," he remarked.[11] The following month he called at Roehampton to find Harriet and Duncannon happy together, and the children being fed sweets by Lord Bessborough. "It is quite a pretty picture to see Lord Bessborough giving them some bonbons and little Fred, who can just go by himself, stretching himself out on tiptoe to reach the bonboniere."[12]

Harriet's letters to her mother from this time do not survive, but Lady Spencer's responses suggest that her younger daughter was much preoccupied with her children and that maternal and domestic concerns dominated her thoughts. Were John's pallor and thinness symptoms of worms? Should John and Frederick be inoculated against smallpox before the winter? Lady Spencer answered all these queries readily but often rather bluntly. "Has John ever had any real symptoms of worms? If he has I imagine they might easily be got rid of." And, rather startlingly, "If you inoculate the children in town I will certainly come and attend them and you through the alarming part of it—if it is at Roehampton it would be inconvenient to you and painful to me."[13]

Inoculation was a subject of concern to every mother of small children. Smallpox was a dangerous disease that claimed thousands of young lives every year, but inoculating against it was also not without peril. The procedure, which had been introduced to the West by Lady Mary Wortley Montagu, wife of the British ambassador to Turkey, involved deliberately infecting the patient with a mild dose of the dis-

ease. Children were prepared for treatment by being fed a specially restricted diet for one month, to make them susceptible to the disease,
after which the doctor would make two small incisions on each arm
and insert infected "matter" from someone who already had the disease by drawing a piece of string doused in blood between the two cuts.
There then followed a tense wait, during which the child was isolated
from the rest of the family, until a fever came and a pustule developed
on the incisions—signs that the treatment had been effective. On
some children the inoculation did not work and they showed no signs
of illness; others contracted the full-blown disease and died from the
very measure that was meant to protect them.

Harriet's anxieties over the matter were far from unusual; she
sought advice from Dr. Warren as well as Dr. Dimsdale, London's leading specialist in inoculation, who told her that the inoculations should
not be given if the child was teething or otherwise ill. In the event Harriet and Georgiana—who had to put Little G through the same ordeal—decided to wait until after Christmas. Although they worked
themselves into a frenzy of worry beforehand, the procedure went
smoothly. "The dear child is quite well and the arms have gone through
the regular process—with a good large pustule on each but not one
more over her whole person—there is however not the least shadow of
a doubt of her having had the distemper tho' she had no eruptions and
we have had a child inoculated from her arms yesterday,"[14] wrote Lady
Spencer of Little G's recovery.

HARRIET'S MARRIAGE WAS less solid than it had seemed and, despite
the promising signs, within a few months of their return from Weymouth evidence of strain once again began to appear. Duncannon was
not devoid of kindness; he adored his children and loved Harriet in his
way. When he was in good humor he was capable of being affectionate
and tender toward her, and at such times, to judge from the frequency
and ease with which Harriet conceived children, the pair must have
had an active sexual relationship. Problems arose, however, from Duncannon's immaturity and irresponsibility, and above all from his
volatile temper. Friends remarked on his tendency to criticize Harriet
(or "tease," in eighteenth-century parlance) and his extraordinary capacity for angry outbursts. Mrs. Damer believed Duncannon was "a

peevish little mortal who *teases* without correcting . . . Abuse has been lavished on [Harriet], without reserve."[15] In later years Harryo, Harriet's niece, was further witness to Duncannon's prickliness. "The sunshine of my uncle's temper [is] somewhat cloudy," she remarked of one incident when for no apparent reason he had flown into a rage. Duncannon, she further damningly declared, was irritating even when he wasn't in a foul mood. "He is really . . . foolish beyond permission, and when he adds to his natural defects vociferous or noisy mirth or as during our last visit to him, childish ill-humour, quite insupportable."[16] Scattered in family correspondence there are also more sinister remarks that hint at physical violence. Some refer to Harriet sustaining injuries after falling down stairs, or suffering from mysterious swellings and bruising, which she tried to hide from her mother. "I saw her . . . with a colour and very little swelling left just a suspicion under one side of her chin, and she was out yesterday,"[17] reported Mrs. Howe to Lady Spencer on one such occasion after visiting Harriet in April.

At the root of the problem lay Duncannon's passion for gambling. In his straitened financial circumstances, losing as often and severely as he did threw him into rages—although it never spurred him to stop. The wit and politician James Hare, a close friend of Georgiana's and Harriet's, remarked that when the cards went against Duncannon, "[He] seems to take such sly revenge on the cards, giving them a bounce unawares, and that at Brooks's he says, after having swore in a violent way, in the meekest voice to the waiter: I'll thank you for a cup of weak tea!"[18] While the family were settled in Roehampton, Duncannon could not prevent himself from being drawn to the city to pass long hours at Brooks's. The Spencers were well aware of what was going on. "The hours at Brooks's this winter have been dreadful—the Duke of Devonshire and Lord Duncannon for a long time hardly ever come home earlier than six or seven or eight in the morning. The Duke is come a little of it lately—but I fear the other [Duncannon] continues there and I suspect has lost but I am not sure of it—I do not like to enquire or show idle curiosity where I can do no good,"[19] Lady Spencer told George. Even when Duncannon had time to see Harriet, he was distrustful of her family and friends and, as ever, prone to tampering with her correspondence. "Dear brother, do give my sister ye inclosed if you see her as I don't like to write by ye post on account of Lord Duncannon,"[20] wrote Georgiana, revealingly, in a letter to her brother.

Harriet loved her children passionately; she responded to Duncannon's affection when it was offered; but passing days and nights with the aging Lord Bessborough and his cronies was no entertainment for a vivacious, alluring twenty-five-year-old. Long periods of neglect interspersed by domineering criticism, and perhaps physical abuse, wore Harriet down, increasing her emotional neediness and making her receptive to temptation. Other men's flattery boosted her flagging spirits, which encouraged her flirtatiousness, which in turn spurred admirers to further pursue her.

Among Harriet's circle—the young, rich, beautiful, and morally free who frequented Devonshire House—extramarital affairs were far from unusual. The ton did not expect marriage and love to go hand in hand and took an easygoing view of infidelity. According to the rules of the game, having provided a husband with heirs a wife might seek love elsewhere, provided she did so discreetly. Many women had a succession of passionate affairs with various members of the group while continuing to share their husband's bed for the sake of appearances. But appearances were all: once passion became the subject of gossip, scandal would ensue, a woman's reputation would be ruined, and, by association, her family would also be disgraced.

Harriet knew of numerous aristocratic ladies who dabbled in *amours* discreetly enough to avoid scandal. Georgiana's friend and mentor, the glamorous Lady Melbourne, had a string of lovers, including the Prince of Wales, the Duke of Bedford, and the Earl of Egremont. Lady Jersey, one of the most beautiful, fascinating, and unprincipled women of the town, was married to a man twice her age and had conducted an illicit affair with the Duke of Devonshire; Mrs. Crewe, the society beauty who had helped Fox in his election, was presently involved in an affair with Sheridan, who had dedicated *The School for Scandal* to her. Lady Oxford, another infamous socialite, had indulged in so many liaisons that her children were dubbed "the Harleian Miscellany." Nor were those closest to Harriet immune to passion. Georgiana's best friend and confidante, Bess Foster, was secretly consorting with the Duke of Devonshire, while Georgiana herself had been linked to Fox and the Prince of

Wales (perhaps unjustly) and would shortly fall for the charms of the dashing young politician Charles Grey.

One side of Harriet disapproved of such licentiousness. Her mother had instilled in her a sense of propriety and strong religious principles and had never been unfaithful. Harriet had taken her marriage vows equally seriously. As she would later write, marriage was "a solemn vow given before God," and she was "deeply impress'd with the great guilt of breaking it."[21] Harriet's friend the diarist Mrs. Arbuthnot would later excuse Harriet's infidelities by claiming she was the innocent victim of "the seductive examples of clever but unprincipled men."[22] Somehow, though, Harriet seems too intelligent to have been duped into another man's arms. Vibrant, sensual, and needy as she was, it appears more likely that she responded to overtures that earlier she might have discouraged, in part to bolster her beleaguered self-esteem and in part because, having produced two children and being surrounded by friends and family who were likewise pleasurably engaged, she could no longer see a reason to resist.

A glimpse of what her life now became is provided by one of the most famous engravings by the draftsman and caricaturist Thomas Rowlandson—*A Scene at Vauxhall.** Vauxhall was the modern-day theme park of the age; it boasted rockeries and colonnades and sham pastoral scenery, including a miniature mill and stream that echoed Marie Antoinette's famous *hameau* at Versailles. It was an ideal place to conduct a clandestine affair, and as such found favor with Londoners of every rank, as a contemporary ballad described:

> *Each profession, ev'ry trade*
> *Here enjoy refreshing shade,*
> *Empty is the cobbler's stall,*
> *He's gone with tinker to Vauxhall,*
> *Here they drink, and there they cram*
> *Chicken, pasty, beef and ham,*
> *Women squeak and men drunk fall.*
> *Sweet enjoyment of Vauxhall.[23]*

---

* The gardens remained open until 1840. The site has since been developed, but was located between Goding Street, St. Oswald's Place, and Kennington Lane.

For Harriet and her peers, Vauxhall offered freedom from social barriers, a place where you could pay a shilling to promenade down leafy lantern-strung walks, gaze upon illuminated faux cascades, sip tea in rose-festooned arbors, or admire the paintings and sculptures of Milton and Shakespeare in the celebrated Rotunda, a large circular building that glittered with crystal chandeliers and vast looking-glasses. As the darkness began to deepen, decorous visitors retreated to alcoves decorated by Hogarth and other eminent artists to take supper and sip wine while the strains of an oratorio by Handel or a ballad sung by the celebrated John Beard competed with their chatter. Meanwhile those of a sexually adventurous character slipped away into the shrubberies to indulge in illicit *amours,* enjoying the frisson of rubbing shoulders with courtesans and stable hands who were all similarly occupied. "What astonished me most was the boldness of the lewd strumpets who came in by the half-dozen with their go-betweens, shamelessly begging one glass of wine after another,"[24] reported Carl Moritz, an astonished German visitor to the gardens.

Rowlandson's engraving shows us the full spectrum of the glamour and seediness of London life. The Prince of Wales whispers to the actress and poet Mary "Perdita" Robinson,* his erstwhile love, whose arm is linked with that of her ogre-like husband. Behind, ladies in voluminous hooped skirts and gentlemen in tricorns gossip and stare. To the right Dr. Johnson, James Boswell, Goldsmith, and Mrs. Thrale tuck into supper in a box, while, above, an opera diva, the celebrated singer Mrs. Weischsel, holds forth from her box. Georgiana and Harriet stand arm in arm in the foreground of this jostling fashionable crowd. Georgiana, dressed in white, gazes affectionately at Harriet, who looks slender and girlish in a blue riding habit and matching

---

* Mary Robinson dedicated "To Simplicity," one of her poems, to Harriet. The final verse reads:

> *The spotless MIND, the brow serene,*
> *'tis THINE, enchanting Maid, to boast!*
> *The sweet, benignant, humble mien,*
> *And all that VIRTUE values most!*
> *Thy blushes paint DUNCANNON's cheek,*
> *Thy light hand weaves her golden hair,*
> *Around her form, THY charms I'll seek,*
> *FOR ALL THE GRACES REVEL THERE!*

plumed hat, apparently oblivious that she is being ogled by the mono-cled Major Topham Beauclerk and several other men, and unaware of the fact that behind her a pair of courtesans ply their trade with eager drunken customers.

For all the beguiling air of innocence with which Rowlandson por-trays her, Harriet was by now well aware of the potency of her sexual allure. Another man, who does not appear in this scene, had entered her life. Lord John Townshend epitomized the morally lax and seduc-tive men by whom she was now paid court. The second son of George, Marquess of Townshend, he was charming and good-looking, with an aquiline nose and a thatch of luxuriant hair that he wore in the latest fashion, swept back from the forehead and tied in a tail. Townshend was an avid supporter of Charles James Fox and had become friendly with Georgiana soon after her marriage. "Jack Townshend is really a very amiable young man, he has great parts," Georgiana wrote on first becoming acquainted with him, ". . . and I daresay he will make a very good figure hereafter."[25]

Harriet knew how to draw Townshend to her, but she was unprac-ticed in the art of sustaining a clandestine relationship and paid little regard to the perils she faced. Among the fan-twitching frequenters of Devonshire House, the attraction was swiftly remarked. Sheridan would later jealously implore Harriet not to "listen to Jack's Elegies."[26] Rumors must also have reached George Spencer, who was furious at her foolhardiness and swiftly intervened. He told Harriet, bluntly, to keep away from Townshend if she did not wish to bring ruin on herself and her family. Loving George as she did, Harriet was mortified to have incurred his disapproval and grew deeply distressed. Georgiana tried to calm her brother. "Ld J [Townshend] has been here and I should think has given up all thoughts about H, at least this I am certain of, that after what has passed he will not think of risking anything that could hurt him with us—however I am certain from her conduct about it that he has it no longer in his power to give us any uneasiness or make her talked of,"[27] she soothed.

In the event, Townshend was no sooner dissuaded from pursuing Harriet than he embroiled himself in an illicit affair with Georgiana Fawkener, a married cousin of Harriet's on her mother's side. The af-fair with Georgiana Fawkener, who was known as "Jockey," brought shame to the Spencers when, despite their intervention, she moved into lodgings at Hampstead with Townshend. "I cannot allow either of you to see her till her ideas alter. I need not beg you . . . to be more cautious than ever in your conduct, the cruel lesson you have before your eyes will teach you both I am sure the unspeakable value of prudence and discretion,"[28] Lady Spencer warned her daughter darkly, little realizing how close Harriet had sailed to a similar fate. Jockey was eventually divorced by her husband by act of parliament, after which she married Townshend. The union turned out to be an unhappy one, however; Townshend developed mental illness (perhaps a form of schizophrenia, although he called it "gout of the head"), in which he suffered hallucinations and thought he was possessed by devils. He became obsessively jealous of Jockey and often made her life a misery, yet he continued to pursue Harriet at every opportunity.

Harriet's chastening experience with Townshend did nothing to curb her determined pursuit of pleasure. In February she looked "vastly pretty" when she attended an assembly at the prince's new residence, Carlton House. She and Georgiana were dressed identically in the newest fashion. "Our gowns were night gowns of my invention," Georgiana proudly boasted to her mother. "The body and sleeves black velvet bound with pink and fasten'd with silver buttons. The petticoat light pink, and the skirt, apron, and handkerchief crape bound with light pink, and large chip hats with feathers and pinks."[29] Few men could resist such temptation and within weeks Harriet had entangled herself in a friendship with such reckless abandon that she became the subject of gossip once more. "I am sorry to say Lady Duncannon and Charles Wyndham seem to be too good friends," remarked the beady-eyed Lady Mary Coke.[30]

Wyndham was the third son of the Earl of Egremont, and one of the Prince of Wales's most disreputable friends, notorious for his wildness, drunken debaucheries, and fondness for the horses. Lady Spencer had always detested him. The summer before he and Harriet became involved, Georgiana had gone to the races at Derby and danced "country dances" on two consecutive nights with him. "Why did not you rather dance with some of the gentlemen of the county than with Mr. Wyndham the second night,"[31] her mother complained.

Two months after Mary Coke had remarked on Harriet's penchant for Wyndham, Harriet announced that she was pregnant with her third child. Lady Spencer sensed that something was dreadfully wrong. "I am anxious to know how both you and your sister do and whether you are by degrees withdrawing from the glut of dissipation you have lately been plunged into," she wrote in a vain attempt to deflect Harriet and Georgiana—who was also pregnant—from their destructive course. Harriet made no response other than to complain of the crush of people at a hot-air-balloon flight, which only incensed her mother further. "Is it necessary that you and your sister must be in every crowd—of every party—let off every balloon. You see I am cross."[32]

For much of her pregnancy Harriet ignored her mother's admonitions and continued to live a wild life, evading the scrutiny of her family because other concerns distracted them. One afternoon at the end of March a serious fire broke out at Wimbledon Park. George was away hunting at the time, but Lavinia and Jack were staying in the house. When the alarm was sounded, there was temporary panic because nobody could find Jack and his nurse. It later transpired that the nurse had taken Jack to a local inn to "drink tea." As the fire took hold, the local gentry joined forces with Spencer servants and local tradesmen to try to salvage what they could. Miraculously, no one was seriously hurt and most of the valuable paintings, books, furniture, linen, and plates were saved; even the valuable mahogany doors were unscrewed and carried to safety. But the house itself, said George, was "entirely demolished, there not being . . . a single piece of wood remaining in any part of it."[33]

By summer, however, Lady Spencer had recovered sufficiently from the shock of the fire to grasp the danger Harriet was in. "I cannot like your Cumberland Lodge party . . . there was no other harm in it than its being a scrambling sort of thing which you had good excuse to have avoided if you would . . . Do you go to the Prince of Wales's ball—for God's sake take care of your conduct . . ."[34] Two months later, she warned. "You are in a dangerous situation surrounded by snares and temptations and those of the most alluring kind."[35] George, meanwhile, had decided to take Lavinia for a nine-month tour of Europe, leaving Lady Spencer in charge of three-year-old Jack and—far more challengingly—the reputations of her daughters. Neither sister showed any inclination to curb the bustle of their lives, despite their advancing pregnancies. Without George to lend weight to her arguments, Lady Spencer made valiant attempts to stem the tide of excess, issuing frequent warnings and criticisms that always made Harriet distraught—especially when they were close to the mark. Suffused with guilt, she invariably wrote back with assurances that she would reform. Yet there is no evidence to show that her determination lasted long, if it ever existed in the first place.

Harriet's clandestine activities were curtailed only by the arrival of Lady Spencer in town for the birth of Georgiana's baby. Her second daughter was "quite a little brown girl, with dark hair"[36] and called Harriet after her sister.* Two and a half months later Lady Spencer was summoned to Cavendish Square. Harriet's labor had not properly begun but she had been taken so seriously ill with "twinges" and other unspecified ailments that Dr. Denman was afraid to leave the house. The pains continued throughout the night and into the next day, growing stronger as the hours passed. Eventually, at half past four, after "two or three sharp pains" and thirty-six hours of exhausting labor, Harriet gave birth to a girl.[37]

Harriet had longed for a daughter and this tiny, fragile baby with her delicate features, large pale-brown eyes, and hair that would soon grow into a mass of wheaten curls immediately delighted her. Even from the earliest days of her infancy the baby, who was named Caroline after Duncannon's mother, proved an awkward child. She cried frequently and did not suckle as lustily as either of her brothers. Lady Spencer supervised the lying-in, taking up residence in Harriet's room and, when Caroline grew fractious, rising to take her into her own bed so that Harriet could sleep.

The fact that Harriet's affair must have been taking place at the time of Caroline's conception, and resumed soon after her birth, inevitably raises a question about Caroline's paternity. Was she fathered by Duncannon or Wyndham? There is no firm evidence to support either claim. Duncannon does not seem to have doubted that he fathered Caroline, and he would become dotingly fond of her in later years. Yet Harriet would have by no means been the first to pass off her

* Within the family Harriet Cavendish was known as Harryo; to avoid confusion with her aunt, she is so called here for the remainder of the book.

lover's child as her husband's. If suspicion crossed the minds of some, they kept it to themselves. It was in everyone's interest to maintain a conspiracy of silence. There could possibly be a signal of unease in an unexpected aside of Georgiana's in a letter to Bess. "Harum [Duncannon's nickname—perhaps a reference to his fondness for boisterous pranks] I really believe is in love with Harriet,"[38] she wrote in the middle of a paragraph about her own flirtations, thus implying that there were whispers about the affair. Nevertheless, all this taken together suggests there is at least a possibility that the future Lady Caroline Lamb—the child who would turn out to be so wayward and different in her unruly temperament and physical appearance from her brothers—was Wyndham's child.*

CAROLINE'S CHRISTENING TOOK place as soon as Harriet's lying-in was over. "[I] had my six grandchildren all there . . . John Ponsonby was in breeches as he has been some time, the rest were all dressed in lilac satin ribbons and sashes and looked very well,"[39] recorded Lady Spencer, basking in the pride of now being a grandmother six times over.

Harriet was still nursing Caroline when a further sexual drama diverted London society. Two years earlier, the Prince of Wales had fallen passionately in love with Mrs. Fitzherbert, a respectable Catholic widow. So ardent were his feelings that when Mrs. Fitzherbert refused to become his mistress he had halfheartedly attempted suicide by running himself through with a sword. Afterward Mrs. Fitzherbert had fled abroad to escape the prince's attention, but he persisted in writing to her, and eventually, after a barrage of pleas and threats, in November, just as Harriet was giving birth to Caroline, Mrs. Fitzherbert returned to London. The prince had persuaded Mrs. Fitzherbert to agree to a secret marriage with him, even though the Royal Marriages Act forbade any descendant of George II from marrying before the age of twenty-five without the king's consent; and everyone knew that the king would never consent to the heir to the throne marrying a Catholic widow. In the eyes of the law, therefore, the marriage would not be

---

* Some writers have suggested that Sheridan may have fathered Caroline. However, I could find no documentary evidence that Harriet was conducting an affair with Sheridan at this time.

legal, and, more seriously, if it were discovered by the king the prince would forfeit his right to the throne. None of this bothered Mrs. Fitzherbert. The marriage was legitimate according to Church law and in the eyes of God—and it was this, chiefly, that concerned her. For his part, the Prince of Wales's only thought seems to have been to lure the object of his affection to his bed.

"Most people suppose a private marriage or some contract has taken place," Lady Spencer told George. "[Mrs. Fitzherbert] has taken a whole box at the opera to herself, she receives his visits constantly at her own house, some people say his chariot is often seen there in a morning to carry him home. He sits with her at the opera, goes into the room to her, carries people up to her, shows her picture or her eye which is much the same thing to people and in short there is every mark of the utmost intimacy—many people are very serious on the subject and see nothing but future civil wars in it . . . at all events it is a disagreeable business and the least consequence will be ruin to her and disgrace to his character as a man of probity or honour. Such are the effects of ungovernable passions."[40]

Conscious of the delicacy and potential dangers of the situation, Lady Spencer tried frantically to persuade her daughters to disassociate themselves from Mrs. Fitzherbert and thus preserve their reputations. "If you and your sister would but give up going to the opera or any public place this one winter on the just pretence of nursing your children, how easily might all this still be avoided; or if you are pressed, as I conclude you will be by the Prince of Wales, why not ask him and Mrs. Fitzherbert what you are to say to me and to the world, and on that score to beg they will excuse your taking any part,"[41] she urged.

Georgiana agreed, perhaps partly because she was far more worried about her sister's antics than those of the prince. No sooner had Harriet weaned Caroline than she had plunged back into a frenetic social whirl, and rekindled her alliance with Wyndham. Rumors of Duncannon's neglect and Harriet's amorous interests were so rife that word reached Lady Elizabeth Foster in Naples. "Why won't you tell me if all I hear of dear Harriet and Harum is true. I suppose and swear always it is not,"[42] she pressed the ever-loyal Georgiana.

Lady Spencer also had an inkling that something was amiss and begged Harriet to tell her honestly what was going on. "All I can discover is that one or both of you are in some imprudent scrape which I shall know when it is no longer in my power to remedy it. You talk of writing from the heart but the truth is you never did nor do you know how to set about having a fair open confidence,"[43] she wrote reproachfully. When neither appeals nor threats persuaded Harriet to confess the truth, Lady Spencer sent a flurry of letters to Georgiana and George, pumping them remorselessly for news. "I am miserable about your sister," she pleaded with Georgiana in late June. "God grant my fears may be without foundation, never suppose though that I suspect her of anything wrong—I only think her very silly in not putting an immediate stop by a thorough change of conduct to reports that have been and are so prejudicial to her."[44]

George was livid to return from his travels only to learn of Harriet's affair with Wyndham. Furiously he took his sister aside and warned her of the risks she ran. As usual when confronted with a misdemeanor, Harriet apologized profusely, sobbed beguilingly, and promised to behave with more circumspection in future. And as usual, George softened and forgave her. "Harriet as far as I have seen is going on very right, they lead a much less bustling life than usual and are a great deal together at home,"[45] he reassured his mother.

Yet Harriet's remorse was far from genuine. A fortnight later George heard whispers that not only had the affair continued, but that Harriet and Wyndham were contemplating eloping together. Worse was to follow: articles appeared in the press claiming that Harriet had already left Duncannon. "We are informed that the sprightly Lady D has left her lord's house being tired of the habitation," declared *The Times* on July 10. There is no evidence to suggest that Harriet ever made serious plans to run away with Wyndham. Most likely the newspaper reports were simply fabricated on the basis of Jockey's misdemeanors. Nevertheless, George could not avoid reaching two unpalatable conclusions: first, his sister had deliberately lied to him; second, her indiscretion had placed her at the center of a whirlwind of rumor and gossip, which would reverberate unfavorably upon the Spencers' reputation.

George confronted Harriet in a rage more intense and manner more severe than she had ever witnessed. She was so terrified and remorseful that she found herself unable to speak. This time, though, George was unmoved. Certain that she was again being less than candid, he ordered her to go to St. Albans to stay with their mother until he and Lady Spencer decided what should be done. Harriet, by now in a state of nervous exhaustion and on the verge of collapse, realized that her silence had made George think she again intended to defy his instructions. That evening she penned an anguished apology. "I must write one word though I have hardly power to do so. I will do everything you desire. I was resolved before I saw you yesterday to tell you everything and to follow your advice exactly, but I was so much agitated at the time and so miserable to think of all the pain I had given you that it was quite impossible for me to speak to you. I am so much afraid from some things you said, that you attributed my agitation to a wrong cause, indeed it was not owing to any improper sentiments in me, but to the hurry of seeing you and of finding how unable I was to express myself. Do dearest brother write me a line to tell me you are not displeased with me . . ."[46]

Georgiana was beside herself at her sister's torment and degradation and added her voice and that of the duke to Harriet's plea for forgiveness. By shrewdly reminding George that if he persisted in exiling his sister for long he would only succeed in damaging his aim, heightening rather than smothering the scandal, and, even worse, running the risk of Duncannon discovering the truth, she added further weight to her argument.

> My sister . . . is determined to do everything you wish and not only that—though she for a great while saw it in too slight a way she sees it now in its true light. You know how much I think it necessary that a great alteration take place, but I think and I find the Duke does too that her never speaking to him would certainly make it be supposed that something had passed which had required our exertions . . . therefore at the opera he shall never come into the box nor speak to her long together at any place—but just speak to her that it may not so is [not?] forbid.
>
> She sees it all now as she should do and she is anxious to do anything that you can wish and though even speaking to him a little she

would not do if you disapprove—I need not tell you my dear dear brother how much especially in her present situation she requires every kindness and soothing from us.

Georgiana's letter contains the postscript "I forgot to say that my chief reason for thinking speaking should be allowed is as Lord Duncannon don't know it might be informing him of it in a very unpleasant way."[47] According to Georgiana, Duncannon was so absorbed in his gambling and drinking that he remained oblivious to the dramas unfolding on his doorstep. Given the articles in the press, his total ignorance seems implausible, but presumably he kept quiet to save face, and Georgiana used this to her advantage—to engineer Harriet's reconciliation with her brother. Her strategy worked. Once he had time to reflect, George saw the sense in this argument and swiftly relented. He was, in truth, far from unsympathetic to Harriet's plight, being well aware that Duncannon's behavior had contributed to Harriet's downfall and that, until he changed, the danger would not be entirely passed. "Her sweet husband never comes home till eight, nine, ten, or eleven o clock in the morning and that is really poor encouragement for living at home. They were at the play last night as I understand with your leave and their box was filled with other people. C[harles] W[yndham] was not there I believe. I trust this matter will end right but when it is ended her situation still continues a most dangerous one and requires the strictest attention on her own part as well as all ours,"[48] he told his mother bitterly.

Filled with remorse, Harriet also wrote to her mother, promising to leave London and dramatically reform her way of life. Lady Spencer responded encouragingly, seeing her daughter as a penitent Magdalene. "Your letter . . . fills me with satisfaction . . . you have a husband who you love and who loves you—the life of dissipation that London has drawn you into detaches you too much from each other and I am sure you will both find the comfort of living more together—do not let false reasoning drag you back again to noise and nonsense."[49]

A few days later the Duncannons and Georgiana and her children, together with Lady Spencer, traveled to Southampton to pass a few weeks by the sea while the furor died down. Lady Spencer thought it tactful to keep herself apart from the rest of the party, staying in lodgings at the Dolphin Inn. Despite this gesture, Duncannon perversely refused to leave Harriet alone with her mother for a minute—perhaps he knew something of her misdemeanors and felt his earlier neglect was to blame. So grating did Lady Spencer find his possessiveness that by the end of the month she abandoned her usual rule of never criticizing her children's spouses, and grumbled to her friend Mrs. Howe. "I see very little of Harriet for Lord Duncannon has hired a buggy which he and she drive out in every half hour that is not allotted to some management scheme—I long for a little quiet and am quite unfit to enter into scenes of mirth and jollity."[50]

The family had hoped for peace and tranquillity in which to recover from the emotional dramas of the past weeks, but they were to be sadly disappointed. Public scrutiny refused to subside. "Her Grace [Georgiana] and party were received with bell ringing etc., and the inhabitants in general are very anxious to show every mark of respect and attention . . . not more from the general benefit they are likely to receive by the additional company this will naturally draw to Southampton,"[51] announced *The Times.* Furthermore, in London, the rumor mill ground remorselessly on. When Lady Melbourne, a leading Whig society hostess and Georgiana's close friend, received a letter from Lady Salisbury—a rival doyenne of the Tories—the letter contained the unwelcome news that she had been "assured yesterday that Lady Duncannon was gone off, surely it cannot be true?"[52] Lady Melbourne was well versed in quelling scandals (she was still respectably married despite the fact that only one of her five sons had been fathered by her husband). She decided to offer her help to salvage Harriet's reputation. Writing to Georgiana, she told her of the reports circulating town:

There has been a report for this last week about Lady Duncannon which I would not write you word about as I was in hopes it would not have gained credit. But as I find it has in a most surprising manner I think I had better venture to make you a little uneasy than run the chance of your not knowing it and being by it prevented from taking any measure of checking it especially as I think it probable you may know something about it. There have been some paragraphs in newspapers to say she was gone off but as there were as I thought no name or initials I was in hopes it would not be known who was meant, which indeed I did not know myself till March told me there was such a report . . . Yesterday Mr. Greenville came to me to ask me if I had heard it and mentioned it to you, as he met Lady Beauchamp coming to town who asked him of news in a very curious manner which he did not understand till Lord William Gordon told him that she actually believed it and did not enquire of them whether it was true but how it happened, etc.

The only way for Harriet to allay the rumors, Lady Melbourne suggested, was to return to town, with her husband, and behave as if nothing had happened. She was holding a party the following week that might serve Harriet's purpose. "I . . . shall ask everybody I can pick up. If you think she had best come she might be seen there and I will ask or not ask anybody you please—if you don't intend to do anything you had better not tell her as it will make her so unhappy."[53]

When Harriet learned rumors of her elopement were still appearing in the London press, as Lady Melbourne had feared she grew deeply distressed. George tried to console her. "I think it is so easy a thing for anybody to find out the falsehood of it that it cannot be of any consequence and may perhaps by proving how much those kinds of things are made up of in the world have its good effect."[54] Harriet bravely decided to take Lady Melbourne's advice and face London society.

Fortuitously, her return coincided with a much more shocking event that deflected press attention. Harriet stood among the crowd at St. James's Palace, watching as the king descended from his carriage to attend a levee, when a woman approached and offered him a piece of paper. As the king stepped forward she produced a knife and lunged at him. "The knife hit his waistcoat but did not wound him," reported a shocked Harriet to her mother. "I have seen the woman and she is very well dressed and perfectly composed."

Then, as if remembering her own recent shame, and afraid her mother should think her in danger of again falling prey to the perils of London society, she ended with a penitent note: "I will make it my study for the next three months to become what you wish me."[55]

SIX

Sheridan
1787 – 1790

ARRIET WAS IN THE EARLY STAGES of pregnancy with her fourth child when George Spencer called at Cavendish Square and discovered his sister in a state of emotional turmoil. Duncannon had just told her that he had lost a monstrous sum at faro. The debt needed immediate settlement and he had angrily ordered Harriet to find the necessary loan, but to keep the reason she needed the money a secret "from everyone who was in the least likely to be of any use to him." Harriet was "at a loss to know where to begin" and, since Duncannon had threatened her with dire repercussions if she failed, "very apprehensive of the consequences of his disappointment"—another ominous reference to his foul temper and perhaps too his capacity for physical abuse when thwarted.

Duncannon's obsessive desire for secrecy was less a matter of damaged pride than fear. This was not the first time his gambling had resulted in dire losses, and his father, Lord Bessborough, had "threatened very much in case of anything of the kind happening."[1] So terrified was Duncannon of incurring his father's disapproval that he had not only ordered Harriet to find a loan; he had tried to force her to sign over her marriage settlement to him. For the time being she had stalled him by claiming that even if she signed the money over, her brother as guardian would also have to give his agreement—something he would be unlikely to do. George was uncertain whether or not the excuse would bear scrutiny, although he was prepared to do all he could to keep the settlement out of Duncannon's clutches and safe for Harriet's children.

George's sympathies now swung unequivocally with his sister, but he was uncertain how best to help. He did not believe ceding to Duncannon's bullying was a wise solution, and refused her plea for financial assistance, telling his mother what he told Harriet: "I myself have not the money to lend it but that I had I should not be willing to do it unless I could be convinced that he would play no more in that manner and at that game."[2] Yet on further reflection he became increasingly unsure. He wanted to protect his sister, but also prevent Duncannon's appalling behavior from continuing, and in this uncertain frame of mind he wrote to his mother.

Lady Spencer's reaction was one of shock and dismay; nevertheless, she was sure George's initial response was the correct one, and that he should remain unyielding. "I grieve for my poor Harriet; with any character but [Duncannon's] one might hope in expedients, but as much as I should rejoice to relieve both him and her I cannot advise giving assistance or even being security—future help (when ruin which I fear is inevitable sooner or later makes it necessary) may be of essential use but nothing else."[3] Two days later George told his mother that Duncannon had been helped "in a temporary way"[4] by his uncle Lord Frederick Cavendish. Yet to judge from Harriet's subsequent gratitude to her brother for "the kindness of [his] behaviour"[5] it seems likely that this version of events was only half true. George, unable to bear the thought of his pregnant sister at the mercy of Duncannon's volatile temper, probably stepped in to lend him the money, but kept the intervention a secret from his mother.

In the immediate aftermath of this crisis Harriet's health once again took a turn for the worse. Duncannon allowed her to spend a few days with her mother. Confronted with the effects of Harriet's ordeal firsthand, Lady Spencer was again filled with foreboding. "She has a shortness of breath a cough and a pain either in her side or across her breast which added to several other weakening and disagreeable symptoms make me fear she is in a bad way." Lady Spencer could not forgive Duncannon for the distress he had caused her daughter. "The truth is I still think everything has been made too easy to Lord Duncannon—nor do I find there has been any attempt to make him promise to leave off Faro. There is no comfortable prospect in this whole matter." She was terrified to let Harriet return to Duncannon alone in such a fragile state, yet uncertain what else to do. "I must go to town as I cannot possibly part with [Harriet] in such a situation," she wrote.[6] The dilemma was twofold. If she returned to London to stay unexpectedly with Harriet, Duncannon might think it was to spy on him, and this would only make Harriet's predicament worse. Georgiana offered to have her mother to stay at Devonshire House, but Lady Spencer was reluctant to do so in view of "the obstacle"—Georgiana's confidante and the duke's mistress, Bess Foster, whom Lady Spencer detested. In the event Lady Spencer conveniently persuaded herself that Harriet was strong enough to return alone to Duncannon.

Harriet's health had improved but the family's financial problems were far from cured, as *The Times* reported the following month: "The gaming houses of St. James's have of late been fully attended and the play deep though but little ready money stirring. Among the losers stands Lord Duncannon who left of £5,000 [approximately £300,000 today] minus a few evenings ago though report hath made it £50,000."[7]

Duncannon was not alone in steering his family toward the rocks of bankruptcy. Harriet now spent more time than ever at Devonshire House, where playing cards for vast sums, and often losing heavily in the process, was a favorite pastime. Georgiana's passion for "deep play" had become entrenched since the early days of her marriage. Her debts had reached a catastrophic level and only three months earlier she had been forced to reveal to the duke that she owed an unscrupulous moneylender more than £100,000[8]—the equivalent of £6 million today. With Sheridan's help Georgiana managed to settle her debt with the moneylender, but her addiction to games of chance remained uncurbed.

Harriet's financial circumstances had always been very different from her sister's. What then made her indulge in such a dangerous vice? Unhappy in her marriage, with a husband and sister and friends who all gambled with reckless abandon, perhaps she hoped to earn enough to pay off her own or Duncannon's debts, to make them both rich, or to make him love her; then, inevitably, as her losses mounted, she found herself forced to continue. But the suspicion remains that it was not simply desperation that drew Harriet to the tables. Gambling was ingrained in her, as it was in Lady Spencer and Georgiana. A hand of cards had been part of her life from childhood, as routine as attending balls, making elegant curtsys, and polite conversation over tea. Virtually every wellborn woman injected a frisson of excitement into the dreary formality of her day with a shilling on a hand of whist. For Harriet, as for Georgiana, gambling was a lure that became impossible to resist—a pastime that went hand in hand with illicit *amours* and political intrigue.

By May, when Harriet was seven months pregnant, she decided to join Georgiana, the Prince of Wales, Lord Foley, the Duke of Rutland, Lady Harrington, and others to form a faro bank. Faro was the most popular gambling-house game in England. The game is not dissimilar from roulette; players bet against the dealer on what cards will be turned over, but since only alternate cards are winning cards, the odds are heavily stacked in the favor of the banker. London buzzed with stories of the large gains made by bankers such as Lady Buckinghamshire, who was said to be so wealthy as a result of her activities that in order to protect her hoards she slept with a blunderbuss and a pair of pistols beneath her pillow.

No doubt it was the promise of similar riches that drove the sisters to embark on such a scheme. But the venture did not run smoothly. While Harriet and Georgiana were in Bath, their stake still unpaid, their colleagues began operating the bank on a small scale without them. Desperate not to be left out, Georgiana scratched around her friends, trying frantically to raise her stake; Harriet, equally eager to participate, borrowed money for hers at an exorbitant rate, gambled with it, then promptly lost it. Daniel Pulteney unsparingly detailed the debacle to one of their supposed business partners, the Duke of Rutland.

Some of our allies at Bath [the Duchess of Devonshire and Lady Duncannon] are in a rage at our having suffered Sir Watts Horton to set up a mushroom bank of £500 in their absence. Little as I can pretend to any great knowledge of fine ladies, I cannot foresee what obstacles the very proposers may suffer in future. All I know is that it is as much their interest as mine, and . . . as much their inclination. Lady Duncannon sold £200 a year for £1600 to a Jew about six weeks ago and showed me overnight a £1000 note which she was determined to keep for this subscription, and in three days it was all gone; though as to her share of the subscription, that can easily be borrowed for her.[9]

Not surprisingly, the press interest in the Duncannons' rocky marriage and financial shenanigans showed no signs of abating. "Lady Duncannon is far advanced in her pregnancy, to the great mortification of her lovely sister, and the inexpressible chagrin of the noble idler, *caro sposo* [i.e., Duncannon], who, after seven years indolence feels more delight at Brooks's than in the earthly Elysium of his 'lady's bedchamber,' "[10] one newspaper declared unkindly.

Duncannon's continuing neglect piled upon mounting financial worry made Harriet listless and low. Her cough became increasingly troublesome; twinges in her chest and side became more severe, and by mid-July, a month before the baby was due, the onset of sudden pains made everyone think her labor was beginning prematurely and fear the worst. In fact the pains subsided and the baby—a boy called William— was born without complication a fortnight later. According to Lady Spencer, who was as usual on hand to dispense advice, he was a large child "and sucked like a leech."[11] But concern over Harriet's health did not diminish during her lying-in. Breast-feeding the baby made her grow worryingly thin and exhausted, and her cough and the pains in her side and chest showed little sign of improvement. Worst of all, Duncannon refused to seek proper medical help, instead choosing to treat Harriet with "terrible medicines" himself.[12]

The precise reason for his behavior remains unclear. Physicians were expensive—especially when their patients were well-connected aristocrats—and Harriet's symptoms no doubt would have allowed her doctors ample opportunity to prescribe treatments that were both exorbitant and protracted. Not only that: the medical profession adopted a holistic approach to medicine, which may have led Duncannon to fear that any diagnosis of Harriet's condition would involve investigation into the cause of her depression—in large part his own irresponsible behavior—and his own weaknesses would thus come under scrutiny. Mrs. Damer, a prominent Whig and a friend of Harriet's, subscribed to this view: "doubting not that [Harriet's illness] was owing to his conduct, and the vile company he kept, [he] used to carry her the medicines, and being ashamed and wishing to screen himself endangered her life by preventing her from having proper advice."[13]

Yet Duncannon's avoidance of the medical profession and his decision to treat Harriet himself is not as outrageous as it may seem from a modern perspective. In an age in which medical knowledge was in its infancy, educated laymen frequently dabbled in medical matters, often publishing articles in publications such as the *Gentleman's Magazine* alongside those of professional doctors, who were happy to divulge remedies for readers to make up at home and to recommend proprietary medications. Duncannon may thus have easily convinced himself that he was not just acting in the interests of economy, but that he might succeed in improving Harriet's condition where others had failed.

Chronic ill health did nothing to dim Harriet's fascination for politics. By the following summer, when a by-election in Westminster was announced, she was sufficiently well to declare her intention of canvassing in support of the Whig candidates. Recalling the horrors of the 1784 election, Lady Spencer immediately feared the worst—that Georgiana would join Harriet, and once again their reputations would be besmirched. As she saw it, the only method to safeguard them was by preventing them from partaking in any political activity. To this end she wrote to the Duke of Devonshire, begging him to send Georgiana out of London and, since she was too afraid to approach Duncannon directly, to use his influence with his cousin "to consent to send Harriet here [to St. Albans]."[14] As a further measure she wrote directly to Harriet. "Pray give me the comfort of telling me now . . . that you interfere as little as possible in the sad confusions that are going forwards."[15]

Georgiana acquiesced to her mother's wishes. "You may be quite secure—I shall not canvass and indeed I don't go out of the house," she declared slightly disingenuously.[16] Within the confines of Devonshire House she busied herself frantically writing notes to supporters and organizing meetings, but, remembering the horror of the press assault four years earlier, she was happy to remain behind the scenes.[17]

Curtailing Harriet's activities was a different matter entirely. She had not been subjected to the same level of vitriol as her sister and, feeling she had less to lose, was unafraid to return to a more public role.

Fobbing her mother off with vague assurances, she donned the Whig colors and launched herself into the throng of Westminster to rally support. This time she worked on behalf of both Fox and her erstwhile admirer John Townshend. "Lady Duncannon is most violently busy at this business—she is about all day and has done infinite good to the party," wrote Lavinia to George Spencer.[18]

The election was no less fraught than before. There were riots in Bond Street as Hood's supporters confronted the Irish supporters of Townshend. Almost immediately, the glamorous entourage surrounding the Whigs became the focus of press criticism. "Lord John Townshend's party is indeed most popular, if it may be guessed at from the Ladies of Covent Garden who all sport the blue and orange cockade. Scarce a barrow woman is to be seen without them," declared *The Times,* openly accusing Townshend and his supporters of "barefaced perjury . . . shameless corruption . . . open and avowed bribery—votes were publicly sold to the canvassers . . . and what is more iniquitous, perjuries . . . purchased at the price of 10s 6d an oath."[19]

The cartoonists were quick to join the fray. One particularly offensive example, titled *Falstaff and the Merry Wives of Westminster,* depicts a portly candidate seated on an ass wearing the Prince of Wales's feathers, flanked by a pair of bare-breasted aristocratic ladies, one of whom is probably intended to be Harriet. In the background a pair of gloomy men wearing antlers imply that Townshend was having affairs with his canvassers and cuckolding their husbands. Another print, titled *Battles of Venus and Battles of War—Contrast of Two Candidates,* shows Townshend drunk in a tavern with dice and cards and broken bottles on the floor, with his arms around two elegantly dressed ladies, one of whom is bare-breasted. Facing him stands Hood, dressed as a naval hero in battle, brandishing a sword.

Presumably, as before, Harriet had joined the canvassing with the support of Duncannon, and he was not unduly perturbed by the adverse comments in the press. The two prints described above are pasted into his print album and are still in the family collection. But once again Lady Spencer did not view the crude remarks directed against her daughter in quite the same manner. "I am afraid Lady Duncannon has been very ill-treated in the newspapers . . . though I myself have seen nothing of it,"[20] wrote an ever loyal George, who could not ignore the fact that Harriet, along with other glamorous female supporters, once again greatly aided the Whig cause. When the polls closed, Townshend had beaten Hood by a comfortable majority of eight hundred, and the election was triumphantly concluded with a long cavalcade.

SCARCELY HAD ELECTION fever died down than a new political subject engrossed society. The king had become unwell during the summer and retreated to Cheltenham in search of a cure. By autumn, on his return to Windsor, reports emerged that, far from improving, his condition had deteriorated further. His speech was at times incomprehensible. He suffered bilious attacks and agonizing pains in his legs that made him weaker day by day. Furthermore, his behavior had become increasingly erratic. He was said to have mistaken an oak tree in Windsor Park for the King of Prussia and to have assaulted the Prince of Wales over dinner. Doctors called in to assess and treat his mystifying symptoms gave a pessimistic prognosis: the king might never be well enough to rule again, and he might die. Pitt reluctantly began negotiations to establish a regency, while the Whigs hastily dispatched a messenger to Italy for Fox, who was enjoying the sights in the company of his mistress, the once notorious courtesan Mrs. Armistead.

Pitt was reluctant to install the Prince of Wales as regent with all the powers of a monarch because, having publicly allied himself to the Whigs, he assumed that the prince would dismiss the present administration and promote Fox and Portland in his stead. To preserve his political position Pitt played for time, proposing a regency without the proper powers of king, hoping meanwhile that the king might recover.

In Fox's absence, Sheridan took on the role of the prince's political confidant, advising him how best to counter Pitt's demands. Sheridan had none of the benefits of a noble birth and, as the impecunious, roguish, hard-drinking, Irish-born son of an actor manager, was on the surface a surprising choice for a princely adviser. Sheridan was an arch manipulator; he had married the beautiful singer Elizabeth Linley and through her inveigled his way into Devonshire House, the ton, and the prince. Tall, with a long face, twinkling eyes, and a high forehead, he loved an audience, and at Georgiana's assemblies and suppers held court and entertained everyone with his sparkling conversation, un-

ending supply of witty stories, brilliant political arguments, and outrageous flirting. Sheridan's meteoric rise to fame was founded on his au-
thorship of two of the cleverest and most successful plays of his
age — The Rivals and The School for Scandal: comedies that throw a window
on the decadent world of late-eighteenth-century aristocratic life.
Since then he had become the proprietor of the Drury Lane Theatre,
and — thanks to the influence of Georgiana — MP for Stafford, where
he had used his position at the theater to woo voters, resorting to unscrupulous methods where necessary, as one contemporary account
testifies:

> His voters, being fully convinced that they ought to receive a quid
> pro quo for their "most sweet voices" [votes], every one had a favour
> to ask. One had a son who had great dramatic talent, another was an
> admirable scene-painter, others had cousins and nephews who
> would make excellent door-keeprs, lamp-lighters, check-takers, or
> box-openers ... Sheridan listened with his usual bland smile to
> every request, and complied with them all ... on their arrival they
> were favourably received and each person obtained the situation that
> he had desired ... Scarcely, however, had the member of Parliament
> left the town than ... it was found that upon application for the pay-
> ment of the salaries due to the different persons employed there was
> no money in the treasury. On Saturday night the receipts were care-
> fully handed over to Sheridan, who carelessly spent the money.[21]

In the elegant saloons at Devonshire House and the seedy smoke-
filled rooms of Brooks's, the prince, like the voters of Stafford, had
been captivated by Sheridan's urbane cleverness, his passionately expressed political views, his reckless gambling and drinking to excess,
and his habit of embroiling himself in injudicious romances. Without
any private means, Sheridan needed a government position more than
anyone; to this end he attempted to persuade the prince to accept Pitt's
restricted terms of regency and then try to change them later. But
when Fox galloped back to London — after an exhausting journey
across Europe — rifts in the Whig faction began to appear. Sheridan
was renowned for Machiavellian plotting and scheming behind the
scenes. Fox distrusted Sheridan's motives in advising the prince to

accept Pitt's terms and, when he learned that Sheridan was also court-ing members of Pitt's government, feared he was trying to usurp him. The prince, Fox claimed thoughtlessly, had "as clear a right to assume the reins of Government, and to exercise the sovereign power during His Majesty's incapacity, as he would have in case of a natural demise."

This bald declaration seemed to contradict the fundamental Whig principle—to keep royal power in check—and handed Pitt an unex-pected advantage. As he had over the ill-fated East India bill, Pitt again accused Fox of acting in self-interest, and turned the tide of public opinion against Fox. Meanwhile, amid the plotting and wrangling, re-ports began to emerge that, far from being untreatable, the king's health had begun to improve; his new doctor, the Rev. Dr. Willis, thought he would recover completely within three months. The re-gency bill, with its restrictions on the prince's authority, was passed through the Commons in mid-February; but in any case the prince would enjoy no change in status; less than a fortnight later the king was declared restored to health.

The prince's extravagance, coupled with Fox's tactless remarks, had tainted the Whig cause in the eyes of the public, and the country re-acted to the news of the king's recovery with general rejoicing and fes-tivities. As the much-needed government post slipped from Sheridan's grasp, he reacted with characteristic dissemblance. "Let us all join in drinking to His Majesty's speedy recovery," he declared before setting out to organize a gala evening on behalf of Brooks's club.[22]

But beneath the insouciant façade the Whigs were bitterly disap-pointed. They had become a laughingstock in society, jeered at and derided even at the most elite gatherings. The queen, who had strongly disapproved of their actions during the king's illness, treated them with icy condescension at the first "drawing room" she held at St. James's Palace after the king's return to duty. Harriet was among the mêlée of aristocrats who attended the event. "The Queen stood near the middle window with a small space around her, through which everybody passed one by one. She did not speak to any of the principal opposition people, Fox, Sheridan, Tierney, Grey, and very cold to the Princes . . . She was dressed in blue and orange and had 'God save the King' in her cap, as almost everybody else had except us; she looked up at our heads as we past her. Nothing ever equalled the crowd, one heard nothing but screams and women carrying out in fits. The whole ground was strewed with different coloured foil and pearls and diamonds crumbled to pieces."[23]

Sheridan's motives for visiting Devonshire House during the Regency crises were not merely political. He had a penchant for glamorous wellborn ladies, and over the weeks his conversations with Harriet crossed the boundaries of friendship into something more. Sheridan's methods of seduction were not dissimilar to those he had used to beguile the Prince of Wales and his voters: "He employs a great deal of art with a great deal of pains to gratify . . . and he deals in the most intricate plotting and underplotting, like a Spanish play,"[24] wrote Sir Gilbert Elliot, one witness to his devious technique.

His unscrupulous methods were experienced firsthand by the eighteen-year-old Lady Webster* when she, briefly, became the subject of Sheridan's attentions. "He took it into his head that there was something between me and a person for whom I certainly did not care the least—and he used to say 'I can get possession of your letters to—— and I can ruin you by means of these letters, if you will not listen to me favourably'—when I defied this threat he took another most extraordinary method—I was told one day that a servant had brought a message which he would deliver to no one but myself, and before I could order him to be admitted, in entered Sheridan, wrapped up in a great watchcoat, and after my servant had quitted the room he rushed up to me and with a ferociousness quite frightful bit my cheek so violently that the blood ran on down my neck—I had just enough sense to ring the bell and he withdrew."[25]

Throughout the Regency crisis Harriet, as staunch campaigner of the Whigs and close friend of the Prince of Wales, had been party to many of the most delicate discussions and moments of drama. There were many evenings when Harriet and Georgiana dined or supped alone with Sheridan and Charles Grey, the dashing young Whig politician who had Georgiana in his thrall. Sheridan and Grey were rival pretenders for ascendancy within the Whig party, but Sheridan was sharper and more quick-witted than Grey, and in such an atmosphere of heightened passion it is easy to see how he might have persuaded

---

* Later Harriet's close friend Lady Holland.

Harriet to succumb to his attentions. By March, soon after the king's recovery, when Harriet went to stay with her mother, rumors had already begun to swirl. "The accusations against me quite bad, told Ca* . . ."[26] Harriet wrote in her journal.

However it began, the love affair between Sheridan and Harriet was the most serious in which either had hitherto been involved. It was an affair based not merely upon sex (or gallantry, the euphemistic eighteenth-century term for it) but upon a deep-rooted friendship in which each recognized the other's faults as well as virtues. An undated love letter from Sheridan to Harriet, written when the affair was at its height in the mannered language used by the intimates of Devonshire House, gives a revealing insight into their passion. The letter alludes unsparingly to Harriet's past sexual misdemeanors, implying that Duncannon's neglect was their cause. With shades of Milton mixed with *Romeo and Juliet,* the letter hints too at the romance and danger of their passion, implying that Duncannon had already warned Sheridan against attempting to seduce his wife.

> I must bid 'oo good Night, for the Light passing to and fro near your room I hope you are going to bed, and to sleep happily, with a hundred little cherubs fanning their white wings over you in approbation of your goodness . . .
>
> Grace shines around you with serenest beams and whispering Angels prompt your golden dreams and yet and yet—Beware! Milton will tell you that even in Paradise Serpents found their way to the ear of slumbering innocence.
>
> Then to be sure poor Eve had no watchful guardian to pace up and down beneath her windows or clear sighted friend to warn her of the sly approaches of T's and F's and W's and a long list of wicked letters. And Adam I suppose was—at Brooke's—"fye Mr. S"—I answer fy fye Lord D." Tell him either to come with you or forbid your coming to a house so inhabited.—Now don't look grave. Remember it is my office to speak truth.
>
> I shall be gone before your hazel eyes are open tomorrow, but for the sake of the Lord D. that you will not suffer me to blame—do not

---

* Presumably Canis—Devonshire House nickname for the Duke of Devonshire.

listen to Jack's elegies or smile at F's epigrams or tremble at C.W.'s frowns but put on that look of gentle firmness, and pass on in maiden meditation fancy free — Now draw the curtain Sally.*[27]

When Sheridan's long-suffering wife Elizabeth — whose own suitors included the lascivious Duke of Cumberland — discovered the affair, she recognized instantly that it was more meaningful than any that had gone before and confronted him. Sheridan still loved Elizabeth in his way and lied repeatedly to her, promising to end the affair and then surreptitiously returning once more to Harriet's arms. Certain that separation, something she had never previously considered, was inevitable, Elizabeth plunged into despair. She and Sheridan no longer lived "in fact" as man and wife, she wretchedly told her friend Mrs. Canning. "The world, my dear Hetty, is a bad one, and we are both victims of its seductions. Sheridan has involved himself by his gallantries and cannot retreat. The duplicity of his conduct to me has hurt me more than anything else, and I confess to you that my heart is entirely alienated from him, and I see no prospect of Happiness for either of us . . ."[28]

Sheridan was a master of dissimulation. In public he and Elizabeth put on a show that convinced even those closest to him that all was well. In June the couple attended a lavish fancy-dress party, at which Harriet — inappropriately dressed as a nun — was also present. Betsy, Sheridan's sister, was delighted to note Harriet "casting many tender looks across the table which to my great joy did not seem much attended to."[29] In fact, despite Sheridan's apparent indifference, his feelings for Harriet were anything but cool. Days later Harriet and Sheridan were apparently caught "in flagrante," and Duncannon, unable to bear the humiliation, instigated divorce proceedings at the Doctor's Commons.†[30]

Although infidelity was commonplace among the circles in which Harriet and Sheridan moved, divorce was still a rare and costly occurrence. Available only to the rich, it tainted entire families with disrepute. Georgiana was in Brussels with the duke when the news of

---

* Sally Peterson was Harriet's loyal maid.
† The London court that dealt with suits of divorce.

Duncannon's impending action and her sister's disgrace reached her. She was expecting her third child and had intended to return to England in time for the birth, but the scandal surrounding Harriet upset her profoundly and irrevocably altered all plans. The duke was equally distraught, fearing a scandal not only because it would bring shame on his family name, but, more crucially, because it might cause Georgiana to miscarry from worry and, if she were carrying a boy, dash his hopes of a legitimate heir. Leaving Georgiana in Brussels, he hurried back to London to try to calm matters down. "As for my return I believe I safely might now, and I ardently wish to lie in at least in England; and more I believe I *shall* and that the Duke's journey will determine him; but circumstances too long for a letter; it is impossible for me to urge him (and you would agree with me). I have nothing to do but to leave it to his determination . . ."[31] wrote Georgiana helplessly to Lady Melbourne.

The duke arrived in London at midnight and met Harriet the next day. Overwrought with emotion and shame, Harriet quickly agreed to give up the affair and do whatever the duke deemed necessary in order to salvage her marriage. She had never intended Duncannon to discover her infidelity but her decision to capitulate was inspired less by disenchantment with Sheridan—they would remain close throughout the rest of Sheridan's life—than by what she had witnessed of Bess Foster's existence. Divorced and separated women existed in social limbo, ostracized by scandal and shame not only from friends, but often (as in Bess's case) from their children too. This was a sacrifice Harriet could never contemplate, and to avoid it she would take whatever steps were necessary to placate Duncannon.

Having satisfied himself of Harriet's remorse, the duke turned to the task of soothing Duncannon's hurt pride and persuading him to drop his suit—a far more tricky undertaking than anyone expected: Duncannon was still fuming at Harriet's indiscretion, and was set upon revenge. Only when the duke pointed out that the scandal of a divorce would certainly cause his elderly father immense distress and the shock might hasten his death did Duncannon decide to drop his suit and reluctantly agree to return with the duke and Harriet to Brussels while the fuss died down. His acquiescence was far from wholehearted, however. He made it clear to the duke that his feelings of grievance remained unaltered. He had dropped his suit temporarily, on the understanding that once Lord Bessborough was dead he would resume it. Harriet would thus live with the threat of impending shame, uncertain when it would strike and unable to avert it.

While the duke was smoothing Duncannon's wounded pride, the irrepressible Sheridan, uncertain whether he was about to become "an object of ridicule and abuse to all the world," hurried to his wife to beg her forgiveness.[32] Elizabeth was staying at Crewe Hall* and Sheridan joined her there, only to be caught a few days later in yet another compromising situation. An exasperated Elizabeth wrote:

> Can you believe it possible that at the very time when Sheridan was pleading for forgiveness from me on this account, before it was certain that it would be hushed up, at the moment almost in which he was swearing and imprecating all sorts of curses on himself on me and his child, if ever he was led away by any motive to be false to me again, he threw the whole family at Crewe into confusion and distress by playing the fool with Miss FD [little Emma's governess] and contriving so awkwardly too, as to be discovered by the whole house, locked up with her in a bed chamber in an unfrequented part of the house.[33]

As so often in the past, however, the strain of events had taken a toll upon Harriet's health, and there were worries that she would not be well enough to make the journey to Brussels. "The Duke still remains perfectly undecided about your sister's coming over and says he will not determine till he sees again how she is. He talks of staying about a fortnight longer in town,"[34] Lady Spencer worriedly reported. By the end of March, however, Harriet was well enough to travel, as Elizabeth Sheridan bitterly recorded. "Lady Duncannon is, thank God, gone to Bruxelles. I should not be sorry to hear she was drowned on her way thither."[35]

---

* The home of Mrs. Crewe, another of Sheridan's erstwhile mistresses.

SEVEN

The Root of All Evil

1791

A S HARRIET TOOK UP the threads of her life at Roehampton and Cavendish Square, it swiftly returned to the same fraught pattern. Fighting ill health, she tried to pacify her creditors and live in some semblance of harmony with Duncannon. But since he still seethed with the humiliation of being publicly cuckolded and gave no sign that his intention to pursue divorce had changed, this cannot have been an easy existence. On the surface she put on an impressive show that deceived most people. "Lady Duncannon...is in great beauty, *et plus aimable* than ever, it is not saying much to say that she is the only woman in London worth speaking to,"[1] wrote Lady Jersey, enthusiastically extolling Harriet's charms to Georgiana the summer after her return. But away from the public gaze the reality was very different. Harriet was deeply disenchanted with herself and her life; guilt and remorse had ripened into self-hatred interspersed with periods of folly, in which, ignoring reality, she immersed herself in further self-indulgence and consumption.

Like many aristocratic women, Harriet attached great importance to how she looked and what she wore. Among the *haut ton* a woman's clothes and jewels were a source of great competitiveness. "The nobility seemed to vie with each other in the taste, richness and elegance of their dresses," reported *Lady Magazine* in January 1790 of the sumptuous ensembles worn to court for the queen's birthday. Those deemed lacking in taste ran the risk of ridicule both among their circle and in the press. Sometimes the condemnations were so scalding that they caused the unfortunate subject to retire from society, as in the case of the unfortunate Lady Mary Coke, who "was determined that no muscle should contract itself into risibility at her expense this day, as it did on a former occasion by the juvenile fancy of her dress; and therefore she very wisely remained at home, saving her credit as an old woman, and her money likewise."[2]

Harriet would never be subjected to such a fate. Blessed with an innate sense of style, she enjoyed a further coveted advantage after her recent journey abroad—that of knowing the latest trends. Women's fashion had long been centered in Paris, but since the advent of political turmoil few female travelers had ventured to the city, and the usual influx of luxurious novelties had been interrupted. Thus starved, the clothes-conscious hungered for news of the latest modes in dresses and wigs. Before Harriet's journey to the Continent had been arranged in the wake of the Sheridan affair, Georgiana had written to her to bring her up to date with the latest Parisian innovations. "The hair is dressed, narrow high—long curls on the chignon—light crêpe caps . . . I send you a fan . . . I am quite well in health and was very well dressed today . . . I have been obliged to have a few caps of Mlle. Gausset and so have been faithless to Mlle. Bertin a little; and likewise to Leonard, for there is a much better hair dresser."[3]

In almost every respect, Georgiana and Harriet discovered, women's appearances had undergone transformation. In place of the high-powdered coiffeurs, hair styles had become simpler and more natural, curled about the head or flowing down the back—perhaps tied with a wide ribbon or a bandeau of gauze. Dresses too were radically altered. Parisian ladies had begun to abandon the cinched corseted waists and billowing hooped skirts, instead donning ensembles inspired by Grecian antiquity: high-waisted gowns with flowing skirts made of flimsy, body-revealing fabrics such as muslin and gauze. The new fashion dispensed with the need for tight-laced underclothes—indeed there was no longer a need for any underwear at all—and echoed the informality and moral freedoms of the age. This was ideal garb for lounging alluringly on a daybed—a pose almost impossible to accomplish in a corset—or for wafting through a parkland while admiring the beauties of the scenery, or for arousing the sexual appetites of men.

While Georgiana remained in Paris after Harriet's departure to await the birth of her new baby (Marquess of Hartington, or Hart, the son and heir everyone had longed for, was born on May 21, 1790), Harriet, in London, had fewer maternal distractions. Ceding to the advice of George Spencer and other family members, she and Duncannon decided to send John, by now aged nine, to school at Harrow, while Frederick, aged seven, was sent to a boarding school in Wandsworth. Caroline and William were well cared for by their nurses. Thus, having soaked up every detail of Parisian modes, there was little, apart from an inconvenient lack of money, to prevent Harriet from embarking on a spending spree.

At the king's birthday celebrations *Lady Magazine* observed that "the earrings most in fashion were clump ear-rings, in the shape of a large button, of gold. This fashion was lately brought over from Paris by Lady Duncannon."[4] At a royal assembly in January, Harriet had been widely admired, glamorously clad in a gown with "a gold body and white crêpe train, ornamented with gold and black velvet, petticoat of white crêpe strewed with green and gold leaves, a rich border of variegated tulips intermixed with seaweed and trimmed at the bottom with black velvet and gold fringe."[5] Enticed by the willingness of dressmakers, milliners, stay-makers, hosiers, cloth merchants, coiffeurs, and the raft of other purveyors of luxury goods who catered to a well-to-do woman's needs to provide their wares on credit, Harriet had no need of ready money to pay for her orders. Overspending added to the losses she had already made from gambling and thus her debts and unhappiness grew. By the beginning of the year Harriet was besieged by unpaid tradesmen's accounts, unable to confide in her husband, brother, or mother, and unable to see any way to save herself from the financial abyss.

Only Georgiana—whose own financial situation was far worse—knew the truth. On her return from France she tried to stave off her sister's creditors as well as her own, borrowing from her friends and family and cultivating her friendship with the long-suffering banker Thomas Coutts. More worryingly, in their desperation she and Harriet were persuaded to turn to various dubious investment schemes that promised easy riches, borrowing unwisely from unscrupulous money-lenders to make investments in stocks and the lottery that resulted in further loss. "Two of our finest ladies, sisters, have descended into the basse cour of the alley with Jews and brokers and waddled out with a large loss of feathers," Horace Walpole remarked of their spiraling descent.[6] Lady Mary Berry claimed that Georgiana's loss of fifty thousand pounds on stocks was "the conversation of the town" and that her name was to be "posted up as a lame duck": in other words, she would be publicly declared insolvent.[7]

As the illicit transactions spiraled beyond Harriet's control, the effect on her mental well-being was devastating. She grew increasingly overwrought, shadowed by the constant terror of public shame and Duncannon's wrath should he discover the truth of her predicament. Georgiana, witnessing her sister's anguish, increased her efforts to protect her from the worst demands. She persuaded Harriet to move her account to Thomas Coutts's bank, hoping he might view her sister's plight sympathetically. The extent of Harriet's losses is visible in the account books at Coutts, where for the year 1791–92 (against her annual pin money of £400) more than £10,000 of expenditure (equivalent to £600,000 today), most of it bills to moneylenders, is recorded.

Georgiana's efforts to help did not succeed in halting Harriet's mental and physical decline. In early February Harriet was probably several months pregnant when she began to complain of dizziness in the head. Over the next two weeks her condition deteriorated dramatically. Exact details of what happened are veiled in uncertainty, but from the reports that survive it seems that her cough worsened and she began spitting blood and suffering from a rapid pulse and strange convulsions. As the muscular spasms became more severe, Harriet probably suffered a miscarriage and then contracted some further form of respiratory infection and suffered a serious illness, all of which left her semi-paralyzed and gasping for breath. Everyone thought her death was imminent.

Harriet's illness shook Duncannon. If, as many reports suggest, she was pregnant, they must have resumed normal marital relations at some stage after the affair with Sheridan; but there were no other outward signs to show that there had been any proper reconciliation, nor that his desire for a divorce had wavered, and this uncertainty had exerted a terrible strain in addition to Harriet's anxiety over her spiraling debts. We cannot entirely blame Duncannon for his earlier frostiness toward his wife. In the light of his long wariness of the Spencers, his resentment of their influence is understandable in the wake of the Sheridan affair. Georgiana had conspired with Harriet in her infidelity, allowing intimate meetings to take place at Devonshire House. Lady Spencer had interfered constantly in day-to-day matters. The family had closed ranks over Harriet's transgressions. Worse still, even *his* cousin, the Duke of Devonshire, had forced him to drop his suit for divorce, apparently beguiled by Harriet's charm.

But the sight of Harriet clinging to life by a thread jolted Duncannon and wrought a remarkable transformation. He summoned Lady Spencer to London and wrote urgently to Harriet's brother, notifying him of her condition. Lady Spencer, presumably with Duncannon's agreement, called in Dr. Warren. After ten days, Harriet was still seriously unwell—unable to walk or move her left arm or leg, which were completely numb, suffering severe pain in her side, and still troubled by a hacking cough. But her condition had stabilized and there was slender reason to hope her life would be spared. "I was much alarmed by Lord Duncannon's letter about my sister," wrote George, clearly still terrified yet trying to be optimistic for his mother's sake. "I was in hopes this attack would go off like some of the others she has had, which though at the moment very alarming have not been attended with bad consequences."[8]

ANY STORY INVOLVING a glamorous aristocrat with a colorful past was a newsworthy item, and Harriet's illness swiftly attracted the notice of the press. Some reports were content merely to detail her mysterious symptoms. "Lady Duncannon's late illness has ended in a kind of paralytic malady by which she has been deprived the use of her limbs," reported *The Times,* declaring her condition "a circumstance of misfortune, which every person must lament."[9] But others probed further, hinting darkly that her condition was in some way linked to her unhappy marriage, that Duncannon had tried to imprison her and that a miscarriage, mental instability, or failed suicide attempt lay behind it. Friends and acquaintances were similarly puzzled by her plight. Many saw her as the unhappy and innocent martyr of Duncannon's cruelty. Georgiana tried to suppress the more fanciful rumors, claiming that Harriet had fallen ill as a result of a miscarriage and inflammation of the womb and bowels.

However, few were persuaded that the truth was so simple, or that Duncannon was innocent of involvement. "Abuse has been lavished on her, without reserve. Last winter she had a most violent illness, the precise cause of which the physicians could not account for—some inward disease, and, at the time, she was breeding. This uncertainty the world good-naturedly took up, and made clear, some that she was not ill at all, but confined by her husband; some that she was mad; some that she had poisoned herself, and assigned all the necessary and plausible causes . . . she is now in a wretched state . . . having lost the use of one side totally, and bearing this miserable state with a resignation and goodness of temper that would almost touch the heart of a newspaper writer,"[10] wrote Mrs. Damer in a later summing-up of the extraordinary speculation surrounding Harriet's illness.

What exactly was wrong with Harriet? Even with modern medical diagnosis of the various symptoms mentioned in reports and correspondence, it is impossible to be sure. The coughing and spitting of blood were probably symptoms of tuberculosis, a slow-progressing disease that she may have contracted many years earlier. The paralysis of Harriet's left side suggests right lobal damage to the brain, although what could have caused this is harder to establish. The traditional explanation, that Harriet had suffered a stroke, seems most likely, although at the age of thirty this was unusually young for such a malady. If, as several sources suggest, she was pregnant at the time of her illness, the onset of sudden dizziness, the heightened pulse and spasms leading to miscarriage could perhaps point to eclampsia, a life-threatening but common complication of pregnancy that could also have led to the damage in her brain and the resulting paralysis. Alternatively, it is not beyond the realm of possibility that Duncannon did, as the whispers suggested, play some part in her illness by assaulting her, thus causing her miscarriage and brain damage.

The novelist Fanny Burney subscribed to the view that Harriet's wretchedness had made her try to take her own life, referring in her journal to "[Harriet's] intended suicide."[11] However, since this remark was added in brackets some years later, after a meeting with Mrs. Damer—who, as we have seen, recounted the same rumor—her opinion must be regarded with suspicion. Certainly, though, in the acknowledged manner of an abused wife Harriet always felt culpable for incurring Duncannon's displeasure and intensely grateful for any gesture of kindness from him. The only clue she provides to the mystery is in a confused letter written to Lady Melbourne during her stay at Bath:

> I know not whether I gave it [her illness] myself or whether it might not have come otherwise but I am very certain had it been just on Lord D[uncannon], good as he is, I never could have rallied. I should have died first. I am but ill humouring and scolding but I cannot [in] all kindness and generosity [deny] if he would always be as good [as] he is now [he] never never should have had the smallest reason for being angry with me.[12]

Harriet's turmoil is clear, but her professed uncertainty as to the cause of her ailments appears to contradict the suicide theory and support the notion that either Duncannon was directly involved or that her troubled state of mind over her financial affairs was to blame. But even here there are doubts: given that "self-murder" or suicide was a crime against God and law, she may have been too ashamed to admit the depths of her desperation.

Whatever the secret truth, we know that debts had played a large part in Harriet's mental anguish and that these did not disappear. Throughout the worst throes of her illness, when she lay helpless in bed, creditors continued to harass her, sometimes bursting into her room to demand the immediate payment of a bill. Georgiana was terrified that if their claims were not met, Duncannon or Lord Bessborough would learn of the outstanding amounts and their anger would make Harriet suffer a relapse. Hampered though she was by her own monstrous debts, Georgiana borrowed more money to save her sister, writing emotionally to Thomas Coutts, begging for help. "In Lady Duncannon's state you may imagine how money plagues torment her; she has a call this day that must be complied with for £500 ... Can you send me 500 today on my faith of repaying it you Tuesday from her? ... I was present when the insatiable dunn [creditor] forced his way into her room and, in spite of her debilitated state, told her he must have 500 today. I confess to you I bid her sleep in peace, she should have it."[13]

Harriet's financial predicament was worsened by the unscrupulous moneylenders she had used, who now resorted to extortion to recover their debts. Georgiana, who had been involved in similar scrapes herself, hid the truth from her sister and bravely managed to curtail their claims, confiding to Thomas Coutts: "I did not dare mention the swindling story to my sister; but I have I hope put a stop to any proceeding of the kind."[14] Coutts was not unsympathetic, but he had already been swamped by countless tradesmen's bills on Harriet's behalf and, having advanced Georgiana large sums against promises to repay that had not been fulfilled, he understandably questioned her story. There was probably some truth in his suspicions, but Georgiana was incensed. "You cannot conceive how shocked I am at your suspecting me of any money transaction of any kind. Since the twentieth of last December I have not borrowed one guinea . . . I have not bought one article I have not paid for . . . You cannot blame me for wishing to assist my sister. Mrs. Murray [who was owed £500 by Harriet] I never will see, nor have. Lady Duncannon is in her hands still, and is too ill for me to insist on her breaking through it, as I dare not vex her . . . I am astonished at what you tell me of the tradesmen, and am certain it is without Lady D's knowledge . . . Should I refuse to assist my sister I should be a monster indeed. How could I assist but through you . . ."[15]

When Coutts was unyielding, Georgiana was forced to beg friends and acquaintances for loans that she had little hope of repaying. The inventor Sir Richard Arkwright was among those beguiled by Georgiana's poignant story and promises to repay. "He advanced the money [£5,000, equal to £300,000 today] at a time, when in the management of my sister's affairs, during her illness I was always obliged to be watching lest Lord Bessborough's* notes should fall upon him and I generally lost near half in the immense discount and interest I was obliged to pay to keep things quiet . . . The debts of honour amounting to £1500 are some that pain me because at the time of borrowing I had no idea of not being able to repay very soon, and I should, had not the annoying cheating about some of Lord Bessborough's notes taken all my money." When friends or family could no longer be persuaded to help, Georgiana repeated Harriet's mistakes, turning to dubious sources to

---

* By the time she wrote this, Duncannon had succeeded to the title the Third Earl of Bessborough.

raise the necessary funds. "I owe another person something but I am not sure how much but think £150, this is Mr. Vaughan of Grafton Street—and this was owing to his having done some of Lady Bessborough's notes, he will wait,"[16] she wrote of one typical transaction. There were countless more.

Two months after the onset of her illness, Harriet's condition was scarcely improved. She had still lost the feeling and use of her arm and leg and remained wheelchair-bound. Dr. Kerr, a new medical expert, was called in by George Spencer. "He thought when he felt her side (which however he said he could not do as much as he would have wished on account of the pain his touching it put her to) that he perceived a sort of hardness that seemed to extend from the kidney to the uterus . . . I only mention it that when her side gets to be less susceptible of pain the attention of Mr. Crofts or whatever surgeon attends her may be turned to this point as it is most probable that this whatever it is is the cause of the complaint in her leg by affecting the origin of the muscles that are used moving it,"[17] wrote an anxious George. Kerr was as mystified by Harriet's condition as everyone else, and his only suggestion was that "the pumping of some mineral water . . . to the part"—in other words, hydrotherapy, a treatment on offer at spas such as Bath and Buxton—might help.

Eager to try anything that might restore Harriet's health, Duncannon immediately set about making travel arrangements and finding lodgings in Bath, even though he, like Harriet, was riddled with debts and desperately short of money. The usually reserved Duke of Devonshire also wanted to do something to help his pitifully ill sister-in-law, perhaps because she had accepted his friendship with Bess Foster without criticism or jealousy (unlike the other hostile Spencers). He generously decided to rent two houses in Bath: one in which Georgiana, Bess, and most of the children could stay, and where Harriet and Lady Spencer could spend the day; and the other for the use of his fourteen-month-old heir, Lord Hartington, and his nurse.

Lady Spencer, still deeply concerned about Harriet, was no less wary of her son-in-law, despite the apparent change in his manner. She had no intention of leaving Harriet to make the journey to Bath alone with Duncannon and insisted on nursing Harriet herself. Duncannon responded by announcing that, in the interests of economy, there would be no room for Lady Spencer's servants.

The sad party arrived at Bath in late May. The city was one of glamour and charm to which aristocrats, merchants, quacks, and ne'er-do-wells had long flocked in search of health, diversion, and rich pickings, and by the end of the eighteenth century it had become the seventh-biggest city in England. Alongside the elegant honey-colored stone terraces, assembly halls, pump rooms, and grand villas that had always drawn the affluent, new developments now clustered on the peak of every hill and descended to every valley. "Its buildings are so unfinished," complained Fanny Burney, "so spread, so everywhere beginning, and nowhere ending, that it looks rather like a space of ground lately fixed upon for creating a town, than a town itself, of so many years duration."[18]

The journey from London had taken a week, during which Harriet contracted a fever and suffered acute discomfort with every jolt of the carriage. Lady Spencer, terrified that Harriet's life was again in danger, refused to leave her daughter alone at night, instead sleeping in a small bed in her room. She was already fatigued by the strain of looking after an invalid and of managing without servants, and Bath always awakened sad memories of her husband. A day after her arrival, she was, she confessed, "as low and uncomfortable as possible and the more so from the necessity of appearing otherwise to [Harriet]." Although food and other domestic services were provided by their lodgings, she was unused to dressing herself, a time-consuming, awkward procedure that could take an hour or longer. And there was a further irritation: Harriet was now in the care of a new doctor who was reluctant to commit himself when it came to giving his prognosis. "Doctor Fraser does not know me and I do not know him so I have no guess what his sentiments are," she frustratedly reported.[19]

Over the next few days Harriet began her treatment. Each morning she sipped a glass of the foul-tasting sulphurous waters in bed, then visited the pump room to force herself to drink further glasses. The first signs were far from auspicious. "Harriet has taken four glasses of the water, which has no other effect than not feeling disagreeably upon her stomach," Lady Spencer gloomily recorded.[20]

Ten days after arriving at Bath, Harriet began to bathe as well as drink the waters. It is hard to understand the confidence the eighteenth-century medical profession placed in this unhygienic and undignified procedure. Men and women wallowed side by side in warm, foul-smelling pools while spectators gawped at them. Harriet would have worn a voluminous gown of yellowish canvas that filled with water on immersion, thus disguising the shape of her body beneath. Little attention was paid to the dangers of cross-infection. The waters were believed to prevent contagion; thus people suffering sores and sexual infections soaked in the same waters as everyone else. Tobias Smollett somewhat exaggeratedly described the scene in *Humphrey Clinker:*

> 'Twas a glorious sight to behold the fair sex
> All wading with gentlemen up to their necks,
> And view them so prettily tumble and sprawl
> In a great smoking kettle as big as our hall;
> And today many persons of rank and condition
> Were boiled by command of an able physician . . .
> You cannot conceive what a number of ladies
> Were washed in the water the same as our maid is . . .
> So while little Tabby was washing her rump
> The ladies kept drinking it out of the pump.

The "pumping" that had been recommended involved squirting the hottest waters available onto Harriet's paralyzed limbs and took place on an island in the center of the King's Bath while everybody else watched. These indignities apart,[21] Harriet found the process of bathing "rather pleasant than otherwise," and there were small signs of improvement afterward: "she sits up with less support and bears motion and noise," observed Lady Spencer.[22] Dr. Fraser told her that he had tended patients more incapacitated than Harriet who had made full recoveries, and her youth was much in her favor. But his encouragements failed to shift Lady Spencer's pessimism. She had noticed that Harriet's right leg was wasting from lack of use, becoming "as useless as the left and the knee is contracted so that she cannot straighten it without pain."[23] Harriet, she feared, would never walk again.

Over the following weeks Harriet and her entourage settled into a routine. Lady Spencer rose at six, spent an hour dressing herself, then walked to Marlborough Buildings, an apartment some distance away where Georgiana and her party were staying. There she spent a short while talking to the Devonshire children and Miss Trimmer, their governess, who was also a close friend. She returned to the Duncannons' lodging in time to breakfast with Harriet at ten, then accompanied Harriet in her wheelchair the short distance to the pump room, where Harriet drank the waters. Afterward they took sedan chairs to Spring Gardens, a fashionable private parkland latticed by elegant walks, cascades, and flowerbeds, where concerts and dances were often held. Here they passed the time reading until the early afternoon, when Georgiana arrived to relieve her mother and allow her time to dress for dinner. The evenings were spent with Georgiana and, as far as Lady Spencer was concerned, were less tranquil. She was often disconcerted by the company that frequented Georgiana's house, and tried to shrink into the background. The presence of Bess Foster was a constant irritation, especially since one of Harriet's favorite pastimes was playing piano duets with her. "Lady Elizabeth plays the base or the accompaniment and [Harriet] plays the upper part and sings delightfully to it,"[24] Lady Spencer told her friend Mrs. Howe. When forced to join in, Lady Spencer consoled herself with a hand or two of whist with the duke and Duncannon; she often lost, although she claimed that since she had "scarcely betted the whole is but little."

Harriet's progress was painfully slow, but there was progress nonetheless. By the end of June, Lady Spencer was able to move out of Harriet's room. In the baths Harriet was "able to stand with very little assistance."[25] Everyone agreed that it would be in her interest to remain at Bath and continue with her treatments. Since money remained a worry, Duncannon decided to move to less expensive lodgings, renting a small house on the Queen's Parade. Lady Spencer, claiming she wanted to save Duncannon additional expense, "which I think a serious matter whatever he may [say],"[26] decided to rent a house of her own. She still felt unable to leave Harriet for long, although after two months without servants and little in the way of privacy, she craved the comforts of home.

Among those who met Lady Spencer and Harriet that summer at Bath was the novelist Fanny Burney. Lady Spencer called at Fanny's lodgings one afternoon, having heard she was in town. A stern moralist, Fanny had risen from a middle-class provincial background, achieved fame as a novelist, and become a lady-in-waiting to the queen. She viewed Harriet, whose "history current of her worthlessness had been so general," with a disapproving eye, deploring her political alliance to the Whig opposition. Stories of financial and sexual misdemeanors that were the talk of London only compounded her aversion. Despite these reservations, Fanny was flattered at receiving a visit from such an illustrious figure as Lady Spencer and agreed to receive her.

After their first conversation, Fanny concluded that although her visitor was "a sensible and sagacious character intelligent polite and agreeable," she was too quick to advertise her charitable occupations. And when the subject of Harriet was raised, Fanny was truly flummoxed. Lady Spencer showed no embarrassment whatsoever over the scandalous subject of her daughter. Her fervently held religious beliefs had helped her interpret Harriet's disgrace and illness as a manifestation of divine fate. Harriet had accepted her suffering with stoicism and resignation and had, in her mother's eyes, acknowledged it as punishment for the error of her ways. She had thus transformed herself into a model of virtue. This was too much for Fanny, who questioned Lady Spencer's grasp of reality. "The dreadful accounts I have heard of the cause of that lady's sufferings, and the want of all principle in her conduct, rushed so forcibly upon my mind, I could scarce give her even the tacit concurrence of silent complaisance: can it be that she is after all innocent?—or is her mother deluded?—or does her mother only aim to delude others?"[27]

Two days later Lady Spencer invited Fanny to Georgiana's lodgings for the birthday celebrations of Harryo, Georgiana's six-year-old daughter. Believing that Harriet was confined to her bed, Fanny accepted the invitation. During the afternoon, however, Harriet was suddenly carried into the room by two servants and laid on the sofa. Unable to leave politely, yet overwhelmed with "an unconquerable repugnance," Fanny contrived to distance herself from Harriet by avoiding eye contact. When Lady Spencer introduced her, she behaved with cool detachment, pointedly making conversation with one of the other visitors as soon as she was able. Nevertheless even the sanctimonious Fanny could not resist the allure of Harriet's notoriety. From time to time she stole a glance at the figure lying languidly upon the sofa.

Even in her illness, she remarked, Harriet was fashionably attired. "Her dress was extremely becoming, though simple, and in part, that of an invalid; in part, I say, for to a close cap she added a hat and feather, and to a brown green round gown, pink ribbons." For all her intended chilliness, Fanny gradually became mesmerized.

> . . . in point of beauty she never looked in my eyes, to so much advantage. Sickness has softened her features and her expression into something so interesting and so unusually lovely, that I should by no means have known her for the same lady I had so little admired in her early days. The tone of her voice, too, modified by the same cause, is soft, sweet and penetrating. She never spoke, without catching all my attention, however unwillingly, and her words and her manner enforced its power by expressing constantly something cheerful about her own wretched state, or grateful for the services offered or done her.[28]

Fanny's gradual conversion was not enough to stop her recoiling with horror when Lady Spencer rose from her seat next to Harriet and offered it to Fanny. "This was too much; this was leading to an intimacy I peculiarly wished to avoid: and neither respect for the mother nor pity for the daughter, could operate; I excused myself, as civilly as I could . . ." Even so, she could not bring herself to leave, and was further intrigued when Duncannon joined the party. Fanny had heard that, having discovered Harriet's infidelities, Duncannon was only waiting for his father to die, "lest the grief of such an event should shorten his days," before proceeding with his divorce. She was astonished, therefore, "to see him hasten up to his wife, enquire tenderly how she did and take the seat I had declined!" Duncannon's kindness also struck her. "[Harriet] wished to look to the garden and see the children; he lifted her in his arms to move her nearer the window; she wanted her cadeaux ready for the little lady Harriot [Harryo], he sought for them, and brought them ready . . . He would let no one but himself lift her into [the wheelchair] and was so silent, quiet, and still in all he did for her, that I plainly saw his assistance was the result of affection."[29]

It is easy to be skeptical of Duncannon's behavior. He was canny enough to have realized that Fanny, with her wide circle of correspondents, would relate the details of this visit. This would not have been the first time he had put on a show of solicitude only to turn on Harriet in private. But there are other signs that his manner toward her had radically changed. "Nothing ever was so kind as Lord Duncannon has been. He is the only good-natured person I know in the world and I really am quite touched with it,"[30] Harriet would write a few weeks later to Lady Melbourne. Lady Spencer also confirmed that Duncannon's attitude had undergone a transformation, remarking to her friend Mrs. Howe that he "was very attentive and good humoured with her and as obliging as possible with me."[31]

Of course the family may all have been clutching at straws, trying to convince themselves as well as others of the change in Duncannon. Certainly, for all her protestations Harriet remained unsure of him, especially when it came to matters of money. If there was something she wanted but could not afford, she preferred to tell him half-truths rather than risk arousing his displeasure, and then covertly appeal to family or friends for help in her subterfuge. George was often asked to help, but was reluctant to act behind Duncannon's back, on one occasion telling Lady Spencer about Harriet's secret request for money, "I am clear that it was right that Lord Duncannon should know everything of that kind and she had proposed in her letter not telling him of it . . ."[32]

By September Harriet had been bled by leeches, and the latest costly electrical treatment was added to the list of remedies she had tried. According to a report in *The Times,* electricity "never produce[d] more than momentary effects."[33] Nevertheless, her condition had continued to improve. Sensation had returned in her left hand, and even though her muscles were wasted and weak she was able to walk across the room on crutches. Dr. Warren, summoned down from London, advised that in order for her recovery to continue Harriet should cease taking the Bath waters for six months and go abroad—perhaps to Lisbon—and spend the winter in milder climes. The advice threw Harriet into despair. She could not bear the thought of leaving her family, and a long sea journey and the discomforts of foreign travel filled her with dread. She persuaded Warren to recommend Devon or Cornwall instead, and with Duncannon's approval it was decided that Harriet, with Georgiana to nurse her, would spend the winter in Penzance.

No sooner had this plan been settled than calamity overturned it. Georgiana had long been infatuated with the young ambitious politician Charles Grey. He had begun paying court to her several years earlier but their full-blown love affair probably began only after her return from France, once she had provided the duke with his heir. The affair had continued throughout the months of Harriet's illness.[34] Georgiana had invited him not only to secret suppers at Devonshire House, but, recklessly, to call on her at the house in Bath when the duke was away, without worrying about who saw him come and go. Harriet and Bess had known all along of the affair, and had tried to warn Georgiana of the dangers. "I begged she would not depend on Lady S[pencer]'s blindness to it, which would not last . . . The storm however broke . . . and her commands are you know absolute and her vigilance extreme,"[35] Bess recounted. Lady Spencer had learned of the affair from an anonymous letter and furiously forced Georgiana to send Grey away, assuming then that the affair was over and would never be discovered. She had not realized something that Harriet and Bess knew: Georgiana had continued to see Grey secretly and was now six months pregnant with his child.

Georgiana's pregnancy lay behind the sisters' desire to move to the quiet of Cornwall. The stay would have enabled Georgiana to give birth to Grey's child in secret, without the truth escaping. But before they could leave for Penzance, the Duke of Devonshire, who had been away for a month on a tour of his estate in Derbyshire, received an anonymous letter advising him to call on his wife. Arriving at Bath late one evening and finding Georgiana now visibly pregnant, he flew into a rage. Harriet, lying in the room next door, overheard the confrontation—the duke shouting and Georgiana sobbing; then he stormed out and began pacing up and down his room without speaking.

Harriet was too terrified to dare ask what he had decided, but, over the days that followed, the duke presented Georgiana with a stark choice. She could leave her children and go abroad with Harriet until the baby was born, when it would have to be immediately given up for adoption. She would then have to wait for the duke to recall her. Or she could stay and face a public separation—and, by implication, a scandalous divorce.

Georgiana had little alternative but to agree to the duke's terms, and Harriet, despite being devastated at the thought of leaving her two older children behind, never wavered in her loyalty to her sister. "I would go to the world's end to do her good," she declared, writing to Lady Melbourne to explain their suddenly revised plans.

> We must go abroad immediately, nothing else will do, neither prayer nor entreaties nor representations will alter him. He says there is no choice between this or public separation at home. Bess has very generously promised to go with us. I urged her to it almost as much on her own account as my sister's. It must have been ruin to her to stay behind.[36]

Frail though she still was, Harriet now had a heavy burden of responsibility to bear. Duncannon was presently away in London and Lady Spencer had returned to Holywell for a few days. The duke did not want either of them, or anyone else for that matter, to discover the reason for the change of plan. Instead, he insisted, Harriet must appear to suffer an unexpected relapse, which would persuade Warren to change his mind and order Harriet abroad. The duke expected Harriet to feign sudden illness, but Harriet, terrified she would not be able to convince Warren, went one step further, deliberately making herself ill. "This sounds very foolish I know but it is not so, in attempting to act it I should have felt so guilty that . . . I should have discovered myself in a moment . . . my health is now so good a trifling cold cannot hurt me, it is only . . . a little the complaint I always have on my breast and it will smooth a thousand difficulties," she told Lady Melbourne. The scheme worked; Warren was easily convinced to change his advice and tell Duncannon and Lady Spencer that Harriet must go abroad.

It was one thing to convince a paid doctor to fall in with their scheme, but quite another to alter Duncannon's and Lady Spencer's plans so dramatically. Duncannon had made arrangements for the move to Cornwall, and, apart from not wishing to have to arrange the practicalities of going abroad, was reluctant to leave his aging father. Georgiana was terrified he would block their plan. "There was never anything equal to Lord Duncannon and Lord Bessborough's absurd obstinacy," she fretted; "there is no chance of moving them but Warren's taking it on himself entirely."[37] Again she pleaded with Warren to put forward their case more strongly. He complied convincingly and after much bitter complaining Duncannon eventually acquiesced to the new plan and agreed to take charge of the party.

Masking the truth from the ever-vigilant Lady Spencer was even more difficult. Having received a sudden letter "to tell me . . . Harriet *must* go abroad,"[38] she rushed back to Bath from Holywell and immediately grasped that the real reason for the scheme was not Harriet's illness but Georgiana's pregnancy. She was furious with Georgiana for her deception, and also with Bess, who she felt had helped to cover the affair. "My mother is come and our difficulties increase—when I see all the vexations and unhappiness that surrounds me I almost wish myself at the bottom of the sea,"[39] a wretched Harriet told Lady Melbourne. Lady Spencer was further incensed to be told that one of the duke's stipulations was that she should remain behind in England while Harriet and Georgiana went abroad. This may have been intended as an additional punishment for Georgiana, or to shield Lady Spencer from Georgiana's pregnancy, which the duke hoped she would never discover. Either way, Lady Spencer refused absolutely to countenance such a plan, and majestically announced her determination to join Harriet and Georgiana in their exile.

The decision had a worrying repercussion. Bess had at first promised Georgiana and Harriet that she would go with them. But Lady Spencer's animosity toward her had worsened in recent days. "Lady S has begun as bad as possible about me even so as to say I should not travel with them," she told Lady Melbourne.[40] On learning that Lady Spencer was to go too, she began to prevaricate. Harriet was well aware of the importance of Bess in their party. As the duke's mistress, if Bess took up residence with him in Devonshire House, what incentive would there be for him ever to allow Georgiana to return to England?

Harriet had a long conversation with Bess, which ended in a "half quarrel" and left Bess still wavering. To Lady Melbourne Harriet wrote, "I really believe it is nothing but the fear she has of my mother and the constraint she feels when with her that makes her hesitate but it is the only thing in the world to reconcile her."[41] But over the days that followed, the crucial question of whether Bess would come away with Georgiana and Harriet and brave the fearsome Lady Spencer was one that preyed heavily on everyone's mind.

EIGHT

A Test of Loyalty

November 1791 ~ 1792

OVER THE WEEKS THAT FOLLOWED, Harriet's fate seemed more uncertain than ever. Having ordered Georgiana abroad, the Duke of Devonshire prevaricated, unable to decide whether he wanted Georgiana to go into exile in Penzance, Lisbon, or France, and refusing to agree to any travel arrangements while he dithered. "If the Duke had purposely intended to perplex and torment us he could not have done it better!"[1] Harriet wretchedly told Lady Melbourne. Her mother was equally frustrated by their helplessness, but for once she bided her time, not daring to interfere. "I never felt altogether so great a depression of spirits or saw anything in so gloomy a way as since my return to Bath," Lady Spencer confided to her friend Mrs. Howe.[2]

Eventually the duke resolved that Georgiana and Harriet must go abroad, and that southern France rather than Lisbon was preferable from Harriet's point of view. This was because the sea crossing was shorter and would entail less risk should she be taken ill en route—even his fury with Georgiana did not extinguish his fondness for her sister. Knowing where she was going did little to lessen Harriet's dismay. At the heart of her unhappiness lay the thought of separation from John and Frederick, her two oldest children, who would have to stay behind at school. Adding to her misery, Duncannon decided that William, now aged five, should remain at Roehampton to keep his eighty-eight-year-old grandfather company. Since the duke would not waver from his decision that Georgiana should be forced to leave her three children in London as a punishment for her transgression, the only children in the party would be Harriet's daughter, six-year-old Caroline Ponsonby, and, if Bess decided to come, Caro St. Jules, her illegitimate daughter by the duke of the same age.

The discomforts of foreign travel and her own fragile condition also preyed on Harriet's mind. Duncannon was in London when the plan to travel to France was finally settled, and she took matters into her own hands, making secret arrangements to buy a carriage. She enlisted the help of Lady Melbourne, claiming that secrecy was important to save Duncannon from further financial worry. "I have already got him to such inconvenient expense by my illness that I cannot bear adding to this which is more than an indulgence, this is really necessary for me."[3]

Duncannon was conscious of her fear of traveling abroad and tried his best to reassure her. "You have wrote me a sad melancholy letter, but I hope by the time you receive this you will be in better spirits. I begin to be reconciled to our expedition and you must be so too."[4] To calm her he detailed the arrangements thus far. He had commissioned a packet boat with a Captain Caldwell to sail them across the Channel, and he'd arranged to borrow a coxswain from one of the guardships at Portsmouth. Despite his reassurances to Harriet, there remained a lingering distrust between them. While he was in London a letter arrived addressed to Harriet in an unfamiliar hand. Unable to help himself from opening it, he uncovered her secret attempt to buy a carriage.

But instead of flying into a rage, as he might have done a year earlier, he controlled his temper, issuing only the mildest of reprimands. "I find by O'Ryan's answer to your letter you have been proposing to buy his carriage, this is a little in your mysterious ways without telling me, but I forgive you."[5] It is impossible to know how Harriet would have read such a rebuke. Were his words of forgiveness genuine, or was this gentle admonition a possible presage of further violence when they met?

Whatever the truth, Harriet's secret scheming did not stop with the carriage. She wrote also to her brother, imploring him to lend her £300 to pay for a doctor to go with them, again begging him to keep the matter a secret from Duncannon. "He dislikes so especially the having it supposed he is the least distressed that probably he would be displeased with me for having mentioned it to you, and yet I cannot bear to think I am exposing him to the inconvenience of borrowing on my account." Again the mention of Duncannon's displeasure rouses the suspicion that Harriet still feared his temper, and yet she carefully reassured her brother that "nothing can equal the kindness [Duncannon] has shown me throughout the whole of my illness but more especially in his ready acquiescence to what I fear must be unpleasant to him."[6] George Spencer agreed to supply the loan for a doctor, although he could not bring himself to act behind Duncannon's back. He tactfully explained the arrangement and offered the services of his steward Townsend to help with the practicalities of travel. Duncannon accepted both offers.

The party then divided. The Duncannons, together with the newly recruited Dr. Nott and several servants, including Harriet's loyal maid Sally Peterson, left Bath for Southampton on October 31, meeting Lady Spencer, Georgiana, and their servants en route before crossing to Le Havre, where they landed on November 4. Bess, much to everyone's relief, had finally decided to join the party; she and the two Carolines and their attendants were to travel a day or two later via Dover and Calais, after Bess had made a final trip to London. The two parties were to meet in Rouen and then set off south for Nice.

In a grimy hotel in Rouen, Harriet and her entourage waited uneasily for Bess and the children. A week later, Bess had still not arrived and no word had reached them of her whereabouts or intentions; anxieties over her loyalty surfaced once more. "We know nothing of Lady Elizabeth but are in hourly expectation of seeing her as we think . . . she left London on Friday—it is very odd that there should be no letter from her and that nobody should mention when she set out,"[7] Lady Spencer wrote with more restraint than she usually displayed when the subject of Bess was raised. A few days later the conditions in Rouen became intolerable and they set off again to wait for Bess in the outskirts of Paris, where the hotels would be more comfortable. They found the city in a state of uneasy suspense, yet filled with a surprising number of English visitors. Five months earlier the royal family had been intercepted at Varennes while making a desperate bid to escape France's revolutionary upheavals and were now held under arrest at the Tuileries. Their predicament had cast a shadow over the city's well-to-do inhabitants. The streets, Harriet remarked, were empty of any sign of ostentation. There were no grand carriages to be seen; instead, people drove about as inconspicuously as possible in "little open chaises like the cabriolet only with one horse."[8] Even gentlemen drove themselves about and wore no hats.

Almost three weeks dragged by before word came that Bess had at last landed safely at Calais. When she reached Paris on November 21, Harriet was both relieved and sad to see how torn she had been. "Poor little soul, I felt for her from my heart, for I am certain the effort was as much as she could bear; but she is better now; she is our only security. I do not think she will go back without us now . . . though I had very great doubts whether she would have [the] resolution to tear herself away."[9]

Bess's arrival marked a shift in Lady Spencer's attitude toward her. "My Mother is very good humoured and civil to Bess," Harriet reported to Lady Melbourne. "She seems pleased and touched with the proof of her friendship for us." But while Bess's arrival brought relief in some ways, it also highlighted a problem they had hitherto ignored. The duke had implied that he would send money for Georgiana with Bess, but now it became clear that he had failed to make any financial provision for her whatsoever. "He has not sent her one farthing . . . what makes it worse he has . . . bound her by the most solemn promise never to borrow any money on interest," Harriet complained. The only way to avoid a breach of promise, or for Georgiana to avoid selling her belongings, was for Harriet, whose own finances were unstable in the extreme, "to *buy* everything she has." Apart from apprehensions over money, Harriet worried that Georgiana's raw nerves would break under their mother's excessive attentions. Ever since they had left England, Lady Spencer had taken it upon herself never to leave her alone. ". . . my sister has literally not an instant to herself, she sleeps in my mother's room, travels in her chaise . . . and cannot send or write a line that is not seen by everybody except now and then that I take her into the room with me and pretend to be asleep,"[10] Prior to Harriet's illness it had been Georgiana who had adopted the role of protector, trying to shield her sister from the worst demands of creditors, to offer reassurance, and to soothe her frayed nerves. Now the situation was reversed. Harriet, frail, weak, and depressed by the journey ahead, rallied her strength to help her sister face the frightening thought of giving birth in a foreign land in secret, and the anguish of giving up the child as soon as it was born.

EAGER TO BE away from the oppressive atmosphere of Paris, they made for the south of France in early December. The party was too large for most inns to accommodate them, and they traveled in separate groups, meeting up every two or three days, taking the journey in slow stages to avoid tiring Harriet. En route, Harriet began the correspondence to Frederick and John that she would maintain throughout her years abroad. Her letters reveal her love of writing and her fascination with the places she visited. Crammed with detail and anecdote, they are tailored to amuse as well as to educate, and many were illustrated with little drawings or watercolors or enclosed small samples of local crafts or plants or stones. "They make all sorts of little bead boxes and chains here," she wrote to John of Nevers, a town south of Paris. "I send you one, but it is not very pretty and is more fit for a girl than for you, but it is just to show you the way of it." Harriet's capacity for humor surfaces constantly in her reports. "From thence we came to Moulins . . ." she told John. "There is a great manufactory of cutlery here, and the women who sell them plague one to death with their knives and scissors. I had fifteen in the room at once and as many in the passage, all talking at once, and making such a noise . . . that it was hardly possible to help laughing . . ."[11]

Harriet was usually too concerned with recording the details of her journey to dwell on the difficulties of travel. By contrast, Lady Spencer's correspondence elaborates upon the indignities of filthy rooms, inedible food, slovenly servants, treacherous and sometimes impassable roads. Even aristocrats in straitened circumstances did not travel light; in this instance Lady Spencer was accompanied by her maidservant Jenny and two footmen. On one of the rare occasions when she allowed Georgiana out of her sight, she arrived at the sole inn in the vicinity to find that the only available accommodation was a room with three beds and no door. Lady Spencer later confessed to a friend that the thought of sharing a room with her footmen "startled me a little at first, but upon reflection I made [the landlady] nail up blankets . . . and both Jenny and I were very glad to have [the footmen] there..." As an afterthought she warned, "Talk of this only among friends or it will make a history in England."[12]

From Lyons the group traveled by boat down the Rhône to Avignon, then on by road to Marseilles. They needed two barges to carry all their luggage and carriages, and passed the journey on deck huddled against buffeting gales with little more than an open canvas awning for shelter from the driving wind and rain. As they disembarked, Harriet's carriage became mired in quicksand up to its axles and had to be dragged out by oxen. In Marseilles the group divided once more. The Duncannons, with Lady Spencer, Dr. Nott, and Townsend, turned southeast toward the Mediterranean coast, since Harriet had her heart set on passing the rest of the winter at Nice. Having convalesced there from illness as a child, she was convinced that the mild climate and pleasant surroundings would once more help her to recover. Georgiana and Bess meanwhile traveled westward to Aix and then Montpellier. The reason for the separation, Lord Duncannon told his father, was that "we are so many" and so that the women could visit "some relations of that little French girl* you have seen at Devonshire House, who were very desirous of seeing her."[13]

Duncannon remained oblivious that Georgiana was now in the advanced stages of pregnancy and needed to find somewhere to have Grey's child away from the public gaze. Nor did he realize that secrecy was paramount. If word of Georgiana's parting from Harriet filtered out and aroused suspicions of a hidden scandal and the rumors reached the duke, this might anger him and prevent her being recalled from exile. Georgiana's vulnerability and her fears of damaging gossip are all too clear in a letter written to her friend Lady Melbourne. "If anybody asks you about me," she implored her, "say that we follow [Harriet] to Nice as soon as her house is taken. But I don't suppose it need be much known that we don't go all together. Oh my love—God bless you I am so nervous and moved I can write no more , , , Tell me all the news— all you do, all you hear; either of me or others but only talk to Black† much of me."[14]

---

* Caroline St. Jules, the Duke of Devonshire and Elizabeth Foster's illegitimate daughter.

† Her nickname for Grey, the father of her child.

Having settled in a house in Montpellier, Georgiana and Bess could do nothing but wait in trepidation for the baby to arrive. Childbirth alarmed Georgiana—as it did every woman of her day—but with so much at stake she was more than usually terrified that she might die. She wrote a letter to Hart, the son she had been forced to leave behind in England, using her own blood as ink, and she drafted a will in which she left everything to the duke apart from a few personal bequests to those who were dearest to her. Among them she bequeathed, "to my dear sister a garnet string as a mourning necklace; a green antique ring and as a mourning ring the one I now wear of the siege of Ismael and the Dante on my table in London."[15] Even in her most unhappy moments Georgiana's love for Harriet was unwavering.

Georgiana's baby, a girl whom she called Eliza Courtenay, was safely delivered on February 20, 1792. Soon after, she was handed to a foster nurse to be taken to England and brought up by Grey's parents. Georgiana would later be granted limited access rights and visited her as an unofficial godmother, and Harriet also maintained contact. But, as part of her agreement with the duke, no one told Eliza the true identity of her mother.[16]

IN THE PLEASANT seaside town of Hyères, south of Toulon, Harriet watched the New Year festivities, waiting apprehensively for news of her sister. Her hopes to settle in Nice had been temporarily frustrated because the town was full of tourists and finding a suitable house had proved more difficult than expected. Time passed slowly and she tried to allay her unease by writing long illustrated letters to her sons. "The Greek woman is the prettiest; all that I have painted yellow about her was gold in reality . . . The man was an Armenian, a sort of pedlar . . . The place is by the seaside . . . New Year's Day when I was there, the shore was entirely covered with people all dressed as fine as could be, and most of them were going to feast aboard a boat which is kept near there for that purpose."[17]

She drew comfort from the fact that Duncannon continued to behave kindly toward her. Throughout their travels through France he had treated her with patience and consideration, and now that they were settled they began to take long rides into the countryside, Harriet on a donkey, with Duncannon on horseback beside her. Already her health had begun to improve. "I now cough very little and the day be-fore yesterday walked down stairs, twenty steps, with crutches and some people to hold them,"[18] she told her sons. Duncannon's letters to his father also always contained encouraging reports of Harriet's progress. "Harriet has more motion of the arm than she had," he wrote in February,[19] and again, a few weeks later, "Harriet is certainly much better and she has had a great deal of pain in her bad leg . . . which we think is a good sign."[20] Lady Spencer, by contrast, struggled under a burden of worry over Georgiana that infected her view of Harriet's condition. A lighted candle spilled hot wax on Harriet's hand and she was unable to feel it: this, she told one of her correspondents, had con-vinced her that Harriet would never be cured.

By early February their steward Townsend had found a suitable house in Nice and as soon as the weather was fine enough the family set out for it. The journey involved taking the treacherous route cross-ing the Esterel, a mountainous region that lies between Hyères and Nice, which was known to be infested with bandits. In places the roads were so severely damaged by the rain that no one could ride in the car-riages. "Lady Duncannon rode the whole nine miles and . . . I walked the greatest part of them that the child [Caroline] might ride my *bour-rica* [donkey]," reported Lady Spencer. Despite the hardships and dan-gers and her constant fears for Harriet and Georgiana, she was captivated by the scenery and by the spectacle of their procession, and her gloom lifted. "Our caravan made a very picturesque appearance—Harriet's *bourrica* and mine ornamented with bridles tufted with red and green worsted, the saddles covered with pieces of old carpet—the baggage mule with his load and the servant men and women by turns on foot and the carriages following."[21]

In Nice, Harriet thought the house Townsend had found them was enchanting. "I wish I could carry it to England with me," she told Lady Melbourne. "There is a garden upstairs from my windows quite to the sea, crowded with every sort of flower and everything that is delight-ful."[22] In the mellow Mediterranean climate, her health continued to improve, and Duncannon's enduring kindness had added to her happi-ness. "It has given me pleasure to see the unaffected marks they both show without design or even perceiving that they are observed of their tenderness and affection for each other,"[23] Lady Spencer remarked.

LIKE MOST ARISTOCRATIC travelers of her day, Harriet devoted much time to maintaining contact with those she had left behind. Hours were passed in writing not only to her children but to other family members and friends, and since letters were her only link with her old life and the woman she once had been, the arrival of the post was something she eagerly awaited. She was touched by how many people remembered her:

> I have been remarkably lucky not only in my friends, but even my acquaintances, most of them I mean, the time of my illness and my long absence has shown those who really cared for me and those who only affected it. But with regard to writing, people really have been very good.

The recipient of this letter is not named, and the only clue to identity lies in Harriet's lines "I do not put you down in the list of friends, I should think it as unnatural for you to forget me as for one of my children to do so...".[24] Was this intimate correspondent Sheridan? Despite the scandalous conclusion of their affair two years earlier, they had remained close. Sheridan had been in touch with her throughout her illness, often addressing letters intended for Harriet to Georgiana to avoid rousing Duncannon's jealousy. Now his wife Elizabeth was ill with consumption and his letters reflect his grief at her gradual deterioration, but imply too that his feelings for Harriet were still far deeper than mere friendship.

> Why have I not written to you lately?—F,* I shall now prove what your regard for me has been and is. *Forgive my silence, and write kindly to me when you receive this.* In the most melancholy hours I have ever known, for I never felt so without Hope on a point that interested us before, I find my mind turning towards you as the only creature whom I find it a relief to think of, or with whom it is an ease to me to communicate, or from whose words I can look for anything consoling or reconciling. O... however negligent, mysterious or unaccountable my

* Harriet's name was Henrietta Frances. Sheridan often referred to her as Frances.

conduct may have appeared to you, let me now find that I am not deceived in the opinion I have of the unalterable kindness of your heart and nature.

I am writing to you on the road to Bristol, while E[lizabeth] is in bed very, very ill—eager to get there and sanguine of the event. But many glaring omens have told me our hopes will be disappointed... Dear F, shall you I wonder think it selfish in me now to share so many gloomy thoughts and melancholy moments with you as I must if I write to you?[25]

Over the following months Sheridan's correspondence continued to chart Elizabeth's illness, until her death in July, when his letters ceased for a month before he wrote again. "I will write to you now constantly, and now... you cannot write too much to me. I shall know then that you are not estranged from me. And pray tell me a great deal, and everything about yourself. How strange I feel it to be that I should know so little... I will say little of the past, when I have once sent you a melancholy detail I wrote on purpose for you. I exert myself in every way, and avoid remembering or reflecting as much as possible, but there are thoughts and forms and sounds that haunt my heart and will not be put away... write to me now constantly. I entreat you do..."[26]

Harriet was understandably disturbed by such pleas. Fond though she had become of Duncannon, he could never rival the sharpness of Sheridan's mind when it came to describing political intrigue, or his wit in recounting a joke, or the poetry and pathos of which Sheridan in a melancholic mood was capable. "Now I am just returned from a long solitary walk on the beach," he once wrote. "Night, silence, solitude and the sea combined unhinge the cheerfulness of anyone, where there has been length of life enough to bring regret in reflecting on many past scenes, and to offer slender hope in anticipating the future."[27]

Despite her disquiet, distance altered her feelings. At the age of thirty, as she reviewed her life and turbulent marriage thus far, Sheridan and the other men who paid court to her appeared in a different light. *"Ne craigner rien pour moi, je vous assure qu'il n'y a pas de danger,"** she reassured a friend who was worried about the intentions of another ad-

---

* Don't worry about me, I assure you I am not in danger.

mirer, nicknamed the *"ambasciatore."* "I was once foolish in my life and I suffered enough for it my heart is now *steeled* or rather worn out and my principle resolution thus far for the *serious* part for the nonsense of talking and flirting, I am afraid it will last as long as I can find anybody to talk and flirt with me—but I am not coquet enough not to take care to let them know completely what my intention is."[28]

In other words, Harriet still enjoyed male flattery and challenging conversation, and perhaps too would never be able entirely to resist leading men on. But after the turmoil of the last years, tranquillity with Duncannon was something she had grown to cherish more than fleeting sexual frisson; there was only so far she would allow her male admirers to go. With Sheridan at a distance, Harriet might enjoy his letters—and adoration—without danger. She saw no reason to sever the connection, and so the correspondence continued.

In addition, Harriet found plenty to stimulate her among the many well-to-do English who had also come to Nice in search of health and warm winter sunshine. There were old acquaintants to renew and new ones to make. Among the familiar faces who were a "great reassurance to Harriet who really loves her" was the beautiful Mary Graham.[29] A close friend of both Georgiana and Harriet for many years, one of the many from whom Georgiana had borrowed money, Mary Graham was now critically ill with tuberculosis and, like Harriet, had come to Nice in the hope of regaining her health.

Another ailing English friend, the Duchess of Ancaster, introduced Lady Spencer and Harriet to her physician, Dr. Drew, a keen amateur scientist and philosopher and an entertaining dinner companion. Drew was a man of short stature and comical appearance, with boundless energy, a capacious memory, and an eccentric sense of humor. Described by Lady Spencer as "a little encyclopedia in Duodecimo,"[30] Drew loved nothing more than holding forth on subjects such as botany, ancient history, and geology, all of which appealed strongly to Lady Spencer's and Harriet's desire for self-improvement. His easygoing charm and quick intellect were in marked contrast to the characteristics of the dull but well-meaning Dr. Nott, and they quickly began inviting him to spend evenings and afternoons lecturing them on his favorite subjects.

Harriet also struck up an alliance with the beautiful, willful, and brilliant Elizabeth Webster, who was on holiday in Nice with her two-year-old son. Elizabeth Webster, the only child of a wealthy Jamaican landowner, had married at the age of fifteen a man twenty-three years her senior. Sir Geoffrey Webster had a reputation for wild extravagance and a tendency to drink and gamble to excess. He was prone to bouts of depression and fits of jealous temper in which he often resorted to physical violence against his wife, who was herself far from a malleable character. Acid-tongued, quick-witted, and ambitious, Elizabeth Webster hated the quiet country life that her husband preferred, describing her home in Sussex as "the detested spot where I have languished in solitude and discontent the best years of my life." She was no doubt attracted as much by Harriet's notoriety and social elevation as by any genuine empathy toward her. But Harriet always drew unlikely people to her, and in Elizabeth Webster's case there was much common ground. Harriet knew exactly what it meant to be caught in an unhappy relationship, and over the following weeks a friendship between them grew.

But friends old and new and pleasant surroundings were not enough to allay Harriet's unease over Georgiana. As the days dragged on with no sign of her return, Lady Spencer's animosity toward Bess resurfaced. "I know she thinks Bess has a hundred and fifty children and is now lying in of twins," Harriet told Lady Melbourne. Georgiana's prolonged absence had also begun to give rise to gossip among the English community. Harriet thought her sister had been unwise to stay away so long. "The mysterious manner in which all the people here inquire after them would be quite ridiculous if it did not provoke one ... I shall have no peace till they are here."[31] By the time Georgiana and Bess sent word that they were ready to return, civil unrest had erupted all over France and gave rise to further concern. They were faced with frightening riots in Aix and Toulon and were so afraid of encountering brigands or looters on the mountain road across the Esterel pass that they wrote asking for Townsend or their cousin William Poyntz, who had joined the party in Nice, to be sent to escort them.

Not until early March did the pair eventually arrive in Nice. "They are come and I never saw her look in greater beauty in my life, but grown so thin it quite frightens me," wrote Harriet. Quite apart from the distress of the enforced parting from her baby, Georgiana remained fraught over money matters. The duke still refused to communicate with her or to make any financial provision, and had even stopped Bess's allowance. "I never heard such a thing,"[32] Harriet stormed after Georgiana had tried to cash a note for £20 and been refused.

Even before Georgiana's arrival, Harriet, Duncannon, and Lady Spencer had begun to think longingly of their return to England. They had now been away for five months. Duncannon had secured his aged father's approval for the voyage abroad only by promising that he would be back by May. Lord Bessborough's subsequent letters had often reminded him of the pledge and hinted at his loneliness. His grandsons, he claimed, were "the only comfort I have for I am quite alone and very melancholy."[33] Harriet was equally anxious to return to her children but would not contemplate leaving Georgiana, realizing that if she did so the myth that her illness was the reason for Georgiana's sudden departure abroad would be shattered. "I cannot bear myself for having a wish against her interest, when I would sacrifice my life for any good to her—but yet my heart yearns for England and my children," she told Lady Melbourne.[34]

Lady Spencer thought Georgiana's chances of being forgiven by the duke were slender and determined that neither she nor Harriet should return until this happened. Instead of stating her fears openly, she pretended that for the sake of Harriet's health they should stay another year and allow her to recover fully. She raised this matter gently with Duncannon, and when he expressed his determination to return to England and his father she remembered how quickly his anger could be roused and did not dare press further. Instead she wrote to George to ask him to speak to Dr. Warren about the matter. "If [Warren] was to write strongly to Lord D[uncannon] on the subject of your sister's staying . . . it might perhaps have some effect."[35]

Warren did as he was asked, but the wording of his letter to Duncannon made plain Lady Spencer's involvement and when he questioned her over the subterfuge she was overwhelmed with shame, blaming poor George for the misunderstanding. "It looks as if underhand I was settling plans for him without consulting him."[36] This was exactly what she was doing, although George tactfully did not say so. Not long after, Lord Bessborough heard of Warren's advice, which came as "a heavy stroke upon me," and wrote to his son, demanding his return as soon as possible. "As I intend to put all my affairs into your hands. I am too old to go on with any business."[37] Harriet, meanwhile, took an equally intransigent stance. "Nothing but absolute force shall make me return without [Georgiana],"[38] she stalwartly declared.

Faced with such an impossible situation, the Duncannon of old might well have flown into a rage. Instead he mustered his self-control and, although Lady Spencer admitted "we had a blackish cloud for a day or two,"[39] he agreed to comply with Dr. Warren's advice. Harriet and her mother were to spend the summer in Switzerland while he returned to England. He would reside with his father during the summer months and then rejoin Harriet and Lady Spencer in time to travel to Italy for the winter. All in all, declared a quietly triumphant Lady Spencer, "Lord Duncannon is as reasonable and as indulgent as possible in whatever he thinks material to Harriet's health or comfort."[40]

Duncannon was still unaware that the true motive behind Lady Spencer's manipulations was not Harriet's welfare but Georgiana's reputation. Indeed, this was a subject that even among the women was scarcely ever broached. As Harriet attested: "[My mother] has put it entirely on my health and indeed she always does to me—now and then she gives hints about my sister as if she knew I knew everything but was unwilling to talk upon the subject and I am glad enough to feign any pretence to escape so unpleasant a topic."[41] It was easier for all concerned if the masquerade continued.

Georgiana wanted to return as badly as everyone else, but she could not do so without the duke's permission and he seemed to have forgotten her existence, never writing and ignoring all her pleas. In desperation Georgiana begged him to let her return temporarily with Duncannon, to see her children, and then rejoin Harriet abroad. When this letter too was ignored, an infuriated Lady Spencer took it upon herself to write. In early April the duke replied. "I think that the Duchess had better remain with Lady Duncannon, whether she comes to England or stays abroad. I suppose she will be decided in that by her physician. If she stays abroad I mean to meet you abroad some time in the summer."[42] By now the duke must have heard that Warren had advised Harriet to spend another winter in Europe, but the obliqueness of his reply was enough to leave Georgiana with a slender hope that she might still be permitted to return, if only temporarily. And so the party left Nice in May, this time heading for Genoa, Turin, and Geneva, where Duncannon planned to leave Harriet to begin his journey home, with or without Georgiana and Bess.

It was not an auspicious time to attempt such a journey. Civil unrest in France had spread through Europe, and their carriages rattled along roads that thronged with columns of soldiers and their equipages. "This place looks very much like war, there are patrols constantly going and they seem to be troops,"[43] Duncannon reported to his father in Turin. A day later he was advised to delay traveling to Geneva because ten thousand French troops were believed to be massing near the border with Switzerland. It was while they waited in the city that further unwelcome news arrived. Reports of the political confusion had provided the duke with a convenient excuse to claim it was too dangerous for Georgiana to travel, even with Duncannon to escort her. She should stay in Europe until he came to fetch her later in the summer, he declared. Bess was to make up her own mind whether she should risk traveling with Duncannon or remain with Georgiana. In the event Bess, like Harriet and her mother, decided her first loyalty lay with Georgiana and stayed. Harriet tried to be equally resolute, although underneath she was devastated as much for herself as for her sister. "I lose all courage and spirit," she confided to Lady Melbourne. "England and everything is, it seems, removed twice as far."[44]

NINE

Unexpected Departures
1792-1793

FROM GENEVA, A MONTH LATER than intended, Duncannon at last set out for England. Harriet bade him farewell with a heavy heart. "I feel very sorry and very low partly at their going and partly at not going my self to that little vile spot of earth that contains so much good and so much bad with it,"[1] she told her friend Elizabeth Webster. Yet Switzerland had much to distract Harriet from her melancholy. The country was famed for the health-giving properties of its mountain air and the cleanliness of its spas, as well as for its dramatic landscape. There was also plenty of society to entertain her. The summer months were popular for tourists and that year visitors from all over Europe had converged on the country to mingle with the local residents and enjoy the sights. In Lausanne Harriet and her party called on the famous historian and author of *The Decline and Fall of the Roman Empire,* Sir Edward Gibbon, who had taken up residence on the shores of the lake and was an old friend and admirer of Bess's. Gibbon was now "a melancholy object,"[2] his limbs so swollen from infirmity that he could walk only with difficulty, but the attentions of three glamorous ladies and the illustrious Lady Spencer helped him forget his ailments and when they rented two houses near his, in the small town of Ouchy, he became a regular visitor.

The next two months passed idyllically, with promenades and picnics and visits to sample the waters in local spas and view the most famous sights. In the evenings Harriet, Georgiana, and Bess held open house. Harriet played on the harpsichord for the entertainment of friends such as the Palmerstons and Bess's brother Lord Hervey; Felix

Giardini, the violinist who had played for Georgiana at Chatsworth, gave recitals, and in the intervals the latest news from Europe was discussed. "We keep a kind of coffee house where people bring all the sights all the news and all that seldom go together,"[3] Harriet happily recorded.

The sisters also devoted much time to pursuing the passion for science that had first begun to enthrall Harriet in Nice while she waited for Georgiana's return. Dr. Nott had returned to England with Duncannon, but the Duchess of Ancaster, who was staying nearby, permitted Dr. Drew to monitor Harriet's health and to spend days and nights "philosophising, chimycising, mineralising... and witticising above all."[4] The group were still besotted by the doctor's charm; to Lady Spencer he was "our great treasure... he has not only an immense fund of universal knowledge but the clearest manner of communicating it."[5] To Harriet, "dear darling Drew" became a "comfort and delight" and "the most delightful little creature I ever met with."[6]

The scientific passion Drew had sparked in Harriet and Georgiana gave them the confidence to seek out other scientists who were staying in the region. The eminent physician Tissot was asked to advise on Harriet's ailments and was charmed by her intellect. Physicist and geologist Horace Benédict de Saussure, the father of mountaineering, who was the first nonguide to make the ascent of Mont Blanc, advised the sisters on mineralogy and was similarly impressed. Charles Blagden, assistant to Duncannon's reclusive relative the scientist Henry Cavendish and secretary of the Royal Society, put on chemical demonstrations and thought Harriet "very good tempered, but a little awkward from shyness"; and the botanist Struve, who held forth on the local flora, afterward loftily declared that while Georgiana was "rather indifferent as she prefers minerals to plants!... the... unfortunate and interesting Lady D[uncannon] seems to have some aptitude."[7]

With so much stimulating company even Lady Spencer's customary low spirits lifted, and rather than worrying about the health and tarnished reputations of her daughters she too began to immerse herself in the quest for knowledge. As well as attending lectures on science, she took German lessons every morning before breakfast. The language was one she found difficult but her tutor was a "very agreeable" gentleman friend and before long the relationship between them had developed to something more intimate than the usual one of pupil and teacher. "[He] has almost prevailed upon me to break a thousand resolutions I have made," she bashfully admitted to her friend Mrs. Howe. "We pass . . . two hours together every day except Sunday when I do not allow myself to see him—he is a German but speaks French . . . is of a good family and is well-informed and to own the truth I have already entered into some engagement with him that I fear you will not quite approve. I have not ventured to own this yet to my son and I beg you will keep my secret."[8] The gentleman in question is never named, and after this confession the references to him are sparse and oblique— usually charting the progress of her lessons rather than the liaison itself. "I go on very leisurely with German," she reported in July,[9] but then ten days later she sadly recorded "my poor German master is very ill. I hope he will recover or he will be a sad loss to me."[10]

There are no further references to the German master, and it is impossible to know how the relationship resolved itself. He may have succumbed to his illness, or, more probably, perhaps the budding romance perished as clouds from the world beyond the shores of the lake intruded. In July the first blow came. News reached them that Mary Graham had finally succumbed to consumption and died onboard ship on her way back to England. Both Harriet and Georgiana were distraught, Harriet especially so, since she and Mary had grown deeply attached to each other during the months they had spent in Nice.

The following month they were shaken by further news of events of an ominous and far-reaching nature. The Tuileries, in which the royal family had been held under house arrest, had been stormed by a mob of more than twenty thousand revolutionaries armed with sabers and pikes. Forced to flee for their lives, the king, queen, and their children had taken refuge in the Legislative Assembly. The bloodthirsty revolutionaries had then begun to attack the Swiss Guard, the only soldiers who had remained loyal to the royal family. Foreseeing a bloodbath, Louis XVI had ordered the Guard to lay down their weapons, but the gesture had failed and nearly nine hundred Swiss had been massacred, along with anyone suspected of being a supporter of the king. Over the days that followed, Robespierre installed himself as the head of the newly formed Paris Commune and challenged the authority of the Legislative Assembly, insisting that the king and his family should be stripped of any royal privilege and locked up as common prisoners in the fortress prison known as the Temple.

All Europe looked on aghast, fearful that the insurrection in France might infect their own countries. Prussian forces reacted swiftly by invading France. In early September they were encamped at Verdun and their proximity to Paris brought fear of reprisals to the mob, who rampaged through the streets of Paris, breaking down the doors of prisons where aristocrats and royalists were held. At least fourteen hundred of them—almost half the entire Parisian prison population—were murdered in cold blood, and England and France moved a step closer to war.

Lady Spencer recorded the devastating effect as reports of the massacres filtered to Switzerland. For her as well as for Harriet and Georgiana, who had regarded the royal family as friends since childhood, the news was deeply distressing. Nearly all among their circle knew someone caught up in the turmoil who had been brutally murdered or whose life remained in danger. To make matters worse, accurate information was sparse and those who carried letters that criticized the new regime ran the risk of severe penalty. "You have no idea of the horror of being at Paris since the tenth . . ." wrote Lady Sutherland to Georgiana. "You have before this time heard the particulars of the . . . cruelty of the Marseillais and Parisians. The King and Queen are confined in the Temple and not suffered to have servants . . . in short it is to bad . . . I wrote a letter a fortnight ago to you meaning to send it [with] my Lord Palmerston, but upon second thoughts I thought it was better not to hazard it, as he certainly would have *suffered* for being the bearer of it had it been opened."[11]

The terrifying events unfolding in France impinged upon Harriet's convalescence. Switzerland was far from safe: with French troops already massing on the borders, everyone believed an invasion was imminent. Duncannon had originally promised to return in time to escort Harriet south to Italy for the winter, but the political tumult and impending war made Lord Bessborough alarmed and he ordered his son to delay his departure. Duncannon ceded to his father's wishes, instructing Harriet and Lady Spencer to leave for Italy without him, as soon as the steward Townsend had arrived to settle their bills and organize their luggage. The tedious Dr. Nott was traveling with Townsend and would once again supervise Harriet's medical treatment, something she did not relish after a summer spent in the sparkling company of Dr. Drew. Within the group Nott's seriousness had become a subject for ridicule: "I will make much of him, shine him in gloss and give him to M. de Saussure [the mountaineering mineralogist] for his cabinet as the best specimen of Terra Ponderosa ever known,"[12] joked Harriet at the doctor's impending return.

Yet such moments of lightheartedness were increasingly rare over the following weeks. Amid scenes that were more frightening by the day, Harriet waited to depart. "We have been going, going, going, like goods at an auction for this month past but we are not yet knocked down,"[13] she wrote with feigned insouciance when no horses were available and they were again delayed. Her mother found it harder to disguise the trepidation she felt. "The scenes here are dreadful, the swarms of French emigrants as well as of Savoyard families are incredible," she fretted shortly before their departure. "There is neither room nor provision for them here, they are forbid to stay more than forty-eight hours; they know not where to go nor can they find horses or conveyances... Geneva is fortifying itself with all possible diligence... from the numbers of disorientated people... the frontiers are preparing for defence in every part of Switzerland."[14]

Even when transport could be arranged, their problems were not over. Fear of French revolutionaries forced them to take a huge detour and made the journey far more arduous than it would otherwise have been. "The French have entered Savoy and are in possession of Chamberry," Lady Spencer recounted; "all hope therefore of passing by Mount Cerni is at an end—we must go by the Tyrol. It will be seventeen days constant traveling that way before we can reach Verona and we then have a very long... troublesome journey before we can get to Pisa."[15]

They left Lausanne in early October, gazing from the windows of their carriages on scenes of heartrending human misery. The Swiss had regarded the French with animosity ever since the massacre of the Swiss Guard at the Tuileries and made little distinction between revolutionaries and supporters of the monarchy who had lost everything and were fleeing for their lives. As Lady Spencer recorded: "[The French] are driven from town to town in perpetual danger of being insulted by the common people who are exasperated by the cruel massacre of their countrymen and do not know how to distinguish between Frenchman and Frenchman."[16]

The depressing situation, coupled with the rigors of travel and nights spent in uncomfortable, ill-heated, and unsanitary lodgings, made Harriet contract a fever, and her cough worsened. As always at such low points, she began to think ruefully of her children. A year had passed since she had left England, and the date of her return seemed as distant as ever. Instead of the cheerfulness that characterized her usual letters to her sons, regret overwhelmed her. "I told you I was not well," she wrote to John and Frederick, "and I believe the lowness of spirits that I felt was a good deal increased by recollecting that on that day year I quitted you all, my dear loves . . . to quit poor England and come and wander over hills and mountains far from my dear, dear children for so long. I hope you still remember me and continue to love me, but I should be very sorry your little hearts should ever feel the bitterness I have suffered at this long separation from you. But I will not write on so sad a subject."[17]

In early November, Harriet reached Florence. Many other English travelers escaping the dangers of France had flooded into the city, and after the wholesome activities of Switzerland and the traumas of their journey the city offered a tempting world of indulgence that she had always struggled to resist. "Science and philosophy are all fled . . . while we are seduced by the magic of Florence wasting in idleness and dissipation hours that ought to be better employed and yet I must confess it is [a] very pleasant place,"[18] she admitted. Bess's brother Jack Hervey was Britain's envoy at the Tuscan court and introduced her to local dignitaries and secured invitations to court occasions. But they did not linger long. Conscious of the dangers, Lady Spencer hurriedly ushered Harriet, Georgiana, and Bess away to Pisa to await Duncannon's arrival.

Pisa seemed quiet, melancholy, and very provincial after the glamorous cosmopolitan mix of Florence. There were only a few English, "but no troublesome ones," and the group befriended men of letters from the university, passing their mornings studying Italian, drawing, and music, driving or walking in the countryside until dinner. Evenings were spent quietly; "this way of life if we can keep to it will do much towards Harriet's cure," wrote Lady Spencer hopefully. Harriet had now regained her strength and had taken to cantering eight or ten miles or more on her pony in a morning, but the worsening situation in France preyed heavily on her mind. "I have literally fretted myself quite ill about French affairs," she confessed to Elizabeth Webster; "the last account of the King and Queen breaks my heart."[19]

Harriet had heard that the king had been brought to trial from Duncannon, who had left England in early December, fearful until the moment of his departure of some news "which may make my father want to put off my journey." Incredibly, despite the horrors of recent events and the precariousness of the regime, he had stopped off in Paris on his way to rejoin her. He was not the only visitor to the city. English travelers continued to stay in the French capital until war was officially declared following the execution of Louis XVI on January 21, 1793. Among the friends with whom Duncannon dined was Crauford, one of the old habitués of Devonshire House. Duncannon also took the opportunity to take in the latest gruesome tourist attractions. "We went today to look at the Temple.* It is a very picturesque high tower but I did not draw it as you may imagine," he recorded, adding, "I propose going to take a peep at the awful procession tomorrow" (when the king was to be taken to trial) "but not to the Assembly as I suppose the crowd will be very great."[20] His letters to Harriet reveal that the fondness that had grown between them during her illness had not waned over the months he had been away from her. "How I long for the day when I shall embrace you," he told her from Paris. Having left "that unfortunate miserable country," he reckoned it would take three weeks to reach Pisa. "Nothing but such a reward [as seeing her again] could carry one through such a journey."[21]

The party decamped for Rome soon after Duncannon's arrival. Harriet was eager to see the processions of Holy Week, but yet again the worsening political situation created unforeseen problems. France's declaration of war on England and Holland jeopardized all Dutch and English ships, including Lord Hood's fleet in the Mediterranean. Italy, previously a safe haven for the British, was also threatened. "If any mischief is attempted in Italy it will probably be

---

* The fortress tower where the royal family were being held captive.

immediately and where in that case we can go is not very easy to decide," Lady Spencer remarked.[22]

In the midst of all this anxiety Duncannon received the news of his father's death. According to a tactless letter from his brother-in-law, Lord Fitzwilliam, Bessborough had grown so depressed after Duncannon's departure that he had fallen into a decline and succumbed to a fatal illness. Fitzwilliam's letter echoed recriminations voiced by Bessborough. Shortly before Duncannon had left, his father had declared bluntly that the whole protracted journey to Europe was pointless—Harriet might just as well have recuperated at home since she was still far from cured. Lady Spencer was vexed by the unkindness of both comments. "God knows," she wrote, "we none of us engaged voluntarily in this hateful banishment but it is now our duty . . . to bear it as well as we can."[23] Unusually, her sympathies lay as much with her son-in-law as with Harriet. "Lord Duncannon is far from being without faults and foibles but I do think his behaviour both to his father and wife ever since she left England has been exemplary."[24] Despite her mother's support, the effect of these harsh words upon Harriet was severe. She felt blameworthy for being the cause of Duncannon's leaving his father and thus hastening his death, and as a result became overwrought and ill herself. "It is impossible to describe what poor Harriet suffers from feeling herself the innocent cause of Lord Duncannon's leaving his father," wrote an anxious Lady Spencer; "she continues very unwell."

The death of his father meant that Duncannon, now the Third Earl of Bessborough,* had once again to make the long journey back to England to settle his estate, only two months after his return to Italy. Both he and Harriet were distraught at having to separate again so soon. "I need not describe to you what I felt at parting from you this morning," he wrote that evening from his lodgings.[25] Harriet had broken down when he left and became further distressed when the family began addressing her as Lady Bessborough. The war with France meant that Bessborough had to take a circuitous route through Germany, and then

---

* Henceforth Harriet's husband is referred to as the Earl of (or Lord) Bessborough; Harriet is formally addressed as the Countess of (or Lady) Bessborough; and their eldest son, John Ponsonby, is called Viscount (or Lord) Duncannon.

to Belgium to cross the Channel at Ostend. He was in Flanders when more bad news reached him.

The bankers Forbes and Gregory, with whom the family had much of their money invested, had been declared bankrupt. Thomas Coutts had already written to Georgiana, warning of such an eventuality: "This country is at present much distressed by bankruptcies among various sorts of people. There are some old established houses who have been very unwisely employed . . . as bankers—but . . . exactly what bankers should not be viz speculators and schemers—some of them have failed for great sums. I hope Lord Bessborough is not among the sufferers."[26] Lady Spencer had long suspected that the Bessborough finances were in a more serious state than anyone yet recognized and was troubled by the effect the news might have upon Harriet. "This added to the embarrassment of the present Lord's affairs will I am afraid prove a most serious inconvenience to them . . . I know when Harriet comes to know this she will be sadly hurt at the vexations it may occasion Lord Bessborough and perhaps the influence it may have in deciding her staying abroad."[27]

At first, Bessborough failed to comprehend fully the implications of the failure, casually declaring, "I know he [his late father] had a good deal of our money in his hands but I should hope I shall not lose much of it."[28] Within days of his return to London the truth became impossible to avoid. The bank had made investments on his behalf in the Liverpool firm Charles Caldwell & Co., which had also failed; the losses were grave and, to add to his woes, he also now discovered that Harriet had taken out loans of which he had known nothing. She owed the bank £1,100 (£60,600 today), while Georgiana owed a further £1,600 and, since the bank had been declared insolvent, both their names would be publicly posted unless the debts were paid immediately. Amazingly, despite these worries, Bessborough's tenderness toward Harriet seemed to increase. "I can think of nothing but you,"[29] he declared with uncharacteristic openness, before writing again a few days later to reassure her that he had paid both the outstanding sums so that she and Georgiana would be saved from scandal.

Bessborough had always lived his life in the belief that on taking up his father's mantle, funds in the bank and a sizable income from the rents of property in Ireland, Leicestershire, and Roehampton would allow him to clear the monstrous gaming debts he had accumulated and live in comfort thereafter. His expectations had enabled him to raise credit easily whenever he required it and his own personal debt now stood at £5,500 (the equivalent of £390,000). But he now found himself in a very different situation from the one he had anticipated. Within weeks it emerged that £9,000 (£450,000 today) was lost from the failure of the bank, and much of his rental income was in arrears. All this compounded to make the bankers who survived regard him very differently. "I am afraid I shall have great difficulties in arranging my affairs, as it is very difficult to borrow money now owing to this blow to credit. I don't know yet what the value of the estate in my own power is, but hope Mr. Caldwell will be here in about a week to inform me of it."[30]

Added to the tangle of his own finances, Bessborough had also to deal with more of Harriet's debts. Over the next weeks he found himself besieged by countless unpaid tradesmen on Harriet's account as the true extent of her profligacy in the months after her affair with Sheridan and before her illness became clear. The tone in which he first raises the subject with her is not one of anger, but suggests rather his bewilderment at the situation in which he found himself. "For God's sake tell me all your debts, there is no use in concealing them. I don't say I can pay them, but we might make some arrangement of them to make them less ruinous,"[31] he wrote; and then again, "I trust you will send me an account of all. There is your Mr. Speed for £26 [who] is very pressing; a Mr. Thompson, Haberdasher in Oxford Road, has sent a bill [for] £172. Don't fret about these things but tell me if the sums are right."[32] Five days later, another clutch of bills arrived at Cavendish Square and he wrote more urgently. "I am sorry to plague you about your bills and don't mind my mentioning that they come in very fast. Thirkuup has sent a great one of £167 and said he should be ruined if I did not pay him some of it this week, so I have sent him £100 of it and a Mr. Dovey twenty odd pounds." This time too there is a note of suspicion; of a letter that had arrived for Harriet from Lord Fitzwilliam he asks, "I wonder what you can have corresponded about."[33]

In Naples, Harriet opened each new letter from her husband, recalled each embarrassing extravagance, and plunged deeper into an abyss of misery, self-hatred, and terror that he would abandon her. In this overwrought state, she wrote to her brother-in-law Lord Fitz-william to beg his advice. Perhaps she secretly (and naively) hoped that he would help her without Bessborough's knowledge—and that her past follies might be erased. She had always prayed she would be able to settle her debts without her husband discovering the truth, and distance had made them seem less pressing. Georgiana's assistance had also reinforced this hope. She had frequently shielded Harriet from financial demands, imploring Thomas Coutts for help on her sister's behalf in the interest of her health. "I must ask you a favour—one for my sister . . ." she wrote in April; "she has been very ill and very much affected by her father in law's death. I have no doubt Lord Duncannon will do something for her as soon as he can—in the meantime I was obliged to draw for her £100 on you . . . And I must entreat you if she has not so much to pay these drafts for the present."[34] But at present Georgiana could do little to help; estranged as she was from the duke, she had insufficient credit to cover her own bills, let alone those of her sister, and Coutts often responded sternly, warning her that if the duke discovered how seriously she and Harriet were indebted "the effect must be very prejudicial to you."[35] There was nothing more Georgiana could do for Harriet.

Fitzwilliam, though sympathetic, did not offer any easy way out either, instead advising her to send Bessborough a full statement of all her outstanding debts and conceal nothing. Harriet read his response with a heavy heart, wondering how many more of her extravagances were to be exposed and how Bessborough might react when he uncovered them. In this state of heightened anxiety she wrote both men letters full of contrition and promises that she would reveal all her follies, no matter the cost.

> I will not deny that the thoughts of my great imprudences and their consequence to my family have long weighed most heavily upon my mind and preyed upon my spirits—and two posts ago I wrote to Lord B[essborough] in consequence of his very kind enquiries stating to him the situation of my affairs—which is hard enough God knows—I am still suffering under the consequences of the agitation this effort occasioned. I most earnestly hope he will arrange nothing

till he has seen me, and still more that when he does see me, he will allow me to pay off myself as far as I possibly can the great debts I have accumulated by my folly and extravagance—for it is impossible for me to express what misery it would be to me to see him distressed and landed with the consequences of my mad imprudences and thoughtless squanderings, for which I can plead no excuse . . . I must only trust and hope that neither you nor he will see me in the light I do myself and I will only allow myself to add that no words can express either how unworthy I feel or how grateful I am to him for all his . . . kindness to me.[36]

In Cavendish Square, the mist gradually cleared over Lord Bessborough's depleted inheritance. There were credits in bonds and dividends amounting to £52,000 (£3,120,000 today), but against this were set losses from failed stocks, outstanding annuities to members of the family, and his own debts, plus a string of bequests and expenses that totaled nearly £45,000 (£2.7 million). In theory there remained a credit of nearly £7,000 (£420,000). The problem was that much of this sum was inaccessible, held in failed banks and in rental arrears, and it was uncertain how much of and when (if ever) the money might become available.

The situation was far from rosy, and yet as in the past, when Harriet had fallen ill, shouldering responsibility seemed to bring out the best in Bessborough. He rose to the challenge without losing his temper and in the process discovered a new self-awareness and maturity. "It is a sad piece of business having to settle so many things," he confessed to Harriet, "especially for me who has never been used to manage any thing."[37]

Bessborough could no longer escape the realization that despite her assurances Harriet had been less than candid regarding her debts. Far from London and the clamor of creditors knocking, she had found it easier to dissemble than tell the truth, less painful to forget and deny, than fully to acknowledge the faults of which she was guilty. And yet, as more and more of Harriet's creditors came forward to plague Bessborough and he faced up to his wife's persistent dishonesty, the discovery did not enrage him. Instead, her flaws and vulnerability seemed to kindle a new passion in his heart and his letters from this time became increasingly reassuring, expressing affection for her in a way he had never done hitherto. "Don't disturb yourself about this, my dearest Harriet, I have no wish on earth but to make you comfortable and happy, and I should not mention this if it was not lest you should pay them over again,"[38] he writes.

Yet even now Harriet could not bring herself to do as he asked; perhaps she remembered how quickly his affection could turn to rage, or the Duke of Devonshire's angry reaction to Georgiana's disclosure of her debts, or Bessborough's threats of divorce—or perhaps she was simply unable to face her own shame. In July, just as Bessborough was preparing to leave for Ireland to survey his estates, a further £3,000 (£180,000) she owed came to light.

Bessborough wrote to tell her of the fact, no longer bothering to ask her to reveal her debts honestly, still calm but begging her never to become indebted again, and reiterating words of reassurance. "At all events you may make yourself easy on the subject which you mention, that you fear you shall lose by it my love and affection, for be assured I have no wish so earnest as your happiness, and if I have the power, I have the inclination to free you from your incumbrances. I really believe you are become sensible that we cannot go on as we have done, and that for the future you will be firm in a resolution to contract no new debts. You must see that in exhorting you to this I am pleading not only for ourselves but our children."[39]

The letter bears testimony to a new authority in Bessborough. In comprehending both her frailty and her financial duplicity, he seems to have felt his control of her had been affirmed. Love simmered beneath the talk of money, as if by saving her from financial disaster he had tied her more securely to him, and this enabled him to express freely the depth of his feeling for her. Thus any idea of divorce was banished from his thoughts. He wrote: "I find what I have always thought, that no happiness can be complete without you, whether I am in a hurry or a calm. You are always present to my mind, and though I may be stunned for a moment by the noise and tumult I am in, something is always wanting and that something my heart tells me is you . . ."[40]

In Ireland he stayed briefly in Dublin to take his seat in parliament before setting out for the family seat, Bessborough House, in Kilkenny. The house, set in grounds of twenty-seven thousand acres, was a large rambling building with eleven bedrooms and a surprising collection of art, including a Claude Lorraine. On his arrival some five hundred tenants congregated in the courtyard to welcome him with dancing and singing. It was the first time he had ever visited the house; he was enchanted by what he found, and wished Harriet was with him to share his delight. "The mountains are beautiful over fine wood and the verdure is the finest that can be seen . . . would to God you were here and that I could stay some time; I am sure you would like it."[41]

Bessborough's increasingly passionate remarks salved Harriet's tormented conscience, but aside from the details of her debts his letters contained a further bitter pill: she was to be separated from her sister. The Duke of Devonshire had finally decided to forget his grievances, and summoned Georgiana home in May. The sisters had always planned that when this long-awaited moment came they would travel together. But worry had once again damaged Harriet's health; she had been unwell ever since her father-in-law's death, and now had all the full-blown symptoms of consumption, spitting blood and headaches and muscular spasms. Bessborough had consulted Dr. Warren, who concluded she was too frail to risk the journey home and recommended another winter in southern Italy. In June, Bessborough wrote, ordering Harriet not to accompany her sister; he would join her in Italy as soon as he returned from Ireland. His decision, although he never says so, was probably also due in part to their straitened financial circumstances. Living in rented accommodation in Europe was much less costly than living the life of an aristocrat in London, with two large houses to staff and the temptations of Brooks's close at hand. Perhaps too, now that his ardor for Harriet had been so strongly ignited, he simply wanted to exercise his rights and have time alone with her.

The instruction came as a profound blow to everyone concerned. Lady Spencer refused to leave Italy without Harriet, even though she admitted the thought of another year away from home "has unhinged me a great deal."[42] For Harriet, the thought of not seeing her sons or her sister for another twelve months seemed unbearable. When Georgiana and Bess set off to make the long journey home two months later she wept bitterly. "It is impossible for me to express half the misery I felt," Harriet wrote, "but what is our life but a continual succession of vexations and miseries, follies and imprudences."[43]

Afterward Harriet and her mother decamped to Bagni, a spa in

Umbria famous for its mineral waters, where it was hoped the treatments on offer would help her to recover from her relapse. Bessborough rejoined them in late September, bringing with him their youngest son, six-year-old Willy. By then Harriet was greatly recovered and, according to Lady Spencer, she "bore seeing Lord Bessborough and Willy with much less hurry than I expected, which is proof of her nerves being much stronger."[44]

Supplanting worries over Harriet were concerns for the well-being of her eight-year-old daughter. Caroline, or Caro as she was called within the family, had always been a lively and demanding child, and throughout their travels her behavior had often been the cause of embarrassment and irritation. On one notable occasion in Switzerland she had told Gibbon he was so ugly he terrified her puppy. Such rudeness had been partly checked by the company of Bess's placid and impeccably mannered daughter of the same age, Caroline St. Jules. But since Caroline St. Jules had returned to England with Bess and Georgiana, Caro no longer had a playmate or good example to follow, and had grown increasingly demanding.

Lady Spencer was fond of her granddaughter and thought she had "a thousand amiable traits," but even she acknowledged that Caro was "one of the most difficult children to manage" and despaired of her ever improving. "Both Harriet and I have tried every sort of indulgence, encouragement and severity to no manner of purpose—she will persist in asking foolish questions with a perseverance and obstinacy that would be quite comical if its sad effects upon her temper and upon the comfort of our lives did not make it serious ... if either Lady Bessborough or I give up our whole day to her she is well contented but if she sees us employed or in conversation it is then she begins—she was so very perverse and so very pert yesterday that I was obliged to whip her, which I did as smartly as I could,"[45] she confided to her friend Selina Trimmer, the governess to Georgiana's children.

In November Caro fell gravely ill. Within days she was a shadow of her former self, unable to eat, barely capable of speech, tossing listlessly in her bed, and growing frailer by the day. Dr. Drew at first diagnosed worms, but when the fever continued to rise with little respite for most of November everyone realized that it was something much more serious (perhaps malaria) and that she would be lucky to survive. "Our sweet child is very, very bad," wrote Lady Spencer; "this is the fifteenth day of her illness and her fever is not the least diminished . . . I think it hardly possible she should get through it."[46] Harriet put on a show of calmness and hardly left Caroline's bedside. In early December her efforts were rewarded when Caroline recovered and began to sip wine bark and eat calves'-foot jelly. There were further setbacks, but by Christmas she was well enough for the family to move to Naples, and could get out of bed for short spells and run around.

In Naples the Bessboroughs wasted little time in setting out to see the sights. Although James Boswell claimed that Neapolitans were "the most shocking race: eaters of garlic and catchers of vermin," the city held many attractions for eighteenth-century tourists. The winter weather was clement, the landscape fecund — "old fig-trees, oranges in full bloom, myrtles in every hedge, make one of the delightfullest scenes you can conceive" — and the food excitingly unfamiliar. "The most excellent, the most incomparable fish I ever ate; red mullets, large as our mackerel, and of singularly high flavour; besides calamaro or ink-fish, a dainty worthy of imperial luxury," rhapsodized Mrs. Thrale, one gastronomically inclined visitor.[47]

Willy was enthralled by the sights of the Neapolitan streets decked out for Christmas. "There is one street in particular, Strada Toledo, that looks like one continued fair, the whole length of it, and it is very long. The fruit shops are remarkably pretty, the fruit is hung in festoons round a king of arbour set up in the street — and the butchers hand their meat in the same manner, gilt in many places and stuck all over with ribbons and flowers. Every shop has something even to the macaroni that is hung in patterns,"[48] wrote Harriet.

There was also an abundance of cultural and social attractions to enjoy — visits to the newly excavated sites of Pompeii and Herculaneum, the palace at Capodimonte, Virgil's tomb, the catacombs, caverns, and lakes. By night there were masked balls, assemblies at the Neapolitan court, theatrical and operatic productions (Neapolitan operas were famous for the performances of castrati). But it was the sight of Mount Vesuvius in eruption that provided the most memorable experience for many tourists. Intrepid visitors — including Lady Spencer, Harriet, and Willy — rode mules up the slopes and braved red-hot lava flying about to picnic on the rim of the crater while gazing into the exploding heart of the volcano. Harriet collected samples of lava for her mineral collection. Her excursion had been fraught with danger and she was terrified when one of her friends "saw the smoke rising and before he could escape [the volcano] threw up a great volley of stones, and he with great difficulty got away with only two or three good bruises."[49]

The British community in Naples was presided over by the envoy Sir William Hamilton—an old friend of Lady Spencer's who was not only an expert on the eruptions of Vesuvius but a connoisseur of Greek and Roman art. At the Hamiltons' glamorous parties, Emma, his beautiful young wife, by whom Nelson was later beguiled, was renowned for dressing up in a loose white chemise and shawl, with her hair flowing loose, and striking "attitudes" in which she imitated the poses of figures from antiquity that adorned her husband's artifacts. As in Nice and Switzerland, Harriet's vibrant personality and sympathetic manner drew people to her, and she was rapidly encircled by friends old and new. Elizabeth Webster, now expecting her second child, arrived in February; the Palmerstons and Lord Grandison were also visiting. Then, in February, a group of amiable young aristocrats on their grand tour arrived in the city. Among them was a handsome twenty-one-year-old, Granville Leveson Gower, the man destined to change irrevocably the course of Harriet's life.

TEN

The Meeting

1794

GRANVILLE LEVESON GOWER was a tall young man with thick dark hair that flopped over his forehead, a sensuously drawn mouth, and heavy-lidded lustrous dark-blue eyes that made him seem both serious and sensitive. His manners were perfectly polished and he had an air of distinction about him that some thought bordered on haughtiness and others attributed to shyness. As one later acquaintance described him, he was "a figure remarkable for symmetry and grace . . . His features were regular, and his countenance expressive of mildness and good-nature. He was one of those men who, once seen, leave an impression on the memory: he belonged to a race of gentlemen of the olden time, that seems almost extinct in our present free-and-easy days."[1] Even as a small boy he had been bright and adorable to look at, and as his mother's only son and the baby of the family he had been much cosseted and lavished with praise. A painting by Romney shows him at the age of six, cherubic and blond-haired, dressed identically to his sisters, Anne, Charlotte, Georgiana, and Susan, dancing barefoot and hand in hand with them in the Arcadian grounds of Trentham, the family home in Staffordshire.

Like Harriet, Granville was born into the cream of British aristocracy. He was the second surviving son of the Second Earl Gower, created Marquis of Stafford in 1786,* and his third wife. A distinguished

---

* Lord Stafford married three times. His first wife, Elizabeth, died of smallpox with her infant son a year after her marriage. By his second wife, Louisa, he had three daughters and one son, George Granville, Lord Trentham, who married Elizabeth, Countess of Sutherland. His third wife, Susan, bore him three more daughters and Granville.

courtier, Granville's father held several high offices, including Master of the Horse and Lord Chamberlain. When Shelburne's administration collapsed in 1783, the king had offered him the post of first minister; he refused, later bolstering Pitt's establishment by serving as President of the Council. Granville was thus raised in a household that was the political converse of the Devonshire House Whigs. Correct in their habits, his parents were Tory traditionalists, staunchly supporting the king and his government, and shuddering at the dissolute freedoms—the drinking, gaming, and sexual shenanigans—of the Whig opposition, especially Fox, Sheridan, and their wayward friends, such as Harriet and Georgiana.

As the second son, Granville was not destined to inherit his father's title or estate, but his parents took for granted that he would pursue a political career and with this in mind began to hone him from an early age. When he was eight, "dearest little Leveson" was dispatched to boarding school in Hammersmith with a hamper full of partridges and pineapples and buns to supplement the meager school fare. After his departure his mother and sister Susan "shed tears . . . in the powdering room without restraint."[2] Despite such lapses into sentimentality Granville's mother, Lady Stafford, was a formidable, highly principled, intelligent woman, and one who was not afraid to express her feelings. She doted on her children and husband and after twenty years of marriage still wrote lovingly of Lord Stafford "there is not a day passes that I do not feel and admire his good humour and constant flow of spirits."[3] Lady Stafford had close connections within court circles, having been a lady of the bedchamber to Princess Augusta, one of the king's sisters. Like Lady Spencer, she saw playing an active part in her children's education and encouraging their self-improvement as fundamental to her maternal role, and so raised political and moral subjects with her son at every opportunity. Pitt, the youngest man to head the government in history and a frequent dinner guest of the Staffords, was constantly held up as a golden exemplar of all his parents admired. "Mr. Pitt has gained himself great credit by his two or three last speeches . . . his passions are all guided by reason," she pointedly commented in a letter that began by informing her son that she had ordered a quantity of "the best oranges that could be bought" for him and his friends at school.[4]

Lady Stafford's strict moral code made her anxious that her beloved son might succumb to dissipation; gambling and sexual laxity were her dual terrors, and the extravagant, womanizing Prince of Wales embodied all she most feared. When the king was first taken ill in 1788, she was fiercely critical of the Prince of Wales and Fox for their efforts to usurp power and establish a regency, and fulsome in her praise for Pitt for doing all he could to limit it. "The debates [in the House of Commons] have proved the principles and wickedness of the leaders of that party," she commented to her son. Mr. "Pitt . . . never was in such high estimation . . . indeed, he is a most wonderful being for with all the extraordinary endowments of judgement, understanding, perfect good temper and unassuming manners, his heart is full of integrity, truth and justice . . . and he is so kind, so attentive a son to his old mother."[5]

After school Granville spent three years at Oxford, where he became close friends with the future prime minister George Canning. His mother's exhortations continued throughout these years. Already she could see he was not without his faults; in particular, his aimlessness troubled her. "I want you to be stout and active, not to have an iota of listlessness nor indolence belonging to you,"[6] she told him shortly before his education was rounded off in the conventional manner, with the eighteenth-century equivalent of a gap-year trip—a grand tour of Europe. In Paris, in 1791, he stayed with his sister-in-law, Lady Sutherland, before moving on to Berlin, St. Petersburg, and Dresden. Here his path crossed with the beauteous Lady Webster, who thought him "remarkably handsome and winning,"[7] although she had heard whispers that his mother's fears had already been partially realized. While he was in Paris, Granville's sister-in-law had "initiated him in the orgies of gambling." It was in Paris too that Granville—aged eighteen—first began to show a marked interest in older women. "Tell him how invidious it is to talk much to *married women* particularly when they have been living so long quietly and without scandal,"[8] his sister-in-law advised Lady Stafford, after Granville began to pay noticeable attention to the Princesse de Hesse. Granville's friendship with Lady Webster in Dresden only added to her concerns. "I saw her in bad Company, with bad connections—I mean bad for domestic happiness—and her husband never near her, and I then feared they would not long continue happy," she loftily declared, adding pointedly: "When you get a wife, I trust you will *go* and *come* together, and not think it necessary that she should live with the fashionable bad wives about London."[9]

Lady Stafford's stern admonishments could not alter the fact that, having been raised by a forceful mother in a predominantly female household, Granville was drawn to women, and in particular to ladies of a certain age with strength of character and charm as well as good looks. Fortunately, however, from Lady Stafford's point of view, Granville's acquaintance with Lady Webster was interrupted by England's declaration of war. He returned dutifully home and joined the Stafford militia, only to form another unsuitable attachment with a married lady, Mrs. St. John.

But Granville's tour of Europe remained incomplete; Italy, the highlight of any young gentleman's travels, had yet to be explored. Thus when his two trusted friends Lord Boringdon and Lord Morpeth invited him to join them there, Granville begged his parents to let him go. With a mixture of relief at his loosening the grip of Mrs. St. John and misgivings at the political turbulence in Europe, the Staffords agreed. They persuaded Granville's commanding officer to grant him six months' leave of absence. Since they were worried for his safety if he crossed Europe by land with only a manservant to accompany him (as Lord Bessborough had done), they arranged for his passage on the *Dido,* a frigate due to lead a convoy joining Lord Hood's fleet at Toulon.

Travel at sea, as Granville soon discovered, was not without its attendant perils. Bad weather delayed his ship and three months later the *Dido* had still only reached Majorca when the news arrived that Toulon had been attacked by the English and evacuated, and that the whereabouts of Lord Hood's fleet was now unknown. The *Dido* parted from the convoy in search of Hood, only to be intercepted off Minorca by a fleet of thirteen ships. Fortunately the fleet was British and headed by the ninety-eight-gun *St. George* under Admiral Gell.

During the rendezvous Granville discovered that a contemporary of his from Oxford was a passenger on board the *St. George.* Lord Holland was the wealthy young nephew of Charles James Fox and shared many of his charismatic uncle's traits. Friendly, jovial, and unaffected by nature, although far from good-looking ("His complexion partakes of the Moresco hue," Lady Webster would later scathingly write),[10] Holland had not until now numbered Granville among his close friends—Granville's hauteur was alien to Holland's outgoing ebullience. But being confined onboard ship for three months had smoothed Granville's affectations and perhaps too made Holland less choosy about the company he kept. "I think Leveson much improved both in intellect manner etc., and has lost that reserve which however laudable and prudent always prevents my liking a man much—I fancy my reason for not liking in this instance, what good sense must approve, must originate from *self love* and that I cannot much esteem a quality of which I am not much possessed,"[11] Holland told his sister. Within hours of renewing their acquaintance Granville decided to leave the *Dido* to accompany Holland for the remainder of the trip to Leghorn, then to travel with him through Italy to rejoin his friends in Naples.

Lady Stafford was far from pleased when word reached her (significantly, via Granville's servant rather than from a letter he wrote to her himself) that her son had befriended Holland, nephew of one of the leading lights of the Whig opposition. Holland was reputedly a supporter of the French revolutionaries—"a veritable *sans culotte*," she sternly warned him in her next letter. As Granville rushed to Naples, the perils of older women also preyed on her mind. "Remember my dear Granville," she worriedly reminded him, "there are passions which must be restrained by reason and religion. An artful woman may draw the best disposed into horrible scrapes, and may outwit a better understanding than her own. Professions of attachment, interest in your happiness, sincerity of affection and a thousand plausible ensnaring ways which that sort of woman possesses are not easily withstood."[12] Her worries were soothed when Granville's first proper letter arrived from Naples. He was, he assured her, socializing, studying, and sightseeing as busily as even she could have hoped. "Every other day is generally occupied in seeing the different curiosities in and about Naples. The intermediate days I generally rise between nine and ten, sit at home till two, an hour and a half of which time is occupied by an Italian Master. Then I walk or ride, dine at five, go to the Spectacle, and then play a rubber at Whist, and sup at Lord Bessborough's or Lord Grandison's or Lord Palmerston's."[13]

Granville had already learned the art of deception where women were concerned. His report neglects to mention that one of his mother's bêtes noires, Lady Webster, had also recently arrived in the city. Significantly, he too omits the name of Harriet, with whom he was by now also on familiar terms. Elizabeth Webster was more candid in her journal, recording that for the next six or seven weeks "gambling and gallantry filled up the evenings and mornings,"[14] and that Granville often kept her company in the evenings because she was pregnant. Her journal records that Harriet, now greatly recovered from her ailments and able to walk with only a stick for support, had two young men in her thrall. Holland's bosom friend Charles Beauclerk, who was as silent and sulky as Holland was sunny, "was deeply in love with Lady B[ess-borough], and abhors Lord Granville, who is his rival."[15] In other words, Granville—despite being first smitten by Elizabeth Webster in Dresden—had also fallen under Harriet's spell.

It is easy to see why Harriet's charms might have eclipsed those of the beautiful, youthful but demanding Elizabeth Webster. The twelve-year age difference between Harriet and Granville—Harriet was now thirty-three—was no deterrent for a young man who had always had a penchant for older women, and Harriet's openness, warmth, and lack of affectation melted his reserve and made him easy with himself as well as with others. Holland was also much taken with Harriet. "Though I do not think her pretty I like [her] excessively for I think her very interesting and unaffected," he told his sister. Commenting on Beauclerk's passion for her, he added: "I never saw anyone but him in my life who answered to the description of a lovesick swain. He thinks of nothing else, is melancholy, and seems to have lost his relish for every worldly pursuit."[16]

Over the following weeks there were rides through the countryside; excursions to Pompei, Paestum, Capri; extravagant masquerades and assemblies; and countless intimate evenings spent in conversation over hands of cards. Morpeth, Boringdon, Beauclerk, Holland, Harriet, and Lady Webster were invariably together, along with the Palmerstons and an Irish family, the Moncks. Lady Spencer was also charmed by the youthful visitors, little suspecting that her daughter had become an object of their adoration. "Lord Granville Leveson is beautiful but is shy and silent, and as I have never seen him but at the whist table I cannot say much of him, but Lord Holland is delightful, I never saw so pleasant, so conversible and so good tempered a young man,"[17] she told her friend Mrs. Howe.

Holiday friendships have always developed at an accelerated rate. To Harriet it now seemed that Naples, instead of being a place of penance, bubbled with excitement. The influx of admiring young Englishmen and the whirl of social engagements that followed in their wake came as welcome distraction from financial worry and the prolonged separation from her two oldest children. "I long to see them— it is terrible to me to have two boys with whom I am hardly acquainted,"[18] she told her brother. Unsurprisingly, though, the attention she paid the young men caused her relationship with Bessborough to grow strained. "I write to say I cannot write for I am in a high dudgeon and mou over going to dine out," Harriet told Lady Webster, confessing that she felt "so low and solitary,"[19] presumably over a disagreement with her husband.

Despite her distance, the ever-vigilant Lady Stafford was also uneasy. When weeks passed and Granville neglected to write home, she had a strong inkling that he was in danger and began making strenuous efforts to persuade him to return. "You are a sad villain," she told him, furiously resorting to emotional blackmail. "If your father could be in a rage with you, he really would, for every mail he has longed for, and every mail has brought him disappointment."[20] Lord Stafford, she informed him, felt Granville's patriotic duty lay at home, "when battalions and companies are raising in almost every county for the internal security of these kingdoms." His father and his commanding officer wanted him to return with Lord Boringdon by the beginning of May. To Granville this order came as a bitter disappointment; he had hoped to stay longer than he'd first planned, bearing in mind "the hardships I have undergone at sea, and . . . the cruelty . . . in calling me home at the moment when I had arrived at the sweets and pleasures."[21] But the Staffords were unrelenting, and by early April he had bowed to their wishes and begun his journey home.

Harriet and Lady Webster and many of their friends, including Lord Holland, Lord Grandison, and Beauclerk, had also made plans to return, but at a more leisurely pace, via Rome, Florence, and Venice. By now Lady Webster had a new admirer to replace Granville. Having initially dismissed Holland as "not in the least handsome; he has, on the contrary, many personal defects," she soon allowed that "his pleasingness of manner and liveliness of conversation get over them speedily."[22] During her stay in Rome, when her husband was increasingly ill-humored as a result of "a sharp fit of gout, brought on by drinking Orvieto wine," Holland became her escape. She and Harriet went out every morning to see the sights with him. "His delightful spirits cheered us so much that we called him *sal volatile,** and used to spare him to one another for half an hour to enliven when either were melancholy."[23] In the midst of the jollity and sparkling conversation it was not only Sir Geoffrey Webster's cantankerousness that sounded a discordant note. Beauclerk's lovesick admiration for Harriet riled Bessborough, and the relationship between them worsened. When the group visited Tivoli, Bessborough's temper exploded, "and from a fit of jealousy about Mr. Beauclerk, [he] compelled us all to return to Rome, and disquieted our mirth."[24]

Secretly, however, Harriet was less interested in Beauclerk than in her absent admirer, Granville. She had made a "half promise" to write to him, and the first letter in the long correspondence that lasted throughout the rest of her life dates from her stay in Rome. In it Harriet's tone is gently flirtatious, an older woman lightly adopting the role of confidante to a younger man. "What a list of sins you will have to confess before we meet again, if you do retain me for your confessor, and put yourself into the *palais de la verité,*" she writes. Along with the lightheartedness there is a discernible intimacy. "Absence is the only cure for quarrelling friends; I think you recommended it on all occasions as a good receipt for being loved," she teases, saying of his friends, "We continue quarrelling and making it up again twenty times a day." Nevertheless, underlying the frivolity is poignant self-awareness. "Like many others, I occupy myself very much with other people's business that I may not have leisure to think of my own."[25]

Harriet's letter must have crossed with one from Granville, who wrote as soon as he returned to London in early May, to tell her that he had called on Georgiana and to inquire jealously which of his friends she liked best—Beauclerk's proximity to Harriet was preying on his

---

* A solution of ammonium carbonate and alcohol used as smelling salts.

mind. Harriet was in Venice when she responded. The tone of her reply is more serious than that of her first letter. Granville's intensity must have alarmed her and, rather than being flattered by his attention, she is typically self-deprecating, although determined to cool his hopes. "I trust and hope I am grown old and wise enough to be certain of never again involving myself in the misery of feeling more than the common interest of friendship for anyone . . . at present at least I know I am in no danger . . . *C'est assez parler de soi ce me semble, surtout quand on n'est plus très jeune ni très jolie, et qu'on écrit à un jeune homme entouré de tous ce que la beauté et la mode, on de plus aimable; le rôle de gouvernante me sied encore assez bien, mais tout autre serot un ridicule.**²⁶

In England, Lady Stafford's anxieties crystallized when Granville returned home. Markedly changed, he was distant with her and rude to his friends, who began to comment on his airs. She guessed that something must have happened in Italy to effect such a transformation — and she never doubted it was a romantic adventure of some kind, but she did not know with whom. "Why will you, *from whim,* give people reason to believe you an affected character . . . I intend to tell every body that you left your heart in Italy; therefore every other place must appear insipid and tiresome till the delirium is over . . . believe me no Italian, nor no other woman, loves you with more affection than I do."²⁷

After such an admonishment Lady Stafford expected that Granville would come to his senses, but two months later he was still neglectful and she began to wonder if the distraction was not in Italy but closer at hand. Had the friendship with Mrs. St. John resumed? Her next letter contained a thinly veiled anecdote of "a young officer":

> He is not ill looking, tolerably sensible, intolerably indolent . . . not apt to be dissatisfied with himself, rather exigeant and easily caught by the artifices of flattery. Well this same young man . . . does his duty as an officer . . . but (*par malheur*) a lady, not a very young one, has got possession of his mind, some think of his heart. Others believe that

---

* That's enough talking of oneself, especially when one is no longer very young or very pretty and when one writes to a young man who is surrounded by all that beauty and fashion can offer; the role of governess seems to me adequate — anything else would be ridiculous.

by flattery, professions of friendship, and how much she is interested about him and all his family . . . that he looks upon her as his best friend, the depot of all his thoughts . . . so this shackled young man loiters away all his mornings . . . with this fair one.[28]

The story brought home to Granville the depth of his mother's concern. He responded immediately, but with a rather feeble defense. Without openly acknowledging that he recognized himself as the young officer in question, he gently pointed out to his mother that things might not be as bad as she supposed: the influence wielded by the lady may have been exaggerated by idle gossip. He also, disingenuously, reassured her that he liked Mrs. St. John only "nearly as well as . . . last year."[29] His feelings for that lady were waning because Harriet, whose arrival in England was now imminent, occupied his thoughts. But Granville made no mention of Harriet and so, for the time being, Lady Stafford remained ignorant of the new woman who had entered her son's life.

Harriet, Viscountess Duncannon, later Countess of Bessborough, with her two sons, John and Frederick. John Hoppner's glamorous portrait, painted in 1787 and showing Harriet in her mid-twenties, is the best surviving record of her unusual beauty.

Left Margaret Georgiana, Harriet's mother, with her oldest child, Georgiana. She was a constant presence in Harriet's life, although her well-meaning interference caused friction in Harriet's marriage.

Below Design for a monument to Harriet's father, John, First Earl Spencer. He died at the age of forty-nine after suffering frequent bouts of ill health.

Above Harriet's only brother, George, painted in his teens by Reynolds.

Opposite
Althorp (*above*), Wimbledon Park (*center left*), and Spencer House, London (*below*), the three main Spencer residences. Lavish entertainments took place in all three, and the grand interiors such as the Great Room at Spencer House (*center right*) also provided a suitable backdrop for the Spencer art collection.

Above Rowlandson's lively watercolor of Harriet and Georgiana reflects the sisters' love of music. Harriet continued to play the piano while she was recovering from serious illness in Bath and living in exile in Europe.

Opposite
Above A gaming scene at Devonshire House. Rowlandson shows Harriet standing at the table wearing a fashionable wide-brimmed hat. The contrast between the sisters' youth and beauty and the grotesque appearance of the other players hints at the corrupting influence of the pastime that would ruin their lives.

Below Vauxhall Gardens, by Rowlandson. Harriet is in the center, dressed in blue and surrounded by a group of other illustrious visitors, including Georgiana and the Prince of Wales.

Above Lord Bessborough's villa at Roehampton. It was designed for Harriet's father-in-law by William Chambers in a restrained classical style that reflected his passion for antiquity.

Above William Ponsonby, Second Earl Bessborough, Harriet's father-in-law, painted in Turkish costume by his friend Jean Etienne Liotard, who went with him to Constantinople.

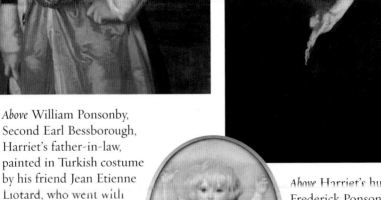

Above Harriet's husband, Frederick Ponsonby, Viscount Duncannon, as a young man.

Left Harriet's daughter Caroline, whose elfin appearance belied a tempestuous nature, even from an early age.

Above left Georgiana's daughters, "Little G" and Harryo. Harryo lacked the good looks of her sister, but her wit and good humor were widely admired.

Above right The Two Duchesses of Devonshire: Georgiana and her close friend Bess Foster.

Left George Spencer's wife, Lavinia, Second Countess Spencer, with her son Lord Althorp. Lavinia's unpredictable temper was often the cause of upset.

Among Harriet's lovers were Lord John Townshend (*above*), shown here with Harriet and Georgiana as the Whig candidate during the Westminster election of 1788, and Richard Brinsley Sheridan (*right*). Harriet and Sheridan became lovers during the 1788 election.

Left Granville Leveson Gower was Harriet's greatest and most enduring love. He was a child in the 1780s, shown here with his sisters at the center rear of the group.

Friendship
1794~1796

As Harriet embarked on her long journey home she could barely contain her craving to see her two oldest boys. "Every step that brings me nearer to you adds to my impatience and longing to see you and I know not how I shall ever hold out till I get to England or bear the joy when I do get there,"[1] she told them. Bessborough had planned the route, taking account of the "motions of the French" and trying to cross the Alps at a time when there would be less likelihood of bad weather that might damage Harriet's health. In June they left Venice, heading, via Milan, for Switzerland, Germany, and Flanders, where they intended to cross the Channel.

Their journey was no less fraught than the one that had taken them to Italy two years earlier, and by the time they reached Germany they were surrounded by the world of war. Roads were filled with Austrian troops and emigrants, many of whom could not get lodgings or horses; streets were crammed with carriages in which, in the absence of lodgings, people slept and ate. In Munich they learned that the French were encamped ten miles from Brussels and poised to encroach farther eastward. The news made Lady Spencer wonder whether they should pass the summer in Germany before completing their journey, but Bessborough decided to press on, taking a route farther north than originally planned via the Rhine, with the aim of crossing the Channel at Hellevoetsluis, near The Hague in Holland.

They reached The Hague safely in early August, but even there danger from the French threatened. Privateers had made several attacks on British shipping off the coast and it was dangerous to cross without the protection of a naval convoy. Frantic as Harriet was to be reunited with her children, she was forced to wait for an escort and favorable weather and tides. To add to the general tension, Georgiana—who had not seen Harriet or her mother for a year—had hurried from Chatsworth to Harwich the moment she'd heard they were in The Hague, and waited impatiently to welcome them home. Not until three weeks later, at the end of August, did Harriet reach Harwich.

Exhausted but ecstatic to be back on British soil after nearly three long years away, she must have been disappointed to find that John and Frederick were not waiting for her at the port. Lady Spencer had been fearful of the effect on her health of seeing them, "as I think the expectation is a bad thing for agitated nerves,"[2] and had ordered them to wait at Roehampton for their mother's return.

HARRIET HAD SCARCELY time to settle back into her old life before Granville began once more to pay suit to her. He delayed returning to his regiment in Plymouth in order to call at Cavendish Square, but Harriet was distracted by family commitments and hurried him away, saying her carriage was waiting. Unaccustomed to being treated so carelessly by the object of his affections, Granville read her preoccupation as a snub and departed in ill humor, afterward lapsing into petulant silence and refusing to write. Underneath, though, he was torn. Perversely, Harriet's brisk friendliness, her hurrying him away when he wished to stay longer with her, had fanned his feelings more effectively than if she had responded warmly to his overtures. No doubt he expected Harriet to apologize for her hastiness, but she took his silence in her stride and waited until he eventually succumbed and resumed their correspondence. His first letter after this telling rift does not survive, but Harriet's reply does: "I began to think I should never hear from you again, and was determined *coute que coute* [cost what it may] not to write till I did," Harriet wrote artlessly, continuing with a lively description of how she had helped canvass support for her brother in an election at St. Albans.

Conceive being dressed out as fine as I could at eleven o'clock this morning, squeezed into a hot assembly room at the Angel Inn, cramming fifty old Aldermen and their wives with hot rolls and but-

ter . . . and to crown all a mad Mr. Cavendish* . . . in the midst of the
ball room, and after demanding silence, repeated . . . a long copy of
verses, in which he compared me to Venus . . . let me hear from you.
Remember my letters depend upon yours, therefore whenever you
wish me to write you will take the means of making me.[3]

The instruction, albeit tongue-in-cheek, shows that Harriet remembered the lessons of her past. She had no wish to return to the
scandals of her affair with Wyndham or Sheridan and convinced herself that whatever Granville's intentions, platonic friendship was feasi-
ble and all she would allow him. The rules of their relationship were
firmly written in her mind. She might, as in the letter above, obliquely
remind him of what drew him to her in the first place—attractiveness,
elegance, and, above all, the poise that comes with maturity; she might
encourage his confidences, dispense advice, flirt gently with him; but
any hope he expressed for a physical or romantic affair would be swiftly
quashed. Literature was a common bond and, perhaps naively, Harriet
cast Granville in the role of courtly lover: she would grant him favors—
a lock of her hair or her portrait—if he earned them by keeping to his
promise never to gamble, to write regularly, and to confide which
young ladies drew his eye. Such a promise, she tried to persuade him,
was neither unreasonable nor improbable. "Some hundred years back
you might have been ordered to kill Giants, overthrow castles, or keep
an uninterrupted silence for four or five years, to be permitted at the
end of that time to sing a lamentable complaint under the high walls of
your lady's castle."[4]

In the first months after Harriet's return to England, maintaining
this firmly circumscribed friendship was made easy by Granville being
at a safe distance in Plymouth. Meetings were brief and few. Harriet
was still dogged by a troublesome cough and rather than face the
weather in London, on Dr. Warren's advice Bessborough decided to
move the family to the milder climate of Teignmouth for the winter.

---

* Probably a reference to Frederick Cavendish (1733–1812), younger brother of the
scientist Henry Cavendish, grandsons of the second Duke of Devonshire. Frederick
suffered a serious head injury in a fall from an upper window while at Cambridge,
leaving him mentally impaired.

Granville was allowed a day's visit before the New Year —but he was invited with his friends Boringdon, Morpeth, and his rival for Harriet's affection, Beauclerk. Afterward, when he wrote effusively wishing he might have stayed longer, Harriet reminded him sternly of the boundaries of their friendship. "Pray do not quarrel with poor *amitié*; it is a very good word and a very good thing. I write it so often, because you always seem to forget it, and as it is *all* I have to offer, if you reject that you reject me."[5]

She knew his infatuation was growing, and tried to make him recognize that his expectations were unrealistic and foolish. "Having pictured out in your imagination something very delightful which at present you call me, you refuse getting acquainted with a thousand other objects twenty times more deserving your love and attention, more able to return it, more suited to you in every way . . ." Yet, however she masked her feelings, she was already fonder of him than she chose to acknowledge and had begun to worry what would happen when his infatuation paled. "Some day or other, when you open your eyes and the sad reality appears stripped of all the bright colours your fancy has dressed it in, you will dislike as much in proportion as you now fancy you like."[6]

When they were not arguing over the limitations of their friendship there were politics to discuss. Harriet was conscious that the political activities of her younger days had attracted adverse comment among Tory circles, where women were increasingly discouraged from participation. Granville, like his friend Canning, looked sternly on females who dabbled openly in politics and proclaimed, "A woman has no business at all with politicks, or . . . if she thinks at all about them, it should be at least in a feminine manner as wishing for the peace and prosperity of her country."[7]

Harriet could never concur with such a sentiment; nevertheless, she had no desire to seem strident in her political views, and thus claimed, "Nothing can be much more ridiculous than a female politician."[8] In truth, this was simply Harriet at her most persuasively disingenuous; she would always prefer to appear to agree, then add a tempered codicil of dissent, rather than engage in open confrontation. Underneath her acquiescence, though, she still viewed herself as part of the Whig faction, and nothing would prevent her from expressing her opinion if she felt so inclined. When Granville was elected as member for the family constituency of Lichfield, Harriet was gracious in her congratulations, though conscious of what his victory would mean. "I know it is to enable you to vote against all my opinions."[9]

But politics had changed during her absence. The Whigs had never been a united opposition party in the modern understanding of the term, but merely a group loosely bound by common creeds. Events in France had shaken those creeds and called old alliances into question; in the process, the old Whig opposition faction had been eroded and boundaries separating it from government tenets blurred. Fox's supporters had dwindled to fewer than forty as, following the execution of Louis XVI, many leading Whigs, including the Duke of Portland and Harriet's brother, George, had joined Pitt's government and been handsomely rewarded with government positions; George was now First Lord of the Admiralty. Bessborough had taken his seat in the House of Lords and offered support to the government, seconding an address that insisted on the prosecution of the war on the grounds that "the enemy would require concessions too dishonourable to be granted"[10] and that England's prosperity and naval and military force compared with the depleted French resources would give her the advantage.

Harriet was torn between her loyalty and affection for Fox, who still favored the democratic ideals that lay behind the French Revolution, and her links to the French aristocracy, whose sufferings she had felt acutely. Granville teased her for being "a democrat" and pro-Jacobin, but her position was ambivalent and she emphasized their common ground rather than their differences. "I quite agree with you," she told Granville; "it is the glory and safeguard of England that every one from the highest to the lowest, has a right to give his opinion free and uncontrolled and the frequent discussion of political subjects among friends, who differ on those points only, seem to moderate both sides, and lessen that bitter acrimony, that prejudiced violence, which does so much harm."[11] When their stances seemed irreconcilable she made light of them and thus defused the argument. "I do not think we shall ever quarrel upon politicks," she assured him blithely after a heated exchange of views over the slave trade, which she, like Fox, believed should be abolished, and Granville did not. "I assure you I am not so great a democrat as perhaps you imagine, and I flatter myself you are not so aristocratical as you tried to appear the day you were here."[12]

GRANVILLE BECAME MORE demanding of Harriet's attentions when she returned to Roehampton the following spring, but she remained as determined as ever to keep to her resolution. "In the end real friendship is a thousand times to be preferred to the thorns and briars of love. It is almost as affectionate, more equal, more lasting, and more disinterested,"[13] she argued whenever he wanted more. She took pains to prevent him from monopolizing her, letting him know that she still had other male friends and admirers and relished their company. Beauclerk called on her regularly, much to Granville's annoyance; so too did his friends Morpeth and Boringdon. And when Lord Bessborough was distracted, old dangerous friends such as Charles Wyndham gained occasional entry into her orbit.

One questionable encounter Harriet described to Granville took place during a journey to Bognor. Harriet and her family were to spend a night with Wyndham's brother, Lord Egremont, at Petworth. Georgiana and Bess were also expected to join the party but were delayed, and rather than face Egremont alone she decided to wait at an inn a few miles from Petworth, telling Bessborough to take the children ahead without her. Harriet's trepidation may well have been genuine: Egremont was a famously eccentric host and a notorious womanizer. But she may also have been covering a secret assignation; it would not have been the first time she had been less than candid with her husband on the subject of her male friends. A few minutes after Bessborough left, Charles Wyndham—who had a house nearby—appeared at the inn.

Harriet and Wyndham were discovered some time later by Mr. Grenville, a friend who also happened to be passing. Harriet told Grenville she had tried to make Wyndham leave but could not get rid of him. Grenville—clearly aware of Wyndham and Harriet's history—advised her to "conquer fears and come on, very justly observing that other people might pass, and perhaps not have the good nature to believe that my stopping in so odd a place, sending Ld. B. on, and meeting with Mr. W. was all pure accident." The meeting may well have been no more than the accident Harriet claimed, but the fact that she chose to recount it to Granville was significant—a reminder of her checkered past and of the perils of attracting scandal. Her letter concluded pointedly: "See how little things are to be misrepresented in this world."[14]

THE RIFT IN Granville's relationship with his family and friends widened as his obsession for Harriet took hold. Lady Stafford had hitherto prided herself on having his confidence, and was mortified to see how secretive and vague he became with her and other old friends. Harriet's spell, she now recognized, was more insidious than the allure of any of Granville's previous unsuitable attachments; the situation had become far too delicate for open criticism. Rather than openly acknowledging the fact he had been ensnared by one of the most notorious and glamorous of Whig ladies, her complaints at first attributed his neglectful behavior to less specific causes: "ladies, late hours, cards, house of commons, sensible companions, dissipated friends, St. James's Street, the church, Hyde Park, good intentions, broken vows, repentance, love and operas."[15] In her heart, however, she knew the truth and was deeply wounded by Granville's failure to confide in her. "I once thought that you knew me to be indulgent to faults or failings; that although I use strong expressions, and represent them in odious lights to prevent them, yet when committed no one can make greater allowances."[16]

Matters came to a head in the summer of 1796, when a sexual scandal concerning another couple brought her fears into the open. Elizabeth Webster and Lord Holland returned to England. Elizabeth Webster had spent several months in Italy without her husband and with Lord Holland staying nearby, living openly as her lover. She was now pregnant with Holland's child and made no attempt to conceal the fact. Her husband, Sir Geoffrey, immediately began divorce proceedings, demanding the return of his children and seizing control of her fortune. Knowing how close Granville had become to Lord Holland and Elizabeth Webster in Italy, Lady Stafford could hardly fail to see similarities in his attachment to Harriet. Terrified he might contemplate following Holland's example, she wrote, lecturing him of the dangers he faced: "misery, disgrace and ruin . . . follow such connections," she warned, "carrying on with Secrecy . . . absorbs the mind . . . every other pursuit is neglected . . . every thought is employed; the converse of those who are not mixed in the affair become vapid and tiresome, business intolerable, and all sort of application detestable drudgery."[17]

Granville consolingly promised that Holland's actions were as reprehensible to him as they were to his mother. This was just what Lady Stafford wanted to hear, but she no longer believed him. "Are you not drawn on and on by a passion that absorbs all your faculties, that employs your every thought, and that draws you from every laudable worthy pursuit, and weans your affections from all those who are not connected in this unfortunate affair?" she pressed. Convinced that Harriet had already embroiled her son in a physical relationship that would endanger the reputations of both, she urged him to end the affair, for Harriet's sake as much as for his own. But even as she wrote the words she knew they were futile. "I own that it is difficult for a young man to break off such a connection, and yet the danger of a discovery to the lady, as well as to yourself, should be a reason, independent of every other consideration, to make you put an end to this affair."[18]

Harriet, meanwhile, took a very different view of her friend's plight. She had known of the pregnancy before Elizabeth Webster's return to England and had advised her to have the baby secretly, as Georgiana had done, and thus avoid a scandal. Lady Webster had taken her advice, stating her intention to have the baby quietly and then to agree to an amicable separation with her husband. Her scandalous flaunting of her condition had only been spurred by the interference of George Ellis, a friend of Sir Geoffrey's, who had discovered the truth before it became public knowledge and threatened to expose her. Harriet told Granville that she regretted her friend's action, but she could not bring herself to condemn her wholeheartedly—perhaps because memories of her own shame lingered. Elizabeth Webster had written her a contrite letter, which "proves how falsely she is accused of braving the world and rejoicing in carrying her point. On the contrary it is full of expressions that show how strongly she feels all that is painful and humiliating in her situation."[19]

But Harriet's concerns for Elizabeth Webster were eclipsed by more pressing worries the following autumn. Georgiana contracted a painful infection that swelled one of her eyes to the size of a fist. "O dear Ld. G. how you would have pitied her, I am sure, if you could have known half what she has suffered." Harriet had rushed to her sister's bedside and sat with her as leeches and various other harrowing treatments were administered with no proper anesthetic. Having heard her screams, Harriet was so distressed afterward that she was forced to take laudanum to calm herself. "After hearing what I did tonight I can bear anything," she told Granville. "Her illness has made me as strong as Hercules."[20] In fact, she was far less robust than she led him to believe. Cold weather always adversely affected her and made her susceptible to disease. Granville was distraught to learn from a mutual friend, Lady Elizabeth Monck, that "Lady Bessborough has been very ill—on Saturday night she was seized with violent spasms and has had them from time to time ever since . . . However though it is very painful you need not be the least alarmed."[21]

While Harriet recuperated she occupied herself with drawing an illustration for *Elegiac Sonnets,* a volume by Charlotte Smith, an eminent novelist and poet, whose novel *Emmeline* had brought her to fame. "Lady B[essborough] is so good as to undertake the drawing . . . this I apprehend will be an advantage to the work,"[22] Smith told her publisher, acknowledging the kudos that Harriet's illustrious reputation would bring. Smith had further reason to be grateful to Harriet. Publishing an illustrated volume was a costly business, and authors commonly offered subscriptions to cover the costs. Smith had raised £150 from a large number of prominent subscribers, including Harriet, Bessborough, Georgiana, and the Duke of Devonshire, but was worried that the costs of illustrating and engraving her work would come to more than she could afford. Harriet's drawing, offered free of charge, was thus doubly welcome.

The drawing echoes the picturesque style of the times and illustrates "The Female Exile," a poem with which Harriet easily identified. The illustration shows a pensive woman, with more than a passing resemblance to Harriet herself, seated on a rocky shore, watching three children playing. Beneath it is inscribed a verse from the poem:

> *The gilt, fairy ship, with its ribbon sail spreading,*
> *The launch on the salt pool the tide left behind;*
> *Ah! Victims—for whom their mother is dreading*
> *The multiple miseries that wait on mankind.*[23]

Meanwhile Lady Stafford's misery remained centered on her desperate desire to break Harriet's spell over her son; in this she was helped by political events. The progress of the war with France had attracted increasing criticism in England. Napoleon, in command of the French forces in the south, had rampaged through Italy, although the French contingents under Generals Moreau and Jourdan had suffered serious defeat against the Austrian armies on the Rhine and were now in retreat in Germany. At this delicate stage Pitt ceded to opposition demands for peace. Declaring that the newly formed Directory was a milder governing system with which Britain might do business, he decided to send a peace mission under Lord Malmesbury to Paris.

Hearing this news Lady Stafford resolved that her only hope of severing Granville's attachment to Harriet was by sending him abroad, and the possibility of securing Granville a place on so crucial a mission seemed too good to miss. Behind the scenes the family drew on every connection, urging Granville to do likewise for the sake of his career and reputation. Granville needed little convincing. His friend George Canning, a recent convert to Pitt's government, was to accompany Malmesbury. Granville had barely seen Harriet since her sister's illness and was frustrated by her inaccessibility; the chance to play a part in such a key political moment seemed a welcome alternative to romantic stalemate. "Ld. Malmesbury . . . promised to speak to Ld. Grenville again upon the subject and to urge him strongly to allow me to accompany him. Pitt also promises to second the application,"[24] Granville assured his mother, after an evening of furious networking. The next day his place was confirmed. "I cannot express my delight at having succeeded. Every person seems to envy me my situation," he declared.

Granville reached Paris a week later. After all the horrific recent events he was surprised to find that the city had an eerie air of normality. "The word *citoyen* seemed but very little in use, and hair powder being very common, the appearance of the people was less democratic than in England,"[25] he reported. Above all he was relieved that "the desire of Peace seems to be universal." His letters to his mother are stiffly formal and noncommittal—a tone that came easily to him. He claimed that the lack of information was an essential part of his duty; he was under strict instructions to divulge no sensitive political information in case his correspondence was intercepted. Lady Stafford could not quibble with such limitations.

Harriet, by contrast, would not tolerate such lackluster correspondence, and gently ridiculed any hint of pomposity. Before he left, Granville had asked her for a portrait of herself; "I suppose you may tell me [where to send the drawing] . . . without any sin against ministerial mystery or state secrets,"[26] she teased. Platitudes or cursory news were less mercifully received. When he wrote, "Do not be angry but I have very little to say . . . I am desirous of knowing particularly how you are, and how your sister's eye goes on," Harriet's response was unequivocal. "How I hate anybody beginning a letter with 'I have nothing to say.' At all times, and especially when from a distance, which makes trifles interesting among friends; and from the peculiarity of the scene which makes everything from thence interesting, there must be so much to be said, if you were not idle—yes, sir, very idle, for all you boast so much of your reading."[27]

To pacify her and buttress the bond between them, Granville offered to buy Harriet presents of books and a fashionable wig, and to perform delicate commissions such as retrieving jewelry from a moneylender. Interspersed with talk of these favors are sparse attempts at lightheartedness and stilted protestations of affection. Harriet's cool response to all this shows she still held the upper hand. When he wrote, "Interesting as the scene is at present, I should feel little contented to remain here if I could see much of you in town," Harriet responded by asking which of the French ladies he had met had most impressed him and reminding him once again of the boundaries of their friendship. Candor and honesty she valued above all. "Remember, whatever *loves* you may have, I shall always claim your friendship and in that light I shall be glad."[28] Granville wrote back, defending himself and repeating his avowals. "Although my attention is much occupied by my present employment, yet regrets at being absent from one whose society is most dear to me very frequently intrude."[29]

Despite appearances to the contrary, though, there was weakness in Harriet's resolve. When Lord Malmesbury told her brother that "the profligacy, licentiousness, and *seductions* of Paris were such that no young man could remain there without total ruin," Harriet's next letter to Granville warned: "remember that I could not like a coxcomical or a profligate friend . . . Do not impute what I say to a wrong motive; I am writing to you as I would do to my son if he was in the same situation . . ."[30] In taking a maternal role she pretended that friendship remained her only desire. But the balance between them was shifting. Whatever she professed, she no longer thought of Granville as a platonic friend or a surrogate son: sexual jealousy had begun to intrude.

TWELVE

The Start of the Affair
1797

EVERYTHING CHANGED WHEN Lord Malmesbury's peace mission ended abruptly and Granville came back to London. In his absence Harriet had spent her time quietly at Roehampton, looking after her younger children with her friend and companion Lady Anne Hatton, and nursing Georgiana at Chiswick after her eye problem again worsened and culminated in a painful operation. On Granville's return Harriet launched into a more sociable existence. Granville and his circle were often invited to Roehampton or to Cavendish Square, along with old friends such as the Townshends and Sheridan and his new wife. At these diverse gatherings, news of the latest calamities and triumphs in the war inevitably dominated the conversation.

The French, under General Hoche, had prepared an invasion of Ireland even as the doomed negotiations in which Granville had played a part had taken place. Bad weather had prevented the French landing at Bantry Bay, but elsewhere their campaigns were more successful. After his victorious campaign in Italy, Napoleon turned his attention northward. Austria swiftly followed Spain, Prussia, and Holland and agreed to peace, leaving Britain facing France alone. Harriet and other Whig friends vehemently opposed the war, which had already resulted in the deaths of forty thousand—"a calamitous waste of treasure and of blood,"[1] pronounced Sheridan, who believed Britain should also seek a peaceful resolution to hostilities. Both Sheridan and Fox censured Pitt for offering monetary support to Austria to help her continue the war and bringing the Bank of England so close to bankruptcy that it had been forced to suspend payments. But most of Pitt's supporters—

among them Granville's family—remained resolute in their support of his ministry. "I shall die, I do believe literally give up the Ghost, if Mr. Pitt cannot procure a loan for the Emperor,"[2] proclaimed Lady Stafford.

In May the gloomy atmosphere further darkened when sailors at Spithead began to mutiny. The sailors were aggrieved at harsh discipline, inhuman living conditions, and poor pay—they had received no increase in their salaries for over a century. Harriet's brother, George, as First Lord of the Admiralty, hurried to assess the situation. The commission that followed his visit concluded that the demands should be sympathetically viewed, but a second, more serious mutiny erupted soon after at Sheerness, among sailors manning a fleet due to intercept Dutch ships believed to be heading for a further assault on Ireland.

At Harriet's soirées discussion of how such dramatic events should be dealt with might easily have erupted into quarrels. Yet when the mood grew heated Harriet was drawn to the role of mediator, creating rapprochement rather than rifts and helping each side comprehend the other's point of view. "Tell me whether there was anything in Mr. Fox's or Mr. Grey's speeches that I should have disliked much, and whether on the whole it seemed to go well for my brother. Tell me the exact truth, and not as an administration person, but fairly and impartially,"[3] she demanded of Granville after a debate in the Commons concerning the mutinies. Knowing that openly to declare her views risked incurring Granville's wrath, Harriet's tactful policy of manipulation continued. Declaring, "No woman has any business to meddle with that or any other serious business, farther than giving her opinion," she excused her political involvement partly on the grounds of her upbringing and partly because of the closeness between them. "From my childhood I have been accustomed to hear politicks the constant and eager subject of conversation, and that when with persons I like and am at ease with, to think a thing and say it is the same with me."[4]

Fearful of seeming "violent," and losing Granville's respect, she heavily downplayed her political influence. She was alarmed that her friend and companion Anne Hatton had tried to persuade Lord Morpeth to vote with the opposition and thus against her brother over the treatment of the rebellious sailors, telling Granville with characteristic modesty: "My sister and I have certainly neither the wish nor had we the wish, the *power* of swaying any of our friends' voices, but I own I should feel mortified if the *first* opposition vote of a person who lives so much with us should be against my brother."[5] Nevertheless, underlying Harriet's self-effacement was the knowledge that she did wield real power. In the end Pitt, with Sheridan's support, passed two emergency bills in which mutineers or those inciting sedition became liable to the death penalty. Meanwhile, Admiral Duncan headed off the threatened Dutch invasion with only one other ship in support, managing to confuse the enemy by signaling to a fictitious fleet. One by one the mutineers returned to their duties. The ringleaders were arrested by the authorities, and twenty-three were sentenced to death.

The insurrection at Sheerness was still rumbling on when Pitt decided to try again to make peace with France. Once again Granville was dispatched as secretary to Lord Malmesbury; once again Lady Stafford was delighted, still hoping against hope that if Granville were sufficiently occupied he would forget his unsuitable alliance with Harriet. "As I think it unlikely you may ever have so advantageous an opportunity again, I am more ardently anxious that you should make the best use of this . . . You are now exposed to the notice of these kingdoms, and you may cause the occurrence of so extraordinary an advantage to bring you into publick life,"[6] she urged. Granville responded, as he always did, with mollifying promises to follow her instructions, confiding that this time the signs of the mission succeeding were auspicious. "An opinion has been so unequivocally declared by the Council of 500* in favour of peace that I cannot conceive the Directory insisting upon terms too dishonourable for us to accept."[7]

Lady Stafford's unease at Granville's infatuation with Harriet by now had just cause. Politics had not been the only topics of conversation between them in the long hours they had passed together since his return. Harriet had come to view Granville as more than another besotted admirer, encouraging rather than dampening his ardor. What had brought about this change? No doubt the tumultuous events taking place in the world at large played a part in weakening Harriet's resolve. England's alarmingly vulnerable situation, the frequent threats of

---

* France's lawmaking body during the Directory.

invasion, the political clashes, the disappointments and victories created a feverish mood, a sense that since anything might happen, life should be lived to the full.

But it was not only the wider world where changes had been wrought. Harriet's own circumstances and perspective had changed during the three years that had passed since she and Granville had met. Then she had been a fragile invalid, barely able to cross the room without support. Now she could dance until dawn, or ride for hours through the grounds of Roehampton, or stay up all night talking animatedly about the latest books or plays. She had always been tactile and emotional, and good health had enhanced her looks and rekindled her appetite for physical as well as intellectual excitement. At the age of thirty-six she was a woman of seductive allure, but conscious that her youth was fading. Granville, twelve years her junior, must have made her feel alive in a way she longed to remember.

We may guess too that time and familiarity had increased Harriet's belief that the differences in their characters were perfectly complementary. His intensity and brooding passion made her feel dazzling and witty; his youthful inexperience enhanced her sense of her own wisdom; his reserve melted in the presence of her easy warmth. There are few glimpses of Bessborough during this time, so perhaps too the temptation of Granville was made harder to resist by his frequent absences. Since their return from Italy distance had again widened between them; he had once more taken to spending long hours at Brooks's and on excursions to which she was not invited, and when he did return he was either uncommunicative or ill-humored. "I believe Ld. B. leaves me here tête à tête with the Duke," she told Granville from Woburn, as if he had barely told her their plans; and elsewhere, of an evening spent with three of her women friends, she wrote, "soon after three Ld. B. returned not in very good humour, and sent them [her friends] away and me to bed."[8]

It is impossible to be certain of the motive behind Bessborough's disappearances that ultimately drove Harriet to Granville's arms. Perhaps he faded from her life because seeing her flirting and holding forth in the intellectual milieu in which she thrived made him uncomfortable. Or perhaps the relaxed male environment of Brooks's and hunting parties seemed preferable to the challenges of his wife's company. Either way, he must have told himself, in the way of many other aristocratic husbands of his day, that Harriet had given him four children and secured the Bessborough lineage. Both of them might now live their separate lives and choose their own companions, provided they did so discreetly and within the limitations of the family's straitened finances, and provided Harriet performed the outward role of a wife whenever required.

So, in the expectation of finding a more fulfilling relationship, Harriet returned to the temptations of infidelity. She ignored Granville's darker side: his self-absorption, the gossip that still linked him with other women, the fact that his family was violently opposed to her. She convinced herself that bitter experience had taught her how to conduct an affair discreetly; that her husband would not uncover the secret; and that she would safely avoid scandal. Her biased judgment and flawed reasoning in all of this reflect Granville's place at the center of her life. Harriet in such a mood could persuade herself of anything; she was too intoxicated by desire to resist any longer.

We do not know when exactly the turning point came, but the letters Harriet wrote to Granville after his first mission and return from France and before he left for his second are markedly different in tone from their earlier correspondence and suggest that it must have been then that the affair began. Henceforth there are no more protestations of friendship; instead, she writes in an openly romantic vein, often mentioning her longing to see or hear from him. "It has just struck eleven, and the whole house, excepting Sally and me, have been in bed near an hour," she wrote from her mother's house in St. Albans. "We have sat at the open window listening to the nightingales and watching for the post man with the most eager impatience."[9]

Soon after this, Granville left for his second mission and Harriet plunged into depression—a further sign that their relationship had changed significantly. Sheridan, her old friend and lover, was one of the first to notice her melancholy and guess the cause. Calling Harriet "the majesty of grief" and teasing her for plunging into low spirits, "he assured me you would be back in less than ten days, that all the farmers in England meant to send a petition, for there was no hope of any harvest now those bright beams* they used to warm and vivify our atmosphere were withdrawn,"[10] she told Granville. Throughout the worst throes of her despondency only Sheridan could amuse her. "I was vexed, and received him crossly, but, Demon like, he was so abominably entertaining that I ended by being glad he came, and letting him stay till almost dinner time," she wrote of a later encounter.[11]

A fortnight later, Harriet had mastered her feelings sufficiently to put on a masquerade of lightheartedness. "I am glad you have found out that republican hands can cultivate the land, and that a state may flourish even without a despotic monarchy to govern it . . . How lucky Lord Malmesbury is to have such wise counsellors; the French have no chance."[12] But beneath the wit there is discernible vulnerability, an awareness that the balance of the relationship had changed. Where once Granville clamored for her attention and begged for her favors, now he was in the ascendant. "Pray write a few lines every night . . . bid me good night once-twice—a hundred times if you please,"[13] she implored, as if the separation was unbearable.

Granville had been in France for little more than a month when he was entrusted by Lord Malmesbury to return to England with a confidential account of the progress of discussions too delicate to entrust to a written dispatch. "I can depend on the correct memory and faithful report of Lord Granville Leveson, and also on the satisfactory manner in which he will answer your questions and explain your doubts,"[14] wrote Malmesbury to Lord Grenville in his dispatch. Granville spent the next fortnight closeted in discussion with Grenville, Pitt, and Canning, expecting to return at any moment to France and with barely a moment to see Harriet. But the deteriorating political situation and "confusions in Paris" were such that there were fears for Granville's safety, so two other messengers were sent. As fate would have it, both were drowned when they attempted a landing in France. "We feel the mercy of your not having gone in that boat," wrote his thankful mother.[15]

Lady Stafford's detestation of the opposition had only hardened with Granville's continuing friendliness toward Harriet and she grasped

---

* This was no doubt an allusion to Granville's soulful gaze, which led to his nickname, Beamer.

every opportunity to criticize the actions of her Whig friends. "I heard at Lichfield that the Democrats are hard at Work to poison the minds of the miners in Cornwall, in the hope to make them rise,"[16] she warned of a threatened insurrection. Harriet had tried to counter her animosity by sending Lady Stafford news bulletins while Granville was away, but they did little to soften Lady Stafford's dislike of the woman she saw as being a morally and politically corrupting influence on her son. Instead, much to Harriet's distress, Lady Stafford widened her attacks by enlisting the support of her Establishment friends. "All that Charles Ellis said to you pains and perplexes me; I am sure he has the sincerest regard for you, and I feel that all my affection and all I can do for you neither can or ought to make up to you for the loss of so good a friend, yet he seems to think your friendship for him and your regard for me incompatible,"[17] Harriet told Granville after a particularly vitriolic attack by one of his friends. Canning also regarded her suspiciously—as he did any woman professing an interest in politics. Granville tried to ignore his animosity, pretending it was Harriet's prejudice and not Canning's that created the coolness. "You are unjust to me about Mr. Canning," she defended herself. "If you will bring him to see me, I shall be very glad of it, and receive him *de mon mieux*. But I doubt much whether he will come, and, as to laying aside my fears, how can I . . . I know myself too well not to be certain that, when tried by strict justice, I must be disliked and condemned—and who knows what effect this might have upon you?"[18]

Harriet countered most onslaughts by refusing to rise, instead responding amiably to attacks. "Pray whenever you see C. Ellis again say a great many kind things for me to him," she instructed Granville apropos his cruel words. She also endeavored to show that she was objective enough in her politics to acknowledge the merits of Pitt and Canning. The Duke of Bedford had told her that "if I could imagine the purest, most correct, forcible, and eloquent language spoke in the most harmonious voice and animated manner, seizing with incredible quickness and ingenuity all the weak parts of the opposing arguments, and putting the strongest ones of his own in the most favourable point of view, that I should then have some faint idea of what Mr. P.'s speaking was."[19]

Mostly, however, in the early months after the affair began, Harriet was too overwhelmed with physical and emotional longing to think of anything apart from when they might next see each other or when Granville's next letter would arrive. During their separations she relived their previous meetings. "I have been riding, and hated it of all things; it reminded me with so much regret of our two rides," Harriet wrote from Chatsworth in November. "How different the most trifling things appear enjoyed with those we love, or seen without them, the same objects that appeared beautiful before, the same circumstances that afforded pleasure."[20] From Hardwick, where she slept "in a black velvet room as large as the State rooms at Chatsworth, with the moon shining through the casement and making me see ghosts and goblins," she begged Granville to write constantly. "Remember that every heavy post that comes in without a letter will give me a sleepless night and consign me over to Mary and all her damsels sweeping about my great room."[21]

We do not know how Granville responded to such letters—his replies are among the missing correspondence—but his letters to his mother from this time show that, although Harriet's presence in his life was never openly acknowledged, her influence on him was potent. He began to view the opposition less dismissively. When Fox ceased to attend parliament in disgust at Pitt's refusal to introduce a bill for electoral reform, taking Sheridan, Grey, and others with him, Granville was surprisingly affected. "I am not quite sure that thus overwhelming the present insignificant champions of the opposition is quite right; it looks somewhat like bullying, when they are left unprotected by the more able leaders of their party."[22]

AT THE YEAR'S end, Granville was offered a further opportunity to advance his career—to become British Ambassador in Prussia and congratulate the new ruler, Frederick William III, on his accession, in the hope that this would sow the seeds of a possible alliance with Britain in the war against France. Lord Malmesbury had offered to write to Pitt on Granville's behalf, recommending him for the post, but Granville, still intoxicated with passion for Harriet, had little inclination to leave London; he told his parents he did not feel experienced enough for a task that might also involve delicate negotiating on the subject of alliance with the court of St. Petersburg.

The Staffords were incensed by the thought that he might turn down so important a promotion, and immediately laid the blame at

Harriet's door. "Can you believe it possible that Granville could think of declining such an opportunity? Without an attachment at home makes him unwilling to stir from London it would not enter his mind. He talks of timidity. That is all a farce,"[23] raged Lord Stafford. Harriet's response was calmer. Dismal at the thought of losing him yet knowing what he should do, she retained her sense of humor, first teasing him, "Your reasons for declining it, dear Granville, are most noble, and do you the greatest honour, and make up in my mind for *half* your idleness," then talking him around gently: "If Lord Malmesbury (who must know you well enough to judge) did not think you capable of executing such a charge he never would have proposed it to you," she reasoned. "You say it is an honourable appointment, and surely it is a laudable ambition to wish to distinguish oneself in useful and honourable employment."[24] Faced with such compelling arguments from both his parents and his mistress, Granville's hesitation crumbled. In early January he left London for Berlin.

In his absences Harriet lived for Granville's letters, "to keep unbroken that chain of confidence which makes one know each other's thoughts, and reunites in spite of distance."[25] She knew the passage to Berlin would take ten days by sea, and it would be a further ten days for the ship's return before she could expect any news. The thought was insupportable. "What, twenty whole days (almost a month) without hearing! Alas, alas, alas, how shall I bear it!"[26]

The duties of motherhood provided the only solace for her loss. No sooner had Granville left than Caro and Willy contracted chicken pox; nursing them helped Harriet to fill her days. Willy was so ill that he lay on her lap for hours, while Caro looked in the mirror, saw her face covered in spots, and fretted that someone "as fine" as Granville would no longer wish to look at her. Lord Bessborough, meanwhile, busied himself shooting hares, partridges, and pheasants at Wimbledon, leaving Harriet alone "every day and all day long, and I am in perfect liberty," she wrote. Days later Harriet too began to feel feverish and unwell; she summoned the apothecary, who "bled me very plentifully, but tho' it made me faint, it has relieved me wonderfully,"[27] Soon after, she woke to find herself covered from head to foot with chicken pox.

She passed the days of her illness by reading a newly published volume of Lord Chatham's (Pitt's father's) speeches. "I was surprised to see how much more *jacobinical* his language is than anything ever ventured now. I question whether some of his speeches repeated would not bring the speaker within reach of some of his son's new bills!"[28] she quipped, in teasing reference to Pitt's draconian laws against sedition. Harriet had always founded her political opinions on extensive reading of the latest publications. She finished Chatham to embark on three thick volumes of Sir Robert Walpole's life. "Attacking three thick quartos frightened me a little," she confessed, "but it entertains me very much. I see all times, all parties, were the same, all Ministers and all Oppositions actuated by the same little motives in half their measures, so we must not complain so bitterly of the present age."[29]

Only a tantalizing few of Granville's responses survive, but those that do reveal glimpses of his longing. "I did not know your little girl had been ill. I am flattered by her mention of me," he remarked of Caro's comment during her bout with chicken pox. "I like her very much; but, indeed, every one to whom you are attached must interest me." He had arrived in Berlin to find the king in bed with measles and unable to receive him; "How I do repent of having accepted this mission!"[30] he told her in a sentence that is cut off by later editing. After a few days there had been a glimmer of hope that his audience would be granted, but this was soon dashed. "To my utter dismay I was told that in all probability it could not be accorded to me under a fortnight. To use your own expression, 'my impatience is grown past enduring.' Even Frere, who cannot have such reasons as I have for longing to return, talks of going mad if we are to stay much longer."[31]

The difficulties of sustaining a clandestine affair became apparent soon after Granville's return in March. Before rejoining his regiment at Plymouth he had called at Cavendish Square and found Harriet arguing with Lady Anne Hatton over a planned visit to an aged lady friend. Having expected to find Harriet alone and ready to receive him, Granville felt slighted when she refused to alter her plans. Losing his temper, he joined Lady Anne, berating Harriet so harshly that she burst into tears. This had infuriated him even more, and he stormed off, only to return later and continue criticizing her frivolity and mercurial temperament. Harriet by then had regained her composure, and even after his second diatribe remained airily unrepentant.

Indeed I pity you for being attached to a being so fantastical, but if the picture you draw is like, I think it would cure me in your place. A person whose whole delight is frisking round London, visiting acquaintances and non acquaintances, and without informing you of the important event of a new visit; who takes every opportunity to teaze and irritate you, now sullenly silent, now oppressively gay (or full of glee, as you call it), capriciously attentive to a game at chess . . . or voraciously hungry and impatient for supper; now lost in careless indifference, and now a scolding virago whom nothing can please. Is the picture like? Am I all this? Or is it not possible that a little ill humour like the jaundice may discolour every object that it looks on . . . Dear Granville, what makes you judge so harshly and write so gravely to me? What are the mighty offences I have committed? My visit this morning was certainly neither from pleasure or choice . . . I never understood that selfish indulgence that cannot endure the slightest inconvenience to serve or please a friend; it is often more in trifles that a kindness is shown than in acts of greater effort or generosity . . . when you came in—which I had almost despaired of—I gave way to the pleasure of seeing you and the sort of spirits I always feel when I am surrounded by people I love . . . You soon, it is true, dampened my good humour, but still I endeavoured to laugh you out of your grave looks . . . *mais en vain.* Here is a long explanation about nothing. Good night, Dear Granville, as I am very much inclined, in common with all my sex, to think myself in the right and you in the wrong—*faite penitence, Monsieur,* and write me an answer by return of post.[32]

For all the benefits of experience, Harriet was rediscovering that the path of illicit love rarely runs smoothly.

THIRTEEN

Extravagance and Ruin
1798-1799

T HE NEWS FROM IRELAND is indeed tremendous my dear Harriet, as I conclude Lord Bessborough has constant private letters pray let me know any details you get, for everything from thence is at this moment highly interesting,"[1] demanded Lady Spencer on the subject that had gripped the nation with dread and fascination ever since the French had tried to invade at Bantry Bay. On that occasion the assault had been foiled, thanks to a stormy night and poor seamanship. Since then the situation had worsened, making a further attempt seem increasingly likely and everyone, including Harriet and her mother, edgy as a result.

The problem as Harriet and many Whigs saw it was the way in which Pitt had handled Irish grievances. Despite relaxing certain anti-Catholic legislation and easing trade restrictions, he had baulked at granting full emancipation. Discontent had thus festered, strengthening the Society of United Irishmen, a subversive organization determined to achieve Irish independence that looked to France to support their fight. In the spring of 1798 English fears were realized when the organization engineered a revolt that started in Dublin, then seeped outward to Wexford and elsewhere. French backup did not arrive until August, by which time most of the trouble had been brutally quashed by government troops. A body of seven hundred French eventually landed in the west of Ireland at Killala but gained little assistance from the Irish, most of whom had been suppressed; after fierce fighting they too were forced to surrender. By then more than thirty thousand people had perished.

Harriet was holidaying in Margate with her family when the French landings took place. Her response reflected the sophistication of her political views: Ireland should be prevented from falling into French hands, but the rebellion had been provoked by government failure to respond properly to Irish grievances. That a relatively small force could cause such mayhem was both astonishing and further proof of the government's inefficiency. Harriet was skeptical of the reports put out by official sources, blaming the administration rather than the rebels or French for the turmoil. "It is a disgrace to all Englishmen to have a handful of French keep a whole country in arms and remain so long unmolested. The French are fools if they don't send more with this encouragement . . . this is only a proof the more that Government people never can speak truth and Gazettes are not to be depended on. If we trust to them, seven hundred French, not joined by the inhabitants have their landing good, march on, and remain safe in an enemies' country, have beat General Lake and his army, and keep Cornwallis with fifteen thousand men at bay!!! Bravo Duke of Portland,"[2] she declared provocatively to Granville.

Her interest in the troubles was made all the more keen because they touched her family directly. A substantial part of the Bessborough income was derived from the rents of Irish estates. The authorities' wrath had been largely vented upon the peasant yeomanry; if Bessborough tenants, like those elsewhere in the country, had been penalized by floggings and hangings, their cottages burned and crops destroyed, many might fall into arrears with their rents.

All this added strain to family finances that were already severely overstretched. Since Bessborough and Harriet's return to Britain, the pledges that both had made on the death of the second Earl—to live carefully within their means—had been forgotten. Bessborough's fondness for the tables and Harriet's sociable nature had once more triumphed over prudence. They had returned to their old irresponsible ways and their debts were once again a talking point among the ton. "Lord and Lady Bessborough it is expected must go abroad on account of extravagance. He stays at Brooks's till three or four in the morning gaming and she goes out at one in the morning . . ."[3] remarked the beady-eyed artist Farington in his diary. Like many, Farington assumed they would settle abroad, since this was the usual method for penurious aristocrats to reduce their expenses, the cost of living being cheaper overseas. But even if Harriet had agreed to it (which, given her affair with Granville, is doubtful), with war engulfing Europe such a move was too dangerous to consider.

Harriet complained that she was not chiefly to blame for their spiraling household expenses. When Bessborough was not rashly gambling away his family fortune, he was carried away on a tide of social extravagance, inviting an endless train of people to lavish dinners, multiplying household expenses rather than allowing her to economize. This was not entirely true: Harriet had happily thrust herself to the forefront of the social scene, entertaining on her own account as well as her husband's. Mounting debts now forced Bessborough and Harriet to turn to friends and family members for loans against promises of rent. Lord Holland was frequently generous; others too yielded to their pleas—accounts show records of substantial loans from Lady Spencer, George Spencer, the Duke of Bedford, and Bessborough's brother-in-law, Lord Fitzwilliam.

Compounding Harriet's disquiet were past debts, many of which were still unpaid. Over the last four years Georgiana had helped shelter Harriet from the truth, making repayments on Harriet's behalf and telling her friend Thomas Coutts to send all correspondence to her. But when Georgiana fell ill and a promised payment was not made, Thomas Coutts wrote to Harriet directly. The letter came as a harsh reminder of the true state of her affairs, a *coup de foudre,* according to Georgiana, that pitched Harriet into such hysterical despair that there were fears she would suffer a further serious relapse. So concerned was Georgiana for her sister's well-being that she wrote from her sickbed, begging Coutts's forbearance. "I have always told you that what I did for my sister, the trouble, anxiety and pain I suffered on her account was to save her the pain I knew to be destructive."[4]

Bessborough, meanwhile, wrote eagerly to Ireland for news, worried that the political mayhem would worsen his problems. The news, when it came, was not as dire as he had feared. "Notwithstanding that rebellion has openly broke out and some hard fought battles have taken place within a few miles of your Lordship's estate in this country . . . in general Bessborough and the whole Barony of Iverk have remained quiet. There are two reasons my Lord to be assigned for this. The one is the industrious and peaceable disposition of the inhabitants and the other is the uncommon exertions of the yeoman cavalry . . . who by un-remitting patrols both by night and by day, kept strangers and rebel parties from entering the barony and contaminating the minds of the people . . ."[5] wrote his steward William Shane. But keeping such an ef-fective force created additional expenses that Bessborough could ill af-ford. "The corps have been acting these two years without pay," Shane went on to remind him, pointing out that on a recent assault on Wex-ford the rebel forces had been within four miles of Bessborough House and that if he "should think proper to come forward with some liberal offer of accommodation and support . . . it would add to that high re-spectability and esteem in which the Ponsonby family have always been held in this kingdom."

Frustrations over money sparked Bessborough's temper as they had in the past, and his frequent bouts of ill humor, coupled with Harriet's burgeoning affair with Granville, had all served to help Harriet detach herself mentally from her husband. He was someone to be tolerated, obeyed, and manipulated if possible, but with whom she had little in common and barely communicated. "We come to town tomorrow," she writes typically to Granville. "I have known it only within this half hour, so could not tell you yesterday, when he rather gave me to under-stand we should stay here a month."[6] Here and elsewhere, we sense Harriet's frustration at her inability to alter or influence his decisions. Another glimpse of Bessborough's failings comes in a letter from Har-riet's friend Lady Anne Hatton. "I was too cross to go to town today. Lord Bessborough puts me quite out of temper," she told Granville. "I have no idea of any man's being so selfish as to wish so ardently to sac-rifice everything to his own convenience."[7]

During the time Harriet and Bessborough spent together in a cliff-top villa in Margate, there were further signs of strain. Harriet rode, played chess, and sang "from morning till night, and almost from night till morning"[8] with friends who were also on holiday in the town, leav-ing Bessborough free to go out driving his carriage and sketching. But one night, after an evening out, he drove Harriet and Caro home in a curricle, lost his way in the dark, drove off the road, then flew into a temper with Harriet and Caro for becoming fearful. Minutes later the horses panicked and Bessborough was forced to halt the vehicle and

196 ☞ *Janet Gleeson*

hand the reins to Harriet while he tried to calm them. Squinting through the gloom, Harriet saw why the horses had taken fright: the carriage was teetering on the edge of a deep chalk pit. A few feet farther and they would plunge into the abyss. In the midst of this crisis Caro slipped, unnoticed, out of the carriage and ran back to town to summon help. The misadventure became the subject of gossip in the town and was soon reported in *The Times,* although, interestingly, to spare the blushes of such prominent visitors, there was no mention of Lord Bessborough's involvement.

There were moments of rapprochement but they were fleeting. Tellingly, when Bessborough fell ill and showed his reliance on Harriet, speaking kindly instead of ordering her about, Harriet's sympathies were roused. "[He was] very good natured to me, [he] paid me a great compliment this evening, for he told me I took off half the pain and all the *desagrement* by my attention to him, and that he almost thought it worth while to be ill to be so well nursed,"[9] she told Granville after nursing her husband through a bout of illness.

How much did Bessborough notice or care about the friendship between Harriet and the dashing Granville? Late nights at the tables, crowded dinners, long shooting parties, keeping debtors at bay: such preoccupations did not leave much opportunity to watch Harriet closely, and his failure to remark Georgiana's pregnancy six years earlier shows that he was never an observant man. If he ever questioned the friendship, Granville's distance—after his spells abroad and a brief stay in London he returned to his regiment in Plymouth—probably helped to allay any doubt. Harriet had further disguised his importance in her life with an abundance of other male admirers, whom she kept at arm's length. In a teasing verse she wrote to Granville she attests:

> Tho' Sheridan with treacherous art
> Should strive t'ensnare my foolish heart,
> Tho' William Lamb in prose and verse
> His growing passion should rehearse,
> Tho' Rob Adair with tearful eyes
> Should whisper forth his amorous sighs
> And Hamilton caresses proffer

From thinking I accept his offer,
Tho' Sol himself my faith should prove . . .

The verse prefaces a letter in which Harriet continues: "Pray remember that all these lovers of mine are very good for poetick fiction
but do not exist in sober prose." Nevertheless she adds: "Pray in the
next list of lovers you write me add the Prince de Poix, *il y a de quoi se van-
ter de cette conquete là,** his praises of me (to my face) are so extravagantly
ridiculous that if they did not distress they would amuse me."[10]

Certainly Harriet had learned from her previous affairs. She was
unfailingly discreet in public; private meetings took place without her
husband's knowledge, with close friends such as Lady Holland† and
Georgiana providing alibis. Intimate correspondence was sent secretly
through friends and trusted messengers and Bessborough remained
unaware of the constant flow of letters. "I walked to Cavendish Square
this morning with your letter. They were just going out of town but to
return tomorrow and I was promised an answer when she came back so
hope next post to send one,"[11] wrote Harriet's friend Lady Elizabeth
Monck to Granville of a typical arrangement.

When Granville did openly visit Harriet, her companion Lady Anne
Hatton provided a convenient cover. Anne was an attractive and flirtatious Irish widow—or, as Lady Holland put it in her journal: "frol-
icsome . . . bewitched, very pretty, very foolish, and very debauched."
Harriet trustingly encouraged Anne's affection for Granville, often
claiming her friend was as fond of Granville as she was herself, presumably in order to disguise the reason for Granville's visits. Perhaps
she would have been less happy to encourage their closeness had she
known of the openly inviting letters, sometimes in Devonshire
House patois, that Anne wrote to him. "[I] know not how to fill up
the whole day without seeing you—I hope in God you will not stay
longer than you at first thought,"[12] Anne wrote on one occasion, and
on another: "I wonder you can suspect me of feeling that passion for

---

* There's something to brag about in this conquest.
† Elizabeth Webster married Lord Holland in 1797, two days after her divorce from Sir
  Geoffrey.

any one on this side of the water, you are all in life to me [and you] know it."[13]

The semblance of marital harmony was shored up by extraneous distraction. Harriet and Bessborough were living through momentous events, against which family intrigues and financial distress sometimes paled into insignificance. In October, when Harriet returned to Roehampton, she breakfasted with her brother, who "amused me very much"[14] by relating details of Nelson's victory at the Battle of the Nile, which had taken place on August 1. Nelson had captured eight ships of the line, and the French Admiral's ship *L'Orient* had been blown up in the action, along with her commander and most of her crew. Confirmation of this decisive victory had taken nearly two months to reach England and caused a surge of patriotism throughout the nation. "Our seamen are glorious people, it must be owned and I am delighted at every proof of it," Harriet wrote, wishing she was in London to see the celebrations. Even in Roehampton there was "such a *tintamarre* . . . with bells and squibs and bonfires, that . . . one cannot hear oneself speak."[15]

At Margate, next summer, evidence of war was stark and unavoidable. The Prince of Wales rode into town to review his troops, who were due to embark for Holland. The sight of soldiers setting off for war moved Harriet profoundly. "I cannot tell you the anxiety I feel for our poor soldiers. It makes me miserable to see them go."[16] Women wept on the dockside as they bade farewell to their sons and husbands. Harriet imagined how she would feel if John or Granville were to embark. She had witnessed a woman with two young children who had been desperate to board the ship with her husband (only a few women were allowed to accompany their men; lots were drawn for the places) but had been refused consent. The woman had waited until the transport rounded the pier, then thrown one child to her husband and jumped aboard herself, clutching the second child to her breast. The officer in charge had been so moved that she had eventually been granted permission to stay.

AWAY FROM SUCH poignant scenes, the reality of Harriet's life was increasingly fraught. Income from Ireland continued to dwindle as debts rose, and she and Bessborough had to face an unpalatable truth: they teetered on the brink of bankruptcy. Unless dramatic changes were made, their estates and livelihood would all be lost. Few understood the full extent of the predicament. Lady Spencer naively believed that a few small economies were all that was required. "I can only wish you would do everything possible to curtail your expenses—would it not be possible to fix one or if necessary two days in every week for giving dinners, this when known would make it far easier and less expensive . . . I am sure the comfort of your lives depends so much upon some plan of this kind till you have once got clear of debts, that I am most anxious to recommend anything that can contribute to your spending less,"[17] she blithely advised. Harriet hated to come under her mother's scrutiny; the subject of money was one that easily distressed her, and rather than explain the true gravity of the situation she found it easier to fob her mother off with false assurances. "You gave me much pleasure by saying your affairs were a better aspect. God grant you may be enabled to settle them so as to live considerably within your income," wrote a temporarily deceived Lady Spencer.[18]

Even with Granville, Harriet rarely discussed her financial problems; the only signs of her distress are her sporadic exhortations to him to beware of overspending and gambling; he too had developed a fatal fondness for games of chance and for living beyond his means. "Pray . . . let me know that you have not been drawn in to play any more. I know you could not help it the other night; but try to avoid beginning. Is it *necessary* that you should always go to Brooks's?"[19] Then, again, after another stern warning, "I always speak with more *aigreur* [bitterness] on this subject, from sad, sad experience, and dreading for you what I have suffered myself."[20]

Only the closest and most sympathetic of family and friends knew the full extent of the Bessborough debts. Bessborough himself was too ashamed to discuss matters openly with his family; too many of them had lent him money against promises that he had failed to keep. Eventually, with bankruptcy threatening, he must have told Harriet to find a means of resolving matters. Harriet, in desperation, spoke to the Hollands, imploring them for assistance in making proper arrangements to pay off the debts. When Lord Holland responded sympathetically, Bessborough himself became involved. "You have been acquainted I understand from Lady Bessborough with the deranged state of my affairs and the resolution I had taken to put them in order, in whatever way my friends approved,"[21] he wrote weakly to Lord Holland when the basic framework of how the accounts could be reconciled had been settled.

The idea was that Harriet and Bessborough should move out of the houses in Roehampton and London, rent the properties if they could, or at least dismiss their staff to reduce expenses, then live at Hardwick, one of the Duke of Devonshire's properties, for a year. This, according to Georgiana, would leave them "an income clear of all expense of £4,500 [£270,000] which they might there almost save."[22] Meanwhile, with the help of Heaton, the Duke of Devonshire's agent, a trust would be established into which Lord Holland, the duke, Harriet's brother, George, Lord Frederick Cavendish, and Lord Fitzwilliam would invest. The trust would take over all the outstanding debts against a claim on the Bessborough family property, until rent gradually repaid the debt. The final reckoning showed that the family assets—property, works of art, and annual rents—amounted to £105,000 (£6.3 million today), while debts amounted to £101,000 (£6.06 million).

Bessborough struggled to reconcile himself to the terms of the settlement, stipulating that the London and Roehampton houses would not be sold until John came of age and was given the opportunity to decide whether to retain them and the debts or sell. He also insisted that only as many pictures and works of art would be sold as would raise £5,000. Even when Holland agreed to this, Bessborough was often uncooperative, and bitter arguments frequently erupted. "Alas they have all quarrelled. Heaton refused to undertake it on a supposed want of confidence in him [Lord Bessborough] and Lord Bessbrough will not sign without knowing what he is to attend,"[23] wrote Georgiana worriedly to her brother after one such altercation. Eventually the relationship between Heaton and Bessborough became unworkable and, probably at Holland's suggestion, a new "man of business," Mr. Townley, was drafted in.

The disturbing financial situation dragged on, lowering Harriet's spirits, coloring her view of the world around her. Pitt had now decided to protect Ireland from French invasion by reuniting the country with England after seventeen years of independence. In return he offered the promise of Catholic emancipation and a lifting of trade restrictions. In Ireland the move was widely opposed, and the government passed George Ponsonby's resolution objecting to the surrender of independence. Granville had initially intended to speak in the House of Commons for unification, but Harriet warned him against such a move in view of opposition from members of Ireland's establishment. "Your people have certainly managed very ill there. Not that I believe that corruption and bribery were wanting; there was as much as you could wish . . . and indeed, my dear G, let the end be ever so good, the means is so infamous that it ought never to be tried. But the misfortune is, your people in Ireland committed the fault, and bungled it so that it was of no use, which was joining folly to corruption. I find I am writing you as grave a discussion on politicks as if it was my trade; but I am in a fever at the possible chance of your speaking . . ."[24]

The authority with which her views are expressed reflects her altered mood. She still paid lip service to convention, claiming to enjoy playing a submissive role, but now, if she felt so inclined, she flouted Granville's disapproval, sometimes forgetting to tread the delicate path between tact and honesty. Differences of opinion over a woman's right to play a political role were often a cause of strain in their relationship. Usually she wrapped her criticisms in humor to make them more palatable, but there was sometimes a note of bitterness beneath the jest. During the spring election, when Granville stood for the contested county seat in Stafford, she learned that several glamorous females were canvassing on his behalf. Immediately she took him to task for his earlier dismissive attitude toward women who involved themselves in politics:

> So your ladies assist you in canvassing? I thought, my dear G, you were one of the people who thought my sister and my canvassing even for our brother, certainly for Mr. Fox, so scandalous a thing that it never could be forgot or forgiven. How I have heard you expatiate on the subject, and exclaim at the impropriety and indelicacy both of our conduct and the people who could suffer us to do so horrible a thing! Yet, you see, in election fervour you can take up with the same means you were so shocked at in others. This is only a little lesson of candour in the future . . . I suppose you are, of course, in love with Lady Lawley. How can it be otherwise when she

happens to be very beautiful, everything that is amiable, and canvassing for one?[25]

Although the tone of this letter is lighthearted, one senses that Harriet's sensitivity does not merely concern politics, but Granville's attentions to other women. Yet in her heart of hearts none of this came as a surprise. Drawn to women as keenly as they were attracted to him, Granville was an inconstant lover. Even before their affair began, his eye had often strayed and Harriet was aware that, having allowed him to conquer her heart and enter her bed, his attention would inevitably roam. Yet she knew that tantrums and tears were not the way to keep him, and therefore quelled her tendency for emotional outbursts. Instead, whenever another woman threatened she teased him and returned to the role of a sisterly confidante, inviting him to discuss his flirtations with candor rather than conceal them. He might conduct brief liaisons with other women, she told herself, but she would be the sole possessor of his confidence.

She also set about making herself indispensable to him, promoting his career, despite their political differences. Thus when Granville found himself fighting the contested election at Stafford, Harriet begged Sheridan to secure an aide to help on Granville's canvass. Sheridan agreed, laughing at the irony of helping a member of the opposition as well as the lover of the woman he still adored. "Dear Traitress," he wrote to her, "the moment Fosbrook [the aide] mentioned the matter to me I desired him to do every possible thing that Lord Granville wished. I do not care about the opposing man's politics."[26]

Harriet also played mercilessly on Granville's jealousy toward her, frequently reminding him that he was not her sole admirer: others were eager for her favor. Sheridan was once again a constant presence. Despite being happily remarried to Esther Ogle (Hecca), the daughter of the Dean of Winchester and twenty-four years his junior, whom he had met at Devonshire House, he remained half in love with Harriet. She felt little physical attraction for him; he had begun drinking too much and his looks were fading, but when his mind sparkled he still charmed her with his insight into political developments and amused her when she was cast down. For his part Sheridan, unscrupulous as ever, played unsparingly on Harriet's insecurity over Granville, leading her into awkward situations whenever he felt so inclined. She wrote of an evening spent in Sheridan's company:

> He was very pleasant, but—it was not you, and the seeing anybody only increased my regrets, which I suppose were pretty visible, for every five minutes he kept saying how I am wasting all my efforts to entertain you, while you are grieving that you cannot change me into Ld. Levison. You would not be so grim if he was beaming on you. At length, as I thought he was preparing to pass the night as well as the evening with me, and as he began some fine speeches I did not quite approve of, I ordered my chair, to get rid of him. This did not succeed, for . . . he followed me about . . . and home again. But luckily, I got in time enough to order every one to be denied, and ran up stairs, while I heard him expostulating with the porter . . .[27]

The Prince of Wales, a friend since she was a debutante, also paid sporadic suit to her. She described a reconciliation after he had behaved improperly toward her. "Georgiana says I looked very cold and proudly at him . . . I never saw any one take such pains to discompose one's gravity. He told me I received him like a Sultana, and asked whether he might be permitted to kiss my hand, that he could not venture without leave, for that when he took hold of it I made it so stiff and looked so contemptuous that he thought I was going to slap his face."[28] Jack Townshend, her erstwhile lover, who had eloped with her cousin and caused such outrage among the family, was also devoted to her and caused her great embarrassment. "Jack still persecutes me," she told Granville; "do tell me what I can do to get rid of him. I do not like doing anything that could make my cousin uncomfortable or Lord B[essborough] angry."[29]

As the year drew to a close, Harriet looked forward to a new century with a sense of mounting apprehension. Two close friends receded from her life: Anne Hatton married the Earl of Abercorn, and Charles Beauclerk, the man who had been so in love with her in Naples, married Emily Ogilvie, daughter of the Duchess of Leinster. Meanwhile, her hold on Granville seemed less certain. He had decided to become more actively involved in the war effort and raise a battalion of volunteers to fight in Europe. Perhaps it was the threat of losing Granville to the war that spurred Harriet deliberately to take the most risky step of their affair, or perhaps fate intervened. Whatever the truth, Harriet entered the new century knowing that she was carrying Granville's child.

FOURTEEN

The Secret Child

1800

HARRIET WAS WELL AWARE of the implications of her predicament. She had witnessed the ordeals of Georgiana, Bess Foster, and Lady Holland, all of whom had become pregnant as a result of extramarital affairs. She had seen them endure the agony of discovery and separation from their children, not to mention the threat of scandal, divorce, and social ostracism. In addition, having undergone three years' separation from John and Frederick while she was abroad, she must have found the thought of further estrangement unbearable, and she determined to take every possible measure to avoid it.

Nevertheless, Harriet bowed to the conventions of the day. She knew that she would never be able to openly acknowledge herself as the mother of this illegitimate baby. The best she could hope for was to raise the child in secret, to arrange for its care somewhere that enabled her to maintain regular contact and, in the guise of benevolent godmother, supervise the child's education and entry into society. It was an uncertain path, the success of which depended upon Bessborough remaining in ignorance. Harriet's obsession with duping her husband leaves little doubt that the couple no longer shared a bed. There was presumably no way now to pretend that the baby she was expecting was his, and every reason to suppose that if he discovered her pregnancy he would divorce her.

Only a very few—Georgiana, Bess, Anne Hatton, and Georgiana's daughter Little G—were entrusted with the truth. Everyone else was kept in the dark. The caution with which Harriet had conducted her affair with Granville was now redoubled. All communications relating to her condition were swiftly destroyed, and thus, frustratingly, our knowledge of how she felt as the pregnancy progressed and the birth approached is scant. The few of her letters to Granville that remain speak of political affairs and election tactics, of mutual friends and of books—but never of the secret they shared.

Nor do we know how Granville felt. His political prospects had brightened with the dawning of the new century. In July he was appointed a Lord of the Treasury in Pitt's government, an important post marking him as a rising political star. At such a moment, if the news that he had fathered a child by one of the most notorious female supporters of the Whig opposition had broken, it would have done little to advance his prospects. Thus, he too was anxious to avoid scandal and was party to the subterfuge. Any of Harriet's letters he did not destroy were dealt with by later censors.

Harriet's most challenging task was to keep her mother in ignorance. Lady Spencer soon noticed that Harriet seemed less diligent than usual in corresponding, but presumed that this was due to ill health caused by the strain of her straitened circumstances. "I do not expect you to write more than dabs my dearest Harriet while your mind is so ill at ease," she reassured her. Having heard from Georgiana of the arguments between Bessborough, the duke, and his steward Heaton, she was terrified that if matters grew worse the trust would never be resolved. "Be assured no regulation you yourselves can make will be so efficacious as those done by a regular trust," Lady Spencer advised. Nevertheless, she was wary of rousing Bessborough's temper at such a delicate juncture and, much to Harriet's relief, thought it best to keep her distance rather than intervene. "Let me have a line as often as you can about your health. I do not offer to come up because I am confident I could be of no use, and should only perhaps add to your difficulties by urging strongly what others might disapprove,"[1] she wrote, tactfully skirting any direct reference to Bessborough's awkwardness.

As the time of the birth grew closer, Harriet's children were conveniently occupied away from their mother. John, Viscount Duncannon, was now eighteen, tall and pleasant-looking, with his mother's wide forehead and soulful eyes and his father's elongated jaw and aquiline nose. After Harrow he had entered Christ Church, Oxford, and that summer he was sent on his first visit abroad, to Germany—a far from easy undertaking given the war. Frederick, aged seventeen, was also otherwise engaged. He had joined the Prince of Wales's regiment at the prince's invitation, with the promise of his "being soon likely to get promotion." Harriet was "quite giddy" at the suddenness with which Frederick was enrolled, and at the thought of the dangers he might face. "What will become of him if there should be another odious expedition?"[2] she wondered. Caro, at fifteen, was a slightly built girl of elfin looks and unpredictable temperament. Few tutors or servants could cope with her sudden moods and tantrums, and at times even Lady Spencer's patience was tested. "Poor little soul—how difficult it is to know what to do with her—yet at times how sweet a creature she is,"[3] she confided to Georgiana that summer, when Caro was sent by Harriet to stay with her at St. Albans.

Harriet's most painful wrench came when Willy, aged thirteen, enrolled along with Bess's twelve-year-old son, Clifford,* as a midshipman in the navy. George Spencer had secured places for both boys under Lord St. Vincent and the pair left England in July. Lady Spencer, at first filled with misgivings at the thought of young Willy going to sea, wished he had entered the Church—another traditional career path for younger aristocratic sons. Gradually, however, she came around to the idea and began to see its benefits. "I hardly know a body of men happier or more respectable than our sea officers; your lovely boy's sweet disposition added to his natural spirit makes him particularly well qualified for this profession. He is not less under God's protection in the wildest storm or in the sharpest engagement than sauntering down St. James's street or lounging at a play or an opera and probably much safer from pernicious temptations."[4] Despite her mother's reassurances and the fact that "nothing ever equalled Ld. St. Vincent's kindness," Harriet was distraught at the thought of bidding her youngest child farewell, not knowing where his ship was bound. "Ld. St. V. calls it a secret expedition," she told Granville. "Is it to Holland do you think or further?"[5]

As summer drew on, London society followed the usual pattern,

---

* Clifford was the brother of Caro St. Jules; both children were illegitimate and fathered by the Duke of Devonshire.

drifting to their country estates or renting houses by the sea. Georgiana took a house at Bognor, in order to recover after a busy London season during which Little G, her eldest daughter, had made her social debut. Lady Spencer joined her, probably taking Caro too. Harriet, however, did not follow, instead keeping quietly to herself at Roehampton. We do not know Bessborough's whereabouts during this time. Perhaps he spent some time with Georgiana and his cousin the Duke of Devonshire at Bognor; or, given his financial difficulties, he may have occupied himself trying to thrash out some mutually agreeable settlement with the family trust in London. Of one thing we may be sure: wherever he was, there is no evidence that he ever became aware of his wife's advancing pregnancy.

How did Harriet manage to keep her secret safe and conceal the inevitable changes in her figure? There seems little doubt that the fashions of the time assisted—everyone, apart from the very youthful, tall, and slender, looked pregnant in the high-waisted styles of the day. As one wit declared in a poem published in 1801:

> *Both maids, wives and widows, you'd think were all wild*
> *And all look as if they were got with child;*
> *Neither balloons, nor turbans, or all fashions round,*
> *Will fit them unless they've a new body'd gown.*[6]

Harriet might further have disguised her pregnancy with artful half robes worn over the skirt of a dress, and with gathers, ruffles, and shawls. A full bosom was regarded as both fashionable and the height of beauty, and in order to wear plunging necklines women often used padding to enhance the size of their breasts. Harriet's weight had always fluctuated with her bouts of ill health, although in general as she aged she grew increasingly voluptuous; so even if Bessborough remarked any changes, he presumably thought nothing of them.

In late August Georgiana unexpectedly left her family at Bognor for a fortnight and rushed back to town. The reason given for her sudden departure was that Harriet had slipped and fallen on the stairs at Roehampton, and in the process had banged her head so severely that she had to take to her bed. It is impossible to be certain precisely what happened, but it seems likely from the details of Harriet's prolonged illness afterward that the story of the fall was true—heavily pregnant women are easily prone to such accidents—and the tumble may well have induced her labor. Despite her injury, the baby—a girl named Harriet Emma Arundel Stewart*—was safely delivered and swiftly handed over to a foster mother. We can only guess how Harriet felt as she endured her labor, knowing that she would never be able to enjoy her youngest child. Presumably, in contrast to her previous deliveries, which had all taken place in London, she was attended not by an eminent man midwife, but by a local woman and her loyal maidservant Sally.

Afterward Harriet consigned her baby to an unknown foster mother—she was an active patroness of several charitable houses helping women in the vicinity of Roehampton, and it may well have been to one of these that she initially entrusted Little Harriet. Although none of Harriet's correspondence regarding the child's care survives, there is evidence that she stayed in close contact throughout her early years. Surviving letters of a later date show that Harriet corresponded regularly with her daughter, writing long, informative, and affectionate letters, sending her books and presents, in much the same way she had kept in touch with John and Frederick while she was abroad in Italy. While resolved never to tell Little Harriet the truth of her parentage, she did not rein in the deep fondness she felt for her and freely expressed it in her letters. "Your affectionate wishes are not thrown away upon me—you do my dear love, contribute very much to my happiness and I love you most dearly,"[7] Harriet wrote on Little Harriet's thirteenth birthday, in one of the earliest of her letters to her youngest daughter that survives. Even after Harriet's death, the importance of guarding the secret outweighed private emotions. "You will feel it my dearest child and so do we as the loss of a most kind and affectionate friend,"[8] wrote Little Harriet's adoptive mother, who knew the truth but never divulged it.

Granville was kept closely informed of his daughter's progress; however, again, in keeping with the need for secrecy, nearly all references to her were destroyed then or by subsequent members of the family. Among the few references that remain from Little Harriet's

---

* The name Stewart came from Granville's mother, Lady Stafford. Harriet Arundel Stewart was usually called "Little Harriet," and to avoid confusion is always so called here.

childhood years, one concerns a locket for which Harriet asks Granville for a lock of hair. Another, more revealing remark is contained in a letter written by Harriet's flirtatious friend Lady Anne Hatton (now Lady Abercorn): "Your great niece [Little Harriet] is perfectly well I hear but I never see her as Mama keeps her for her own and Papa's inspection. She concludes I suppose he may be tempted to increase the kind and as she seems to be the only one of his loves capable, I think he ought—for it is a precious breed."[9] This implies that Harriet was far from unhappy to have borne Granville's child, and was even anxious for another, perhaps feeling that whatever happened in the future, bearing Granville's children gave her a permanent part of him that none of his other female admirers enjoyed. Anne's comments, however, should be balanced against her jealousy of Harriet, especially where Granville was concerned. She had always felt drawn to him and was undoubtedly irked by his failure to respond to her overtures. "I know *she* writes very often and that whilst you hear from *her* my letters are quite *useless*,"[10] she once stormed.

In the immediate aftermath of Little Harriet's birth, though, the thought of more children was far from anyone's mind. Harriet failed to recover from her head injury. Georgiana visited her sister every day and wrote to Lady Spencer to keep her abreast of Harriet's illness, playing down the gravity of Harriet's symptoms in order to prevent her mother from rushing to Roehampton and discovering the truth. "My sister slept so well the night before last I couldn't help hoping that an evident change has taken place—she has eat partridges for the last two days and I carry her grapes and strawberries from hence daily,"[11] wrote Georgiana blithely from Chiswick. But the truth was that Harriet was far from better; her head injury had not healed, and a few days later she terrified Georgiana by slipping into unconsciousness. At Georgiana's insistence she was rushed to London in order urgently to seek specialist medical opinion.

"I was brought from the carriage *lifeless* and poor Federico [her manservant] stormed and raved like a mad man," Harriet later told Granville.[12] Five eminent doctors were summoned, including the royal physician Sir Walter Farquhar. None knew what had caused Harriet's symptoms, but her head was shaved in preparation for a possible brain operation. Such procedures were fraught with risk, undertaken without antiseptics and only the most rudimentary of anesthetics. Harriet was terrified, knowing she might not survive, and Georgiana, remembering her own ordeals with her eye, became equally distraught. "O my G, write me what you know and how you think your dear M[other] and poor dear aunt are in health, and how your aunt bears all this,"[13] wrote a worried Bess to Little G, who had come to Devonshire House to offer her mother much-needed support. Eventually, to everyone's relief, the doctors decided Harriet's illness was owing to the violence of the fall "and the weak state I am in" but that an operation was unnecessary. Even so, Harriet suffered haunting nightmares. "Mr. Home [was] standing over me with the instrument to open my head. I waked quite cold and trembling. He says he must come and see me very often and take of the impression of horror I seem to have of him,"[14] she later recounted.

Georgiana too remained deeply upset by her sister's illness, and by the vulnerability of her situation, which must have reawakened her own memories of secretly giving birth to Charles Grey's daughter Eliza Courtenay. Granville's reputation as a ladies' man had long been a subject for general mirth, but Little Harriet's arrival altered Georgiana's view. "I might seriously suppose you to be really the Love of My Love. In short I am miserable, for I have caused a person pain [Harriet] without meaning it . . . Remember then . . . that I forbid your flirtation . . ."[15] Georgiana wrote sternly to him apropos a misunderstanding regarding Harriet and another of his many female admirers.

It was nearly two months before Harriet was well enough to leave her bed and could travel with Bessborough to join her sister and mother and a large house party at Chatsworth. The party consisted of twenty-three guests, including Lord Moira, a distinguished soldier and Whig politician and confidant of the Prince of Wales; John Townshend and his wife; the politician James Hare; the family of the late Mme. de Polignac, one of the members of Marie Antoinette's court who had escaped to Switzerland in the Revolution; and Granville's friend Lord Morpeth, who was by now paying serious suit to Little G.

Having stayed in London while Harriet was in the worst throes of illness, Granville too traveled north to his family home at Trentham, and from there made a visit to Chatsworth, where he was reunited with Harriet. As soon as he left the party, Harriet became a focus for

Townshend's unwelcome advances. "We had a long set to, in which he prosed sadly about his love for me ever since I was fourteen, and that I always scorned him. Then a violent attack on you [Granville], chiefly, I think for being handsome . . . He flew into a violent passion, and began protesting and vowing . . . he was so violent he frightened me, and while he was beating his head and acting a fit of despair . . . I ran into Sally's room, and remained there till he went away."[16] The irony, as Harriet saw it, was that Townshend had also been making advances to another relative, Mrs. Spencer, while declaring himself insanely jealous if his wife so much as spoke to anybody else.

Townshend's unpredictable behavior was soon eclipsed by family rejoicing when Morpeth proposed to Little G. Meanwhile, Harriet flippantly told Granville that Georgiana's youngest daughter, fifteen-year-old Harryo, also fancied herself in love—with him. "[She] cries after you and wants a horse to ride after you and fetch you back. But, oh *disgrazia*! She took Lord Ossulton for you this evening at dessert."[17] Such were the everyday intrigues and dramas of the grand country-house party.

FIFTEEN

Peace and Love
1801 - 1802

I LONG FOR YOUR COMING and to tell you fifty thousand anecdotes," wrote Harriet to Bess, apropos a sudden political eruption
that had captivated her attention. Ireland had once more come to
dominate British politics. Pitt had implemented the Act of Union in
1800, reuniting Great Britain and Ireland in the interest of security,
with the intention of also giving Irish Catholics full emancipation—
the right to vote. But the king had other ideas: to him the admission of
Catholics to public office clashed irreconcilably with his role as up-
holder of the established Church. He furiously made known his determination to oppose Pitt. "I will tell you, that I shall look on every man
as my personal enemy who proposes that question to me."[1] After seventeen years' premiership, at the age of forty-one Pitt thus found himself at an impasse and tendered his resignation. The king, infuriated
but resolute, accepted on February 5, 1801, turning to Addington, a
friend and ally of Pitt's, to form a new administration.

Pitt did not expect his supporters to follow him by resigning. Nevertheless, several leading members of the government, including
those in charge of directing the war—Harriet's brother, George
Spencer, Lords Grenville and Dundas—did so, prompting Sheridan
to declare stingingly that "when the crew of a vessel was preparing for
action, it was usual to clear the decks by throwing overboard the lum-
ber, but he never heard of such a manoeuvre as that of throwing their
great guns overboard."[2] Amid this tumult George III became mentally overwrought and was once more stricken by his old malady. Some
said his illness was less severe than before—merely a slight attack of

"whimsy"—although Lady Holland and most opposition supporters declared him "as mad as the winds." As in the previous crisis, messengers were sent galloping off to recall Fox, amid rumblings about the introduction of a regency. Meanwhile Pitt, terrified that Fox's alliance with the Prince of Wales would finally help him to seize power, decided to delay his departure.

The king's illness continued throughout February, but in early March he rallied unexpectedly, once more foiling Fox and the prince's hopes. George III returned to the political fray, declaring that it was worries over the question of Catholic emancipation and Pitt's behavior that had caused his sudden decline. In response, the anguished Pitt promised never to raise the subject again in the king's lifetime, although he was unwavering in his decision to leave office.

To Granville the news of Pitt's resignation just as his prospects had begun to shine came as a hammer blow. "A more calamitous event to the country is about to take place than all the victories of the French; I mean the resignation of Pitt," he told his mother. Pitt had expressed his support for Addington's administration but Granville felt unable to serve an inferior leader. "Pitt is the object of my political idolatry and it is impossible to have any opinion of any Government of which he is not at the head," he declared as he prepared to leave the Treasury.[3] Ever the dutiful son, however, he asked his parents' permission before tendering his resignation. The Staffords' initial response came by return; they were "more dismayed, hurt and astonished than words can express" by the news of Pitt's resignation, and, despite their loyalty to the king, had "no doubt of your judging and acting right."[4]

Alongside these unfolding crises the Bessborough financial problems were at last inching to their conclusion. In February Harriet traveled to Christie's and watched the hammer fall on works of art by Kneller, Van Dyck, Schalken, Giordano, Dürer, Poussin, Raphael, and Liotard—a friend of the Second Earl, with whom he had traveled to Turkey. The most expensive painting, a port scene by Claude, fetched a mere £300—the modern equivalent of only £18,000 (today such a work would fetch many millions). In April a further sale was held; Harriet glibly told Granville "the marbles at Roe[hampton] were sold yesterday—very well I think for between £4,000 and £5,000 and we have kept back several that we wanted besides."[5] There is little hint in this account of distress at losing such family heirlooms, but for a woman of refined taste such as Harriet, let alone Bessborough, who had grown up surrounded by these works of art, the pain of seeing family treasures dispersed must have been considerable.

As soon as the deeds for the trust were finalized, Harriet packed up a few of her most precious belongings and set out for Hardwick Hall,* the Duke of Devonshire's house near Chesterfield in Derbyshire, which was built for his ancestor Bess of Hardwick. For the foreseeable future Harriet and Bessborough planned to spend as little time as possible at Roehampton or Cavendish Square in order to curtail expenses. The move came as a distressing wrench. Whereas Roehampton was light and elegant, with rooms that were ideally suited for family life and entertaining, Hardwick, as Harriet saw it, was a sprawling, dingy edifice of endless corridors and staircases, dark hangings, and rattling windows. There were no books or musical instruments and it would take several weeks before the possessions Harriet dispatched from Roehampton were unpacked. "If it was not for chess and one volume of La Harpe's correspondence we should all die,"[6] she grumbled after one evening bereft of the usual diversions. But it was not the absence of home comforts that above all depressed her, but the difficulty of seeing Granville. "My despair is merely founded on not seeing you, for I do not join in the cry against poor Hardwick. I delight in its gloom, its black velvet furniture, casements grown over with ivy . . . and could live here happy and contented were you to be one of its inhabitants; but to be shut up in a dismal prison when I might be with you . . . is a situation as provokingly tantalising as imagination can suggest."

She was frustrated too at being away from London just as Addington's government made faltering steps toward agreeing to peace with France. The Whig MP James Hare had written Bess a detailed account of the debate; she passed it on to Harriet, who pored over every detail and then recounted it to Granville—despite the fact that he had witnessed the debate. "Pitt spoke eloquently as he always does, but was much less attended to than usual, and I fancy will soon find . . . that the gift of speech without the gift of place is of little value as to weight or

---

* Hardwick Hall dates from the late sixteenth century. Now administered by the National Trust, it is regarded as one of the greatest surviving Elizabethan houses.

persuasion."[7] Pitt supported Addington's move for peace, believing that Britain had less to gain from prolonging a costly war than from trying to hold on to the territories she had gained. Granville, however, thought the terms made too many concessions to France and, speaking in the house, declared the agreement was "nothing more than a naval armistice, of which all the advantage is in favour of France."[8] His speech once more marked him out as a rising star, although he was widely accused of inconsistency when, after criticizing the proposed treaty, he voted for it, claiming as he did so to reflect his constituents' desire for peace.

Harriet too favored peace, and although she realized that Fox was no longer a suitable candidate to lead the country, like Granville she had little faith in the new administration. "I think you must allow that either justly or unjustly Mr. Pitt has lost a great deal of his popularity, and with all my love and admiration for Mr. Fox, I should not for his sake wish him to be Minister. But it does seem an extraordinary circumstance, with two such men in the country and with many others of great abilities on both sides, to pick out the poor little negative administration they have got now."[9] But as the weeks passed, her fascination with the situation turned to concern for Granville's future career. Pitt's motives in supporting and directing Addington seemed far from transparent, and she fretted that in continuing to offer Pitt support Granville might damage his prospects. "Even you must allow that there has been something very odd and underhand from the beginning. The confidential friends of an open, frank-minded man could not have been in doubt for a moment as to what his real sentiments and intentions were . . . you cannot think how uneasy I feel sometimes as to what your future political conduct is to be—not from any doubt of your judgement, but from the extreme difficulties the strange conduct of your leader has thrown in your way . . ."[10]

Harriet had now left the gloom of Hardwick to travel north to Chatsworth, where she joined another large group of family and friends for Christmas and the New Year. Granville visited her there briefly, and pleased his mother by telling her that he had befriended Lady Spencer, who was also a guest. By now Lady Stafford had resigned herself to Harriet's presence in Granville's life. We do not know what, if anything, other than the passage of time (it was nearly eight years since their first meeting in Italy) and Granville's adamant refusal to give up Harriet, had brought about her change of heart. It seems unlikely that Lady Stafford had been told of Little Harriet's secret birth. Perhaps, though, she had observed how Harriet guided Granville in his political career, or perhaps Harriet's absence from London encouraged her to hope that Granville would soon find a more suitable female companion and marry. Certainly she welcomed the presence of Lady Spencer, realizing she would have a moderating effect on the excesses for which Harriet and Georgiana were notorious. "I am quite glad that she is at Chatsworth; I think she will do you all good. She, somehow or another, has the art of leading, drawing or seducing people into right ways. I wish she would determine to be your guide and counsellor . . . I had an affection for her children, too, when they were very young, and it is not worn away."[11]

To Harriet, Granville's stay seemed all too brief, and she was distraught when he took his leave of her. "How I miss you every hour! Every moment makes me feel your loss more."[12] As if mirroring her bleak mood, the weather at Chatsworth turned harsh, with heavy falls of snow and biting frosts. Harriet watched her fellow guests skating on the canal pond, and sledging and go-carting on the snowy slopes behind the house, sometimes with dangerous results—John "near killed Lord B[essborough]" by pushing him in a chair on the ice, turning too sharply, and tipping him out. Bad weather always undermined her strength and she could not prevent herself from fretting over the temptations that might draw Granville in her absence. "Do not break your neck skating or hunting, do not drink and do not flirt," she implored. Her passion for Granville had been difficult to disguise during his stay and, much to her annoyance, had been remarked by Jules de Polignac. "Think of that fool Jules saying to me today, *Allons donc ne soyez pas si triste il reviendra.*"*[13]

The harsh weather continued well into January, making Harriet's health and spirits so low that she retreated to her room. Letters from Granville became her lifeline, but the needy tone in which she wrote to him suggests it was not only illness that depressed her. Distanced from Granville, she knew it might be months before she saw him again, and

---

* Come now, don't be so sad, he will return.

her vulnerability became all too plain. "Remember that if ever my letters are the least pleasure to you, yours are to me ten thousand times more delightful; they are a proof to me that you do not forget me, that you like confiding in me, that I am present to your thoughts; in short, they give me life and spirits, which both very often seem sinking from me when I am ill and away from you, and only left to my own sad thoughts."[14]

Even when she managed to muster enough strength to return to the bustle of Chatsworth life, there is often a sense that she looked on from a distance, observing every detail only to relate it later to Granville. Fellow guests amused her, and she chatted and bewitched them, then used them as entertaining subject matter for her letters. For her heart was always elsewhere—with Granville. Thus, with a note of typical detachment she described one winter's afternoon at Chatsworth:

Sol and Jules playing at chess, G. and John talking on the couch, Augustus asleep in the corner, Mr. Hare in the great chair reading Dryden and discussing on Alexander's Feast, Bess by the fire reading Chenier, Robinson on the other side of the table grumbling . . . I am writing to you near the fire, and at times disputing with the whole room in turn. The rest of the family are variously disposed of: my sister shut up with Gurdon; the Duke tho' well not up (at past five); Ld. B[essborough] in his room, and Frederick hard at Euclid . . .[15]

Bessborough was in his room because he had been taken ill with gout, delaying the longed-for moment he had promised Harriet—a brief visit to London. Despite her frustration, as in the past, seeing him ill roused her sympathies. One night while he was confined to bed, a severe storm struck; the gales brought down several trees and a torrential downpour flooded the ground-floor rooms. Harriet rose from her bed, worried that Bessborough's room might be exposed to the inclement weather, only to discover a back staircase on fire. She roused the servants—fortunately before any serious damage was done—and gave up her room to Bessborough, moving in with Sally to make him more comfortable. The next day, the party dined in the music room since the dining room and drawing room were awash with flood water and the rooms below full of smoke. "I could scarcely breathe for fright," she wrote of the moment she discovered the fire, "but comforted myself all the time with thinking that if you could see me you would not accuse me, as you usually do, of giving way to foolish fears and fine lady airs, which always affronts me extremely, as I think I never do."[16] No matter the danger or crisis, Granville was never far from Harriet's thoughts.

BY THE END of February Bessborough was well enough to travel to London. Harriet and he arrived to find the city in a euphoric mood. After ten years of hostilities the Treaty of Amiens, finalizing peace with France, was signed at last in March 1802. Old friends from Paris who had settled in London to escape persecution lingered on, reluctant to leave, while English aristocrats made plans to journey to Paris, eager to witness the new regime firsthand and, above all, to glimpse Napoleon. Harriet's views on the treaty were wryly perceptive. "It seems very odd that the very men who loaded Bonaparte with every epithet of abuse should be the first to trust him in the unqualified manner they seem to have done."[17] The peace would last barely more than a year.

Such presentiments of doom did not prevent her plunging into the whirl of London life, but everywhere she went Granville's presence haunted her. At visits to the opera, theater, or assemblies she chatted with old friends or conversed with famous French visitors, but never failed to remark from the corner of her eye any of Granville's other lady friends who chanced to be present.

Sheridan, jealous as ever of her affection, added to her torment, teasing her by telling her "that he knew such things of you, could give me such incontrovertible proofs of your falsehood and not only falsehood but treachery to me, that if I had one grain of pride or spirit left I should fly you."[18] Sheridan's increasingly obsessive and frequently unkind behavior may have been partly due to his own marital difficulties, or to the fact that he was drinking too much and heavily in debt. His unpredictable onslaughts continued whenever he and Harriet met, making her frightened and increasingly anxious to avoid him. "There was a time when I was not afraid of him; he amused me and I could laugh at his manner . . . but now I feel the justice of some of his attacks,"[19] she confessed. Among the wider Devonshire House circle Sheridan's erratic behavior was losing him friends and political support.

"Sheridan clouds his talents by a mean and pitiful love of trick and by way [of] influence, his want of truth, his jealousy of Fox, and his want of integrity about money have really so lowered him in the estimation of men that had he come in for Westminster or did he try to succeed Fox as the leader of opposition he could not command one follower worth reckoning upon,"[20] wrote Bess in her journal.

One summer evening when Bessborough was away Harriet came home early, as ever dreaming ruefully of Granville, "regretting that I had nothing to expect...no chance of hearing your step upon the stair."[21] Suddenly she heard a knock at the door and Sheridan's voice in the hall below. Harriet told Sally to say she was out, but Sheridan insisted that he would pace in front of the door until her return.

Where once Harriet recounted such incidents to Granville to arouse his jealousy, now her motive was different. She was filled with shame and regret that she had ever permitted herself to become ensnared by such a man and was confessing past folly rather than taunting him with her conquests. What had brought about this change of heart? Having recently celebrated her fortieth birthday, Harriet surveyed her past and felt profound misgiving at much that she recalled. She questioned the motives of her old lovers and felt mortified at her own actions. Now when men flirted and made advances toward her, there seemed something unbecoming in their courtship; that she was being mocked rather than genuinely admired. "I wonder how long Sheridan, Ld. John and Fitzpatrick will think it necessary to make love to me whenever we chance to meet, *cela ne sied ni a leur age ni au mien;** and if they mean it for flattery, it has quite the contrary effect, and troubles me more than the worst abuse could,"[22] she wrote. She had learned to differentiate between vanity, lust, and love, and no longer believed in their protestations. "Were they really in love with me they would dread offending me, and be easily silenced...but as probably with Fitzpatrick it is antiquated gallantry, in Lord J[ohn Townshend] madness, and in S[heridan] obstinacy."[23]

---

* It is not becoming to their age or mine.

Yet, tellingly, Harriet was unable to apply such objectivity to her affair with Granville. She knew his failings: he was interested in numerous other females, sparing in his compliments, and often critical or cool. She also acknowledged the fact that he would have to marry soon. Yet nothing dampened her adoration, nor her craving for his love: ". . . but really and truly do you look back with pleasure on the time we have spent together?" she wrote poignantly after a few rare words of kindness; "remember I look upon you as *truth* itself. What from others would appear to me mere words of course, from you I receive as the real sentiments and feelings of your heart, and as such they give me joy or pain."[24]

Maturity also tempered Harriet's view of the world around her. Although her fascination remained undimmed, generally she looked on with wry amusement. When Fox unexpectedly announced that he had married his mistress Mrs. Armistead—once a famous courtesan of the day—eight years earlier in secret she was amused at the angry response of many of his so-called friends. "The odd thing is that people who were shocked at the immorality of his having a mistress are still more so at that mistress having been his wife for so long."[25] Napoleon was another source of fascination, and she devoured every detail of his life. Alexandre de Calonne, the exiled French finance minister and an old friend, had told her that Napoleon "bathes every morning for an hour, during which time a man chose for that purpose translates the English papers to him . . . he devotes twelve hours to travail—that is: to being locked up in his room quite alone, where he forms new constructions, new laws, and . . . he issues out orders from thence written on little slips of paper . . . three hours he allows for meals and exercise, two for amusement, and six for sleep . . ."[26] Harriet's son Frederick had traveled to Paris with the Hollands for the summer and became an invaluable source of news of Napoleon. "Frederick says all the busts and pictures are like, but not very; that his countenance is much better, not near so stern, but has a good-natured expression; that he talks and laughs with the few he speaks at all to, and that his manner is remarkably simple and unaffected."[27]

WHEN LONDON SOCIETY dispersed for the summer, Harriet together with her sister and their children made a brief visit to the Melbournes' country house, Brocket Hall.* Lady Melbourne had long been a close friend of Georgiana's, but Harriet had never felt as warmly toward her, finding her too controlling, cynical, and hard-hearted. The Melbournes had six children: four boys—Peniston, William, Frederick, and George—and two girls, Emily and Harriet. Most of the children were rumored to be the product of Lady Melbourne's various love affairs, which included a brief liaison with the Prince of Wales and a long-standing affair with the Earl of Egremont.† William Lamb, Lady Melbourne's second child, was widely believed to have been fathered by Egremont. Tall and good-looking, enthralled by poetry and drama, yet with a noisy zest for life, he was twenty-two years old that summer when the Bessboroughs and Devonshires, including sixteen-year-old Caro, came to stay.

As a young man William had been fleetingly infatuated by Harriet; now, though, he found his attention drifting toward Caro. With her large, wide-set eyes, strawberry-blond curls, petite figure, and vivacious, unconventional yet artless charm, she was unlike any female he had met. For her part Caro was equally smitten by William's handsomeness, energy, and devotion to her. "They seem, I hear, mutually captivated. When the rest were at games, etc., William was in a corner, reading and explaining poetry to Caro . . . she is already as vain as a peacock about it,"[28] wrote Georgiana's daughter Harryo to her sister Little G, adding waspishly, "He did not captivate anybody else, for he does not look cooler or nicer than of old, and they say is grown very vociferous and boisterous." Harriet looked on with dismay, hoping it would be no more than a passing fancy; this was not an attachment she wished to encourage. Quite apart from her reservations about Lady Melbourne, as the second son William Lamb would not inherit his father's title; and, while she liked William well enough when he was alone, his rowdy and supercilious behavior when he was with his brothers did nothing to endear him to her.

After Brocket, Harriet, Georgiana, their children, and assorted oth-

---

* The house is situated twenty miles north of central London and was built for Lord Melbourne by the architect James Paine in the neoclassical style in 1760.
† Rumor had it that Lady Melbourne's affair with Egremont began after he bought her from a previous lover, Lord Coleraine, for £13,000, and that she shared in the fee.

ers moved on to Ramsgate, where they stayed in two adjacent houses. Harriet complained that there was little respite from the noise of the children and a nearby school. "If you were with me at this moment and many other hours in the day you would go mad. On one side I have a boarding school, where various instruments and voices are playing and solfeggeing so loud that it makes perfect discord; on the other side Harriet is practising on the harp with Mle. Menel, Corisande on the piano forte, Caroline St. Jules on the guitar and my Caro upstairs on the piano forte—all different music, all loud and all discordant. It requires great good temper (like mine) to bear it."[29]

Noise was not the only threat to her holiday tranquillity. The escapades with the opposite sex of her eldest son, John, Viscount Duncannon, also began to perturb her. Lady Jersey—one of the least popular of the Prince of Wales's mistresses—was also holidaying near by, and had picked John out as a possible husband for her pretty and flirtatious daughter Elizabeth Villiers. John was immediately flattered and responded warmly to Elizabeth's attention. Harriet was far from happy at the thought of her eldest son, who she claimed was too young and boyish to marry, becoming involved with the daughter of such an unscrupulous and ambitious woman as Lady Jersey. "It is of all things the match I should most dislike," she protested.

John was also showing amorous interest in his cousin Harryo, whom he had known all his life. In appearance Harryo was no match for the pretty Elizabeth Villiers, being slightly plump and round-faced ("I fear I shall never be rode or bathed into a beauty," she told her sister. "*Tant pis,* but there is no remedy"),[30] but she was warm, clever, funny, and perceptive. Harryo was flattered by John's attention, remarking that he "is desperately smitten with Lady Elizabeth Villers, but sticks to me here with an astonishing good grace." She was unsure whether her warming feelings were enough to form the basis for marriage, although as time passed she felt jealous pangs toward her rival, later declaring herself "more afraid of the Jerseys than of Bonaparte."[31]

As the holiday wore on, Harriet realized she was being outmaneuvered by the rapacious Lady Jersey, who coerced the Duke of Devonshire to invite her and her daughter to dine. Bessborough, who shared Harriet's reservations regarding the match, was so incensed that he announced he would sooner eat in his own room. Harriet was further infuriated to discover that when John refused invitations from the Jerseys, Lady Jersey ridiculed him for being too weak to resist parental influence. Harriet could see where this might lead. John, thus challenged, might easily behave too warmly toward Elizabeth, giving the wily Lady Jersey "a right to complain if it goes no further."

Harriet was not authoritarian by nature, but terror that John would be unwittingly ensnared forced her hand. She spoke frankly to him, warning him of the perils he faced. John's response to Harriet was similarly frank. "Use a better argument, and say you dislike it and wish me to avoid her."[32] Harriet did not deny her dislike but further explained her reasons, which made John "look grave" for several days, and then decide to leave Ramsgate to stay in London until he set off on his grand tour later in the year. Harriet later discovered, with a mixture of pride and sadness, that it was not only Lady Jersey who had mocked him for heeding maternal advice; he had been much ridiculed by the Lambs but had laughed off their comments while staunchly defending her: "if mine was tutelage it was very pleasant tutelage, and he did not wish to throw it off. Pray allow this required some courage . . ."[33]

SIXTEEN

Paris

1802-1803

I N EARLY DECEMBER 1802, Harriet, Bessborough, Caro, and John joined a flood of British well-to-do visitors and traveled to Paris. Harriet's resolve to leave was far from easy, given the prospect of several months' separation from Granville. But with Caro poised to make her social debut and John ready to embark on his grand tour from Paris, maternal duty demanded she should go. By now, Harriet sensed that her eight-year relationship with Granville was approaching a watershed. At the age of twenty-nine he had at last succumbed to his mother's exhortations and acknowledged that he must marry. Harriet's own unfortunate experiences of marriage, and the sacrifice it would entail, did not prevent her from agreeing with this advice and urging Granville to take the plunge. "Marriage . . . is the happiest state for man or woman that can be found . . . and not deviating from it is rewarded with respect and peace on earth and eternal happiness hereafter. It is what I think you particularly formed for . . . "[1] she reassured him that autumn. Yet whatever she advised, knowing Granville would begin a serious search for a bride when she was away, and that when he found one their relationship would inevitably change, must have added to the poignancy of their parting.

The discomforts of travel compounded Harriet's downcast frame of mind. The crossing was wretched—the sea was rough, everyone was sick, and, to make matters worse, at Calais they were forced to unpack all their belongings for customs. But from there on things rapidly improved. They traveled in easy stages, via Montreuil and Amiens, "this city of Peace," then on to Chantilly before arriving at Paris, where they took up residence in the Hôtel de l'Empire in the Rue Cerutti. Bess and two of her children, Frederick and Caroline, had arrived the previous month and greeted Harriet warmly. Little G and her husband, Morpeth, would join them the following month. The three women—Harriet, Bess, and Little G—would soon hold Paris in their thrall.

Before Harriet could test her charms, she had her mother to appease. Even before she arrived in France, Lady Spencer had bombarded her with a list of worries she could barely contain. She wanted the trip to be used to polish Caro's manners in preparation for her coming-out, and issued instructions to Harriet in her usual blunt manner:

> As you are going to Paris I wish instead of running after all the curiosities there as your first and solid object—you would set seriously about the improvement of [Caroline's] manner and maintien—get one of the best dancing masters or mistresses if there are such, to teach her how to go out and come into a room with propriety and without embarrassment—make her your companion and teach her to look upon herself as one of the company to enter reasonably but not pertly into conversation, not to quit the society for any trifling purposes—and to attend while in it to what is going forward—as soon as you cease to treat her as a child she will learn to respect herself.[2]

Lady Spencer's chief concern was to safeguard family reputation. Post-revolutionary Paris was a famous hotbed of decadence; she fretted that Caroline's character might be tarnished before she was even out, perhaps by Harriet's thoughtless conduct. Taking up a contentious political stance, keeping unsuitable company, behaving with unseemly lack of decorum—all were blunders to which Harriet had been prone in the past. Without firm guidance, Lady Spencer told herself, Harriet might easily transgress once again. "As your object is seeing *things* I hope you are careful with respect to *people*. Frequent visits, which your good nature might tempt you to receive, from any particular description of men, might be injurious to them and dangerous to yourself. I know you all carry companionship sentiment and generosity so far that you might easily be beguiled by them into imprudences of which you are unaware. I only beg you to avoid, with the same care that I do, all political subjects and attend to masters and milliners and such sort of objects."[3]

Along with her numerous commands, Lady Spencer divulged a matter of some delicacy that required Harriet's help. During the war, financial restrictions had made taking money abroad difficult, and even the well-to-do had suffered from financial embarrassment. The Queen of Naples and Mme. Talleyrand, wife of the French foreign minister, who had spent much of the most turbulent period of the French Revolution in England, were among several eminent foreign friends who had applied to Lady Spencer for assistance, presumably with a promise of repayment once hostilities ceased and life returned to normal. Lady Spencer had little surplus wealth; ever since her husband's death she had lived in a relatively modest way in order to make ends meet. Nevertheless she was a generous-hearted woman, spending a large proportion of her income on charitable projects, and, like her daughter, she found it hard to say no to friends. When asked for help she had offered more than she could strictly afford and now found herself short of funds, with many loans still outstanding.

Harriet's stay in France offered an opportunity to recoup some of her money, and she implored her daughter to inquire discreetly of Mme. Talleyrand when the outstanding sum might be repaid. "I heartily wish poor Madame de Talleyrand may be able to send me her £100 in January, as she tells me she shall," Lady Spencer optimistically responded, presumably after Harriet had received a promise of some sort. Elsewhere, she told Harriet, the news was less auspicious. She had just had a letter from the Queen of Naples "without a word about money" and concluded, "I am very angry but it cannot be helped."[4] But by the middle of January, no money was forthcoming from Paris and Lady Spencer again asked Harriet to do what she could. "Do you think I am likely to have any money from Madame de Talleyrand?—for I am as usual quite a beggar."[5] Harriet must have tried but made little progress, for a week later Lady Spencer resigned herself to another loss and grumbled, "As to poor Madame de Talleyrand's money it is I think almost as hopeless as the Queen of Naples's."[6]

Aside from chasing her mother's debts and supervising Caroline's grooming, Harriet was immersed in the Parisian social and cultural scene. The connections she had forged with numerous French aristocrats during the war, coupled with her reputation for intellect, charm, and beauty, opened every salon door. Liveried footmen presented invitations to assemblies, dinners, and balls, where she crossed paths with many of the most powerful and brilliant figures of Napoleon's new regime. Harriet's allure, along with the charms of Bess and Little G, who went everywhere with her, brought instantaneous success, and word of their popularity ricocheted back to London. "Camille Jourdain says that you, Lady E and my aunt [Harriet] have all the *cleverness, vivacity,* and *piquante charms* of what he fancies the ancienne noblesse of France to have possessed in their perfection, united to all the *truth, candour* and *solidity* of the English character,"[7] Harryo reported to Little G.

As well as beguiling Parisian society, there were countless cultural delights to enjoy. As soon as she arrived, Harriet hurried to see the grand galleries of the Louvre, which had opened to the public the previous year and now thronged with visitors. She perused the sculpture galleries, gazing at the exhibits that included the Apollo Belvedere, longing for Granville. She admired the paintings but thought the light unfavorable and the hangings too crowded. "I should enjoy ten times more seeing a few of the fine ones separate than in the bewildering manner in which they are placed,"[8] she told him, again wishing he was by her side. In the evening she made visits to the opera, sometimes sitting in Talleyrand's box, or attended one of Paris's theaters — including the Comédie-Française, where the renowned sixteen-year-old actress Mlle. Georges, soon to become Napoleon's mistress,* and the leading French actor François Joseph Talma, were wildly applauded. These outings gave Lady Spencer further cause for consternation. "I hear such accounts of the indecency of the French theatres," she had fretted even before Harriet's departure, ". . . that I think you should enquire a little about them before you take young women especially to them."[9]

Amid all this bustle, Harriet never failed to find time to write to Granville. Some of her letters are filled with the ache of longing:

I cannot tell you how very low the not hearing from England makes me feel, except that one letter of yours the day after I left you . . . I have not had a line . . . the gaeties of Paris fade away before this mis-

---

* Mlle. Georges was notoriously generous with her favors — the Duke of Wellington and the writer Alexandre Dumas were among numerous others who enjoyed liaisons with her.

fortune and I have no comfort but Delphine! . . . I would give anything to stay quietly at home tonight . . .

MIDNIGHT

I am just returned and judge of my agitation and impatience — Ld. Bor[ingdon] says he has a letter for me but alas had forgot it at home — oh how could he! Men are so calm and patient, they never allow for the miseries of expectation which women feel so keenly. I shall not close my eyes all night . . .

Your letter is come. How good you were dearest G to go and to say you regret me. Oh G. Dear Dear G. Will you continue to do so? Will my return be pleasure or trouble to you? How I wish for you if it was but for a moment.[10]

Other letters are crammed with anecdotes of what she had been doing, who she had met, and who had said what to her, rather than how much she longed for him. Their brisk tone suggests that she had resigned herself to his marriage, and any dejection she felt on their parting had been healed by the stimulating world to which she had gained entrée, and her success within it. Occasionally Harriet complained to Granville that the constant round exhausted her. But her buoyant mood and the long conversations she recorded for him do not entirely bear this out; they suggest that her grumbles were little more than token gestures to appease any rancor Granville might harbor. The truth was that she was happier in Paris, surrounded by the dazzle of brilliant men and women, than she had been for years. She might have been physically drained and emotionally bereft, but she was mentally energized.

Being fêted and flattered reminded her that after years of worrying over Granville, at the age of forty-two she was still a woman of irresistible charm and beauty, and she did not hesitate to remind him of this fact. "We opened the door of the box a moment to speak to the Princess Dolgoouki and Madame de Vaudemont, and instantly M. de Naarbonne, Segur, Montmorency, M. de Mun, Noailles, Lord Lauderdale, and General Klyne crowded round the box to speak to us, to the great amusement of Madame de Vaudemont, who tells me I am *très coquette,* and cannot move without a regiment of Generals and *beaux es-prits à mes trousses,*"[11] she wrote, reveling shamelessly in the admiration.

Other letters reflect her sheer enjoyment of Parisian life. She describes a lavish banquet given by Talleyrand in apartments that were sumptuously furnished and perfumed with frankincense. As she and more than seventy fellow guests sat down to dine, "an immense glass at the end of the room slid away by degrees, and soft and beautiful music began to play in the midst of the jingle of glasses and *vaisselle.*" Despite the grandeur of the surroundings, however, not everything ran as smoothly as she expected. "The dinner was, I believe, excellent," she told Granville wryly, "but from some awkwardness in the arrangement it was very difficult to get anything to eat."[12] This was only the start of the evening. She and Bessborough took their leave, then went on to a ball given by the Duchess of Gordon, where Caro made her public debut. Bess and her daughter Caroline St. Jules were also there, and the young girls would not let Harriet leave until four in the morning.

The next day the frenetic circuit continued. Harriet dined with Bess at the home of Alexandre Berthier, one of Napoleon's closest friends and his frequent traveling companion. Berthier, "a little sharp looking man, very gallant," already knew of Harriet by reputation and, having made her acquaintance, offered to escort her and Bess to Versailles. Harriet declined the invitation "and on his pressing us for a reason, told him the true one": memories of the late queen and her family would make it too painful. Berthier was taken aback by Harriet's frankness but was clearly captivated by her. Slowly he won her around, telling her "that he had fought with and admired the English his whole life through." At the end of the dinner, when she took her leave, she was astonished that "he kissed my arm up above my elbow."[13]

That same evening Harriet also met and befriended Baron Dominique de Denon, the newly appointed director of the Louvre. Denon had traveled into Egypt with Napoleon on his campaigns, and his book on his travels, *Voyage dans la Haute et Basse Egypte,* provided illustrations and topographical accounts of unprecedented detail and accuracy of the relics of the ancient Egyptian civilization. Harriet had been fascinated by the book and was enchanted by his stimulating conversation—"like his book, very natural and very interesting"[14]

—and accepted an invitation to see his original drawings and his collection of antiquities.

Not everyone was welcoming. Harriet had met the famous beauty and society hostess Mme. Récamier in London the previous summer. In Paris, her home was to become an informal center for the opposition to Napoleon, and Harriet was drawn by the mixture of glamour and intrigue surrounding her. "It is very curious to see the opposition naissante which is beginning to form here. It is now only in whispers, but seems numerous," Harriet wrote.[15] Mme Récamier's reputation as an icon of classical beauty rested partly on the famous depiction by the painter Jacques Louis David of her reclining on a chaise longue. Prints of the painting had been widely disseminated throughout England, but when Harriet attended Mme. Récamier's ball she was amazed to find her hostess simulating the composition by lounging in her bed in semi-dishabille and allowing anybody, male or female, to admire her. The following day Harriet called again on Mme. Récamier and found her once more in bed and surrounded by men. It was, she told Granville, just as David had painted. "That beautiful bed you saw prints of— muslin and gold curtains, great looking glasses at the side, incense pots and muslin sheets trimmed with lace, and beautiful white shoulders exposed and perfectly uncovered to view—in short, completely undressed and in bed."[16] Bemused and unable to contain her curiosity, Harriet asked Mme. Récamier if she was indisposed. The response was cold, loud, and, to Harriet's sensitive ear, mortifying. *"Oh non seulement,"* she replied, before pointedly explaining to all those assembled that she was not with child.

Amid the descriptions of such colorful adventures, Harriet's letters also reveal shadows. The still-visible remnants of the Revolution disturbed her profoundly. Traveling about the city, she could not avoid noticing grand houses that had once belonged to her friends and were now destroyed or made into lodging houses. As she crossed "that shocking Place de la Concorde, with ye remains of the Guillotine and the Madeleine Church," she shivered with trepidation, remembering the terrible fate of the late king and queen. Napoleon's regime had brought with it an atmosphere of suspicion and fear that pervaded the city and shocked and repulsed her. "It is with the greatest caution any of the people we see venture a word, and always adding *'vous ne savez pas qui peut se trouver dans l'antichambre.'* "[*][17]

Misgivings about Napoleon did not diminish her curiosity about him, however. She remained hungry as ever to glean all she could of his life and character, and having established herself at the heart of British and French society she found it easy to learn the latest gossip. Lord Whitworth, the British ambassador, told her that Napoleon was moving toward establishing himself as emperor, a fact that puzzled her. "I think it interesting to watch the continual little steps towards royalty. Do tell me why so many great men enjoying unbounded sway . . . have yet appeared uneasy and anxious to obtain the empty title of King or Emperor,"[18] Harriet wrote. As a visitor of repute it was expected that she would be formally presented to Napoleon. But her association with Marie Antoinette was one neither she nor French society had forgotten, and the wily politician Hare, who was also in Paris, advised her to avoid attending court. She agreed wholeheartedly. "I do not intend it [presentation]," she told Granville. "Unless I find it a point of etiquette that every body is expected to conform to."[19]

Harriet's first glimpse of Napoleon came in early January, when she stood in a window of the Palais du Louvre to witness a military parade. The vast expanse of courtyard below was filled with cavalry and infantry troops and marching bands. Into the heart of the pageantry and splendor rode France's first consul, astride a white horse that had once belonged to the late king. Harriet could not see Napoleon's face clearly, though she remarked that he rode well and from a distance seemed very like the busts and portraits she had seen. Above all it was his sense of power and majesty that impressed her. "When you view that whole immense place of the Carousel crowded with his troops after so many victories, himself surrounded with all the pomp and splendour of royalty, and half the nations of the world seeming to do homage to him, and reflect what he was a few years past, what the mere force of genius, valour and successful ambition have raised him to, it is impossible not to look with some astonishment . . ."[20] She was struck too by Napoleon's obvious unpopularity with both his troops and the populace. Despite the splendor and magnificence, there were no cheers,

---

[*] You don't know who might be listening next door.

only silence. Harriet had few doubts why this was. "His despotism, his restless ambition, his jealousy of every thing that comes near him, the heavy taxes imposed upon the people and the oppressive plan of the conscript, all combine to make him dreaded and disliked."[21]

Some hours later Bessborough and Duncannon were presented at court. Napoleon questioned Bessborough at some length about his family. Harriet was not present; taking Hare's advice, she had pleaded tiredness and retired to her lodgings. But her reputation was such that her absence did not go unnoticed, and a few days later Napoleon "expressed a wish" to meet her. Harriet was tempted but, mindful of her resolve, remained unyielding. "I will not go, as I said I would not."[22]

Her staunch refusal to meet Napoleon was to have unforeseen repercussions. She had marked herself out as being anti-Bonapartist and, as such, a subversive presence, and she and her friends fell under a cloud of suspicion. A fortnight later she was warned "by a great friend of B[onaparte's]"—probably Berthier or Moreau, with whom she had grown close—"to give secretly a warning to some of my Société—that they were observed closely, that *le ciel est menaçant* . . . two or three particularly of those . . . living a great deal with us are supposed to be in danger . . ."[23] She and Bessborough had planned to leave Paris at the end of January but delayed their departure because Bessborough was once again suffering from gout. Now Harriet feared that they might be forcibly expelled at a moment's notice. "Buonaparte fancies we not only are not presented out of enmity to his court, but that we have prevented the Duchess of Somerset and Georgiana [Little G]. In short there had been a great piece of work, but I cannot tell you now,"[24] she reported to Granville. Despite her mother's warnings, Harriet had once more embroiled herself in a political storm.

In England, meanwhile, Granville had begun to court Lady Sarah Fane, the heiress daughter of Lord Westmorland. To begin with all had seemed promising; Harryo observed him on his way to meet Lady Sarah at a house party at the Priory,* "in tearing spirits and . . . so well pleased with himself, that I think he must have great hopes of success."[25] But at the party he discovered more competition than he expected. Lord Craven and Sheridan's son Tom were also trying their

---

* The home of Harriet's friend Lady Abercorn (Anne Hatton).

chances. Granville put on a brave face. "Lord Granville, seeming to have made a vow that he would take everything for the best, smiling with self congratulation when she turned her back, and walking about the room with looks of complacency and satisfaction when she was too much surrounded for him to get near her."[26] By the end of the month it was clear that there was another contender for Lady Sarah's hand — Lady Jersey's son Lord Villiers was also in keen pursuit and seemed to be gaining ground. Meanwhile, Granville's hopes of marriage were not hampering him from chasing a string of married women, whom he found far easier to please.

> Lord Granville is in great spirits about his proceedings, though no-body can very well tell why, as he has not seen Lady Sarah since the Priory, which I am sure was not a very encouraging meeting; however he likes just as well talking to Lady Cahir, Mrs. Bouverie, Lady Abercorn, etc., etc., who all encourage him about it, *à l'envie l'une de l'autre,* and I begin to think he mistakes them for Lady Sarah, if one may judge from the looks of self congratulation which always follow an interview with any one of these ladies. Lord Villiers and him met in our box last night, and each looked like the favoured lover, and the least successful was certainly the most triumphant, in manner at least.[27]

Throughout her stay in France, Harriet kept abreast of Granville's courtship of Lady Sarah. She told Granville that when she heard Lady Sarah criticized, out of loyalty to him she rushed to defend his potential bride and staunchly sang her praises. Afterward she was forced to admit she was not personally acquainted with Lady Sarah, and one of her friends whispered, *"Vous la craignez et cela reveint au même."**[28] Harriet probably related this story to reassure Granville that she still supported his marriage, but she did not entirely succeed. He was a proud man, unused to rejection, and despite appearances to the contrary he was irked by the obstacles he had encountered in his courtship. His failure seemed all the more ignominious set against Harriet's success. "How odious they all will be when they come back,"[29] he remarked unkindly

---

* You fear her and it's the same thing.

as he gossiped with Georgiana over dinner at Devonshire House. His pique also became clear to Harriet when he told her that after leading such a stimulating life in Paris she would return and find him dull. Harriet wrote:

> There is not much danger of my thinking any society in which you are joined fade or stupid, and you know it but too well; but if you mean for the general run of conversation that one meets at assemblies here, or assemblies in London, I should certainly reckon those at Paris most interesting, both because most of the people are either celebrated themselves or have gone through interesting scenes . . . in England it rarely happens that very clever or very celebrated men deign to mix in common society or talk on trifling subjects; they are usually wrapped up in some pursuit . . . I might move heaven and earth before I could get three words from Mr. Pitt; and Mr. Fox, whom I know and love, I see perhaps two or three times in a year; yet I am an unfair example, for I reckon I live without exception in the best society in London. But clever men in England are too much superior to women; there is too great a distance between them to allow of much conversation; they make them their amusement and sometimes their friends, but seldom their society. In France, from the Generals to the Savants everything goes about . . . [30]

It is clear from this letter that Harriet's taste of Parisian society had done more than flatter her ego. Access to men of power and influence had sparked an awareness of something she had previously accepted— the increasing limitations of a woman's existence in England. Under Pitt, women had become ostracized from political debate, regarded as "strident" and masculine if they expressed views forcefully; thus Harriet had to accompany any proffered opinion with an apology. In Paris the closed masculine world did not exist. Women and men mingled freely; educated women expected and received more than flattery and patronizing conversation. They were neither excluded nor obliged to feign deference; their opinions were taken seriously. To Harriet this way of life came as a revelation, altering her view of herself. There would be times in the future when her confidence would be eroded, when she would yearn for those whom she loved and could not have, but even in such dark hours a core of resoluteness and self-belief would sustain her.

Harriet was not expelled from France; rather, she suffered a series of frustrating delays and difficulties upon leaving the city. Some of the obstacles were undoubtedly a result of the animosity she had aroused. Bessborough asked Lord Whitworth, the British ambassador, to arrange for a British ship to take them across the Channel. This he proved unable to do because British shipping required the personal approval of Napoleon and, as Harriet recorded, "The First Consul is, unluckily, out of humour, on which occasions none of his ministers, or even his own family or his wife, dare speak to him on any subject. *Ce n'est pas aimable;* never was there any character that united such contrasts of greatness and littleness, never one that aroused admiration and contempt, compassion and indignation, so much as this man."[31]

Her antipathy to Napoleon had grown and with it her doubts about the nature of the fragile peace between Britain and France. Whitworth had also failed to impress her. He had neglected his countrymen when they needed his assistance and made a number of social gaffes toward the French that were so crass she suspected they were deliberately intended to give offense. When she heard that Whitworth had failed to attend a dinner with Napoleon at which he was expected, Harriet was both outraged and suspicious. "From something he said I cannot help suspecting their orders are to show slights to the government here, and that is a true Addington Plan." She sensed that Addington was encouraging Whitworth to be rude in order to take revenge for the concessions he had been forced to make to Napoleon. Such underhanded retaliation seemed to her demeaning to the standing of Britain. "As long as we have an Ambassador here it would be much more dignified to have him correct in Etiquette, magnificent and splendid in appearance, obliging in all trifles . . ."[32]

Three weeks after making their request to Whitworth, still with no crossing arranged, Harriet, Bessborough, and Caro took their leave of Paris, accompanied by the Morpeths. They had left Duncannon and Frederick Foster to travel on to Rome on their grand tour, while Bess remained in Paris with her daughter. The journey to the coast was fraught with mishap. One letter Harriet wrote to Granville was addressed from "the worst Inn and worst room etc." She had arrived

there in the midst of a torrential downpour after the axle of their carriage had broken on the road. She and Caro had left Bessborough and
the maids and baggage and taken a chaise to the nearest post house,
from where they organized assistance to be sent back to the rest of the
party. Only after the chaise had been dispatched did Harriet consider
the dangers of her own situation:

> We were left at the mercy of a set of the strangest-looking people
> you ever saw. We were established in a very dirty kitchen, with all the
> postilions and some men smoking. On asking for another room, the
> only other in the whole place was shown us, where we now are; it is
> up a ladder, the bed formed of a rug, and shared with the chickens.
> Another rug covers a provision of mellow apples; the light is admit-
> ted through oiled paper, part of which is torn and stopped with dirty
> rags, some more of which ornament the room by being hung across
> it on a string . . . bad as this is, we could have borne it patiently; but
> our host . . . will sit with us, and two other men have scrambled up
> the ladder first to stare at us . . . [33]

This was not the last misadventure en route. The carriage suffered
further calamities, and when they finally arrived at Calais they discovered that there was no possibility of securing passage on an English
ship, and the only French boats available looked far from promising.
"I . . . have *mauvais augure* for the voyage,"[34] Harriet wrote as she gazed
across the dark-gray Channel and a gale began to blow. In one sense at
least, her foreboding was not misplaced. Less than two months after
her return, the Peace of Amiens crumbled; Britain and France were
again at war.

SEVENTEEN

Intrigues
1803-1804

WHEN HARRIET RETURNED TO LONDON, Granville's courtship of Lady Sarah Fane still hung in the balance, and his mother, Lady Stafford, lamented the effect her presence might have on his "grand-affair." Granville would no longer feel the same impetus to press on with his suit, and his chief rival, Lord Villiers, would thus gain an advantage. "I hope *Arrivals* will not slacken nor cool your attentions; there is no doubt that enemies may urge that the real attachment is come from the continent,"[1] she pointedly remarked before again chivvying him in his pursuit of Lady Sarah. "I know you are attached to her; and though sometimes jealousy may make you see things in a false medium, yet you must feel that you have cause to hope . . . and I do hear that . . . spectators fancy you the favoured lover . . . and [Lord Villiers] scruples not to own himself miserable, but that you are attached elsewhere and follow her for Fortune . . . go on in following her, talking to her, and paying her every attention in your power. You may be agitated with hopes, fears, and anxious doubts—all who truly love experience these contending plagues."[2]

In fact Lady Stafford's fears regarding Harriet were without foundation. Harriet pushed Granville on at every available opportunity, bolstering his confidence whenever he seemed dejected. Harryo, she told him, had reported that she "never saw anything so coquettish as Lady S[arah] Fane's manner to Lord G[ranville] Wednesday night; she never took her eyes off him . . ." Harriet assured him she interpreted this flirtatiousness as a sure sign Lady Sarah could not possibly be in love with Lord Villiers, whatever anyone else might believe. "Real se-rious love completely roots out every vestige of coquetry. She would scarcely know whether you exist . . . and if she is not in love with him you have full as good a chance as he has—I should think better," she reassured him.³ But neither his mother nor Harriet could persuade Granville to muster enthusiasm for a woman he, in his heart of hearts, had little desire to ensnare. "I am inclined to despond. Not to advance is to lose ground and I cannot flatter myself with having in the last week advanced a single step,"⁴ he reported gloomily at the end of March.

Harriet, meanwhile, had set herself another task. Realizing that once she lost Granville to a wife, friendship with his mother would provide insurance of a kind, she decided to demolish Lady Stafford's long-standing coolness toward her by bombarding her with charm. With this objective in mind, Harriet sent Lady Stafford an expensive present from Paris—a *pelisse*—an ultra-fashionable fur-trimmed coat. Granville's mother was genuinely touched by the gift, yet the thought of indebtedness to a woman who seemingly stood between her son and a respectable marriage was anathema. She commanded Granville to "thank Lady Bessborough a thousand times and tell her how much I like it, and pray take money in your pocket to pay it *without delay*."⁵ Har-riet refused any talk of payment for the fur coat, instead dispatching more gifts: political cartoons and an expensive set of Lady Mary Wort-ley Montagu's newly published diaries. She also took other measures to ingratiate herself, making visits to Lady Stafford's daughters so she could report to her on the grandchildren's health, and writing regular letters to keep Lady Stafford up to date with the latest political gossip. The tone of the letters is quite unlike the chatty informality of her letters to Granville and other friends—always uncomfortably subser-vient, apologetic, full of obsequious praise, beneath which her desper-ate longing to be liked is clear. "Any notice you are kind enough to take of me my dear Madam is so flattering and so delightful to me that what you choose to call attention . . . afford me the greatest pleasure . . . at the same time I beg your ladyship will not think I expect you to answer all my nonsense."⁶

In June she wrote, telling Lady Stafford of the French occupation of Hanover and of their refusal to release British prisoners captured at the onset of hostilities. Among the British citizens held by the French were Duncannon and Frederick Foster, who had been apprehended in Fréjus. "I am giving a gloomy account of affairs, but I own that indignation against Bonaparte and anxiety for the fate of my son drive me quite wild."[7] In the event Bess wrote to their friend General Berthier, imploring him to intervene; Berthier immediately organized passports for Frederick and Duncannon and their safe passage home, and attracted Napoleon's wrath for doing so, but they were back in England by the end of July. "My son's arrival in England was an event which astonished me almost as much as it delights me,"[8] she joyously reported to Lady Stafford.

Despite her formidable reputation, Granville's mother was no match for such an onslaught of spoiling, charm, generosity, and intelligence, and Harriet's campaign did not take long to yield results. "Her attention and kindness to me are unceasing," Lady Stafford told Granville after receiving yet more presents. "I am really ashamed of the expense. The *pelisse* and the books are not trifles and I do not believe that she is very rich. That she is generous, benevolent, and of a most affectionate disposition I knew long ago, and I feel her kindness, and I want you to find out something that she would like, and would not bestow upon herself . . ."[9] At last Lady Stafford had admitted to herself and her son that she knew what drew Granville into Harriet's arms. From then on she and Harriet would correspond regularly.

Harriet was never short of political news to divulge to Lady Stafford or to discuss with Granville. Her fascination with the political world had intensified since her visit to France and instilled in her a renewed confidence to express her views. As the nation again confronted Napoleon and the prospect of an imminent French invasion after fourteen brief months of peace, she was caught up in a new mood of anticipation that swept through London. Supporters of Pitt—Granville, Harriet's brother, George Spencer, Lord Grenville, and Canning— fiercely hoped that the events now unfolding might soon bring about a change of government and that, when it did so, "Pitt and more warlike statesmen" would succeed.[10] Meanwhile, Harriet and those adhering to the ideals of the old Whig opposition—with Fox, Grey, and Sheridan at their pinnacle—also revised their strategy. They had offered Addington qualified support in times of peace; now, with a return to war, they began to hope for something better. Fox, however, was no longer at the forefront of political events. Having returned from a visit to France he was presently enjoying a quiet semiretirement in the countryside and was content to watch events unfold from the sidelines. To Georgiana his conduct in the present climate seemed a wasted opportunity and she made feverish endeavors to tempt him back to parliament.

Yet both Georgiana and Harriet knew that now, more than ever, allegiances were in a state of flux. Enlightened members of both political flanks recognized that the most effective way to remove the current government would be to forge a united front or a "junction" against it. Harriet's and Georgiana's friendships with Fox, Sheridan, Grey, and the Prince of Wales had always placed them at the heart of the Whig political debate, but Harriet's position was particularly strong. Thanks to her links with leading Pittites, whom she had met and befriended through Granville, she was better placed than anyone to aid a new alliance between them. It was this delicate mission she now set out to facilitate.

She began by trying to persuade Granville that the aims of Georgiana's erstwhile lover Grey were not so far removed from his own, in the expectation that this message would filter through to Pitt. "Had you chanced to meet and show him [Grey] the resolutions, especially that one which gave some hope of further openings for Peace, I am convinced he would have voted with you and have given up tonight's motion," she reassured after Grey and others tabled a motion of censure against the war. Her letter also included a copy of a highly confidential letter Grey had written to Georgiana. "It is obvious if the oppositions cannot agree between them, Addington must stand," Grey had written; "no recollection of former political differences should have prevented my giving a cordial and unequivocal support to any set of men who had adopted a line of policy which appeared to me suited to the present circumstances of the country . . . Could Ld. Granville have any thing of a political nature to say to me? I would most willingly have met him, and if he had anything of that sort to suggest would have been quite open with him."[II]

Not everyone welcomed the sisters' attempts to bring the two sides together. Sheridan, fraught with financial worry and his mind frequently muddled by drink, had long been jealous of Granville's place in Harriet's heart and detested the thought of any agreement between Fox and Pitt, whom he deeply distrusted. "I had rather see Fox dead than joined with Pitt, and whilst I have life I will never suffer it,"[12] he declared to George Tierney, a Whig supporter who had joined Addington's administration as treasurer of the navy. Sheridan convinced himself that secret meetings were taking place at Devonshire House from which he was being deliberately excluded. Worse still, he felt he was losing his influence over the Prince of Wales, who had grown sympathetic toward the idea of an alliance. Sheridan had little doubt that Harriet and Georgiana lay behind his loss of favor and in a meeting with the prince lashed out against them both:

> He told the P[rince] that he must not give credit to the stories told him by us (calling us by no very gentle epithet) that as to politics we only saw through the eyes of one man [Mr. Fox] which was always bad enough even before it was dashed with the Grenville infection, which we caught from my brother, Lord Morpeth, and you [Granville]. That he himself . . . being the only real good and honourable politician was hated for this reason, and that we by way of serving our mottled party scrupled no lies against him, either as to his public or private character.[13]

The prince handled the situation diplomatically, defending Harriet and Georgiana and reassuring Sheridan of his continuing affection, but making clear that he would have to decide on his own course of action. Harriet no doubt passed details of all this on to Granville, in the hope of making him see the prince in a more favorable light. She also told Granville of something the prince had divulged to her in the strictest confidence—his increasingly strained relationship with the king. With the country facing imminent invasion, the prince wanted to participate in the defense of his realm and had asked the king's permission to command a body of volunteers. The king had not only refused his request but had threatened to take away the regiment of which he already had command. This reaction, the prince told Harriet, was by the direct order of Addington—in revenge for the prince's support of the opposition.*

Harriet's behind-the-scenes scheming was temporarily interrupted in mid-September, when Georgiana was taken gravely ill. For several days Georgiana suffered spasms in her side that were so severe even laudanum could not dull them, while the doctors tried to find what was causing the pain. Eventually she passed "a gall stone of amazing size." Harriet spent the next week at Devonshire House, sitting up all night by Georgiana's bedside and barely daring to leave during the day. "She likes me to sit by her bed and read to her, which I do almost incessantly night and day. To night I have read nearly without intermission since one, and I think have succeeded at last in lulling her to sound sleep,"[14] Harriet wrote from her sister's room at four in the morning.

By the year's end Georgiana was recovered but, still too weak to reenter society, she traveled to Bath with Bess and the duke to convalesce. Harriet was left in London to continue alone on her delicate path. Already the signs seemed favorable. Granville now openly enlisted her support in discovering Fox's intentions, while Canning was trying to coax the same information from Pitt with the aim of finding enough common ground to bring the two great men together. "I am most impatient to know what answer you receive from Fox even more so than I am to hear from Canning upon the state of Pitt's mind," Granville wrote, with reference to the thorny issue of Catholic emancipation, over which Pitt had resigned. Granville wrote: "What I should like best would be that Fox should write a letter intimating an intention of bringing forward the Catholic Question, that Pitt should in answer frankly declare his reasons for not supporting it . . . and that upon this Fox should express his willingness to defer the Catholic Question, seeing that it was not likely to be carried, and that an unsuccessful attempt might . . . be a means of giving strength to

---

* When Addington later heard of the prince's accusation he defended himself hotly, "assuring [the prince] that so far from advising the king on this subject they did not even know of the letters that had passed."

Addington."[15] But Fox was evasive, or, as Harriet put it, "*un enfant difficile à pateliner.*"* Sheridan had laid siege to him with his anti-Pitt stance and Fox was too afraid of being seen to court an alliance to make a firm commitment to any policy at all. "As to politicks I put off the evil day as long as I can," he had written to Harriet.[16] Another letter written soon after offered little more hope. Harriet wrote: "I have seen Mr. Fox and have nothing to tell you. It is quite provoking to have two people sit quietly and say, nothing can save the country but a union of all the talents in it — nothing but a junction can do good, yet neither of them stir a step towards it."[17] At the root of Fox's reluctance lay his distrust of Pitt's motives. Harriet had tried to overcome this, impressing upon Fox that when she spoke of Pitt's intentions she was repeating information she had been given from his closest friends. But even this assurance had not succeeded in altering Fox's view. "He named you [Granville] directly as the person he supposed I got my intelligence from, praised you extremely, and said you were the person through whom he meant to communicate to Pitt . . . and it was his opinion of your good sense and good heart made him think you might deceive yourself . . ."[18]

Among Pitt's supporters Harriet's efforts met with only marginally more success. Canning wrote her an amusing letter, saying that "he must pursue his own place, not listen to the voice of the charmer [Harriet] though her charm [be employed] ever so wisely." But after this unpromising opening Canning went on to make a crucial revelation. Both he and Grenville were losing patience with Pitt's refusal to oppose Addington directly. "I have begged that if Lord Gr[enville] offers to act in concert with Mr. Fox, that my name may be joined as being ready to join in any . . . opposition on a broad basis, but that opposing only a question here and there was vexatious without doing good, that he was convinced that the powers of the continent would feel confidence alone in an administration so formed."[19]

The following month a further layer of complication was added to the political tangle when the king was once more taken gravely ill. "He is quite mad — accompanied with a very bad appearance as to health," wrote Harriet to Bess, who was in Bath with Georgiana. The prince

---

* A difficult child to direct.

had now been informed that a regency was necessary, and this development made his political ally Fox more inclined to reveal his intentions.
He believed that the prince should be given the full powers of a
monarch, and declared that if he was called on to form a government
"his first measure will be an attempt of Peace . . . if the offer is rejected
by France Mr. Fox pledges himself to prosecute the war with the utmost activity and vigour, but only stipulates that it should be a war for
terms of peace not for any interference of ours in the arrangement of
the French government." With the possibility of a regency now seeming more likely, Fox suddenly returned to favor. Harriet wryly added
that Granville had been at Brooks's the previous night and was "extremely amused with the court paid to Mr. Fox by people who for years
had been slighting him."[20]

BUT ONCE AGAIN the king defied his doctors and recovered in time to
avert his son's becoming regent. Meanwhile, despite the cajoling of
both Grenville and Canning to join in opposition with Fox, Pitt's
stance remained unchanged. He still believed that outright opposition
to Addington would lose more supporters than it would gain. He was
prepared to join in government with Fox and Grenville, but only if
asked to do so by the king and with the agreement of the current administration. Meanwhile, he took more positive steps to secure a return to power; over the weeks that followed, Pitt became increasingly
forthright in his criticisms of the government's handling of the war. As
a result Addington's majority dropped rapidly, and at the end of April
he tendered his resignation to the king.

Two days later, Pitt submitted proposals to the king that included
Grenville and Fox in the new cabinet. All seemed well, but four days
later Harriet heard whispers that made her tell Bess, "mischief is growing."[21] Her doubts were not misplaced. When Bess returned from a sitting at the studio of the painter Lawrence she discovered the prince
with Georgiana at Devonshire House.

> "It is all over," said the Prince, "Pitt has accepted without Fox being
> included" . . . the king said he would not object to Lord Melville and
> had named Lord Grenville himself but he must object to Charles
> Fox as having been personally hostile to himself.[22]

After all her efforts the news must have come as a bitter disappointment to Harriet. But it paled into insignificance beside the two personal concerns that now consumed her: Granville had become embroiled in a rash flirtation that seemed likely to jeopardize his future career; and Harriet, meanwhile, had found herself pregnant with his second child.

EIGHTEEN

Separation
1804

THERE ARE NO MENTIONS of Harriet's second pregnancy by Granville in the published version of her correspondence. As when Little Harriet had been born four years earlier, secrecy was paramount. Harriet and her confidants—probably only Georgiana, Bess, and Granville—were ever conscious of the danger of discovery by Bessborough. The fact that he had turned a blind eye to Harriet's friendship with Granville for a decade and was conveniently unvigilant when it came to remarking the changes in her shape lulled none of them into supposing he had fundamentally changed. He still relied heavily on her presence, expecting her to perform the outward duties of a wife and avoid any whiff of scandal. Everyone understood that she contravened these rules at her peril.

Bessborough was also still prone to opening and reading Harriet's correspondence, and it is a sign of the need for discretion that only a handful of letters referring to Harriet survive from these months. Nearly all correspondence that passed between the three women on the subject was destroyed at the time or subsequently censored. "I burned your letter in such a hurry that I don't know if there was anything else to answer,"[1] wrote Bess typically to Georgiana days before Harriet gave birth. Harriet's letters to Granville met a similar fate; any compromising material was destroyed by him at the time or by later censors, and most of what we know must be gleaned from scant references to Harriet's health, or to the handful of surviving letters that she, Bess, and Georgiana exchanged.

Once again we are left wondering how Harriet managed to disguise the later stages of pregnancy from her children and her husband. We can only guess that the task was made easier by the weight she had put on in recent years and, as before, by the high-waisted fashions of the time, which made concealing a thickening waistline easy. What we do know is that as the summer drew on Harriet withdrew from society and arranged to pass the autumn, when the child was due, in a rented house at Hastings. Bess agreed to accompany her. Georgiana, racked with the strain of monstrous debts and anxious to deflect attention from her sister, decided to stay in London.

As if the strain of her secret pregnancy were not enough, Harriet had also to contend with serious tensions in her affair with Granville. In April Lady Sarah Fane's engagement to Lord Villiers was publicly announced. Granville's first serious attempt at finding a wife had failed, but he shed few tears. Lady Sarah had been replaced by a bolder woman who left him in no doubt of her desire for his attention.

Granville had conquered the heart of Lady Hester Stanhope, William Pitt's attractive, strong-willed, twenty-seven-year-old niece. Hester was striking rather than conventionally beautiful—tall, with sensuous heavy-lidded dark-blue eyes, rather masculine features, and a lofty air that concealed the fact that she had never before dealt with the ploys of love. Hester's singular character had been molded by a miserable childhood. Her mother (Pitt's sister) had died when she was only four and she had been brought up by a neglectful stepmother and a father who vacillated between ignoring her and treating her with brutal unkindness. Three years before her meeting with Granville, Hester had left her father's house to live with Pitt's mother, Lady Chatham, where she was happy for two years until Lady Chatham died, leaving Hester homeless. At this point Pitt stepped in, offering his niece a home with him at Walmer Castle near Dover.

Pitt had always been famously uninterested in women, and his generosity was sparked not by any frisson of sexual interest but by kind-heartedness. Now in his mid forties, Pitt found that Hester aroused his paternal instincts; she brought out a warmth that few people ever saw. To him it was unimportant that her strong character did not conform to the usual submissive feminine orthodoxy. He respected her intelligence and uncompromising honesty; her sarcastic wit amused and entertained him; she brought a color to his life it had hitherto lacked.

For her part, Hester was swiftly captivated by the political plottings and aura of power that encircled Pitt's household. During the months of negotiations prior to the fall of Addington's government, she grasped the chance to meet and mingle with her uncle's friends and to immerse herself in the latest intrigues. She adored Pitt and took pains to please him, and as the rapport between them took root Pitt made her his confidante, allowing her to play hostess at his table and thus become the acknowledged queen of one of the most politically influential households of her day.

It is no surprise, therefore, that when Granville came to call to discuss the possibility of an alliance with Fox, he should pay court to Hester. Always drawn to glamorous, intelligent females, he never saw his long-standing love affair with Harriet as an impediment to casual flirtations and launched into a dalliance with Hester, not thinking where it might lead.

Several men had wooed Hester since she had moved in with her uncle and she had never been tempted by any of them. But to her Granville seemed different—better-looking, more worldly, romantic, and reckless. He roused feelings she had never felt and she took his flirting more seriously than it was intended. Unafraid to speak her mind and romantically inexperienced, she saw no reason to hide her attraction, instead openly flaunting her passion in the hope that this might spur him to propose.

Granville, however, had no intention of taking such a step. Lady Hester was wellborn and her political connections certainly added to her allure, but she lacked what to Granville was an essential requirement in a wife: money of her own. He had until now always managed to avoid any association with scandal, and it was Harriet, with her feminine insight and past experience of ill-starred *amours,* who first spelled out to him where the path he was treading might lead. "I must only entreat you to be upon your guard . . . I have very good reason to believe Lady Hester has taken a strong fancy to you and imagined you returned it, and had serious intentions—so much as to have mentioned to Pitt . . . Think how many unpleasant things any thing like a scrape with her might entail upon you—you are a pretty gentleman to be sure."[2]

Jealousy must have played some part in this gentle scolding, but Harriet also had Granville's interests at heart since his career had now reached a crucial juncture. During his visits to Walmer, Granville had risen in Pitt's estimation, and in June Pitt had offered him the key job of ambassador to Russia, with the aim of securing Russia's support in the war against Napoleon. For Granville this was a fortuitous promotion that would place him at the forefront of international politics. Not everyone took the offer at face value, however. Bess thought it was a sign that Granville had dug himself into a political hole. By supporting the notion of an alliance, he had identified himself as a member of the opposition and an ally of Fox's. Sending him to Russia was an expedient way to disarm someone Pitt liked but with whom he essentially disagreed or, as Bess put it: "[Granville's] situation in politics is so awkward a one that it would be a good thing his going, for he supports Pitt from friendship, disapproving all the time of his conduct."[3]

Bess may have been correct in suspecting Pitt's offer was prompted by something more than gratitude or admiration, but the reason she chose may well have been wide of the mark. The indiscreet affair between Granville and Hester was causing disturbances that were embarrassing to Pitt. Having heard his niece's love-torn agonies, Pitt must have guessed that Granville was never going to marry her. Sending him to St. Petersburg would neatly bring the liaison to an end. But if this was Pitt's aim he did not initially succeed. Granville viewed the promotion warily. He was loath to leave Harriet in the final stages of pregnancy and to relinquish his self-indulgent existence for the challenge of crossing war-torn Europe to take on a difficult diplomatic role for which he had limited experience. In the end, though, after seeking Fox's advice, he reluctantly accepted.

Having settled on this course, Granville tried to console Harriet by offering to take her son Willy with him as an attaché. Harriet greeted the news of both appointments with a mixture of delight and dismay. Willy had been miserable at sea; since his return from his last voyage he had looked pale, ill, and depressed and she knew he would welcome an alternative occupation. There was another benefit too. Willy's presence in Russia would provide an extra link to Granville—a legitimate reason for regular correspondence. But the thought of the dangers he might face, coupled with a year's separation from Granville as she prepared to give birth to his child, was something she could scarcely bring herself to contemplate. "I must not think of another departure, but trust in God's mercy to support my sinking spirits,"[4] she wrote sadly that summer.

The wider family knew nothing of her predicament and viewed the prospect of Willy's new diplomatic role with approval. It would be educationally beneficial, declared Lady Spencer—perhaps remembering her father's flourishing career—although she could not help adding a waspish aside: "How far Ld. Granville Leveson Gower is qualified for diplomatic business you are a much better judge than I can be, but I conclude he has some secretary or experienced person goes with him from whom William may get information and he should take this opportunity of acquainting himself with modern history especially that part of it that regards Prussia, Russia, Denmark, Sweden and Poland."[5]

News of Granville's imminent departure did nothing to dash Hester's hopes. As soon as she heard he was leaving she stepped up her campaign to secure a marriage proposal. By August gossip was rife that the couple would marry, and announcements of the impending wedding began to appear in the press. "Everybody is talking of it, I wonder what Hetty will say to it. I dread this subject coming on the *tapis* between you,"[6] Harriet fretted. She had always made efforts to ally herself to Granville's women friends, and Hester was a regular guest at Roehampton dinner parties that summer, often naively confiding her passion for Granville to Harriet in the hope she might aid her pursuit of him. "I hear Lady Hester is in despair and vents it at Roehampton— is that policy or ignorance?" wondered Harryo, who scathingly continued, "*il bel Uomo* [Granville] sits at dinner bodkin, with 'decent triumph and a look serene.' Oh, how many fair Germans, Poles, Hungarians, Livornians, Scavonians etc., etc., will rue this gay deceiver's soft looks and broken vows."[7]

Nevertheless, even Harriet's forbearance had its limits. As the time for Granville's departure approached, she became exasperated to find him spending time with Hester that might have been spent with her. It was galling to long for his visits only to receive notes from Hester telling her that Granville was too busy to call. "I am so disappointed . . . I thought if you dined and spent the evening with her and Pitt you would not mind coming here afterwards, considering how soon I must quite lose you..."[8] she chided him on one occasion. Another letter takes a different tack, scolding him not for her disappointment but for unchivalrously continuing to toy with Hester's feelings.

> Is it quite honourable, Dear G, to encourage a passion you do not mean seriously to return? And which, if you do not, must make the owner miserable? And how can you be certain of what lengths you or she may be drawn into? We know she has strong passions and indulges them with great latitude: may you not both of you be hurried further than you intend? If Mr. Pitt knew even what has passed already, do you think he would like it?[9]

Despite such exhortations, Granville was unwilling or unable to break away from Hester. His last hours on British soil were shadowed by her. As he prepared to leave, she sent him a garbled letter threatening to commit suicide if he refused to marry her. He showed the letter to Harriet, who was flabbergasted by Hester's lack of composure, but could not condemn her outright. "I shall always be kind to her, from a strange reason—she belongs in some manner to you."[10] Harriet later found out that Hester attempted to carry out her threat; after Granville's departure she tried to take her own life by swallowing poison. As soon as she recovered, Hester severed her friendship with Harriet, tearfully claiming she had been advised to do so by the queen and the Princess of Wales. Harriet was deeply wounded, suspecting that Hester was not being frank with her, but did not dare press the matter further, perhaps dreading whispers about the secret baby.

Hester's demands did not prevent Harriet from preying heavily on Granville's mind in the days before he left London. The thought of their imminent separation, the dangers of childbirth, and the heavy burden of secrecy wrought a change, making him lose his usual suave airs and grow openly heated one minute and dejected the next "I feel low and uncomfortable... I am out of spirits at the time approaching of my leaving everything I love or care for. I fear to some of them I shall appear wanting in kindness,"[11] Granville wrote with unusual self-awareness, apologizing for losing his temper with Harriet at supper. Amid their fraught meetings there were practical difficulties to consider. The problem of how to communicate sensitive information by letter loomed over them both, adding to their worries. Post sent overseas was prone to being opened; even mail consigned to special foreign office messengers sometimes fell into the wrong hands. "I am afraid I should not look well in print . . . I should hang myself immediately; I have no notion of how one could support one's poor letters being read and criticised by all Europe,"[12] Harriet would later write.

To avoid such an eventuality, she and Granville arranged code names for the principal people whom they would discuss in their letters. Harriet was "Mrs. Newton," Granville was "Mr. Arundel," Pitt became "my uncle," Hester "my niece," and Georgiana "the chessboard." In all, some three dozen friends and family members were given pseudonyms; others were referred to awkwardly by association with the code. The "sea nymph's husband" was Lord Melville (formerly Lord Dundas); the title was a reference to his new post as First Lord of the Admiralty. These precautions were to prove necessary sooner than expected. In November a messenger carrying several of Harriet's letters, en route to Russia, was robbed of his deliveries by French soldiers. "My patriotism sinks before my selfishness," Granville would write. "I am lamenting more the loss of your letters than the knowledge that Bonaparte will obtain all our secrets with the different continents of Europe."[13] Fortunately there were no adverse consequences. But the thought of what might happen would afterward constrain Harriet's writing. "I hate thinking my letters are read, but it is as impossible for me to write *pour la Galerie* as to fly, and whenever it comes into my head I stop short and won't say another word till the idea is gone again."[14]

And then there was nothing left to do but say goodbye. The painful parting took place on October 10, in the privacy of Cavendish Square. They both broke down in saying their farewells. "You must have seen how I suffered . . . last night—I know not that I ever passed so heart-rending a moment,"[15] Granville wrote from Whitstable in Kent, as he waited for Willy to arrive. "You cannot conceive the anxiety I feel about your health." After all the troubles with Hester and the strain of the last weeks, his distress reaffirmed the depth of his feelings and in this Harriet found consolation. "You know how I dread your suffering, yet I own in this instance, painful as it was, I should have been sorry we could have had such a parting without regret to you. How I shall watch the wind."[16]

As soon as he had gone, Harriet hurried to Hastings to prepare for the birth of her baby. She joined a straggling group of familiar faces: Bess and two of her children, Caroline St. Jules and Frederick; Georgiana's son Hart, who had come in the hope that sea bathing might improve his deafness; as well as Bessborough, John, and Caro. It was late in the season and fashionable society had left the resort to return to London, but the loneliness of the place suited Harriet's wretched mood. She had long ago mastered the art of putting on a show for the benefit of others and masking what she really felt, but for the time being feigning insouciance was beyond her. The torment of Granville's departure was beyond anything she had ever felt. "There is no end to the miseries of separation. How could I ever be unhappy before,"[17] she confessed miserably in one of her first letters to him.

In a mood of desolation she filled the days in taking long solitary walks on the cliff tops or along the beach, or in sitting for hours sketching stormy seascapes for Granville, or in watching meteors light up the night sky. Her behavior was unusually withdrawn and erratic even toward Bess, the one person in Hastings who understood her predicament. "Harriet gave me a fine fright today—she was not returned at half past five—I really was finished . . . the fairness of the weather . . . had tempted her to walk and sit on the rocks later than usual,"[18] Bess reported worriedly to Georgiana.

Yet if ever Harriet had doubted Bess, the latter was to prove her loyalty over the following weeks. Bess had endured similar ordeals (as well as giving birth to two illegitimate children in secrecy, she had recently been parted from her son Augustus, who had left for a diplomatic post at the British Embassy in Washington). She was endlessly patient, sitting with Harriet during her lonely vigils and calming her when she grew agitated at the thought of what lay ahead. "Bess and I sit and watch the sea and frighten one another from morning till night " Harriet told Lady Holland; "you may imagine we are not in any good spirits."[19]

As the time for Harriet's delivery drew near, Bess's courage was tested more severely. A letter she wrote to Georgiana records that the rest of the party—John, Caro, and Bessborough, together with Bess's children and Hart—were due to leave Hastings at the end of October, shortly before the baby was due. This would leave Bess and Harriet free to slip away to a secretly prearranged place for the birth. But a few days before their departure Bessborough suddenly announced that he had decided to alter his plans and would stay on for a week after the rest had gone. Harriet and he would then pay a visit to Brighton before returning to London. Such a scheme was obviously impossible given Harriet's condition, and it threw Bess and Harriet into panic. Bess wrote frantically to Georgiana in London to ask for her advice. Georgiana could offer little practical assistance—she was too overwrought by her gargantuan money worries—but managed to suggest that Harriet and Bess should slip away to Dover for a few days, and the baby could be born there. Bess thought this too risky. It would be safer, she argued, if Georgiana wrote, inviting the whole party to Chiswick. "You have misunderstood me if you think she can go to Dover with me . . . but merely by inviting them to Chiswick, to prevent Lord B[essborough] as his only resource loitering on here . . . the gap will be so great that we shall make that I hope Ld. B[essborough] will not remain . . . and if he promises to be at Chiswick he will be more punctual—keep up your spirits about her—I think it will do well but I think much depends on her going [into labor] from here."[20]

The scheme presumably worked and Bessborough was diverted, but Bess's worries were still not over. Four days later she wrote to Georgiana again, in turmoil now because the two women on whom she had relied to assist with Harriet's labor were no longer available, and it was too late to move. "My ill luck has sent Lady de Clifford away . . . and our German lady is ill—I am afraid there will not be a woman I know, and so fear that my posi[tion] will [be] made up to me."[21]

Harriet's labor must have begun in the first days of November, immediately after Bessborough left for Chiswick, although, predictably, not a single mention of the birth survives. The child, a boy she named George Arundel Stewart, was born safely and given over to a foster mother. Nothing is known of where his early childhood years were spent, although he was probably brought up somewhere near Hastings with his sister Little Harriet, since almost every year from then on Harriet would spend the autumn in the vicinity. Like Little Harriet, George would never learn the truth about his parentage, although both

Harriet and Granville would keep closely in touch with their children's progress and, in due course, as we will see, they would return more openly to their father's life.

By the end of the first week of November, Bess was happy enough with Harriet's progress to hurry to London and take care of Georgiana. Harriet passed the next eight days lying in, which roused Lady Spencer's suspicions. "When do you come back for I imagined the cold weather would have timed your return?"[22] Fearing her mother might arrive and uncover the truth, Harriet traveled back to London to finish her recovery there. The house at Cavendish Square reawakened memories that were still painful. "I am once more in that sad room where I suffered so much a month ago."[23] On the pretext of having a bad cold she stayed in and, except for one brief outing to Chiswick to see her sister, saw few visitors for the next month. Learning of her withdrawal from society, Lady Spencer no doubt feared Bessborough's temper was to blame and grew restless with concern. "I am really uneasy at not hearing of you my dear Harriet and beg somebody will write without fail tomorrow."[24] Harriet replied reassuringly but without giving any indication of what was wrong. Memories of her mother's discovery of Georgiana's pregnancy must have lingered in her mind, and she took pains to keep her mother at a distance until the visible signs of her recent pregnancy were gone.

Unsurprisingly, given the likelihood of post being opened, Harriet's letters to Granville pointedly avoid all mention of their baby and make only the vaguest references to her health. "I did not want any additional anxiety just now, and really feel quite unwell with the constant, constant agitation I live in — *mais ne parlons pas de cela*,"[25] she told him in what must have been one of her first letters after giving birth to George. Instead, her letters chiefly concern themselves with safer subjects: political and social gossip that she had heard from her sister or Bess. For Granville, the words mattered little. He crossed the North Sea and made his way across northern Germany and Poland to Russia, in a fever of expectation for news. Any word, no matter how brief and ambiguous, must have come as a relief — it meant she had survived the peril of childbirth. Granville had always been a reluctant letter-writer, making any excuse to avoid the task, and we must see it as a measure of his mounting anxiety that only four days after leaving England, when his ship passed a convoy returning to England, he sent a letter imploring her for news.

This brief note was all Harriet heard of Granville or Willy for nearly two months. Their party did not reach St. Petersburg until the end of October and from there letters took three or four weeks to reach British shores. Confined to her room, Harriet waited for news with increasing desperation. "Every day brings me fresh disappointment and letters never will come. Surely your messenger must have been taken too, or else why should ships be coming every day from P[etersburg] and none bring letters from you?"[26] When his first letters reached her, they made clear that he was struggling with the demands of his new role. He could write to Harriet only after writing lengthy dispatches, making endless visits to members of the Russian Imperial family, groping his way through a maze of protocol, and speaking in formal French, in which he felt inept and foolish. As if these tribulations were not enough, there was also a disappointing paucity of attractive females. "I am not reconciled to my situation," he grumbled after another round of formal engagements. "I am sick of the punctilio of bowing three times to an Ambassador and twice to a Chargé d'Affaires, etc., of walking out with the former through all the rooms to the staircase, and accompanying the latter only to the door of the ante-room. There is scarcely a pretty woman to be seen, even Ponsonby's [Willy's] tender heart seems in no danger."[27]

Despite—or perhaps because of—these unfavorable surroundings, Granville had warmed to Willy, finding him "delightfully good natured and gentlemanlike." His only complaint was that Willy, like so many teenagers, was reluctant to get up in the morning. "Stuart and myself were gone to church yesterday before he was dressed,"[28] he teased Harriet, forbidding her to mention the matter to Willy. After weeks of waiting for correspondence, Harriet paid little attention to his complaints. "Thank heaven at last there are letters, dear letters, and though not very satisfactory yet the few lines are your hand writing and have relieved me from more pain than I can express."[29]

A week later Granville wrote again. He still detested the diplomatic life as much as ever—"it is impossible to describe to you how bored and wearied I am with being introduced to two or three hundred people with whom I have had to repeat the same conversation"—but his mood had mellowed because at one of the numerous assemblies he had recently attended he had met a woman who attracted him. Princess Serge Galitzin, nicknamed "the Barbarian," was in her mid-twenties, a striking woman with fine black eyes, coal-black hair, "and a strangely powerful and sweet expression of countenance."[30] According to Sarah, Lady Lyttelton, who met her seven years later, she was also a lively and flirtatious conversationalist, but flirting was as far as she went—she had an unblemished reputation as far as illicit sexual liaisons were concerned. Granville seemed undeterred by this reputation, telling Harriet that she merely "afford[ed] the opportunity for conversation which it was impossible to undertake with any other of the ladies who were sitting in a row," although he soothed Harriet, "I am not yet in love nor likely to be so."[31]

Over the following weeks Granville's interest in the Barbarian deepened. He learned that she had been estranged from her husband, "to whom she has hitherto . . . denied conjugal rights," and had returned to St. Petersburg to try to repair the marriage—an aim that did not prevent the princess from regularly receiving Granville alone at her house. Nevertheless, he was at pains to stress that the developing friendship made him no less reliant on Harriet and her letters for contact with the world at home. "I cannot describe to you the comfort I derive from them," he told her after receiving a batch of letters. "Pray, pray continue always to write to me in the same way, communicating to me all you hear and all you think and feel. Let not the distance which divides us cause the least change in that unreserved confidence which has been to me the source of so much real gratification and pleasure . . ."[32]

Protestations of this kind meant little to Harriet; she knew Granville well enough to guess that he would not mention the Barbarian so frequently to her unless he was drawn. But having heard it all before, she was too clever to respond jealously, "I think the little Barbarian and all the other handsome ladies you talk of begin to reconcile you to the society at P[etersburg] . . . I do not wish you to be *ennuié*, but do not amuse yourself too much, do not forget *how* you are wished for at home,"[33] she wrote, obliquely reminding him that the passion she offered was more satisfying than mere flirting.

By now whispers circulating the ton suggested that Harriet had distanced herself from her friends out of sorrow at Granville's departure and, even more irritatingly, that several other ladies had done likewise. "I minded it the more as one of the stories about is that you shut up half London, and that it is the fashion to be ill from despair at your absence. Think!"[34] she fumed before returning to a more active life.

Among Harriet's first outings after her "long confinement" were visits to the theater to see London's newest star. William Henry Betty, dubbed "the young Roscius," was a thirteen-year-old boy of outstanding beauty and acting ability who had taken the city by storm. The first time Harriet saw Betty, he was playing a leading role in *Lover's Vows,* a play by August von Kotzebue, adapted by Mrs. Inchbald, in which an illegitimate child plays a prominent part. The subject matter alone, so close to Harriet's heart, moved her profoundly, and the part played by Betty—in which he braves execution to save his mother from penury—must have made her think of her youngest son's future. "I cried my eyes out," she told Granville. "The detail of all the disadvantages a natural child must suffer would alone have affected me, but it is impossible to give you an idea of what this creature [Betty] is—his tenderness to his mother, his perfect freedom from all affectation and whining . . . are really finer than anything I ever saw."[35]

After the performance Sheridan brought the young actor to her box, only to begin making a spectacle of himself that rapidly descended into the farcical. He tried to speak to Harriet, then stopped himself and sulked in silence in the corner before bursting into tears. "I took no notice, but ought to have exclaimed," Harriet declared firmly. Over the following days Harriet made several more visits to the theater; each time Sheridan's behavior grew more bizarre:

> He says one word to my sister, then retires to the further corner of the box, where with arms across, deep and audible sighs, and sometimes tears! He remains without uttering and motionless, with his eyes fixed on me in the most marked and distressing manner, during the whole time we stay. Tonight he followed us in before the play began, and remained as I tell you through the play and farce. As we were going, I dropped my shawl and muff; he picked them up and with a look of ludicrous humility presented them to Mr. Hill to give me. I took Morpeth's arm and walked away, but he followed, and

then posted himself at the outward door by the carriages. I always pretend not to see, but you cannot imagine how unpleasant it is to *feel* eyes upon one so.[36]

We sense from this description Harriet's unease at Sheridan's behavior toward her. She had good reason to worry: not for long would he allow her to walk away unscathed. Within weeks she would discover the full extent of the bitterness and wrath that simmered beneath the tears.

NINETEEN

Defamation and Disturbance
1805

WHEN A MALICIOUS LETTER arrived at Cavendish Square, Harriet was thrown into turmoil. Addressed to Caro, the communication was "filled with every gross disgusting indecency that the most depraved imagination could suggest—worse indeed than any thing I ever heard, saw, read, or could imagine amongst the lowest class of the most abandoned wretches."[1] Harriet immediately concluded that she rather than her daughter was the intended target and blamed her chekered past, reproaching herself bitterly for her worthlessness. But who had sent the letter? The fact that among the obscenities were references to conversations that had taken place recently at Devonshire House, when only a handful of friends had been present, suggested someone within her circle was the author. The signature was that of Mr. Hill, an old friend and one of the habitués of Devonshire House, but the handwriting was not his. Nor did she recognize it as belonging to any of her friends.

Two days later the situation became yet more alarming. Another poison-pen letter arrived, this time addressed to Harriet herself. Worse still, defamatory articles appeared in the *Morning Post* and *Courier,* slurring Harriet and casting aspersions on Harryo's relationship with Duncannon. In a state of shock, Harriet asked an old friend, Robert Adair, for help in discovering where the articles had originated. Adair could discover no name—the articles had been submitted anonymously—but he brought the manuscripts to show her. One glance was all Harriet needed; she recognized the hand as Sheridan's.

There is nothing to corroborate Harriet's assertion that Sheridan lay behind the letters, but he had always had a spiteful strand to his nature and the letters certainly tally with his persecution of Harriet at social functions. On every front Sheridan's life had spiraled into chaos. He was drinking heavily and falling ever deeper into debt through ill-starred business dealings at Drury Lane. His second wife, Hecca, had become embroiled in an affair with Charles Grey, the rising star of the Whigs;* his parliamentary career was floundering and there was little sign of his former handsome self; "nothing remained of his once expressive face but the remarkable brilliancy of his eyes; his cheeks were bloated, his nose was of a fiery red, and his general aspect bespoke the self-indulgence of the reckless man,"[2] wrote a contemporary.

Those close to Harriet certainly believed she was right. "I suppose that Sheridan is the author, though one should have imagined that, however depraved his morals, and however malignant might be his mind, he would have had *good taste* enough not to have resorted to such a species of vengeance,"[3] Granville agreed from Russia.

But knowing who was behind the malicious campaign was one thing; stopping it was quite another. Over the following weeks a deluge of letters, some containing obscene prints, arrived addressed to Harriet and other members of the family, including Georgiana, Harryo, and Caroline St. Jules, as well as close friends such as Mr. Hill—the supposed writer of the first letter. Articles also continued to be submitted to the newspapers, although thanks to Harriet's connections few of these were printed. The pieces were always in the same hand—which Harriet examined several times and each time identified as Sheridan's.

The hand is dreadfully like one I know very well . . . the abuse is chiefly levelled against me—old stories ripped up about Sh[eridan] C[harles] W[yndham], Ld. Paget and now Mr. Hill consoling me for other diplomatic losses; sometimes cuts at a display of melancholy, but usually accounts of violent dissipation and gaiety. As all this has not even the slightest shadow of foundation . . . it certainly seems like a plan to hurt me.[4]

---

* Once Georgiana's lover and now married to Mary Ponsonby, a cousin of Bessborough's.

Throughout February and March the poison-pen letters continued. Harriet learned to expect them and took to destroying suspicious mail unopened, although since the handwriting of the address, folding, and postmark often differed, recognizing them was not always easy. She never grew immune to the hatred they contained. To her it seemed Sheridan had taken advantage of her present situation. Had Granville been present to defend her, he would not have dared torment her thus. "The world is full of spite and malice, and I hate it, and I hate that you should be away; some of our persecutions, I believe in my heart, would not have arisen if you had been there."[5]

Even when the letters eventually tailed off, Harriet remained haunted by the ordeal and took pains to avoid Sheridan as much as possible. But the world they inhabited was small, and inevitably their paths crossed. In June she bumped into him at a ball and he tried to force her to sit next to him at supper. Luckily, Lord Morpeth knew about the letters and intervened, steering Harriet close to the Prince of Wales on one side and squeezing himself between Harriet and Sheridan on the other.

Other occasions were less easy to control and ended in embarrassing scenes. At a ball in July, at which Granville's two sisters were present, Sheridan sat opposite Harriet and gazed fixedly at her in so obvious a manner that other guests noticed and began to pass comment. Harriet excused Sheridan on the grounds of his drunkenness, then stood to leave the table, but Sheridan grabbed her by the arm, begging her to shake his hand. Harriet extricated herself as coolly as she could and moved away, but he followed, reproaching her loudly for her cruelty and asking why she would not greet him. Harriet told him that "his own sagacity might explain to him why I never would, and that his conduct tonight did not tend to alter my determination," then seated herself in the midst of a group of elderly ladies. But even here the harassment continued. Sheridan loudly begged her pardon for his past offenses and declared "he had never ceased loving, respecting and adoring me, and that I was the only person he ever really loved. Think of the dismay of all the formal Ladies! I really thought I should have sunk into the earth . . . I was told afterwards that I turned so pale they thought I was going to faint."[6]

Sheridan was not the only one of Harriet's so-called friends to turn against her. Hester Stanhope still clung to hope of reconciliation with

Granville. In November, shortly after Harriet's return to London, she had begun to reveal a marked animosity toward Harriet, which the latter indignantly reported to Granville:

> Hetty talks as if she had been ill treated; says Mr. A[rundel]'s [Granville's] notes, language, and manner were such as to induce her to suppose he meant very differently by her, and that she can only attribute the failure to the treachery of Mrs. Newton [Harriet].[7]

Hester claimed not only that her illness (a breakdown and failed suicide) had been caused by Granville's "dishonourable conduct but that he had been deceived and persuaded by that D[amne]d Mrs. N[ewton] who under the mask of false friendship had wormed out his mistress's secrets from her, and then by her arts broke off the match." Harriet recalled the friendship and advice she had offered Hester and her efforts to persuade Granville to treat Hester fairly, and was understandably wounded by the injustice of the accusations. "It is a little hard; and heaven knows the heart aches all this caused Mrs. Newton at the time—and now to be accused of treachery and falsehood."[8]

The following month Hester was again taken ill—probably suffering from a further breakdown. In the midst of her despair she wrote a rambling twenty-page letter to Granville in which she absolved him of any guilt and talked of Harriet affectionately. Despite the mischief she had earlier caused, Granville took the letter at face value and, unusually, felt his conscience prick. Harriet, more knowing and more directly affected by Hester's slanders, was less forgiving and warned Granville to be wary. "I cannot help thinking hopes are entertained that at Mr. Arundel's return he will marry her."[9] Her suspicions were confirmed when soon after this Hester began to spread rumors that she was about to give birth to Granville's child.

Was Hester suffering a phantom pregnancy, or was "the story of the accouchement...upon [which] she affiches" another means to prod Granville into proposing, or a further barbed attack on Harriet? If the latter was Hester's aim, she was to be disappointed. Harriet rarely bore grudges, and talk of childbirth made her realize the hopelessness of Hetty's obsession. Her anger evaporated. "She goes out without rouge, much fairer than she was, and so languid and faint...I do wonder what all this means . . . From my soul I pity her, though sometimes I fear she has been doing very wrong from the mistaken notion that I deceived her—but no matter."[10]

HARRIET COULD NOT bring herself to condemn Hester or Sheridan for long, but their onslaughts made her yearn for Granville's return, particularly since he had yet to meet his son, George. As spring gave way to summer, it seemed increasingly unlikely, however, that he would return as originally planned that autumn. Security forbade discussion of his work or plans in his private correspondence with Harriet— "there are many reasons why I could not write to you all the secrets, and I cannot write to you by halves upon any subject"—although he did say that waiting for responses to his key dispatches gave him "the same sort of feel as when one has a great stake upon a card, which card will not come up."[11] From this Harriet must have gathered that his mission was enjoying slow but significant success. Other influential friends told her that Granville had persuaded Tsar Alexander to accept Pitt's offer of financial subsidies from Britain in return for Russian troops joining an attempt to oust Napoleon from southern Italy. But progress was painfully slow and Granville's role in finalizing the agreement was crucial. Harriet drew her conclusions. "I fear you mean to put off your return, and if you do much longer, it will be too late to leave Russia this winter."[12]

Delay was what she had always dreaded, and it intensified her longing. Amid the social chitchat, the woes, the commentaries on political news, and the reviews of plays and books with which her letters are crammed, there are increasingly poignant references to her yearning for his return. In one moving incident she describes dressing for an evening engagement, when she heard the sound of piano music in a room below. Her heart skipped a beat—this was the way Granville sometimes signaled his arrival. "How often have I flown at that call. I cannot tell you the feel it gave me. Candles were not brought, and as I pushed the door open I only saw the tall figure of a man, which though very unlike you in fact seen so and at that time, made an impression on me I could not recover the whole night."[13] The letter survives only in published form, and the editing at this key juncture implies that Harriet went on to describe her longing so intimately that it was deemed unsuitable for publication.

Harriet had another reason to abandon caution in describing her physical cravings. Granville had given up attending the stilted and stuffy Petersburg assemblies that were supposed to be part of diplomatic life, and instead spent most evenings at the Barbarian's house, deep in conversation. The Barbarian appeared to offer much that Granville looked for in a woman. "She is certainly very clever and entertaining; she talks upon all subjects—politics, scandal, etc.—without that reserve which usually characterises the conversation of most people here." Women of vivacity, openness, and intellect had always appealed to him—these qualities had made him love Harriet in the first place—and the thrill of the chase was what had invariably led him into other amorous skirmishes. Harriet had always encouraged him to confide details of his other affairs to her, deriving a sense of security from knowing rather than being kept in ignorance. In this instance he admitted only that "something of flirtation is mixed up in our conversation; but I see no probability of its proceeding beyond what it is at present."[14] Well used to reading between the lines, Harriet sensed Granville's withdrawal and resented it. Jealousy added to her longing. "What can I say? When you go every night to the Barbarian and stay there sometimes tête-à-tête till three, the *cause,* whatever it arises from, must end in being probably dangerous to you."[15]

Sex was the one thing Granville had so far been refused by the Barbarian. Again Harriet reminded him of the one key advantage she held over the youthful, teasing, but famously chaste Barbarian. "I see and acknowledge the truth and justice of your lecture about the Barbarian," Granville responded, "but I know not how I am entrained; she piques me into perseverance. She is regarded by every body at Petersburg as 'unstained and pure as is the lily white' and the contradictions and inconsistencies of her conduct lead me to be of the same opinion. I think she likes me . . ." In other words, he was drawn by the challenge the Barbarian represented as much as by any real allure; her flirtatious ambivalence kept him in her thrall. The letter goes on, more revealingly still:

I know not whether I have repeated to you before that to you I owe the happiest moments of my life, but a truer opinion was never uttered or written by me; and I am persuaded that if it had been my lot to have been married to you, I should have passed a life of happiness such as is enjoyed by few people. When I used to praise you, I remember you told me always that I viewed you under a temporary delusion. Whether that were so or not, I will not pretend to say, but I can with sincerity affirm that to this moment I look upon you as far, far superior to any other human being I ever met with; and I look forward to the time of our meeting with feelings of impatience such as I cannot describe.[16]

There are two possible interpretations to this. At face value it reads as proof of Granville's continuing commitment to Harriet. Distance and their prolonged separation had not lessened Harriet's allure, he was saying. He still loved and depended upon her deeply; she was, if anything, more indispensable to him now than ever before. In this context his flirtations with other women were meaningless, no more than rituals that passed the time. Harriet, distanced though she was, eclipsed all others in life and still held the preeminent place in his heart. But Granville's repeated claims that he was not in love raise the suspicion that he protested too much. We cannot but wonder whether such a reticent man would have felt it necessary to acknowledge all Harriet had been and was to him, or to declare that he was not in love, were his heart not engaged elsewhere.

If such disturbing thoughts occurred to Harriet she must have tried to disregard them, for by spring she was wrapped up in a series of family crises. Caro's teenage passion for William Lamb had not faded with the passage of time and had been fed by William paying marked attention to her whenever they were together. Harriet had always opposed the match, and her feelings had not altered. Caro was her only legitimate daughter, and although now nineteen she seemed far younger and Harriet, like every aristocratic mother of her day, hoped that she would marry brilliantly. Until now his limited financial prospects had made William hold back from declaring himself, but when his eldest brother, Peniston, died of consumption William became heir to the title and fortune, and with his prospects dramatically altered* he wrote to Caro to ask her to marry him:

---

* William did not immediately reap the benefits of his altered state. His father, Lord Melbourne, doubted William's legitimacy and thus refused to offer him the same annual settlement of £5,000 he had given Peniston, whom he knew to be his son. After a friend's intervention he was eventually persuaded to grant William £2,000.

I have loved you for four years, loved you deeply, dearly, faithfully, — so faithfully that my love has withstood my firm determination to conquer it when honour forbade my declaring myself—has withstood all that absence, variety of objects, my own endeavours to seek and like others, or to occupy my mind with fixed attention to my profession, could do to shake it.[17]

Caro had passed sleepless nights longing for such a letter to arrive; she read it with a mixture of joy and anguish, then passed it to Harriet, who promptly transcribed it for Granville. Harriet had always hated saying no to Caro, and, having read the letter, she was moved by its sensitivity and agreed to mull the matter over with Bessborough. "I have long foreseen and endeavoured to avoid what has just happened," Harriet told Granville. "But she likes him too much for me to do more than entreat a little further acquaintance on both sides."

Despite her misgivings she weighed the arguments in William's favor. If they did not give consent to the union Caro might become seriously ill; furthermore, marriage might make her grow up, calm her tempestuous nature, and subdue the "little oddities of manner and *sauvagerie.*" Against this, Harriet set her ambivalence toward the Lamb family, their lack of social grace and hedonistic amorality—or, as she put it, "creed or rather no creed"[18]—and her particular dislike for Lady Melbourne, whom she nicknamed "the Thorn,"[19] a reference to her acerbic wit and bossy nature.

Nevertheless, the family slowly reconciled themselves to the idea of consenting to William's proposal, but nothing had yet been said when, a few days later, Harriet, Bessborough, and Caro went to Drury Lane Theatre. During the interval William visited their box to pay his respects. Harriet was impressed by his manner toward Caro, and any vestige of reluctance melted. Harriet told him that she and Bessborough had decided on "leaving everything to Caro's decision": in other words, he and Caro might marry. Hearing this, William was so delighted that he threw his arms around Harriet and kissed her. At this moment Harriet looked up and saw Granville's friends Canning and Mr. Hammond staring at her in bewilderment; meanwhile, William, in a fit of embarrassment, ran off down the stairs. "No words can paint to you my confusion," Harriet told Granville later, "but, unable to bear the Pope's

[Canning's] mortifying conjectures even till all was declared, I flew after him, and calling him out, told him the cause of what he saw, and you can have no conception of his kindness; he was delighted, quieted all my fears, assured me my objections were idle—praised William extremely, and did me more good than any one thing I had heard before."*20

The wider family greeted the happy news with mixed response. Even before Harriet's final capitulation, George Spencer had declared that Caro "should belong to his son."† After the incident at the theater, the Bessborough trio went to Devonshire House to announce the engagement. On hearing the news, Georgiana's fifteen-year-old son Hartington—heir to the Devonshire fortune—was visibly taken aback and grew hysterical, tearfully declaring that he had always hoped that Caro would marry him, and that "no plan he had ever formed of future pleasure or happiness was separated from her."‡

There was also Lady Spencer's reaction to fret over. Georgiana had tried to prepare her mother, writing with characteristic exaggeration that William's proposal "has brought... such happiness in her [Caro]—such evidence of the most boundless attachment that I really believe... that any check would be productive of madness or death."21 Caro adored her grandmother—Lady Spencer had always taken a great interest in her, despite her tantrums and nervous crises—and her consent was fundamental to Caro's peace of mind.

Lady Spencer's first response seemed favorable. "My head and my heart are so full my Dear Harriet that I can only say how fervently I hope your dear girl may be happy—she must run some risques—and there seems in the present choice at least the advantage of mutual attachment,"22 she wrote on first hearing of William's proposal. She then proceeded to baffle her family by refusing to give her formal approval until Caro came and stayed with her at Holywell, and she could meet William. No one underestimated the significance of this meeting. "I

---

* Part of the reason for Harriet's embarrassment was that William had been rumored to have been infatuated with her before falling for Caroline.

† Caroline's first cousin, Jack, Viscount Althorp, who was heir to the Spencer estate and fortune.

‡ True to his word, Hart never married, although his bachelor state was more likely a result of his having little attraction for the female sex in general than of an unrequited passion for Caroline.

hope my grandmother approves of it in the first instance,"[23] wrote Duncannon to his sister, while William remarked, "I am much more anxious about it than I can express."[24] Even after she had met William, Lady Spencer remained inscrutable, causing an overwrought Caro to dissolve into noisy tears, whereupon Lady Spencer eventually agreed to give the union her blessing, tersely declaring that Caro was being dishonest in making such a scene, since the match had already been agreed before she came to stay.

Further drama was sparked by Lady Melbourne. Though she was pleased with the Spencer-Cavendish connection, Caro's tarnished family background could hardly be ignored. Also, she was jealous of the warmth that already existed between William and Harriet and cuttingly commented that "she hoped the daughter would turn out better than the mother, or William might have to repent of his choice." Harriet told herself this jibe was intended half in jest, but she was wounded nonetheless. "There are subjects too sore to bear a joke . . . I felt hurt and possibly could have retorted but checked myself however and only said I hoped and believed she would prove much better 'especially (I added) with the help of your advice' (I would not say example)."[25] In the interests of family harmony and Caro's future happiness, Harriet said nothing to defend herself—a resolution that cannot have been easy given Lady Melbourne's own less than virtuous history.*

THE WEDDING WAS to take place only three weeks after the announcement of the engagement, and Harriet hurried to London from St. Albans to set the frenetic wedding preparations in motion. Along with receiving a stream of visitors who wished to offer their congratulations, there was the trousseau to arrange. "My whole day passes in seeing milliners and mantua makers," she wrote.[26] There was also Caro—difficult at the best of times—to handle as tensions mounted. In the run-up to the wedding Caro grew depressed and nervous and even more childishly demanding and dependent on her mother than usual. Harriet took her to Roehampton to rest, and when William came to

---

* If, as was widely supposed, William Lamb was Lord Egremont's son, and, as has been suggested, Caro was fathered by Charles Wyndham—Egremont's third son—then Caro was marrying her uncle.

call, Caro histrionically proclaimed: "My dear William, judge what my love must be when I can leave such a mother as this for you. Girls who are not happy at home may marry without regret, but it required very strong affection indeed to overpower mine."[27]

The ceremony took place on June 3 at Cavendish Square, at eight in the evening. Caroline had been showered with expensive gifts—a wedding dress from the Duke of Devonshire, jeweled tiaras from Georgiana and Lady Melbourne, a topaz cross from Harryo, a pearl-and-diamond cross from Bess, and a parure of amethysts from Lord Melbourne. But she remained taut with apprehension throughout the evening, and when she came out of the house to find a vast crowd had assembled to wave her off her agitation worsened. Harriet was equally moved; by now she had wholeheartedly accepted William into the family—"As I told you so gravely the other day he really appears to me like my natural son,"[28] she said of him, and bearing in mind she had given birth to a "natural" son only seven months earlier, this was high accolade indeed. Warmth toward William did not lessen the blow of losing Caro, though. As the first of her children to marry and her only legitimate daughter, Harriet felt Caro's loss especially keenly. As soon as the couple had mounted into their carriage and sped off to Brocket Hall, where they were to spend their honeymoon, Harriet collapsed with nervous exhaustion. Her first letter to Caro, written a day after the wedding, reflects the turbulence of her emotions:

My darling love your letter made me cry and then laugh at myself for crying, the truth is we are two simpletons and unlike what mother and daughter ought to be. William may pride himself on his good conduct for to nothing one atom less kind and delightful than he is could I have yielded you, I should have forbid the banns at last with anybody else . . .[29]

Harriet visited the newlywed couple a few days later and found Caro happy but still in a state of shock after the traumas of the wedding night. "I never saw anything so kind as he is; but, really, being married is a state of great sufferance to a girl in every way. I do think it very hard that men should always have *beau jeu* on all occasions, and that all pain, moral *et physique,* should be reserved for us."[30] Lady Melbourne was also in residence, and thus for Harriet too the stay at Brocket was an ordeal. "I like William of all things, but I could dispense with some of his *entours* [family] — but this I must not even whisper."[31]

Scarcely had Harriet recovered from the stress of Caro's nuptials than Georgiana became the source of alarm when she was taken seriously ill with a recurrence of the earlier problem with her eye. Harriet, devoted as ever to her sister, sat at Georgiana's darkened bedside until she recovered a week later. In mid-July, Georgiana was again bedridden, this time with overwrought nerves. She had declared her debts to the Duke of Devonshire, spurring dozens more creditors to come forward with outstanding bills. In despair of ever getting to the bottom of his wife's financial mire, the duke gave Harriet the task of making sure that he was told the truth about the full extent of Georgiana's money troubles, and that no new debts were incurred.

The task placed Harriet in an invidious situation. She was aware that the duke was notoriously unpredictable — a wrong word might mean him withdrawing his agreement to help Georgiana, in which case she would descend into despair. But discovering all Georgiana's debts was no easy matter. "I [am] drove mad with every day hearing of some fresh claim on my sister whose affairs are to be put into my hands as the only person she will entirely trust, and K [Canis — the Duke of Devonshire's nickname] says he has so high an opinion of my integrity that if I give him my word that no new debt shall be entered into, and that I tell him the whole sum to the best of my knowledge, he will trust implicitly to me and not enquire the names or circumstances; but you cannot think how worrying this is."[32]

WHILE HARRIET WAS thus mired, in Russia Granville's chief complaint was of boredom. "The dullness of a Petersburg summer is excessive," he groused of interminable days spent rising at eleven, doing nothing all morning and early afternoon except for dressing, breakfasting, and reading the papers and "some idle book" before driving or riding out till five, then dining, attending a public concert, and visiting the Barbarian, "where I stay till two — the last two hours are tête-à-tête; we talk politics, metaphysics, literature, beaux art, scandal, love . . ."[33] To alleviate the tedium he rented a country house three doors away from a lodge rented by the Barbarian. "Do not be alarmed," he ingenuously told Harriet "... [but] her coming to a lodge in this vicinity has created some talk among those inclined to *commérage* [gossip]." Even in the countryside his gripes continued; he was being eaten alive by gnats and mosquitoes, and having followed the Barbarian, he found she had disappeared to another part of the countryside to visit her sister. By contrast he remembered his last summer, racing between Chiswick, London, and Roehampton for secret assignations with Harriet: "it is a melancholy recollection, for my impatience to return is becoming intolerable."[34]

Granville had already decided he could no longer bear to remain another year in Russia and had begun pressing the foreign office to recall him, when his yearning to return was suddenly intensified with an unexpected sad discovery. Reading the newspapers one morning, he found an account of his mother's death. Granville was distraught, but since he had no confirmation of the report tried to persuade himself it was false. A few days later, however, a letter reached him confirming the news of Lady Stafford's death.

Harriet's heart went out to Granville. "I have scarcely heart to write to you, dearest G. No words can tell you how much I regret being from you at this moment—how deeply I feel your loss, and let me say, my own, for I can never think without gratitude and affection of her kindness to me."[35] Despite their past difficulties she and Lady Stafford had reached an accord, and since Granville's departure the two women had corresponded regularly. Naturally, though, she was glad to hear that Granville would return to Britain at the end of September, after visiting the Polish frontier to finalize agreements and take his leave of the emperor. He too looked forward to their reunion with eager anticipation. "What joy I feel in thinking that perhaps in less than six weeks I shall again be with you," he wrote, adding a parting barb: "you will not give the less credit to this assurance because I add that I shall feel very sorry at taking leave of the Barbarian; when I bid her adieu, it will be in all probability the last time of my ever speaking to her, and having for some months passed almost every day three or four hours with her, the idea of never seeing her again will certainly be painful."[36]

HARRIET PASSED THE interval consumed by another drama of family life. This time John, her eldest son, was a source of worry. He had involved himself in various romantic scrapes since his flirtation with Elizabeth Villiers, including a worryingly intense liaison with Mrs. Payne, a married friend of the Abercorns. Throughout this time his relationship with his cousin Harryo remained unresolved. The pair had agreed to wait for a year before deciding "whether they liked each other well enough to marry." In principle the Cavendishes and Bessboroughs were keen on such an alliance, but Harriet was concerned because John and Harryo had spent most of the past twelve months quarreling with each other, mostly over John's inconstancy. Eventually matters came to a head. Harryo, who rarely minced words, gave John an ultimatum that "he must promise to cure himself completely of flirting, for she could not bear it; and *nommément* [in particular], Mrs. P[ayne] and a new flirtation with Lady Maria Fane must be given up."[37]

John was used to Harriet's gentle manner of manipulation and took umbrage at this baldly issued demand, responding petulantly that "he was not over anxious to marry at present, and above all things would not bear rules to be prescribed to him *by any woman living.*" Hearing this, Harriet rushed to Harryo's defense, telling John that her request was reasonable. But John was unmoved; he did not wish "his wife to attempt to govern him . . . he had not been used to it in a mother, and certainly should not submit to it in the person he was to pass his life with."[38]

John was still fuming when Harriet left London to spend an autumn holiday in Hastings. A few days later he wrote announcing his engagement to Lady Maria Fane and asking Bessborough to write to Maria's father, the Earl of Westmorland, to request her hand formally on his behalf. Both Harriet and Bessborough were flabbergasted. Maria was all that Harryo was not. Gentle-natured, quietly spoken, and adoring toward John, she conformed perfectly to the Regency ideal of womanhood, but she was an outsider to the close-knit Devonshire House circle, and Harriet did not much like the Fanes. Westmorland was a friend and supporter of Pitt's, and perhaps too the memory of Granville's snub by Maria's sister Sarah still rankled. To Georgiana also the news came as a profound disappointment; she had hoped Harryo and Duncannon would resolve their differences.

No one could deny, however, that from a financial point of view the marriage was advantageous. Maria stood to inherit a fortune of her own,* which would allow the couple to lead a comfortable life and would greatly ease the financial burden on the depleted Bessborough estates. The tricky subject of money was one that Bessborough and John had already tentatively discussed when it came to choosing a bride. "I never meant to control you in any match you wished to make, neither did I want you to marry a very great fortune," he remarked in his letter to his eldest son. "I only represented to you it was necessary that the lady should have some fortune, otherwise you would have great difficulties in your living, and I should hope in the choice you have now made, there will be that which will remove some incumbrances off my estate and enable me to add to your income enough to make you comfortable though not in affluent circumstances."[39]

Harriet was similarly embarrassed by their straitened circumstances and did not wish Lord Westmorland to think the sum they settled on their son inadequate. "Lord B[essborough] will do all he possibly can . . . and means to share with them every additional increase of income we may have from leases falling in, etc., which for some years to come will be pretty considerable, as we have some leases from the time of Oliver Cromwell; but still, as I hope and trust, Lord B is likely to live many, many years, they have nothing to look forward to but a small income for the best part of their lives."[40]

In fact, the Westmorlands welcomed John as their future son-in-law without quibble, and Harriet slowly reconciled herself to the match. To Granville she gaily wrote: "I hear on all sides such praises of the character and disposition of Lady Maria . . . that altogether it makes me feel much happier than I did, and I really think Dun[cannon] is very lucky."[41] Privately, however, Harriet still struggled to accustom herself to the idea of Maria joining their family. Days before the wedding she sat up with Harryo discussing her future daughter-in-law. "I do not think she [Harriet] seems to like the marriage much," remarked Harryo afterward; "at least she talks of it *en victime*, praises her

---

* Maria's mother was Sarah Child, daughter of the banker Robert Child. She had married the Earl of Westmorland after eloping with him and racing to Gretna Green, pursued by her furious father. After the marriage Child ensured no male heirs of Lord Westmorland would benefit from his gargantuan wealth by stipulating that only female descendants might inherit. Maria had three siblings—one brother, and two sisters with whom she would thus share the Child wealth.

in rather a languid way, says she thinks her very ugly (which is, I think, both ill-judged and ill-natured), and hopes he will be happy and constant, with shrugs and reveries. Then says with a sigh, it is fortunate that from mixing in so new a set, he will be very little in our family."[42]

Throughout these difficult weeks Harriet had been sustained by the thought of Granville's imminent return. But a fortnight before John's wedding was due to take place, she was shocked to learn that the Prussian army of thirty thousand men under General Mack had been surprised by Napoleon and forced to surrender at Ulm. Not knowing Granville's whereabouts, she was terrified. "This man moves like a torrent," she wrote of Napoleon, "and if Mr. Arundel [Granville] is with the Emperor Alexander I shall tremble for his safety; yet I dread his being blamed if he is not, as I hear so much reliance laid upon his keeping the Emperor steady."[43]

The humiliating Prussian defeat was countered by the news of Nelson's epic victory at Trafalgar on October 21, which also reached London in early November. Harriet's interest in Nelson was reinforced by a family connection. It was her brother, George Spencer, as First Lord of the Admiralty, who had defied the opposition of the Admiralty Board and given Nelson command of the Mediterranean fleet. She was overwhelmed by his achievement, yet devastated by the news of his death. "Good heavens! What news!" she declared, flooded as everyone was by patriotic fervor. In London people from every echelon of society wore black armbands or black cockades in their hats. At the Admiralty crowds of women and children gathered, anxious for news of loved ones. "How glorious if it was not so cruelly damped by Nelson's death! . . . what an irreparable loss to England! I wish they would do what the *Courier* [a newspaper] proposes—order a general mourning for him . . . I can think of nothing else and hardly imagined it possible to feel so much grief for a man I did not know."[44] And yet, in the midst of the general mourning, Harriet reported, there were those in the Establishment who felt Nelson deserved to die for failing to observe traditional naval tactics. "The difference of a great or a common man is the knowing when to apply and when overlook general rules,"[45] she resolutely declared.

Harriet might not have praised a disregard for the conventions of warfare so warmly had she known of the great victory such tactics would bring to the French before the year's end, and how this would affect her. Granville had left St. Petersburg for Warsaw, then traveled south to Vienna to take leave of the Russian emperor, who was leading his forces into battle at the front. In early December, Canning told Harriet what she had already heard whispered: Granville would not return as expected because, having heard of his intention to leave, Tsar Alexander had intervened "to entreat him, in consideration of the high esteem they bear him . . . if possible, and if consistent with his health, not to leave them for at least a few months to come."[46]

In view of the dire state of the war, Granville had acceded to the request. Eighty miles from the Austrian capital he had learned of Napoleon's rapid advance; Tsar Alexander was now fleeing to the Austrian fortress town of Olmütz,* and Granville diverted to meet him. Letters arrived a month later describing Granville's increasingly precarious situation. He and a manservant were living in Olmütz with the Russian and Austrian army encamped nearby and the French holding the strategic position of the Pratzen Heights. "A great battle is momentarily expected . . . It is a most critical and anxious moment, for upon the issue of this battle rests the dependence or independence of the continent."[47] Three days later, from Troppau in Poland, he detailed Napoleon's decisive victory over the Russo-Austrian forces at Austerlitz, a nearby village (now the site of Slavkov u Brna in the Czech Republic). "A very bloody engagement, of which the event was favourable to the French, but in which the Russians behaved with great courage, has driven us out of Olmütz . . . and to this place are we miserable fugitives arrived."[48] Napoleon had successfully lulled the allied armies into thinking he was retreating, and then attacked head-on. Within a matter of ten hours the allies lost around twenty-five thousand men—a third of their total number; French casualties numbered nine thousand. Napoleon had never seemed more invincible; nor, in Harriet's eyes, can Granville's fate ever have seemed so uncertain.

---

* Now in the Czech Republic.

TWENTY

Heartbreak

1806

THE YEAR THAT WAS TO BE the saddest of Harriet's life began with a stream of inauspicious news from the Continent. The war against Napoleon had entered its darkest phase. The vanquished Austrians had signed the Treaty of Pressburg, ceding Venice and Dalmatia to the French, and to her chagrin Harriet discovered that although Granville had survived Austerlitz, instead of returning he had traveled to Berlin. His brother-in-law, Lord Harrowby, was frantically trying to entice the Prussians to join the British and Russian alliance in the city. Harrowby had taken ill, probably from the effects of the severe strain he was under, and while Granville was offering his support Willy too became dangerously unwell. So much unwelcome news piled together was more than Harriet could bear and she plunged into tearful despondency. "She is in a terrible state of lowness," recorded Harryo, "and sent Lord B[essborough] to say she had so bad a cold in her eyes as not to be able to stir from her room." Beady-eyed Harryo was not, however, deceived by the reason given for her aunt's decline. "They prepared for her being very unhappy tonight and 'poor Willy' is proxy for all the public and private grievances of Russia."[1]

Harriet's depression deepened with the national grief surrounding Lord Nelson's funeral. When she traveled to London with Maria and Duncannon, she found a city decked in mourning, with crow-black banners fluttering along the route from Greeenwich to St. Paul's. From her vantage point at Temple Bar, Harriet witnessed the funeral procession; carriages crammed the route as crowds looked on in an eerie silence punctuated only by the sounds of muffled drums and cannon fire.

Amongst many touching things the silence of that immense mob was not the least striking... they had been very noisy... the moment the car appeared which bore the body you might have heard a pin fall, and without any order to do so, they all took off their hats. I cannot tell you the effect this simple action produced; it seemed one general impulse of respect beyond any thing that could have been said or contrived...[2]

Scarcely a week later a further public calamity began to unfold. Pitt's health had long been fragile, but the news of the allies' defeat at Austerlitz had coincided with a worsening of his illness, and when he learned that Prussia had reached an accord with Napoleon he slid into an even more rapid decline. Harriet was saddened to learn that in Pitt's moment of weakness those who had once been his supporters deserted him in droves: "the courtiers and ministers who have all turned against poor Mr. Pitt, and because he is ill and unhappy abuse him more than his enemies ever did."[3] Pitt passed the winter recess in Bath, distanced from enemies and trying to regain his strength, but on his return to London in the New Year he was still obviously unwell and losing weight alarmingly. "It is dreadfully painful—gout all over him, attended with such extreme weakness of general health and particularly stomach and digestion, that it will require the greatest care and quiet to restore him."[4]

A week later Pitt had deteriorated further. He could keep nothing down but egg and brandy and a little chicken broth. "He is emaciated beyond anything ever seen alive, and proportionably weak, without any apparent means of nourishing him, as his stomach rejects everything he takes, whether as medicine or food,"[5] wrote Harriet, having heard the latest details from the royal physician, Sir Walter Farquhar, who also attended her family. Day by day the crisis deepened; Pitt developed a fever in addition to his other symptoms. "Good Heavens!" wrote Harriet, "where will all our misfortunes end? For there is no one, friend or foe, that would not think this a misfortune."[6] Two days later, having murmured, "Oh, my country! How I leave my country!"[7] Pitt breathed his last. He was only forty-six years of age, yet his health had been so ruined by heavy drinking and the cares of duty that his doctor declared his death due to old age, "as much as if he had been ninety."[8]

On hearing the news of Pitt's death, Fox, his longtime adversary in parliamentary debates, turned ashen and was lost for words for several minutes. "Impossible, impossible," he eventually declared; "one feels as if there was something missing in the world—a chasm, a blank that cannot be supplied."[9] Yet for all Fox's fine words, the void left by Pitt was quickly filled. A coalition government, dubbed the ministry of "All the Talents," was appointed, with Lord Grenville as leader of the administration, Fox at long last restored to office as foreign secretary, and Lord Sidmouth (the erstwhile leader Addington) installed as Lord Privy Seal.

Fox's return after so long in the political wilderness spelled opportunity for many of those who had opposed Pitt. Harriet watched her friends advance with mixed feelings, delighted on the one hand, yet railing at the "scene of rapacity, self interest, discontent, envy, rancour and heart burnings, this change of administration has occasioned."[10]

Not all those who had once opposed Pitt were anxious for a role. The Duke of Devonshire was offered any post he chose by Grenville but refused. Bessborough, whose financial situation had nothing in common with the duke's, was similarly devoid of political ambition and, strangely, Harriet supported his reluctance to take a post. When he was offered the lucrative job of postmaster general, once filled by his father, she agreed he should decline it; nor did she wish him to take another appointment. "He thinks very much as I do," she wrote, "that however *convenient* a place may be, perfect independence is much pleasanter."[11] We cannot help wondering whether part of her desire to keep Bessborough out of politics was the thought of Granville's imminent return. Perhaps she reasoned that with no public office to fulfill he would be more inclined to stay away from London, leaving her free to see Granville as she chose.

Whatever the reason for her qualms, Fox's role in the new administration represented the culmination of Harriet's political dream—one she had long shared with Georgiana. But the triumph did not lift their lives in the same way as had his great election in 1784. Now, both sisters were beset by personal cares that allowed little room for jubilation. Caro was expecting her first child and had been unwell during much of the pregnancy. In late January, after a bout of influenza, her labor began prematurely and she gave birth to a child who survived only a few hours. The tragedy of losing her first grandchild was one Harriet must have felt keenly, and the following month her misery worsened when Georgiana was taken gravely ill.

Financial worry had never ceased to dog Georgiana. Despite Harriet's attempts at ensuring all her debts were acknowledged, those she had confessed to the duke had resulted only in a further and apparently interminable train of liabilities emerging. The resulting stress, coupled with years of drinking too much, had led Georgiana to suffer blinding headaches and a string of other ailments that with each passing month became more debilitating. "I am most uncomfortable about your sister . . ." wrote Lady Spencer to Harriet in mid-March; "some horrible difficulty is hanging over her I conclude—and what can be done . . . I conclude her illness is owing to the old and hopeless story of money difficulties."[12]

Then Georgiana succumbed to what appeared to be another painful attack of gallstones. Harriet, as usual, dashed to Devonshire House to be at her side. "The events of a sick room can only be interesting to those who witness them, and I have nothing else to tell you, as I rarely quit her room. Yesterday she was very ill, today much better, but tonight a shivering fit has again come on . . . I am very anxious and absolutely pass my life at D[evonshire] H[ouse],"[13] she recorded. A day later Georgiana seemed calmer and Harriet felt happier about her, although her yellowish skin and eyes now suggested she was suffering from jaundice. "After sitting up the whole night I have not yet been able to find a moment when she was well enough for me to go home. It has been a sad day, but she is at length in a quiet sleep and I hope will have a good night . . . I am miserable at her suffering, but do not feel alarmed . . ."[14]

But Harriet's confidence was misplaced. Soon after she wrote this, Georgiana's condition worsened and a fever took hold. For the next three days and nights Harriet sat with her sister, protecting her from visitors, nursing her through fits of delirium and fever, calming her when doctors shaved her head and applied blisters that did little to salve her condition and only worsened her agonies. Georgiana was suffering from advanced liver disease[15] that was beyond the help of eighteenth-century medication. Despite the efforts of Harriet and the doctors, she died in the early hours of March 30, aged forty-nine, in the arms of her beloved sister.

IN THE IMMEDIATE aftermath of Georgiana's death, Harriet was so exhausted and shocked by the ordeal she had witnessed that she was incapable of expressing anything except the classic wish of one who is painfully bereaved—that she too might die.

> You will know, Dear G, by the newspapers—I cannot write—if any thing should happen to me... Mrs. Baker will send you a letter... God bless you—Break it to Willy.
>
> Any thing so horrible, so killing, as her three days' agony no human being ever witnessed. I saw it all, held her through all her struggles, saw her expire... and yet I am alive.[16]

Inevitably, as the initial shock faded, grief gripped Harriet's soul. She remained at Devonshire House while Georgiana's body lay in state, mourning with the duke and his children and Bess until the coffin was removed to Derby Cathedral to be buried in the Cavendish family vault. Harriet and Georgiana had always been physically demonstrative, and Harriet's anguish at Georgiana's death was increased by physical separation from her sister. The thought of never again touching or holding her seemed insupportable: "[I] since have again and again kissed her cold lips and pressed her lifeless body to my heart."[17] She yearned for some tangible memento of Georgiana's presence. Before the body was transported away in the hearse, the sculptor Nollekens came to take Georgiana's death mask. The duke, perhaps urged by Harriet, wanted to commission a bust of Georgiana, but Nollekens refused, saying he could never do her justice; Harriet insisted on keeping the first cast he had made.

Afterward she went to Roehampton and for a while lost herself in reliving each last moment of her sister's death. She had endured the pain of bereavement before when her father had died, but nothing had prepared her for the maddening agony she now felt. Days passed in which she was demented by loss and could barely function or write. "You have never known what it was to lose a friend to whom your whole heart was open, whom you loved with all the strong ties of natural affection and choice, habit, similarity of character added to it," she told Granville in one of her typically tortured letters. "Pray forgive me this strange letter; I am afraid my head is not yet quite right."[18] As if mirroring her desolate mood, for the next fortnight the weather turned unseasonably bitter. Harriet looked out from the windows of Roehampton, across parklands where spring blossoms had been blanketed in snow, and her sense of dislocation seemed to intensify. For hours she could do nothing but weep; there seemed no reason to go on. She searched for consolation in her faith, but found none. "I have been very unwell and my eyes extremely inflamed," she told Granville, "but now I really am not myself; I must trust to time, which I am told will do much . . . Time, submission to the will of heaven, and fervent prayer might do much for others, but what can I hope from prayer."[19]

When the weather eventually lifted and Harriet returned to London, she was still unable to sleep or eat and had little desire to do anything except pass each day with Bess's and Georgiana's children at Devonshire House. Here she walked through echoing rooms in which her sister had once danced, intrigued, and held court, discovering no solace, only memories that swamped her with desolation. Among those who were generous in offering Harriet their sympathy in her lowest moments was the Prince of Wales. He had often referred to Georgiana and Harriet as his sisters, and was distraught at hearing of Georgiana's illness and death. He repeatedly asked if he might call on Harriet. When she eventually agreed to receive him, he gave her an emerald ring "to bind still stronger the tie of brotherhood which he has always claimed,"[20] and then exhausted her by staying for four hours.

The prince also brought a message from Sheridan, begging Harriet to forgive his past misdemeanors. Harriet's reaction, though conciliatory, remained firm; even set against her present torment the pain he had inflicted remained raw. She had no enmity toward Sheridan, she told the prince, "but . . . particular circumstances had made me determine never to have any intercourse with him; that if he only would keep out of my way, or if we happened to meet not persecute me, no one would perceive anything in my behaviour that could mark out a quarrel."[21]

Before dying, Georgiana had asked Harriet and Bess to sort out her papers. Feeling stronger, a few days later Harriet agreed to go to

Chiswick with Bess to begin this task. But the effort of returning to a place so entwined with memories was too much and once again Harriet descended into inconsolable despair. "That place where I have passed the happiest and most miserable hours of my life—where every turn recalls to me all that I have loved best, where remorse and regret equally tear me, and bitter grief from seeing her almost present to me and losing her again. Oh G it drove my mind, already weak, almost to frenzy, and I was brought back to town quite ill."[22]

LIFE WOULD NEVER again be the same for Harriet. In Georgiana she had lost a loyal sister, a conspirator in transgressions, a supporter in illness, an irreplaceable ally in marital and financial turmoils. For weeks Harriet had little enthusiasm for society; she was filled with self-loathing and despaired whenever she thought of the years ahead without her sister, sometimes thinking of suicide. "I see myself in all the follies and weaknesses of youth, on the verge of old age, its infirmities, its desolateness threatening me on every side."

The sense of loss would remain for the rest of her life. The diarist Nathaniel Wraxall recorded a visit to the Cavendish vault in Derby Cathedral five years after Georgiana's death:

> As I stood contemplating the coffin which contained the ashes of that admired female [Georgiana], the woman who accompanied me pointed out the relics of a bouquet which lay upon the lid, nearly collapsed into dust. "That nosegay," said she, "was brought here by the Countess of Bessborough, who had designed to place it with her own hands on her sister's coffin. But, overcome by her emotions on approaching the spot, she found herself unable to descend the steps conducting to the vault. In an agony of grief she knelt down on the stones, as nearly over the place occupied by the corpse as I could direct, and there deposited the flowers, enjoining me the performance of an office to which she was unequal. I fulfilled her wishes.[23]

Adding to Harriet's misery was the delay in sending and receiving the news. It was the end of April when Granville learned of Georgiana's death, and another month before Harriet received his first letter acknowledging her loss. The letter, when it came, showed his open distress—Georgiana had been a close friend to Granville, a colluder in his affair with Harriet (and friendships with other women), and privy to all their most intimate secrets. "I am grieved, most sincerely grieved, but my grief is lost in the consideration of your sufferings . . . Oh that I had been in England! I think I might have been some comfort to you . . ."[24] He took seriously Harriet's suicidal desolation and, though alarmed, did his utmost to bolster her. "Oh let me conjure you to bear up against this sad misfortune; think of *all* your children," he pointedly remarked, "think of all who love you."[25]

Slowly but inevitably, the world around Harriet began to impinge on her consciousness. She would rarely again feel the same sense of connection with public matters; nevertheless, life—the intrigues, confidences, dramas, and tragedies of family and friends—recaptured her. She had always felt bolstered by the confidence of others, and once again her letters to Granville began to contain reports of the latest stories with which fashionable salons buzzed and on which she could shed special light. Prominent among these were the marital difficulties between the Prince and Princess of Wales. For several years the princess had been living apart from the prince, in Montague House, Blackheath. Rumors abounded of her illicit liaisons with various men (among them Granville's great friend George Canning, presently employed by the Board of Control, the naval hero Sir Sidney Smith, and Captain Thomas Manby, a dashing young naval officer). When the Prince of Wales had first mentioned his wife's indiscretions to Harriet two years earlier she had advised him either to ignore the whispers or to ask her for an explanation. The crisis deepened when Lady Douglas, one of the princess's disgruntled ex-ladies-in-waiting, made a deposition claiming that the princess had not only committed adultery, but had given birth to a child named Willy Austin out of wedlock and had planned to pass the baby off as the prince's.

In June, while Harriet was still mourning Georgiana's death, the prince decided to take advantage of the new position in government of his ally Fox by trying to rid himself of the princess. He told Harriet that the king had now decided to appoint a secret commission of ministers—including Harriet's brother, George Spencer—to begin a

"Delicate Investigation" into the claims against the princess. The king had become fond of the princess, but he was a man of high moral values and had long deplored the sexual license of his eldest son. It was the princess's wantonness rather than the fact of her adultery that riled him. "Had it been one serious attachment, even with consequences, I would have screened and protected her through everything," the king had told Lord Boringdon, "but there have been so many and mixed with so much levity, that it proves a determined profligacy of character."[26]

The commission interviewed various members of the princess's staff and eventually concluded that she had not given birth to an illegitimate child, although she was probably guilty of adultery—a conclusion that was undoubtedly accurate, since even her footman noted "the Princess is very fond of fucking." Harriet's reaction to the humiliating broadcasting of the princess's private life was both curious and revealing. "O G how glad I am Mr. Arundel [Granville] was not included! If he had stayed in England I have no doubt he would."[27] In other words, she was in little doubt that, like his great friend Canning, Granville might have succumbed to Caroline's advances.

In addition to charting this embarrassing episode, Harriet relayed somber news concerning one of her long-standing friends. Fox was seriously unwell, suffering from fluid retention, swollen limbs, and pain that the doctors diagnosed as dropsy. "I cannot tell you how much I was affected at seeing him. His face and hands are dreadfully drawn and emaciated, his complexion sallow beyond measure, his bosom sunk—and then, all at once, a body and legs so enormous that it looks like the things with which they dress up Falstaff,"[28] Harriet wrote after visiting the man with whom her political existence had been so entwined. Fox had been pathetically grateful for her visit, kissing her hand repeatedly and thanking her for her kindness. He remained witty and generous-hearted as ever. When his nephew Lord Holland complimented him on looking well, Fox quipped that to judge by the number of similar remarks he had received he must be the handsomest man in England and then, turning to Harriet, said: "Talking of the handsomest man in England reminds me of a friend of yours who has good qualities enough not to want his beauty. I hope we shall have him here soon." Fox's quip was not made lightly. Granville was due to return to British soil in a month's time, and when afterward Fox asked Harriet to lift her veil and saw her haggard face and eyes reddened by weeks of crying he remarked gently, "Come, come, this must not be. You must remember our Russian friends, who will be startled if they see you look so."[29]

Fox's illness became increasingly debilitating and in August, at the invitation of the Duke of Devonshire, he moved to Chiswick House to be treated there. The doctors performed several painful operations to siphon away the fluid that was bloating his limbs to elephantine proportions; on one occasion thirteen quarts of liquid were tapped. But although there were days in which Fox was able to receive visitors and drive about in his carriage, nothing could save him. He died at Chiswick on September 13. Harriet watched his funeral procession, recalling each sorrow she had endured over the past months. "At any time this would have been a most painful blow to me, but now that my spirits are so broke I cannot tell you how completely it overcomes me." She remembered Nelson's funeral, with which the year had begun, Pitt's sad end, and above all her misery at Georgiana's death. "The same crowd, the same appearance . . . but alas, alas! She who was always with me, who shared every pain and every pleasure, I have lived to see borne to the grave—I have lost for ever."[30]

One consolation alone helped Harriet cope: Granville had at last returned. His euphoric mood had helped restore her faith in life, although not everyone was equally restored by his company. Georgiana's youngest daughter, Harryo, had always been deeply critical of him; now more than ever, his manner seemed at odds with the atmosphere of sorrow, and was jarring. He was "gracious beyond the power of caprice, but too playful and gay to be agreeable,"[31] she declared after a dinner given by Harriet at Roehampton.

Harryo's critical view of Granville was colored by difficulties of her own. As a female and the least favored of the duke's children, the adjustments in the household since her mother's death had been hardest for her to bear. She had always deeply resented Bess's presence at Devonshire House, and her rancor had hardened as she watched Bess take on the privileges of chatelaine, sitting at the head of the table in the place that should rightfully have belonged to Harryo. The duke did nothing to curb Bess's airs, and Harryo felt aggrieved to be thus over-looked. Nevertheless, as an unmarried female, she was unable to make her feelings known.

Harriet was conscious of the friction in Devonshire House, but her loyalties were divided. She placed enormous store on the memories she and Bess shared of Georgiana; furthermore, Bess had been a loyal friend to her, not least during the delivery of George Arundel Stewart, her last illegitimate baby. But Harryo, however difficult and outspoken, was her niece and so claimed her familial loyalty and sympathy. Harriet was also conscious of the fact that Bess, living in Devonshire House, unmarried yet giving herself the airs of a duchess, might cast a stain on Harryo's reputation and mar her marriage prospects. Harriet thus trod a delicate path, often inviting Harryo to stay at Roehampton or to dine at Cavendish Square, yet still maintaining a close bond with Bess and refusing to join in any condemnation of her by the Cavendish children.

In the past Harryo had often been critical of Harriet, believing her mannered and overly prone to exaggeration; she also found her obses-sion with Granville ridiculous and faintly embarrassing. But with Georgiana gone and her sister married, Harryo was hungry for affec-tion and attention. Harriet provided a link to her mother, representing a shared history that made Georgiana's death more bearable, and Har-riet's sensitivity and sympathy made Harryo change her opinion of her aunt. "Nothing can be kinder than my aunt's behaviour has been to me and I like the thoughts of being with her in the country very much,"[32] Harryo declared in November. A month later her sympathy had grown when Harriet came to stay at Devonshire House for a few days during the election, in which Sheridan was standing for Westminster. The sight of Sheridan being chaired and brought triumphant to Devonshire House awakened unbearably poignant memories for both Harriet and Harryo. Now there was no Georgiana to organize proceedings or wave victoriously from the balcony. "My aunt was very much overcome by it, as the noise was very great and anything like a procession going out of these gates recalled a most painful scene to her mind."[33]

Harryo's esteem for Harriet had grown, but so too had her irrita-tion with Bess, especially when she thought Bess was trying to manipu-late a match between her and Granville.

Just before dinner Lady Elizabeth came up to see me, with a significant smile, a look full of meaning and a note in her hand. "I suppose you know who is coming tonight?" I said with great naivete, "Who?" "Lord Granville." Will you tell me, my dear G, why she always talks of him to me as if I was so very much interested (to say the least) about him?[34]

Harryo was far from immune to Granville's good looks—few women were—but his loftiness had always irritated her; she also disapproved of Harriet's liaison with him. Her letter goes on to reveal that on the evening in question the Bessboroughs were also expected at Devonshire House for dinner. Bessborough and Willy arrived, but Harriet and Granville failed to appear. To begin with Bess had seen the delay as amusing, winking knowingly at Harryo. But after several hours, when Harriet and Granville did not arrive, Bess grew "most terribly out of humour, wondering in rather an ill natured way at my aunt's not coming." Eventually, just as everyone was going to bed, a note arrived from Harriet, telling Bess not to expect her. By this time Harryo was as furious as Bess. Her letter goes on:

> I think after what you know of my altered sentiments about my aunt, and the real love and admiration I feel for her, you will not suspect me of being actuated by anything like ill nature or unkindness, if I to you regret the imprudence of her conduct. Neither Lord B nor Willy knew that Lord G was in town, as Willy told me, when I said he was, his mother had told him it was quite impossible for him to come now. She had left Willy here, depending on her to carry him home, and he was extremely angry and very sulky all the evening. I dread his taking any fancy in to his head, and it is impossible not to lament that my aunt, with the best intentions, the most exemplary change of manner and a heart quite broken, should by a little imprudence, expose herself to the suspicion of others; for by what even Lady E and Caroline say, one may judge of what others less indulgent will.[35]

This implies that neither Bessborough nor Willy knew of the affair, although Willy's sulkiness and Harryo's dread of his "taking any fancy in to his head" suggests that he may have had his suspicions. Harriet's suffering at the death of Georgiana had seemingly wrought a further dire effect: the caution that had previously governed her affair with Granville had been forgotten. But the fact that Harryo should pay attention to such details, and express such disapproval for the aunt toward whom she had warmed, reveals something else too: Harryo was more than just a casual observer; she too was falling prey to Granville's charm.

TWENTY-ONE

The Rivals

1807 - 1808

OVER THE FOLLOWING WEEKS Granville's whereabouts and visits to Devonshire House were monitored by Harryo. Often he came after dinner and she played chess with him, surprised to find that she enjoyed his attentions. "He is in one of his most gracious moods and certainly improves upon the pleasantness of our evenings,"[1] she reported of one typical occasion. For all her reservations concerning Granville's haughty manner, and her knowledge of his affair with her aunt, Harryo felt a disconcerting attraction for him that she battled to suppress. Letters to her sister mention the evenings when she knew he was in town but did not call, her disappointment unspoken yet implicit. There were times too, she told Little G, when his behavior confirmed her worst suspicions of his character. "He actually gave a loud and contemptuous laugh and made a long Oh, drawing back as if he said, 'indeed, I cannot undertake such messages' . . ."[2] It was not only his ill manners that irked her but his ennui. "He seemed bored, and went off in such a hurry, that I think he will never come again without more attraction. *Tant pis et tant mieux.*"[3] Harryo felt constrained by unfamiliar and increasingly turbulent feelings, and consequently her behavior toward Granville became self-conscious. She was cool when she thought his manners wanting and, even when he was good-humored, less inclined than most women to flirt and flatter him.

Granville was at first puzzled; he told Little G that he thought she had taken a dislike to him, a remark that delighted Harryo. Soon after, much to her annoyance, Granville began to grasp the truth. "Do you know, I suspect Doodle [Granville] of having confided to Lady

Charlotte Greville that I am one of his adorers. I have often told you I am convinced he thinks so of me and half the world beside . . . *O doodle mio, se tu vedessi quell cor che tu chiami fedele!*"*4

Whatever Harryo's hopes or fears, Granville did not consider her a potential partner; he had a more controversial match in mind. The Barbarian had promised him she would try to obtain a divorce from her husband. Granville had returned to England with the idea of testing his friends' and family's reaction to his marrying a divorcee, arguing that the princess's status as a foreign royal would protect her from the social ostracism that such a union would usually incur. He confided his plan to Harriet, who was far from convinced it would work, believing he had underestimated the difficulties involved. Her doubts were further reinforced by a far from encouraging reaction from Granville's sisters. "I am still afraid you flatter yourself too much as to the general opinion and reception of the poor little Barbarian. I judge partly from what in the case of any other person I should have thought myself,"5 Harriet warned.

It was not only social considerations that made Harriet view the match uncertainly. She still supported Granville's desire to marry, but while she felt sympathy for the "poor little Barbarian," whose unhappy marriage reflected the predicament of countless women, not least herself, her religious beliefs had deepened as she aged. Divorce violated deeply ingrained Christian tenets. There seemed little moral difference between marrying a divorcee and conducting an affair with a married woman. Harriet's unease for Granville's future with the Barbarian was therefore colored by guilt at the past affairs in which she herself had become embroiled.

Girls are often married, hardly knowing their husbands or what marriage is, how many there must be who would gladly separate, and still more gladly choose again, if they could do so without ruining their characters. Yet is there really much difference in obtaining a divorce by ye strong hand of power, through the influence of one's personal charms, for the purpose of marrying a man one prefers to one's husband, and being borne away by love for this man, and in

---

* O my Doodle, if you could but see the heart which you call faithful!

some unguarded moment yielding to his passion and your own and thus becoming liable to the punishment of divorce? Parliament or a despotic sovereign may waive the legal part of marriage, but who can waive the solemn vow taken at the altar in the name of the God who made you . . . Whatever excuse or palliation one may endeavour to make to oneself of ill usage or neglect one way . . . or of seduction, passionate love, or momentary weakness the other—there is no denying it, whoever breaks this vow is guilty of a great sin . . .[6]

Meanwhile Granville dithered, perhaps disturbed by Harriet's reservations and uncertain whether his feelings toward the Barbarian were strong enough to withstand the possibility of social ostracism. The relationship was eventually forced to a climax when political events intervened. In March 1807, the ministry of All the Talents resigned over the question of Catholic emancipation. Grenville was replaced as leader by the Duke of Portland, with Spencer Perceval as chancellor and Granville's old friend Canning at the Foreign Office. The following month Granville was offered the crucial role as ambassador to Russia, with the aim of bolstering Russian support in the war against Napoleon. Bearing in mind his romantic hopes, the appointment must have seemed serendipitous; yet Granville disapproved of the present administration and only after cajoling by Canning and his brother-in-law did he finally accept. "Can you be so well, so usefully, in some respects so agreeably employed as by undertaking a mission which will give you the opportunity of settling the affairs of Europe as well as your own?"[7] his brother-in-law urged.

Harriet was unsure whether Granville would return a married man, but she was certain that, once he wed, their intimacy would fade, and so his departure was deeply painful. The cloud that had descended with Georgiana's death had risen and faded a little with his return; it now descended and darkened once more. The possibility of change in their relationship gave their correspondence new significance in her eyes, and she reacted sternly whenever his letters seemed cursory or stilted.

When every little interest and occupation becomes different, and one can no longer guess what those one loves are thinking of and doing, or what kind of people they are living with, absence is increased tenfold;

it is a sort of death, and breaks through all those smaller ties of unlimited habitual confidence that bind affection closer to the heart.
When once anything is thought too trifling to be written, the first
break is made, and writing, instead of a pleasure, will become a task.
Life is made up of trifles, and soon such a multitude will flow between as to lose all knowledge of each other.[8]

She tried to alleviate her low spirits by busying herself with her
family. "I came here again today in the vain hope that change of scene,
change of air, and change of society and occupations, would take off a
little from the depression of spirits I labour under. I look upon it as an
illness, but it must be cured,"[9] she wrote from Brocket Hall, where she
had gone to visit Caro, who, after several miscarriages, was now in late
pregnancy. Yet whatever Harriet's hopes, her family could not provide
an impervious shield from the world in which she belonged.

A few weeks later she returned to London ready to attend Caro,
whose labor was imminent, when Hecca, Sheridan's second wife, sent
word that she needed Harriet's assistance in a matter of urgency. Never
one to refuse a plea for help, Harriet went and was sitting in Hecca's
bedroom talking when Sheridan, much the worse for drink, burst in. In
Harriet's words, "the most ridiculous scene ensued." Sheridan begged
Harriet's mercy and compassion for past wrongs, and declared "he was
a wretch and was even to this moment more in love with me than with
any woman he had ever met with." Hearing this, Hecca interrupted,
exclaiming: "Not excepting me? Why you always tell me I am the only
woman you ever were in love with."[10] Sheridan tried to extricate himself from an embarrassing showdown with his wife, at the same time
trying desperately to flatter Harriet. When, at three in the morning,
Harriet rose to leave, Sheridan grew suddenly violent, grabbing her
with such force that the maid and Hecca had to wrestle him away and
lock him in the room before Harriet could make her escape.

Worries for Granville's safety intensified her depression. He had
sailed to Copenhagen before traveling on to Memel to meet the Russian emperor and she was uncertain of his whereabouts when the first
rumors reached her of the Battle of Friedland, in which twenty thousand Russian troops perished. "What is to become of us? Here is another Austerlitz," she wrote frantically. "I give all up for lost, and

expect to hear of the French standards flying at Petersburg. Would to heaven you were back! I cannot calm my terror."[11]

As it turned out, her wish was to be swiftly fulfilled. Granville had escaped the gunfire but failed to achieve either of the objectives that had taken him to Russia. The Barbarian avoided him for weeks after his arrival, ignoring his communications and refusing to meet him alone. Eventually, in late July, they met at an assembly, where she confirmed what he had already suspected: she could not bear the thought of leaving Russia. Furthermore, she had heard several rumors of Granville's amorous activities in London that made her question his commitment. She no longer wished to marry him.

Granville's diplomatic negotiations with the Russians were similarly doomed. Following the Russian defeat at Friedland, Emperor Alexander signed the Treaty of Tilsit, joining forces with the French and declaring war on Britain. By year's end, only three short months after his arrival in Russia, Granville was on his way back to London.

IN HIS ABSENCE, Harryo, now aged twenty-one, fretted over her marriage prospects. There was talk among the family that her cousin Jack, Viscount Althorp, had fallen in love with her, and for this reason she went to stay at Althorp House in Northampton, tolerating her aunt Lavinia's notoriously uncertain temper while waiting for signs of Jack's attraction to her. Several weeks went by during which Jack showed more enthusiasm for hunting than for Harryo. "He attends to no one person, no one thing, is surrounded with the vulgarest set of men . . . Althorp as he is, no reasonable woman can for a moment think of but as an eager huntsman."[12] Scarcely had Harryo dismissed Jack as a potential husband when her brother Hart arrived, insisting that his best friend, William Rumbold, had fallen for her. Once again Harryo was not deceived. "If Sir William does pretend after three days to be charmed with me, it confirms all the harm we have heard of me and is humiliating to me beyond measure."[13]

By year's end Harryo was back at Devonshire House, with several further unconvincing suitors in tow. Among them was Harriet's youngest (legitimate) son, Willy, who had been "dangling after her" and drawing attention, so that among the family and the servants rumors were rife that a marriage was imminent. Learning of the whispers from her maid, Harryo hardly knew whether to laugh or cry: "Dearest G, was ever unoccupied person so constantly occupied, disengaged person so eternally engaged, proud person so perpetually humbled? In high life supposed to be promised to Frederick Byng [another bachelor with whom she was purportedly linked], in low life to Willy."[14]

Exhausted by her attempts to find a husband, Harryo embarked on a journey north to stay with her sister at Castle Howard. Harriet, meanwhile, occupied herself with arrangements for the christening of Caro's son, who had arrived safely a day after her ill-fated visit to the Sheridans. When Harriet asked the Prince of Wales to stand as godfather, he agreed with an effusive gratitude that reflected their long-standing friendship:

> You never can, nor indeed anyone even ever so remotely belonging to you, can make me so happy, as affording me any opportunity by which either publicly or privately I can testify the real love and affection I have felt for you and yours for so long a series of years . . . Since you desire it, I shall be but too much delighted to give my name to your little grandson. I only pray to God that it may be more auspicious to him than it has been to me, and that none of the ill and hard fate which has attended his godfather may ever fall to his lot. But I will not trespass upon you, my much loved friend, with expatiating upon the numberless vicissitudes to which I have now through a long course of years been continually exposed, as in great measure you know them all, and in some have been no inconsiderable sharer and participator yourself.[15]

The baby was christened Augustus after his illustrious godfather. All ran smoothly until the arrival of an uninvited guest—Sheridan. Prior to the christening he had plagued Harriet, Caro, and Lady Melbourne for an invitation. Harriet and Caro had fobbed him off, telling him invitations were issued only by Lady Melbourne, who cuttingly told him that "if she began [inviting] strangers there was no end." Undeterred, Sheridan secretly approached the Prince of Wales, offering his services as an escort. Harriet described the family's shock at the moment of the prince's arrival: "When we were all dressed, expecting the Prince, the 'double battants' were thrown open with great fracas, and in entered Mr. Sheridan, announcing the Prince, and himself as the attendant he had chosen to accompany him."[16]

The christening was over when Harryo returned from Castle Howard, still with no eligible suitor in view. Harriet now dutifully took on the role of chaperone. Despite her fondness for her niece—"she only needs to be known to be liked"—Harriet found her duties both exhausting and dull. "If Harriet [Harryo] is talking to anybody, I dare not stir though I should be dying to speak to some one three steps from me, lest I should interrupt a tender conversation just at the most interesting moment; or if I happen to have any body by me I like, and am in the *beau milieu* of some animated discussion, I feel a little pull at my arm with, 'Aunt, shall we not go into the next room?' And, dear Girl, she will not let me stir a step without her."[17]

Another reason for Harriet's frustration was that in attending to Harryo she had been prevented from scrutinizing the new object of Granville's marital ambitions. Susan Beckford—"the Sapphire," as Harriet and he dubbed her—was the daughter and heiress of the eccentric sugar millionaire William Beckford of Fonthill. Granville had first shown interest in her shortly before his departure for Russia, much to Harryo's chagrin. "Is Lord Granville in or out of spirits? And what do you think about Miss Beckford? I spent yesterday entirely in crying,"[18] Harryo had poignantly asked her sister in March.

Once again, however, Granville's courtship met with a stony response. When he came to London specifically to call on Susan, she refused to see him, staying in her house for several days to foil any attempt he might make to engineer a chance encounter. Forced to acknowledge that she was avoiding him, Granville gave up the chase for "the Sapphire" and turned his attentions to the woman he and Harriet now dubbed "the Pearl"—the woman who had long struggled against her attraction for him: Harriet's quirky, clever, plump, forthright niece Harryo.

EVEN BEFORE GRANVILLE'S return from Russia, Harryo's secret adoration of him had led to strains in her relationship with Harriet. Harryo thought her aunt seemed unnecessarily touchy whenever they were together.

We [Harriet and Harryo] are very good friends at present but for all I can do, she will fancy that every word I say is meant to convey some meaning of dislike or indifference to her. Yet I do assure you I never before felt so anxious to show her every possible kindness and attention. If I ask what o'clock it is, she gets up and begs my pardon for not recollecting how much she must bore me and says she will not stay a moment longer. If I go out with her in the carriage, she is all the while on the defensive, and if I was always venting the most bitter reproaches upon her, she could not be more constantly hinting at my dislike and her wish to spare me the ennui she knows I feel when I am with her. In spite of this we are, as I said before, very good friends. I have seen more of her than I almost ever do in London and I am sure my manner to her is warmer and more attentive than usual. I flatter myself the style of complaint is grown almost mechanical to her, but though it may please her ear, no words can say how it fatigues my lungs to be obliged every half hour to repeat, "How can you, my dearest aunt? Oh no! my dearest aunt. What an idea!"[19]

In other respects too Harryo began to view her aunt critically. She disapproved of Harriet's subterfuges and her habit of often dishonestly accusing Bessborough of bullying in order to excuse her own transgressions: "My aunt is, of course, anxious to be in town when he is, and if she would be so, with less detour and prevarication, I should not blame her for it; but there is so much contrivance, so much of representing poor yielding Lord B[essborough] as a tyrant from whose commands there is no way of escaping, and herself as a victim to him, that it is really distressing to hear her. I do not know how she contrives to manage him as she does."[20] Tellingly, nothing in the surviving correspondence between Harriet and Granville refers to the difficulties with her niece. We must guess, therefore, that Harryo's criticisms reflect her own altered perspective. Her infatuation with Granville had reached the point where she regarded Harriet as a rival.

TWENTY-TWO

Harryo
1808–1809

HARRIET DID NOT at first realize Granville's altered intentions toward Harryo because she went away on holiday just as his interest in her niece escalated. Together with Bessborough and Willy, she set off on a tour of the north of England, Scotland, and Ireland, a newly fashionable trip whose popularity had been partly boosted by the difficulties of traveling in war-torn Europe. An appreciation of the beauties of the rugged and mountainous landscapes of Britain was intertwined with the notion of romantic sensibility in Regency consciousness, a quality to which every well-educated person aspired. Thus while Bessborough sketched the sublime landscapes, Harriet rambled among the hills and valleys and found consolation for her passionate longing for Granville in the majestic surroundings. "I could have borne no place but this after parting from you, but this wild ruin accords so perfectly with all I like and all I feel, that I could renounce the world, and live and die here . . . it is beautiful, wild, and picturesque beyond anything I have seen in England, and the singularity of inhabiting a ruin adds to it,"[1] she wrote from Bolton Abbey, one of the Duke of Devonshire's residences.

From Bolton they went to Howick, the home of the Greys, where Georgiana's illegitimate daughter, Eliza Courtenay, now aged fourteen, lived with her stern grandparents. Harriet thought Eliza "a fine girl," although she felt she had "such a look of mortification about her, that it is not pleasant."[2] Harriet's heart went out to her sister's child, especially when Bessborough, who was oblivious to the entire Grey/Georgiana interlude, asked whether Eliza was the governess. Her own illegitimate children were still secretly fostered and remained unaware of the circumstances of their birth or the identity of their father and mother. Yet seeing Eliza must have made her think of their future with mounting apprehension. She sensed that among the upper echelons of society the moral ethos had shifted. The presence of illegitimate children, once widely tolerated, was increasingly frowned upon; children were being burdened with the guilt of their parents' profligacy. She dreaded the thought that as Little Harriet and George grew up they too might be overshadowed by the shameful circumstances of their birth.

The Bessborough party left Howick and returned to the perils of the road. In the last week of September they sailed to Belfast, then traveled south. Ireland was a country of unfamiliar traditions, and fraught with civil unrest. Everywhere they went they were faced with horrific tales of the dangers of traveling at night. "I dare say many of the stories one hears are exaggerated," she wrote bravely, "but the whole conversation is reports of robberies and murders, in short, everything that impresses the mind with a state of almost savage society."[3] In late October they arrived at Bessborough House in Kilkenny. This was Harriet's first visit to the family seat, and she was enchanted by what she found. "I like this place extremely," she told Granville; "with a very little expense it might be made magnificent... I feel I could do a great deal of good here."[4] Harriet had been warmly greeted by the tenants on the estate and, conscious of local sensitivity, received "the benediction of both parson and priest" on the same day. She was astonished by the crowd on their way to Mass who waited outside the Protestant church to see her and her family, and even more flabbergasted on entering the church to find a congregation of only eleven.

BACK IN LONDON by year's end, Harriet faced Granville's new romantic hope—her niece Harryo—and was forced to take the relationship seriously. It was not a match she had considered. Harryo had none of the glamorous, showy beauty to which Granville was usually drawn. As one later observer put it, "she rather affected a remarkable simplicity in her dress, was generally attired in black, and would receive her guests in the plainest of caps wrapped up in a shawl," while Granville, even in his mature years, "was the beau-ideal of a high-bred English nobleman."[5] Harriet had long acknowledged that Granville must marry;

nevertheless, Harryo's lack of ostentation was little consolation for the loss of her lover. The thought of her niece married to the man she had adored for the past fifteen years affected her keenly, and the urge to feel sorry for herself was hard to resist. Despite her doubts, over the following months she persuaded herself that Granville's marriage to Harryo, however painful, would be less agonizing than would marriage to an outsider. Harryo knew about their affair, and was also probably aware of the existence of their two children. Family bonds would ensure that Harriet would be able to continue some form of relationship with Granville, and make his contact with their children easier.

From Harryo's point of view, the advantages of Granville as a potential marriage partner were more confused. She had always felt a physical attraction for him, and the feeling had intensified ever since he had begun paying serious attention to her the previous summer. Marriage would provide an escape from Devonshire House, where Bess, whom she detested, and her neglectful father seemed more united than ever. But Harryo's exposure to the sexual laxity of Devonshire House, set against the influence of her straitlaced governess, Miss Trimmer, and her moralistic grandmother, had instilled in her firm principles that characterized the new ethos of the age. To Harryo a whiff of moral compromise was intolerable, and while she had grown fond of Harriet since her mother's death she regarded her checkered love life as a symptom of moral weakness or, as she put it, "an awful example of what self-indulgence and yielding principles will end in."[6] Above all, Harryo had no intention of marrying Granville if his affair with her aunt continued. Thus, the more attention she received from Granville, the more she forgot Harriet's kindnesses toward her and viewed her aunt with disapproval and distrust.

As the year progressed, Harriet forced herself to encourage Granville in his courtship, urging him on whenever he flagged. Nevertheless, she could not bring herself to relinquish her hold over him, and carried on encouraging his confidences in matters that should have been kept private. Harriet was initially unaware of her niece's hostility, and Harriet's influence over Granville only fed Harryo's insecurities. Relations had reached a low point by September 1809, when Granville secured an invitation for Harryo to join a house party at the home of his sister, the Duchess of Beaufort, at Badminton

House. Lady Harrowby, another of Granville's sisters, was also a guest, as was Harryo's sister, Little G.

Away from Harriet, the family atmosphere soothed Harryo, although she was disturbed to hear persistent rumors that her marriage to Granville was imminent when he had yet to propose. "So many people tell me that I am going to be married to him that perhaps it may be as well for me to begin acquainting my friends that I am not,"[7] she complained to her brother. Harryo must have suspected that the rumors emanated from Harriet, whom—much to her annoyance—Granville still continually consulted for advice. It was Harriet who had suggested Badminton as a place to conduct the courtship. "The first twenty-four hours have certainly produced no progress in that which you seemed to think might be the result of our meeting here," he had reported soon after his arrival. "I had a conversation today of some length in which she was very agreeable and showed that good sense which I always knew she possessed, but we talked upon indifferent subjects."[8]

Riled by Granville's dependence on Harriet, Harryo continued to distance herself, neglecting to write to her aunt and urging Little G to be similarly reticent. In London, Harriet was wounded by Harryo's growing jealousy toward her. She had persuaded herself to agree to the match in the expectation of remaining in Harryo's confidence. She began to fret that she had misjudged her niece and the situation entirely.

Meanwhile, a further alliance preoccupied the family: the duke and Bess announced their intention to marry. The Cavendish and Bessborough children and Lady Spencer viewed the duke's decision with dismay, seeing it as a slur on Georgiana's memory. To Hart, Bess was "a crocodile,"[9] while Caroline Lamb railed against the "scene of deceit, plot, iniquity and whiles this serpent has made use of,"[10] and shuddered at the thought that she was to become the duchess. Harriet, however, regarded the marriage less stonily than the rest of the Spencer-Cavendish-Bessborough clan. Bess's moral failings were not so different from her own; their lives and intrigues had been long intertwined; and Bess had proved a trustworthy friend. Thus, for all her devotion to her sister's memory, Harriet put loyalties to the living first and would not malign her. "It will be too hard to have him [the duke] my mother and my niece angry with me as favouring what cannot be to them as painful as it is to me, yet I will not be unjust to Bess,"[11] she bravely announced.

Harriet's staunch refusal to denounce Bess further fueled Harryo's animosity toward her aunt. To Harryo, Bess was an interloper who bore much of the blame for her mother's unhappiness. Thus, as she saw it, Harriet's support of Bess was a betrayal of Georgiana. "My mind was early opened to Lady Elizabeth's character, unparalleled I do believe for want of principle and delicacy, and more perverted than deceitful, for I really believe she hardly herself knows the difference between right and wrong now,"[12] she told Hart. Distress over her father's marriage merged with her own deepening love for Granville, warping Harryo's view. She began to convince herself that Harriet had grown violently jealous of her relationship with Granville and was determined to destroy it. To this end, she believed Harriet had told Granville that Harryo intended to cut herself off from her father on his marriage, thus jeopardizing her marriage settlement. Granville could not afford to marry a wife without income—so, Harryo believed, Harriet was effectively sabotaging her marriage hopes. The dilemma in her mind was not only that she felt unfairly maligned—whatever her feelings for Bess, she had never intended to distance herself from her father—but, more problematically, if Granville was prepared to believe whatever misinformation Harriet fed him, was he suitable material for a husband? In a fever of uncertainty she spilled out her worries to her governess, Miss Trimmer, and begged for advice.

Ought I . . . ever to think of a man over whom [Harriet] has such claims or such influence as this! I found also that she had tried to alarm him by telling him that I meant to quarrel with my father, if any change in Lady E's [Bess's] situation took place. Two days before he left B[adminton] he talked to me in the most serious manner of my extraordinary situation with regard to her and the difficulties it placed me in, begged me not to think him impertinent, but he . . . thought *the way in which I meant to act* was calculated to inflame everything . . . I was astonished and begged him to explain himself. He said he had been told that I had determined to quit my father entirely . . . I answered that not only had I never said anything of the sort but that I had never felt it . . . He seemed as much astonished as delighted—again begged my pardon and so it dropt.

What is it that awaits me at my return, my dearest Selina? Is it

possible Lady B[essborough] should have fabricated an alarm to answer any purpose in frightening him from any idea of connecting
himself with me or are our worst fears indeed to be verified?[13]

There is nothing to corroborate Harryo's accusations against Harriet; rather, toward the end of the Badminton party Harriet wrote of
the impending marriage: "This is a subject I can say nothing on; it is
one of too immense consequence to me even to bear resting my
thoughts upon it. I only know you are both very dear to me, and that I
think I cannot be quite wretched at anything that makes those I love so
tenderly happy."[14] Surely not the words of the scheming mischief-
maker Harryo claimed. Nevertheless, Harryo was not untruthful or
malicious by nature, and her accusations cannot be dismissed as mere
lies; rather, they appear to have been a genuine misinterpretation and a
sign of the strain she felt. It seems likely that in taking on the role of
peacemaker Harriet urged Granville to try to reconcile Harryo to her
father's marriage, but, fraught and emotional as Harryo was, she misjudged her aunt's intentions as "artifice or duplicity." Certainly Harryo
was by now desperate for Granville to propose; and while he wavered it
was all too easy to blame Harriet for his prevarication.

By the end of her stay at Badminton, nothing was resolved and
Harryo remained in anguish. Granville's behavior was affectionate, but
his manner seemed erratic and she was uncertain whether his fine
words could be believed. And behind it all she saw the destructive influence of Harriet. "Lord G's manner varied perpetually . . . he certainly
at times, especially the last evening, betrayed great interest in me, and
seemed to feel more than he was at liberty to show, but if there are obstacles to his seriously thinking of me, it is both weak and selfish to act
so as to place me in a very difficult situation as he does everything to
occupy me and to attract the attention of others, without committing
himself, or making any sacrifice of the slightest gratification to himself.
This conduct does not belong to a character to which I could wish to
trust the happiness of my life. He professes great impatience for my return to Chiswick — my conduct there will not be difficult if Lady B[ess-
borough] does not make it so by jealousies and *tracasseries* . . ."[15] she
wrote in confusion to Miss Trimmer.

Back at Chiswick, Harryo was relieved to find the situation with the duke and Bess, who were now married, less awkward than she had feared. She remained, nonetheless, convinced that Harriet was plotting against her. "You can have no idea of the manoeuvring of her conduct—she has acted fairly by no one person—a directly different part to each and then obliged to have recourse to artifice and duplicity to try and reconcile the whole—what a shipwreck she has made of honour, dignity and fair renown!"[16]

At last, on November 14, the moment came that Harryo had longed for: Granville proposed. Afterward, in his interview with the duke, he renounced "his former follies"—in other words, gambling and womanizing—promising he "did not intend to persevere in them." If the physical affair with Harriet had not ended before now, this moment undoubtedly marked its end. But the emotional tie was not so simply severed; Granville would never cease to regard Harriet as his confidante. That evening, from Chiswick, she was the first person to whom he wrote. "I spoke to H tonight; she was very nervous and so was I. I know not what I said."[17]

Knowing that her behavior over the next few weeks would probably set the mold for any future relationship between them, Harriet greeted the news with a characteristically clever response, adopting a tone of maternal concern tempered with detachment. "Thank you ten thousand times for your goodness in writing. I am glad this nervous moment to you is over and that you found everything as you wished. God in Heaven bless and grant you every happiness; if you are as happy as you deserve to be and as I wish you, nothing will be wanting . . . I think only of your happiness—yours and Harriet's. God bless and preserve you both."[18] Two days later Harriet called at Chiswick to offer her heartfelt congratulations; again her manner was friendly but undemanding, and both Granville and Harryo were touched. The next day Granville wrote to Harriet, reassuring her that he did not intend to forget what she had been to him, and that Harryo had accepted her special place in his heart.

> I talked of you today to [Harryo] and told her how very delightful and valuable a person you were. I said that for a great many years I had had that confidence in you that there was scarcely a thought that passed through my mind or a folly committed by me, that I did not

talk of to you; that I had before she left town last summer, talked to you of my disposition to like her . . . that you had always expressed the highest opinion of her; that you loved her as if she were your own child, and that you had always encouraged me in my intentions of marrying her; that considering the sort of confidence that had always subsisted between us, you had certainly felt nervous at any change of confidence which had subsisted between us. She intimated last night a wish of talking to me about you. She praised you, she said how much she loved you, and how very much happier she was since seeing you here last night.[19]

Granville may have exaggerated the warmth of Harryo's feelings toward Harriet, but there was doubtless more than a pinch of truth in what he wrote. Much evidence shows that once Harryo was engaged to Granville her jealousy and distrust evaporated and she was carried away on a wave of euphoric happiness. Granville improved the strained atmosphere between her and Bess by staying at Chiswick. He was more attentive and generous than she could have hoped—he had given her an engagement gift of a necklace valued at £5,000, made from diamonds presented to him by the Russian emperor. No matter how uncompromising her view of his past life, the future promised all she desired. "Lord Granville's character and attachment give me a security I could not have believed I should ever feel,"[20] she told her brother. If Harryo had learned anything from Harriet, it was that clever women knew the importance of superficial compliance.

The wedding was arranged for three weeks hence; Little G was again expecting a baby, and Harryo and Granville wanted to marry before her lying-in. In a fever of activity Harryo summoned Hart to come with her on an expedition to London to prepare her trousseau. "[Harryo] is going to settle everything in the dress way tomorrow . . ."[21] he told his grandmother. Hart settled on an extravagant pair of pearl-and-diamond drop earrings from the royal goldsmith Rundell & Bridge for his wedding gift.

The wedding took place on Christmas Eve, a fortnight later than was first planned. Granville, unfailingly sensitive, decided to wait until after Little G's baby arrived—so that Harryo would not worry about her sister while on their honeymoon. Equally tactfully he decided that the party should consist only of the immediate family: the duke and Bess, Hart and Morpeth, and Granville's sisters—the Duchess of Beaufort and the Countess of Harrowby—together with Bess's daughter, Caroline St. Jules, who was now married to George Lamb,* "who being in the house could not be told to go away."²² The ceremony took place at eight in the evening in the drawing room at Chiswick House. The couple left for their honeymoon at Woolmer, one of Lord Stafford's houses, an hour later. "We all behaved well," recorded Bess to her son Augustus, "and dearest G was less agitated than one could have supposed . . . crowds of servants and their friends assembled to see her go, but the doors were shut during the ceremony."²³

Caroline Lamb was furious to learn she had been left out of the party and feverish with impatience to know what had happened. "Nothing but a long expressive letter from you can remove the affront I labour under at being excluded from my own cousin's wedding," she stormed to Hart. "Pray send me a favour and cake if not I shall positively turn green with jealousy and yellow with melancholy . . . I have just written to Lady H. L. Gower but shall not visit her at all. Send me an account of the ceremony. No soul writes me word what happened who was affected how Ld. G behaved . . . how she was dressed . . . let me know all these things . . . was Mama at the ceremony?"²⁴

Harriet was not among the guests—but Granville had not forgotten her, nor had the invisible thread of confidence that connected them been severed. Thus, despite being happier than he had expected in his choice of wife, three days after his wedding he wrote to her. "Every hour I passed with [Harryo] convinces me more and more of the justice and liberality of her way of thinking, and of her claim upon me for unlimited confidence. She is indeed a perfect angel."²⁵

---

* Younger brother of William Lamb, to whom Caro was married: the two Carolines were thus known as Caro William and Caro George.

TWENTY-THREE

New Perspectives
1810-1811

G RANVILLE'S MARRIAGE HAD BARELY taken place when the Prince of Wales called on Harriet. Much to her astonishment he berated Granville roundly for marrying Harryo and for his past inconstancy, then made a clumsy attempt to seduce her. "He has killed me—such a scene I never went through," she afterward related. "He threw himself on his knees, and clasping me round, kissed my neck before I was aware of what he was doing. I screamed with vexation and fright; he continued sometimes struggling with me, sometimes sobbing and crying..." In between these farcical lunges and histrionics the lovelorn prince pledged that he would break off with his current mistresses—Mrs. Fitzherbert and Lady Hertford—and, revealingly, that he would look to Harriet in future to be his chief political confidante and adviser—clearly the prince knew how to tempt her. Harriet, though astonished, could see the funny side in all this, describing the prince as an "immense grotesque figure flouncing about half on the couch, half on the ground." The political clout he offered did nothing to alter her view, and she told him firmly and repeatedly, "I never could or would be on any other terms with him than the acquaintance he had always honoured me with."[1]

The lightheartedness with which Harriet related this incident to Granville belied the difficulty she found in coming to terms with the new status quo. Weeks after the wedding she remained obsessed with thoughts of the newly married couple. For the past decade and a half Granville had been her confidant on every subject from her children's ailments to the latest political intrigue. Her letters had also given her an emotional outlet, a means to play up every extravagant feeling, to give free rein to every fancy, to portray herself as a woman of sensibility and turbulent feeling. Now that their intimacy was at an end, so too was this release, and she was utterly bereft. "I have so long been accustomed to say and write everything to you, every impression good or bad as it strikes me at the moment, that I cannot tell you what a gene it is to refrain…"[2] Sometimes she began writing to Granville with the old freedom, but then, feeling suddenly constrained by Harryo (whose name she hardly dared mention), she would destroy the letter for fear of giving offense. At times she felt a sense of loss so acute that it reawakened the emotions of Georgiana's death. "Indeed it is no exaggeration to say I believe I could find no hour in the four and twenty, waking or sleeping, when my thoughts were not in some measure occupied with you—something connected with you, or… the recollection of one also most tenderly loved by me. It is wonderful how often I dream of you, or her, or Harriet [Harryo] and your marriage, etc. etc."[3]

Granville's letters to her remained the only fragile link to what once had been. He had never been a natural correspondent, and she lived in terror that without a sexual relationship to bind them his feelings for her would fade and their correspondence would become more perfunctory with each month that passed. "I am afraid that tho' a woman may feel pure, tender, devoted friendship for a man, without one other sentiment mingling with her affection, no man knows what friendship for a woman is. They are in love with them, and when that ceases—if they think they have been loved and well treated—compassion and something like gratitude forms a sort of attachment, which grows fainter and fainter every day…"[4]

But her fears were unfounded; letters from Granville did continue to arrive. He still sought her advice, took an interest in her children's lives, and discussed the latest political developments with her. When he was in town—which was rarely, because much of the first two years of his marriage was spent staying with his sisters, the Duchess of Beaufort and Countess of Harrowby—he still called. Harriet thus came gradually to understand that the friendship between them would endure, and with this realization her acceptance grew. When Harriet learned that Harryo was expecting her first child she immediately wrote, fulsome in her concerned advice, even though Harryo was apparently suffering from few adverse symptoms. "I long to hear how Harriet [Harryo] bears her journey. Do not let her over do it at Sandon;* it is lucky for her that from your sister's being in the same way she will be inclined to keep quiet."[5]

Tellingly, it was Harryo who replied on this occasion, with a polite friendliness that speaks volumes about her sensitivity to her aunt. "I cannot say how much I am obliged to you for having advised yourself to give me so much pleasure."[6] Harryo never entirely forgot her disapproval of Harriet, or her dislike of Bess — "their society does not particularly suit or please me"[7] — preferring Granville's sisters, whose moral values and fondness for a quiet domestic life were a sharp contrast to the decadent lifestyle she had known as a child. But marriage had exceeded all her expectations, as she delightedly told her brother Hart: "I do nothing from morning till night but think what an angel my husband is, which is more pleasant than profitable."[8] To her sister Little G she confessed, "My attention was taken up this morning with G's profile at chess. I never saw him in such beauty. He looks as if he were rouged and his long blue eyes watching the pawns are quite irresistible."[9] In this blissfully happy state, pleasing Granville took precedence over her own feelings. Her distrust mellowed and she did nothing to prevent the channels of communication between Harriet and Granville remaining open.

Granville and Harryo's first child—a girl called Susan—was born safely at the end of October in London. Caro and Little G were on hand to assist, and kept Hart informed of the progress.

> She is in labour—it began before six this morning, I came here a quarter after and find it going on slowly, no violent pain and now it has only been the beginning pains but Croft says she is doing as well as possible . . . she bears it like an angel and says she does not mind it but that she cannot believe she is going to have a child. Ld. G and I am a great deal with her but nobody else yet which I am glad of—

---

* The home of Granville's sister Lady Harrowby in Staffordshire.

Lady B[essborough] and my grandmother are both in town—she has just peeped in to admire the room . . .

Later Caro recorded that the labor lasted all day, but that only the last three hours were severe, until at ten o clock in the evening the baby was safely delivered. A few minutes earlier Harryo had said, " 'Hope makes everything easy.' Ld. Granville seemed quite overcome when he heard this and was most anxious the whole time."[10]

For Harriet, meanwhile, good fortune of another kind arrived unexpectedly. In March 1810, the money worries that had plagued her and Bessborough throughout their married life were unexpectedly lifted. They received a legacy of £100,000 (£6 million today) from Henry Cavendish, grandson of the Second Duke of Devonshire, a reclusive and immensely wealthy scientist who had undertaken pioneering research into the composition of water, electricity, and the understanding of flammable gases. The money transformed Harriet's existence. Bessborough was able to pay off a mountain of debts at the bank and further borrowings from her brother, whose help only a month earlier she had begged to pay for Frederick's promotion in the army: "it is the last purchase to be made for his promotion—it is very difficult and if he misses then it may be years before he can have another opportunity of rising."[11]

News of their good fortune traveled fast. Harriet was rapidly besieged by pleas from Lady Spencer, who requested financial assistance for various good causes, while at the same time rebuking her daughter for her poor handwriting—"what is the use of £100,000 if it will not enable one to buy a little black ink?"—and advising her to keep the windfall secret. "Pray hold out to everybody that you are not individually rich or you will have innumerable demands made upon you which you must prepare to resist or you will be undone."[12]

Other areas of Harriet's family life were less fortuitous. Caro grew disenchanted with her marriage, feeling William paid too much attention to his political career and not enough to her. Another pregnancy ended with the baby dying hours after birth. Augustus, her only surviving child, was by now two years old but seemed slow in developing and suffered frequent bouts of ill health, including worrying seizures during which he screamed and foamed at the mouth. The doctors said the fits were a sign of his being spoiled and recommended a stricter regimen. Eventually they diagnosed epilepsy and resorted to the only medicine available—sedatives.*

In a fit of depression, Caro embroiled herself in an indiscreet affair with Geoffrey Webster, much to the horror of his mother, Harriet's old friend Lady Holland. Caro's mother-in-law, the flinty Lady Melbourne, was equally outraged, despite her own sexual dalliances. It was not Caro's infidelity so much as her indiscretion and the fact that the affair jeopardized William's relationship with Lord Holland—a key member of the Whigs—that she found intolerable. "Your behaviour last night was so disgraceful in its appearances and so disgusting in its motives that it is quite impossible it should ever be effaced from my mind. When one braves the opinion of the world, sooner or later [one?] will feel the consequences of it."[13]

Lashed by such criticism, Caro soon realized the error of her ways and begged William for forgiveness with the same extravagance and lack of decorum with which she had earlier betrayed him. "On my knees I have written to William to tell him ... the whole disgraceful truth. I have told him I have deceived him; I have trusted solely to his mercy and generosity."[14] Despite her protestations, however, the affair was resurrected and reached the ears of her disapproving grandmother, Lady Spencer: "How has dear Caroline's great imprudence been received at Whitehall?" she wondered. "I hope she recollects the positive promise I had from her of her never riding without her husband ... Dear child, she knows not the pain she gives to you and me, and too probably the misery she is preparing for herself; and all this not from vice but vanity, inordinate vanity."[15]

HARRIET WAS ALSO losing sleep over Frederick, who was now serving in Spain as a major in the 23rd Light Dragoons. He had fought at the Battle of Talavera and distinguished himself in leading his regiment against the French. As assistant adjutant general with the cavalry in

---

* Augustus's epilepsy adds further credence to the theory that Caro and her husband were more closely related than anyone realized. Modern research shows that the incidence of epilepsy is higher in the offspring of close relatives.

Cadiz a year later, in March 1811, he received a saber wound at the Battle of Barrosa, but although he wrote a long account of the battle he played down his injury, telling his anxious mother that he had "often suffered more in a cricket match." Harriet only learned the true gravity of Frederick's injuries from Colonel Macdonald, who called on her in London. "I find poor Frederick had indeed a narrow escape, if he had not very dexterously turned the edge of the sabre it must have cut through his knee, but he says he scarce ever saw a more severe contusion without bones broke; he is also slightly cut across his face."[16] Frederick did not recover as speedily as he pretended, and was still suffering from bouts of fever in the summer—probably caused by malaria. Harriet and his superior officer General Graham tried to persuade him to return home on leave but he refused, saying he saw it as a sign of disgrace. Only when ordered to return by the Duke of Wellington did he eventually comply.

Shortly before his return, on July 29, 1811, the Duke of Devonshire died. Harriet went to stay with Bess at Chiswick, where she learned Bess had "done herself great harm with Hart"[17] by having unrealistically high expectations of the allowance Hart—now the Sixth Duke*—should provide for her. Bess, intent as any widow of her day upon securing her future, claimed that the duke had intended to double her jointure, provide an additional settlement, and let her live on in Chiswick House. As Harriet saw it, Bess was her own worst enemy: by asking for so much she had made an already sensitive situation worse. "I want him both for hers and his own sake to do very handsomely by her, but am afraid the very effort she makes on his account to amuse and prevent his growing out of spirits does harm; it takes off some of the compassion he would otherwise feel for her."[18]

Hart was naturally generous, increasing Bess's income from four to six thousand pounds a year and making an additional payment of two thousand pounds. But he refuted her claim to Chiswick, leaving Harriet to break the news. He also made settlements on his half-brother and -sister, Clifford and Caro George, and insisted that Bess tell them the truth about their father's identity. Harriet must have known that

---

* Despite his new title, to avoid confusion he is referred to as Hart or Hartington for the remainder of this book.

the pair had been fathered by the duke, but she was less certain of the wisdom of the fact being confirmed to the world at large, especially when Clifford began to bring embarrassment to the family by giving himself airs and advertising his connection with the duke. The debacle must also have given Harriet pause. Worried for the future of her own illegitimate children, she had already begun making plans to move them from their foster parents, but, if ever she had doubted it, her decision to keep them in the dark as to their parents' identity must now have been reaffirmed.

HARRIET WAS NOW fifty; her figure had grown plump, although her sexual allure remained potent and, by her own account, she was still "courted, followed, flattered and made love to *en toutes formes* by four men."[19] Nevertheless, reviewing her life and her long affair with Granville two years after its cessation, she had come to recognize her own deficiencies. But if her past was littered with regret, her consolation was that in acknowledging past folly she had arrived at a new sense of peace. She had much to feel thankful for: an enduring friendship and six children on whom her existence would increasingly depend. Now when she wrote to Granville, her letters relayed information as they had always done — the latest political news, social gossip, books, plays, and personal anecdotes — but they did so with a new lightness of touch and less of the extravagant emotion that had characterized her earlier correspondence.

The king's health had deteriorated gradually and by the end of 1810 the prime minister Mr. Perceval had moved to appoint the Prince of Wales as regent, with certain restrictions, for a year. "As you said you had not seen Mr. Perceval's and the Prince's letters, I have put out my eyes and made my hand ache to copy them for you,"[20] wrote Harriet to Granville when the Regency was still in the balance.

From Portsmouth she watched Frederick embark on a ship that would take him back to fight in the Spanish peninsula. The city reverberated with war; cannon shots echoed, the streets swarmed with troops, ships set sail for battle. "Every now and then the gun fires, the streamers point westward, the whole place is in motion, the generals with all their suite, and Frederick with all his . . . hurry on board; the anchor is weighed the ship sets sail, and I watch it with an aching heart

diminishing and disappearing in the mist . . ."[21] The controlled manner
in which Harriet describes this painful moment of separation confirms
her inner transformation. There were still times, though, when sentiment intruded, usually after she had seen Granville. "I will not weary
you with repeating how heavily the time goes with me when I know
you are quite away, for the distance—I scarce know why—makes a
great addition to the pain . . . After you left me I walked to W. St. lest
any one should come to me and see my eyes,"[22] she told him after a
meeting in July, possibly after the duke's death. But such lapses in her
self-possession were rare. Mostly she now regarded the love affair with
Granville from a new, uncompromising perspective:

> For seventeen years . . . [I] loved almost to idolatry the only man
> from whom I could have wished to hear it, the man who has proba-
> bly loved me least of all those who have professed to do so—though
> once I thought otherwise.[23]

TWENTY-FOUR

Love Is Made of Brittle Stuff

1812

HARRIET HAD RENOUNCED all illicit affairs, but for the foreseeable future amorous intrigues would still dominate her existence. In February, Samuel Rogers, a literary friend of Caro's, showed her the proofs of *Childe Harold's Pilgrimage,* a gloomy and decadent volume of verse by Lord Byron. Inspired by the author's extended travels in the Mediterranean, the book relates a pilgrim's encounters with pirates and tales of shipwrecks, erotic love affairs, swimming the Hellespont, and meditation in a Greek monastery. To an inveterate fantasist such as Caro, Byron's mingling of fact and imagination was irresistible. She wrote, telling him how beautiful she thought his writing was, and two days later wrote again, this time sending her own verse composed in his homage:

> Oh that like thee Childe Harold I had power
> With Master hand to strike the thrilling Lyre
> To sing of Courts and Camps and Ladies Bower
> And chear the sameness of each passing hour
> With verse that breathes from heaven and should to heaven aspire . . .[1]

Caro was not alone in being enthralled by Byron; the publication of *Childe Harold* turned him into an overnight celebrity. "I awoke one morning and found myself famous,"[2] he later remarked, although Bess for one remained unimpressed by the furor surrounding him. "Lord Byron's book holds its place in the opinion of the public and he himself is invited, flattered and feted wherever he goes . . . his conversation is very opinionated and entertaining I hear . . . but he is odd, very odd . . . he lives chiefly on tea and vegetables,"³ she recorded in her journal. Caro, though, had always been impressionable; to her the buzz of strange rumors linked to Byron only added to his attraction. She set her heart on meeting him and even when Rogers told her that he had a club foot and bit his nails would not be deterred. "If he is as ugly as Aesop I must know him,"⁴ she proclaimed. Caro's first glimpse of the great man came at Lady Westmorland's house, where she arrived to find him standing in the center of the room, surrounded by a circle of admirers. Caro listened to the conversation for a while, then, irked to find herself one of a crowd, went away without speaking to him. Popular legend would have it that it was at this point that she murmured Byron was "mad, bad and dangerous to know."

Meanwhile, Byron had also noticed Caro watching him. She did not conform to his idea of female beauty, "wanting that roundness that grace and elegance would vainly supply."⁵ But her boyish figure, blond curls, musical voice, and childish manner reminded him of John Edleston, a choirboy with whom he had had a passionate friendship while at Cambridge, and, surrounded as he was by sycophants, her aloofness presented a challenge. Above all, socially ambitious and short of money, he recognized that Caro might provide a useful entrée to the upper echelons of the aristocratic world he wanted to infiltrate.

Two days later they met again at Holland House, and Byron asked Caro why she had avoided him. She refused to answer. Lured on, he called unexpectedly at Melbourne House just as Caro returned from riding, disheveled and dusty. Embarrassed, she made her excuses and left to change. But despite appearances to the contrary, these brief meetings had fanned her feelings as well as Byron's; soon after, she invited him to a waltzing party at Melbourne House and the stage was set for one of the most dramatic and scandalous—and most written about—love affairs of the age to unfold.

Harriet was worldly enough to suspect early on what was happening, and after Caro's recent amorous debacle with Webster she rapidly grew alarmed. To dissuade Byron from pursuing her daughter she told him Caro was in love with someone else. But her meddling proved disastrous; Byron grew resentful and distrustful of Harriet—it was perhaps at this moment that he dubbed her "Lady Blarney"—and his determination to woo Caro was further heightened. Harriet could only watch in dismay as Byron besieged Caro with demands, sometimes writing ten love letters a day or ordering that she cancel her waltzing parties or calling daily on her at Melbourne House, bringing books and staying for hours to discuss them. Bored and disillusioned by her marriage and a husband she felt ignored her, Caro was flattered to receive attention from a national celebrity and put up little resistance to his advances. Byron later wrote: "I was soon congratulated by my friends on the conquest I had made, and did my utmost to show that I was not insensible to the partiality I could not but perceive. I made every effort to be in love, expressed as much ardour as I could muster . . ."[6]

Both Caro and Byron had often chafed against the restrictions of convention. Now, as their grand passion progressed, they ignored these entirely, flaunting their affection and scandalizing society. By May, within two brief months of their meeting, the relationship had reached a highly charged peak. In public they paraded their affection, gazing longingly at each other at grand assemblies, leaving together in the same carriage. In private Caro called on Byron incognito, dressed as a page, and deluged him with letters declaring her passion. Outrageous stories of Caro's indiscretions were soon the talk of London and reached Lady Spencer. Now an old woman of seventy-five, she could no longer muster the anguish that Harriet's amorous indiscretions had once roused. But she was impelled to write stern letters to Caro and Harriet, praying that the foolishness would soon blow over. "How is dear Caroline?" she asked Harriet in May. "She fidgets me sadly as I daresay she does you, but I hope her good sense and excellent heart will in time find out that eccentricity is not a favourite qualification."[7] Other family members were equally mortified. Harryo met Byron when she accompanied Granville to London and, having heard of Caro's liaison, was cutting in her condemnation.

> Lord Byron is still upon a pedestal and Caroline William [Caro] doing homage. I have made acquaintance with him. He is agreeable, but I feel no wish for any further intimacy. His countenance is fine when it is in repose, but the moment it is in play, suspicious, malignant, and consequently repulsive. His manner is either remarkably

gracious and conciliatory, with a tinge of affectation, or irritable and
impetuous, and then I am afraid perfectly natural.[8]

Harriet, revealingly, failed to raise the subject of Byron in her letters
to Granville, instead finding plenty to discuss in what for her had always been an engrossing diversion in times of stress: the dramas of government. On May 11 John Bellingham entered the lobby of the House
of Commons and assassinated the prime minister, Spencer Perceval.
This act in itself was astonishing, but what left Harriet aghast was that
Bellingham had killed the wrong man. His intended target had not
been Perceval but Granville, who "had heard a good deal of [Belling-
ham] when he was ambassador in Russia—he was involved in a suit
which almost ruined him and was imprisoned for some months and
passed his time in importuning and libelling the Russian Government."*[9] Bellingham, Harriet soon discovered, was a deranged timber
merchant from Liverpool who was imprisoned when his business in
Russia went bankrupt and who blamed Granville for his misfortunes.

Perceval's assassination meant a new administration had to be
formed, and Harriet again found herself in the thick of it. With friends
among the Whig high command, Tory allies forged through her affair
with Granville, and wisdom and discretion honed from years of political involvement, she had never been more courted. Politicians in every
camp employed her to pass on information—or, on occasion, disinfor-
mation—to test political temperatures and to extract opinions, all with
such disarming charm and informality that offense was never given.

The Prince of Wales had already made use of Harriet's knack of
smoothing ruffled feathers the year before, when he had finally been
installed as regent. The Whigs had hoped that after years of cultivating
his favor they would at last be summoned to form a government. But
the prince had disappointed them, retaining the government installed
by his father, with Spencer Perceval at its head. He explained his reasons to Harriet, on the understanding that she would make them
known; "a change would drive the king mad again and even endanger

---

* Bellingham was found guilty of murder (even though he was insane) and publicly
hanged a week later, on May 18, at Newgate. Byron was one of the spectators.

his life—had it done so the Prince said he never could have enjoyed a quiet night's sleep again."[10] In fact, his decision was probably influenced by his opposition to their lukewarm approach to the war and policy of Catholic emancipation, but this was presumably a bone of contention that he chose not to declare to a Whig sympathizer such as Harriet.

The regent was also well aware that Harriet had grown close to one of the most fiery and influential Tory politicians of the day, George Canning. Granville's old Oxford friend had left office in 1809, having last served as foreign secretary in Portland's government, where he had been a fierce critic of the war minister, Lord Castlereagh. Their disagreements had climaxed in a duel on Putney Heath,* and since Perceval's appointment Canning had remained in the political wilderness. The regent also had reason to feel wary of Canning—Canning had enjoyed the intimate favors of his estranged wife. But in the interest of political stability, he was anxious to form a government that united the various Tory factions, including Canning. With this aim, he cajoled Harriet to talk the notoriously touchy Canning around, warning her that he "needs as much courting as a woman and a great deal more than most."[11]

Harriet did her best, passing on conversations to Canning, often via Granville. But when Canning remained unrelenting, the regent unfairly blamed Harriet, imagining Whig subversion where none existed. "He accused me of trying to warp you and as much as I could Mr. Canning, and prevent your coming in from the hope of strengthening Opposition," Harriet raged. "I told him, had I any such plan it would be perfectly fruitless, and a great deal more, which ended in his saying the proof would be my giving you the above message. I said I never would give *any message;* that it was not a proper way of treating a subject of such consequence, that I had already refused the same thing to Lord Grey, and that there were means enough if he chose to renew."[12]

Her denials were more than a little disingenuous—she did pass on messages and relay conversations on countless occasions—but they reveal the shifting political climate and the new dilemma faced by women with an interest in politics. Whereas once she and Georgiana

---

* Both men missed their first shots; Canning was slightly wounded in the thigh by the second and the duel was ended.

had openly expressed views and influenced elections, and had been widely lauded for their role, under the long rule of Pitt and the establishments that followed conventions had changed; women had been largely ushered from center stage, and those who remained trod a delicate path.[13]

Harriet had little difficulty adapting to the altered rules of the game. She had no desire to challenge the new political mood, perhaps because she feared that to do so might jeopardize confidences it had taken years to nurture. Besides, confrontation had always been alien to her nature, and she had spent years with Granville feigning acquiescence yet expressing her point of view and acting as an efficient political facilitator. "I am glad you declined being the bearer of any message from the Prince," replied Granville, who understood the unwritten rules as well as she. "As you said, if he wishes to renew, he may find out modes to do it . . . Canning went the whole length he could in the way of concession."[14]

FOUR DAYS LATER, politics were banished from Harriet's thoughts as Caro's affair with Byron reached a new crisis. "Oh G," Harriet wrote, abandoning her earlier reticence in her anguish, "Caroline is gone. It is too horrible. She is not with Lord Byron, but where she is God knows."[15]

The disintegration of the affair had begun several weeks earlier. Byron had never made any pretense of faithfulness; he had made a confidante of Caro's mother-in-law, the highly critical Lady Melbourne, and nurtured a close friendship with Caro's mentor, the sexually irrepressible Lady Oxford. His eye had also been drawn by Lady Melbourne's wealthy and unmarried niece Annabella Milbanke and by the heiress Miss Margaret Mercer Elphinstone. Caro knew Byron was not faithful to her and, as Harriet had once done with Granville, claimed to have resigned herself to his marriage. But her emotions were more fragile than her mother's; she was less accomplished at putting on a front and maintaining it, and her behavior became increasingly hysterical and bizarre. She made suicide threats and once sent Byron a lock of her pubic hair with a note signed "your wild antelope."

All this had convinced Harriet that Caro was on the brink of eloping with Byron, and she begged him to leave London, imploring his friend Hobhouse to intervene. When this failed, she attempted to persuade Caro and William to join her and Bessborough on a tour of Ireland. On the morning of August 12, the day Harriet wrote in such distress to Granville, she had arrived at the Lamb apartment in White-hall to entice Caro to Roehampton for a few days before leaving for Ireland, but Caro had been in a difficult mood and the situation swiftly deteriorated. When Lord Melbourne entered the room and began chastising Caro for her conduct, she clashed so violently with her father-in-law that Harriet rushed to fetch Lady Melbourne. By the time she returned it was too late. Caro had run out of the house while Lord Melbourne screamed at the porter to stop her. But it was too late—Caro had vanished.

Harriet hurried into the bustle of Parliament Street, searched in every direction, and returned filled with despair that can only have been made worse by Lady Melbourne's apparent indifference. Eventually Lord Melbourne revealed that Caro had threatened to go to Byron, "and he bid her go and be——, but did not think he would take her."[16] Hearing this, Lady Melbourne and Harriet hastened to Byron's lodgings. But Caro was nowhere to be seen, and Byron—who until then had known nothing of the drama— was so shaken by Harriet's distress that he promised to return Caro if she made contact with him.

Harriet, meanwhile, widened her search, driving about London for hours and stopping everywhere she could think of. Not until nine that night, in a state of nervous exhaustion, did she concede defeat and re-tire to Devonshire House to seek Hart's advice. She was with Hart when word arrived from Byron: he had discovered Caro's whereabouts and returned her to Cavendish Square.

Harriet later discovered that earlier that afternoon a hackney coachman had taken a message to Byron from Caro. Byron threatened and bribed the coachman to lead him to the author of the message and had been led to a surgeon's house in Kensington. Byron barged his way in, pretending Caro was his sister, and then forced her to go with him to Cavendish Square. As the evening unfolded, Byron continued to be-have more chivalrously than anyone might have expected. On Harriet's arrival he helped persuade Caro to return to Whitehall and her hus-band. William had agreed to take Caro back—he had always assumed her passion for Byron was merely a passing obsession, possibly aware that it was partly his indifference that had led her to ever more outrageous behavior. "All this will end ill," wrote Harriet that evening; "if it does not to her, it will to me."[17] The drama of the day had all been too much for her: she had collapsed on the floor of her carriage, unconscious, after coughing up blood. She was carried indoors by her footmen, "perfectly senseless and her poor mouth drawn all to one side and as cold as Marble." Harriet's maid, Sally, had no doubt where the blame lay and wrote sternly to Caro: "even her footmen cried out shame on you for alas you have exposed yourself to all London—you are the talk of every groom and footman about town."[18]

Ill health worsened Harriet's despair, counteracting any sense of relief at recovering Caro. "I do feel very unwell," she wrote that night, "and have for the last hour spit up so much blood that I think some little vessel must have broken. Why is it not a large one? I do no good to any one and am grown rather a burthen than pleasure to all those I love most."[19] The next day her gloom deepened when Caro announced she could not leave England, as she was expecting a baby and traveling might make her miscarry. William Lamb was so anxious for a second child that he fell for her story. Harriet was skeptical but still at a loss. "I know not what to do! I never saw so distressing a creature, and yet when she thought me in danger almost distracted with grief and remorse, swearing one moment that she will destroy herself if I am ill, then next that if Ld. Byron offers to stir out of London she will instantly fly—if not *with* him, from everyone else."[20] Caro claimed to be stricken by guilt at her mother's condition, but argued that making a journey would be as bad for Harriet as for herself. "I should never have thought of considering myself if Crofts and Sir H. H. had not positively said that it was madness to take Mama on a journey of that sort, far from medical help, at such a time. They said delay it a month; I only ask ten days; and that my motive may not be suspected, lock me up if you chuse during that time,"[21] she appealed to her father.

Adding to Harriet's torment were worries about Frederick, who was fighting in the Spanish Peninsula. Rumors of the Battle of Salamanca (fought on July 22), in which Lord Wellington decisively defeated the French under General Marmont, had first reached London in early August, two days before Caro's disappearance, although Wellington's official dispatch did not arrive until August 16. But the news when it arrived lifted her soul. Frederick had been in command of three squadrons and taken orders directly from Lord Wellington, from whom he afterward received high praise for his bravery and leadership. In her depleted frame of mind the news came as a welcome tonic. "Is not this a delightful thing to hear," she wrote to Granville, "to know that F[rederick] had the advantage of being directed by the greatest general that ever lived, and the glory of being approved by him?"[22]

In early September Harriet, together with Bessborough and William Lamb, finally coaxed Caro to Bessborough House in Kilkenny—but only after Byron had left London for Cheltenham. It had not been an easy journey. Caro arrived in Bristol happy enough, but when she found no letter from Byron she became hysterical. Harriet felt for her, knowing from her own bitter experience what it was to wait for a letter from her lover; nevertheless, Caro's uncontrolled sobbing terrified Harriet. "Were I to give you an account of my child it would only grieve and astonish you," she told Granville. "Indeed sometimes I cannot help fearing that her mind is affected."[23]

At Bessborough the family tensions seemed to lift, but there were other unforeseen obstacles to surmount. Harriet was inexperienced at performing the duties expected of her as chatelaine of the Bessborough estates. This was only her second visit to Ireland in all the years of her marriage, and the crisis with Caro and her own ill health made her pay less attention than was necessary to her duties. The Bessboroughs presided over two neighboring estates—Piltown and Carrick—and there was fierce rivalry between the two. Thus when the Piltown tenants performed a dance for Harriet and her entourage soon after their arrival, the Carrick tenants expected to be allowed the same privilege. Not realizing the significance of this request, Harriet neglected to reply to several communications from "the Carrickers" asking for her agreement to perform for her. It was not long before she received a forthright reminder of her function, which included the lines: "As her honoured Ladyship had not had leisure to condescend to an answer, the inhabitants of Carrick have taken the liberty to write one for her, which they enclose."[24]

The Carrickers arrived soon after, closely followed by numerous Piltowners. Bessborough and William Lamb were absent, and Harriet was alone in the house except for Caro and the servants. She was alarmed by the number of people flooding into the court and park. As the festivities got under way, the rivalry between the two groups grew more marked and the mood turned ugly. Harriet afterward amusingly described the scene to Granville:

> After the dancing was done and various feats of activity, this jealousy began showing itself by the Piltowners . . . [who] began stripping off their coats, saying tho' they were not so finely dressed nor so cock-aded . . . they could hollow as loud and fight as long as they could for my lord and lady. The proof of this was a yell more like what I have heard of the Indian war whoops than anything European, and the old house keeper came running to me, "<u>Och!</u> My own dear Lady, there will be <u>murter</u> below, and we shall all be kilt! And O, the Caters! It's all for love of you, and perhaps if you would make them a bet of a <u>Spache</u> off the stage it would set all right, and save a blessed soul <u>from Heaven</u>" Upon this I sallied forth in some dismay, and stretching my poor voice to its utmost pitch, made them, as she desired, a <u>bet</u> of a <u>Spache</u>, which succeeded better than most Speeches do, for it was not only greatly applauded, but obtain'd all I ask'd. Peace and harmony were restored.[25]

Harriet ordered whiskey punch to be brought and, bravely going among the crowd, drank the first glass herself, toasting her tenants' health and reminding them they were "all equally Lord B[essborough's] tenants" and begging them to go home quietly without fighting. The tenants responded by presenting Harriet with a garland and dancing around her peacefully before returning to their homes without "a single broken head," but, as Harriet perceptively pointed out, "it gave me a little notion of how hard they are to manage."[26]

Throughout the time at Bessborough, Caro put on a façade of normality, dancing and flirting with William, so much so that her fondness became a talking point. "When they say this," wrote Harriet, doubtless remembering Caro's hysterical screaming fits, during which she lay on the floor, drumming her feet, and bewailing her love of Byron, "I want to bellow."[27] Caro's correspondence with her mother-in-law reflects her inner confusion. "Here we are where all are gay one hour and sick with fever the other—as to me I can neither be ill or well, I neither sleep nor eat nor am able to do anything, I am more out of spirits than it is possible to say . . . ."[28] Lady Melbourne was also in correspondence with Byron and made matters worse by repeating his confidences concerning other women and his promises that his affair with Caro was over.

Harriet and her party made their way home in November, stopping en route to stay a few days at Tixal, Granville's country house in Staffordshire. Harryo was shocked by Caro's appearance. "My aunt looks very stout and well but poor Caroline most terribly the contrary; she is worn to the bone, as pale as death and her eyes starting out of her head. She seems in a sad way, alternately in tearing spirits and in tears . . . she appears to me in short, not very far from or rather little short of insanity." The rest of the party did not please her greatly either. "Poor Lord B *me pese sur le Coeur, l'esprit, l'estomac,** etc. William Lamb laughs and eats like a trooper. Rolla [Harriet's dog] is grown super-annuated and makes me sick—he whines, howls, coughs and what is worse in every corner of the room."[29]

Harryo had recently given birth to her second child, but it was not this new addition to Granville's family that made Harriet particularly anxious to call, but rather the presence of another child who had also taken up residence in the house. In August, in the midst of Caro's traumas, Little Harriet Arundel Stewart, the child fathered by Granville and secretly fostered, had been brought from the shadows for a stay at Tixal.

For this reason Granville had looked forward to Harriet's arrival with a sense of pride and anticipation. "I think you will find [Little Harriet] improved, she has lately been taking steel with the hope of curing her of that languor and paleness which seems to be her only complaint."[30] Little Harriet also yearned for the arrival of the benefactress who had always shown such kindness and concern toward her. "How happy it makes me to think that now I shall be able to count the days in which you will be here at Tixal and in the same house as me . . . I hope you do not mean to go a visiting on your way here or else the people will detain you so long that you will not be here before Christmas."[31]

When Little Harriet first arrived it had been for a temporary stay

---

* Weighs down my heart, spirit, stomach.

only, but Harryo had taken to the child quickly and decided to offer her a permanent home; "she really is a most amiable little creature and though she has nothing precose about her, her intelligence and docility make her a very delightful companion."[32] For Harriet, who had always kept in close touch with her child, witnessing the warm bond that had grown between Little Harriet and Harryo must have been both consoling and heartrending. While Little Harriet had lived in a foster home, Harriet had enjoyed regular access to her, and she and Granville had freely discussed her progress—which provided a link to sustain their relationship—and Harriet had complete control over her upbringing. Now all this changed.

When her daughter became a member of Granville's household, Harriet had to tread carefully and defer to Harryo in all that concerned her; decisions regarding Little Harriet's well-being no longer provided her with a pretext for discussion with Granville. To relinquish her child and her lover to the same woman cannot have been easy. "Dear child how I do love her, miss her, long for her," Harriet wrote of Little Harriet, and yet at the back of her mind must have been the image of Georgiana's dejected child Eliza, raised under a cloud of shame. She forced herself to recognize Harryo's generosity of spirit. "But yet I am delighted to have her where she is—and with her improvement and yours and Harriet's [Harryo's] kindness to her," she sadly acknowledged.[33]

A slender bundle of correspondence between Harriet, Granville, Harryo, and Little Harriet survives in the Public Record Office and provides a poignant insight into the continuing constraints and subterfuge. After Little Harriet had been offered a permanent home with Granville and Harryo, she addressed Granville as "her guardian," although Harryo remained "my dearest lady Granville," and Harriet would always be "Lady Bessborough," a concerned friend to whom she had always written regularly without any idea that she was her mother. "The account you give me in your letter of all the fairs and dinners, lodgings of the grand ladies and how busy you have been amused me very much,"[34] Little Harriet wrote in a typical letter.

Such artifice aside, Little Harriet settled happily into her new home. She was much loved by her new family, so much so that soon after her stay was made permanent she was joined by her younger brother, George, who was welcomed with similar warmth into the Granville fold. The packet of letters also contains a verse dedicated to Harriet in a child's hand that is probably Little Harriet's:

> Love is made of brittle stuff
> Nor let it cause the least surprise
> That spite of verse, he has his eyes
> These tales of blindness were untrue
> He proves his sight by seeking you.[35]

Lawrence's dashing portrait of Lord Granville Leveson Gower was painted a decade after his meeting with Harriet in Naples, at the time of his appointment as ambassador to Russia.

The Chairing of Fox—one of the many political satires to appear during the 1784 election. Charles James Fox is being carried by three attractive female supporters sporting foxtails in their hats; the central one is probably intended to be Harriet. "I do not believe there is a man of greater talents, nobler heart, or purer integrity living," Harriet wrote of him.

Above Fox addressing the House of Commons during Pitt's ministry.

Left William Pitt the Younger was Fox's political rival and Britain's youngest first minister. The prince regent (*above*) was a friend of Harriet's from their teens. "I should guide his politics," she told Granville, describing his "immense grotesque figure flouncing about half on the couch, half on the ground."

Above The great eruption of Vesuvius from the mole of Naples, October 20, 1767. English tourists relished the warm climate and sights of Naples. It was here that Harriet and Granville first met.

Below La Place des Victoires, Paris, and the hectic throng of English visitors in pre-revolutionary Paris. Harriet visited the French capital to escape the aftermath of her affair with Sheridan.

Right After her illness, Harriet spent several months convalescing in Bath, bathing and drinking the waters, which she found "rather pleasant than otherwise."

Below Bessborough House in Kilkenny, Ireland, was built for the first earl from local limestone by Francis Bindon in 1744. Harriet visited the house only twice, once with Caroline and William Lamb in the aftermath of Caroline's unhappy affair with Byron.

Below A seaside resort, possibly Margate, with bathing machines. Not everyone concealed themselves in machines. Lavinia Spencer was outraged to see teenage girls with their dresses tucked about their waists romping with stark naked boys.

Harriet's closeness to her mother (*right*) continued until her death. Lady Spencer still dispensed advice to her family well into her seventies.

Center Frederick, Third Earl of Bessborough. He and Harriet discovered a friendship in later life that eluded them in their youth.

Below Harriet, painted in Italy in 1793 by Angelica Kauffmann, a family friend who had painted Harriet and her siblings in their teens.

Above Sir Frederick Ponsonby, Harriet's second son, became a military hero but was gravely wounded at Waterloo.

Above Caroline Lamb's stormy
marriage to William Lamb (*right*)
and affair with Lord Byron (*above
right*) caused great distress to her
family and brought shame that
haunted her for the remainder
of her life.

Granville Leveson Gower's marriage to Harryo proved blissfully happy; the couple's children were brought up alongside Little Harriet and George Arundel Stewart, to whom he also offered a home.

TWENTY-FIVE

Lady Blarney

1813–1815

HARRIET ENJOYED LITTLE RESPITE from family drama when she returned to London. Caro was frequently agitated, threatening to harm Byron or Lady Oxford—his latest passion—or herself. Setting her heart on a meeting with Byron—something with which he was, understandably, reluctant to comply—Caro expected Harriet to talk him around. Harriet had never mastered the art of refusing her daughter anything. Against her better judgment she tried to visit Byron, but his indifference to her pleas, contrasting so starkly with Caro's torment, roused her fury and she vented her outrage in furious letters to him. Even then, Byron failed to respond or to give in, treating Harriet's wrath with wry amusement. "It is odd that her last letter to me . . . contains nothing but more general menaces of vengeance and professions of not unwelcome hatred . . . the closing sentence is awfully amiable and I copy it 'you have told me how foreign women revenge—I will show you how an English woman can,' "[1] he told Lady Melbourne.

In January, Caro's temper subsided and she became more composed and reasonable, offering to return the gifts Byron had given her and asking for the return of her letters. Harriet and Byron managed to reach an uneasy truce and Byron at last agreed to a meeting to discuss how the handover of the letters could best be accomplished. He later described the encounter in some detail to Lady Melbourne:

Ly. B[essborough] was at home this morning and after <u>mutually</u> premising that neither "<u>would believe one word the other had to</u>

say" much civil upbraiding took place.—She lectured pleasantly upon "Soothing," complained that I had deceived you and Mrs. L[amb: i.e., Caro] etc. into a belief that I was a "sober quiet Platonic well disposed person"—added that you was "the best and cleverest of all possible women" . . . She was a good deal horrified at my deficiency in <u>Romance</u>—and quite petrified at my behaviour altogether . . . The result of all this is that I shall restore the brilliant epistles, and get back the baubles . . . To Ly. C[aroline]'s good resolutions I have nothing to say . . . I have already sent her the requested absolutions and remissions . . . In short I wish to hear no more of the matter.[2]

Cordial encounters such as this were rare. For the most part, Byron spent much time away from London, where there was no danger of confrontation. When in town he consciously avoided any social occasion that Harriet or Caroline might attend. "If I had gone to Mrs. Hope's [Lady Douglas] I should have found the only 'novelty' that would give me any pleasure in yourself," he told Lady Melbourne after missing an assembly in March. "But then I should have been checkmated by the Ly. Blarney [Harriet] who ranks next to a breast of Veal, an earwig, and her own offspring, amongst my antipathies."[3] He made many similar claims to detest Harriet as much as her daughter, even though he recognized Harriet's attractiveness and intellect, and there were times—when Caro was quiet and occupied elsewhere—that he confessed to very different feelings toward her mother.

How is the Ly. Blarney?—if that sagacious person knew how matters stand just at present I think her alarms would be at rest forever—if ever I were again smitten in that family it would be with herself and not C[aroline]—but hatred is a much more delightful passion—and never cloys—it will make us all happy for the rest of our lives.[4]

Inevitably, there were formal events at which Byron and Caro's paths crossed—and when they did, angry words usually ensued. The worst fracas came in July, when both attended Lady Heathcote's ball. Accounts of the events vary, but it seems clear that Caro began dancing after remarking pointedly to Byron, "I conclude I may waltz now."[5]

(His club foot made dancing awkward and he had forbidden her to dance during their affair.) As ever, though, her composure was more brittle than it appeared and later in the evening something Byron murmured to her made her rush to the supper room and stab herself with a broken glass. "She is now like a barrel of gunpowder," wrote the unsympathetic Lady Melbourne, who witnessed the entire episode, "and takes fire with the most trifling spark."

Much to the chagrin of the Melbourne and Bessborough families, the scene was reported widely in every echelon of the press. "I see the sharp censures ready to start into words in every cold, formal face I meet,"[6] Caro lamented as the ignominy her desperate actions had brought began to dawn. She retreated to the seclusion of Brocket Hall to spend the next months with her long-suffering husband in the hope that the furor would blow over, and wrote to Byron to apologize for her behavior. "I have received a most rational letter full of good resolves — and a most tempting basket full of excellent fruit,"[7] he reported to Lady Melbourne in August. Despite her shame, Caroline underestimated the effect of what she had done. Not even illustrious connections and disappearing from view could alter the fact that she had transgressed one of the great unwritten rules of her day; such flagrant infidelity and uncontrolled emotion would taint her reputation for the rest of her life.

Harriet harbored no such illusions, instantly comprehending the gravity of Caro's actions. But she never accepted that Caro was at fault and her support never wavered. Other members of the family displayed less forbearance. Granville insisted Harriet censure her daughter; she refused unflinchingly. "I know how bad all this has been, and how much worse it would be were there any relapse; yet when you say that in such a case she would lose all title even to compassion, I am afraid I could not act up to such an opinion. Deserving punishment and ruin does not make them less severe, and I can scarcely conceive a case where parents can renounce their child,"[8] she told Granville firmly.

HARRIET'S REFUSAL TO bow to Granville was a sign not merely of maternal indulgence and the strain she was under, but of a gradual distancing in their relationship. Less patient now with his demands, she spoke her mind openly when she felt inclined. Her indignation was sparked one morning when Granville, alone in her private sitting room, rifled through her desk. Finding several of his recent letters hidden beneath a folder, he criticized her for her carelessness. Harriet did not hesitate to defend herself and tell him his reprimands were unjust:

> When common acquaintances are admitted into a lady's sitting room they do not take up a presse papiers and examine what is under it. You may do this because I have never had anything I wished to hide from you . . . This is too bad, too tantalising, and very unjust, sir, your letters are never left to *traîner.* I value them too much. They are put up as soon as read into my red case, and from thence travel to the famous cedar box, which some time or other you are to inherit.[9]

The incident, though trivial, also tells us something of the new vicissitudes in the male-female divide. Since the hedonistic bed-hopping days of the late eighteenth century, Granville, like much of society (and apparently without any sense of hypocrisy), had become increasingly circumspect and disapproving of sexual transgressions. Nevertheless, nothing had altered the fact that men still made the rules. Thus, although Granville and Harriet no longer shared a bed, he felt able to exert certain proprietary rights over her. He still called without warning and allowed himself freedom to search her desk if he felt like it. Harriet's staunch defiance of his criticisms also reflects the gradual reshaping of her world. Once she might have tried to soften her response, but with family crisis absorbing her thoughts, and Granville no longer occupying center stage, she had little impetus to do so.

Her scrawling correspondence mirrors her multiple preoccupations that summer: Caro, always a source of worry; Frederick, fighting in Portugal with the Duke of Wellington; and, in addition, her mother, who until now had enjoyed robust good health but in June became unwell and needed constant attention. Even when the worst symptoms of her illness disappeared, Lady Spencer's convalescence was slow. She had lost her appetite, had grown thin, and had an "appearance of languor" that worried Harriet. "It is difficult to settle our plan much till she is quite recovered for she is so used to have me near her that I should be unwilling to go far till she is quite stout,"[10] she told her brother, George, whom she joined for a holiday in Ryde, on the Isle of Wight.

The holiday was to prove a great success. Harriet felt secure in the company of her brother. "It is so many years since I have lived as much in his society, that it makes me feel as if we were gone back to the time of Wimbledon and St. James's Place before he was married." Lavinia's abrasive manner had not improved with the passing years, but for once everyone got on well. "She really has been extremely kind, and when she is so it always makes me more provoked at her manner of talking, which, in spite of a sounder understanding, more cleverness and more information than most people, makes her justly very unpopular,"[11] Harriet reported.

Congenial surroundings did not prevent Harriet from being frantic for news of Frederick. His worrisome yet fascinating accounts of Wellington's advances in Spain arrived sporadically and made her so proud that she circulated them among the family and sent copies to Granville. Fears for his safety were magnified when she knew news was imminent. In July she told her brother she had passed a night "filling it up with every horror"[12] after a telegraphic account of a battle had been cut off. She was ecstatic the next day to learn that the French had retreated from Burgos and there had been no bloodshed. "Tomorrow we open forty guns upon St. Sebastian, and in all probability it will be knocked down very soon," Frederick had told her. The following month he was awaiting orders to follow Wellington in his pursuit of a now demoralized French army. "I assure you we all expect to be in a very short time on the other side of Bayonne . . . we army politicians see nothing to prevent his marching at least to Bordeaux."[13]

Back in London in the autumn, Harriet immersed herself in the social whirl that had always beguiled her. The city was alive with visitors from France, escaping Napoleon's regime, and Harriet had enough connections among the high echelons of French society to ensure that many made their way to her door. Prominent among the latest influx was the famous French writer and political activist Mme. Germaine de Staël. Having been an outspoken critic of Napoleon, she was now living in exile and visiting London with her lover, Baron Rocca. (According to Byron, he was the only proof of her good taste.) Harriet had long been an admirer of Mme. de Staël's writing. While in Paris, during the Peace of Amiens, Harriet had sat up through the night to finish her autobiographical novel, *Delphine,* proclaiming afterward, "My eyes are swelled out of my head with crying."[14]

Mme. de Staël was a woman of masculine appearance, with dark flashing eyes and "a thoracic development worthy of a wet nurse,"[15] who paid little heed to personal hygiene. "To air and water, not to mention soap, I think she has an antipathy,"[16] Caro once waspishly commented. Despite this drawback, she and Harriet discovered much common ground. Both loved stimulating intellectual conversation and could discuss politics and literature late into the night. Both admired the doctrines of Rousseau, reveling in expression of feelings as well as opinions and in nurturing intense friendships. Before long Mme. de Staël regarded Harriet as an intimate and became a regular guest at Roehampton and Cavendish Square.

Harriet, to begin with, was enchanted by her new friend's warmth and effortless ability to entertain, describing her as being "at my elbow to *me souffler les anecdotes Histoires, littéraires et Militaires** of all the crowned heads in Europe."[17] When Mme. de Staël's book *De l'Allemagne*—a critique of German literature, which also managed to reveal hostility to Napoleon and imperial despotism—was republished,† she aroused wide comment, not all of it favorable. Harriet secretly thought the second volume "tiresome," but grew defensive when anyone else criticized it. "Any account of metaphysics must be obscure . . . therefore, this first part of the third vol has *des longueurs,* but . . . many of her own observations delight me. I think it so good and often so full of wit,"[18] she censured Granville.

Despite this defense, the underlying strains in the friendship were becoming more marked. Mme. de Staël failed to recognize Harriet's need for time alone with her family, and eventually her demanding nature and intensity became more than Harriet's frayed nerves could take. "She is continually coming here, and sometimes pleasant, but I

---

* To whisper historical, literary, and military anecdotes to me.
† The whole edition had been seized and destroyed on Napoleon's instructions in France three years earlier.

cannot bear morning visits in the Country. A large house full of company is often very pleasant, because people go their own way all morning, and only assemble in society at dinner and night; but in the morning, unless something you are really anxious to see, it just breaks up your walks and plans, and puts you out of all you want to do, very seldom repaying you for this discomposure by its own merits,"[19] she complained to Granville, while to her mother she confided, "Wherever I go she comes . . . I really like her but must own I should have preferred being here quiet with Caro and William."[20]

Lady Spencer was less than sympathetic in her response to Harriet's grumbles. "Madame de Staël is quite in the right to run after you my dear Harriet I would do so too if I could."[21] Perhaps the literary anecdotes Harriet recounted revived for her mother memories of her younger days when she had enjoyed similar friendships with literary giants such as Samuel Johnson, David Garrick, and Hester Thrale. Despite the robustness of her response, however, her health was weakening rapidly, placing an added burden on Harriet's shoulders. George Spencer, though devoted to his mother, was often hampered in his desire to look after her by frictions between her and his wife Lavinia, and he trod a precarious path keeping both women happy. Typical of Lavinia's unsympathetic and imperious manner was a note written to Harriet in December, when Lady Spencer was staying with her at Althorp, and Harriet and her family were expected en route to Chatsworth. "We expect you on the twenty-third I take the liberty to inform you—but pray don't say anything about going away after you are once here . . . You'll find your mother very well, if eating all day long is a proof of being well."[22] Harriet incurred the brunt of Lavinia's fury when sometime during the journey she inadvertently misdirected a letter:

> God knows who this letter is addressed to—not to me is all I can make out, although it was under cover to me . . . are you not too careless? And into what severe embarrassments might such mistakes put you!—to whom has my property gone? For I suppose the letter you intended for me is equally missent—upon my word and honour you deserve a good whipping to impress all this on your memory as a dog is whipped for putting up his leg where he ought not.[23]

Chatsworth was buried in snow but looking beautiful when Harriet arrived. This for her was a poignant visit, the first she had made since Georgiana's death, "but dear Hart seemed to wish it so much I could not well refuse him," she told her mother. She was doubly moved to find that he had put her in her sister's rooms, telling her she could change the room if she wished but that he hated seeing anyone but her or Little G in the room. Once she had got over the shock, Harriet found herself enjoying the sense of closeness to Georgiana it brought, although she confessed to sitting sometimes, looking around and waiting for the door to open and seeing her come in. "But . . . though length of time blunts ancient habits and . . . I do not think it blunts the pain which places and this being past time bring[?] Forcibly to your memory and you see everything remaining as it was except what gave it value."[24]

The pain reawakened by staying in her sister's room was soon to be repeated in Harriet's life. Returning from her visit to Chatsworth, she found her mother's health had worsened. After a lifetime of writing three times a week to her son and daughter, and of corresponding regularly with countless others, Lady Spencer became too weak to hold a pen and had to dictate her letters to her companion, Selina Trimmer. "I have a pretty little pit of a cough which I am nursing up with all possible care. Selina leaves me tomorrow in the hope that you and sometimes a game at chess will do me much good,"[25] she wrote. A few weeks later, she seemed to rally slightly and was well enough to quiz Harriet on her social life. "Selina is out, my dear Harriet, so I am proud to be my own scribe and to say that I really think my cough is better. Was you at the Ball last night? The carriages passed my windows till after five today, and I was sorry not to be well enough to look out, as I should have seen some of their odd dresses."[26] The improvement was to prove sadly short-lived. A few days later, Lady Spencer was once again fighting for breath, and on March 18, 1814, at the venerable age of seventy-seven, she died.

Her death marked the closing of a chapter and irrevocably altered the map of family life. Lady Spencer had been a constant presence in Harriet's life, cajoling, chivvying, and encouraging; a voice of restraint whenever Harriet had veered to excess; a support in moments of darkness and despair. Now the once wayward daughter had to take over the mantle of family matriarch. We can only guess the effect of all this—no letters survive to record Harriet's feelings, although a deferential obituary survives among her papers. "No one was ever better formed by nature not only to become but to shed a grace and ornament upon the high station in which she was placed by this alliance and to exert the noblest prerogative which rank and wealth confer by giving a high example of virtue and piety limited with a proper display of the splendour and a due enjoyment of the pleasures which naturally belong to her situation . . ."[27] it reads.

We can surmise, however, that the sense of loss, though acute, did not compare with the agony Harriet had endured when Georgiana died. Lady Spencer had not been cheated of her life; she had lived to a great age and for all the innumerable tragedies and difficulties she had suffered, by any standards her life had been rich and fulfilling.

There was also auspicious news from the wider world to distract and soften the blow. By the end of February the allied advance on Paris had resumed and Napoleon's troops were melting away like the snow. A month later Paris capitulated and agreed to an armistice with Tsar Alexander, the leader of the allies. In April the elderly Bourbon king Louis XVIII, until now living in exile in Hartwell House, Buckinghamshire, was installed as monarch. Meanwhile Napoleon, retitled Emperor and Sovereign of the Isle of Elba, sailed to exile aboard the English frigate *Undaunted*. After twelve years of war (since the short-lived Peace of Amiens) and living under the threat of French invasion, peace had at last been restored.

Closer to home, there was further reason to rejoice when William made an advantageous marriage to Lady Barbara Ashley Cooper, the only daughter and heiress to the Fifth Earl of Shaftesbury. Neither Bessborough nor Harriet could ignore the significance of the match; like John and Caro, Willy had managed to overcome the financial difficulties that had dogged his parents and secure his own future.

It was thus in a mood of celebration that Harriet and Bessborough, together with Willy and his new wife, Barbara, joined the throng of British visitors traveling to the Continent that autumn. They planned to pass some time in Paris, where they would meet up with Bess, and then to winter in the South of France. They traveled in some style in two luxurious carriages because, as Harriet wrote with bashful honesty, "we are all rather inclined to like our comforts, especially W." Harriet and Bessborough traveled in one vehicle, William and Barbara in the other; a total of eight servants accompanied them, most seated outside on dickeys next to the driver, where they were exposed to the worst of the elements. Uncertain of the condition of the lodgings they would find, they also took with them "all sorts of household goods and kitchen utensils, beds in and out of the carriages," so much so that one of the maids had remarked, "One might almost think we were going to traverse the deserts of Arabia."[28]

Even before they had arrived in Paris, word of their arrival had spread and a stream of visitors called to pay their respects. Among the great and good paying court to Harriet were the Duke of Wellington and Mme. de Staël (the latter sweeping into Harriet's room before she had even finished her breakfast). Harriet could hardly fail to be flattered. "They detained me a good while and were hardly gone before Archibald de Perigord, the Comtesse de la Mare and Giamboni arrived, followed shortly afterwards by Bess and her daughter,"[29] she recorded of the first whirlwind morning. In between making calls, receiving guests, and attending a stream of formal assemblies, there were the cultural attractions that Harriet, as a woman of refinement, could not possibly ignore. She found time to visit the opera and the theater, to see the studios of various painters, and, whenever there was a spare moment, to shop.

A month later, exhausted by the social circus and laden with new purchases, they headed south and reached Marseilles by Christmas. After the winter chill of northern France, the streets seemed sunny and vibrantly alive. "The Quay is very gay, like a masquerade — Greeks and Turks and Jews and Genoese sailors and English tars, mixed with Poissardes and Marseilles Elégantes, parading up and down all day," Harriet told Granville. We may surmise that her colorful descriptions were less for his benefit than because she knew that whatever she wrote would be passed on to Little Harriet and George.

As ever, her letters are also filled with whom she met and what they said to her, one name featuring particularly prominently. In Paris, the Duke of Wellington had provided her with letters of introduction to Masséna, the commander of the French forces in the south, whom she had first met on her visit to Paris twelve years earlier. Masséna remembered Harriet favorably and, eager to renew the acquaintance, one morning burst into her bedroom with another officer in attendance before Harriet had finished dressing. Harriet, consummately accomplished when it came to social graces, concealed her surprise and subjected Masséna to the full force of her charms. He was so captivated that he offered her party every hospitality: free use of his box at the theater, accommodation in a magnificent hotel—no easy feat in a country overrun with British visitors—and introductions into Marseilles high society. Harriet attended her first soirée with some trepidation but soon found herself in her element. Chess, a favorite pastime of hers, was being played at numerous tables; there were also games of whist and musical entertainments taking place. "We are having a very wholesome quiet life here, keep very good hours, are out almost all morning either by the seaside or amongst it round Marseilles. In the evening we generally sit at home and read or write often have a few people to dine with us, sometimes a little music, sometimes we go to the play and sometimes *pour mon particulier* play at chess,"[30] she reported happily to her brother in January.

Harriet was at first flattered by Masséna's attentions, particularly relishing his insights into Napoleon, but, as with Mme. de Staël, his constant attention gradually jarred and she began to feel stifled. "He will not let us stir without him or speak to another human creature, and every attempt we made to walk about he started up offering me his arm, and after a turn or two brought us back prisoners to our old place," she complained after one particularly oppressive evening. For all her growing edginess with Masséna, Harriet refused to submit to ennui, remembering advice given to her by Mme. de Staël: "When conversation lags . . . it is better to risk an impertinence than be bored." To liven up matters, she began probing Masséna on the subject of Napoleon's love life. Masséna was apparently so astonished at her frivolity that his whole countenance changed and after a moment he said, *"Lui! Jamais, il n'a rien aimé de sa vie, femmes, hommes, enfants, rien—rien au monde que lui."*[*][31]

Although she never says so, we cannot help wondering whether behind Masséna's interest in Harriet lay the circumspect hope that their

---

* Him [Napoleon]! Never, he has loved nothing in his life, not women, men, children, nothing—nothing in the world except himself.

platonic friendship might develop into something more. Had he heard of her colorful past and made the same assumption as the prince regent—that Granville's marriage had left a void in her life? If so, Harriet disappointed him, deftly eluding his advances, though no doubt flirting charmingly as she did so. "Poor Masséna labours as hard to make me a good General as if I was to serve him as aide de camp in his next campaign," she declared, "and I interrupt his best planned battles to make him tell me stories of his chief."[32]

In February the weather turned warm and Harriet spent her days outdoors enjoying the surroundings, taking boat trips in the heat of the day, or strolling through shady gardens, drawing and rambling by the shore. "Everything is in full blossom and all the flowers are out," she reported.[33] Yet her blithe descriptions mask her true feelings; she was homesick for England and for her friends. "If ever I live to get back it will be a difficult matter to draw me from it again."[34] A fortnight later her feelings intensified when an English frigate arrived en route from America to Constantinople. "The fair locks, blue jackets, and little dirks of these boys [two midshipmen] made my heart quite beat, and I long to set sail with them, defying storms, Americans, and sickness—to get back to you all."[35] Adding to her unease, she had heard a whisper that Napoleon had left his exile in Elba with a party of supporters and had landed at Fréjus. The report seemed so outlandish that Harriet tried to dismiss it. But two days later Masséna confirmed that Napoleon had indeed landed with eleven hundred men and some arms. He had tried to enter the town of Antibes, and having been repelled had made for the mountains near Grasse with the intention of heading for Paris.

The news threw Marseilles into uproar. The city was a pro-Bourbon enclave—unlike other southern towns. Drums rolled and people stampeded in the streets, chanting slogans in support of the king. Masséna, worried that anarchy would break out, summoned the National Guard to maintain order. Addressing the populace from his balcony, he urged calm and reassured them that a large force was being sent to Toulon (a city known to be sympathetic to Napoleon) to maintain control. Harriet was too exhilarated at the prospect of being in the center of such momentous events to feel fearful; and besides, she had received Masséna's firm assurance that her party was safe.

Events unfolded rapidly. Two days later Masséna confessed he was worried that the army would defect and join Napoleon. Furthermore, Harriet became conscious that among the pro-Bourbon Marseilles populace the British were viewed with increasing suspicion, thanks to Napoleon's claims that he had returned to France with the support of the English government. Compounding the air of confusion were constant contradictory rumors: some said that Napoleon had been captured, others that he had arrived in Paris and that Louis XVIII had escaped to Belgium. Again and again the streets of Marseilles were filled with panic. The shops closed and all commercial activity ceased. "Excepting at a County of Middlesex Election I never saw such a crowd or such a clamour,"[36] quipped Harriet with hollow bravado.

Masséna continued to assure Harriet and her party of their safety, but she now suspected he had an ulterior motive for wishing her to remain in Marseilles. He had often confided his highly critical thoughts about Napoleon to her; if she ever repeated them, the consequences for him might be dire. "In spite of his courtesy he would sooner put me in a dungeon by way of gag than risk letting me go free and talk."[37] Secretly, Harriet and her party began to make tentative arrangements to leave Marseilles and head home. Hampering their decision to leave, and adding further problems to an already complicated situation, was Barbara's condition. She was in the early stages of pregnancy and suffering from sickness; there were fears that travel might lead her to miscarry. Bessborough was also seriously unwell, racked with gout, which made travel extremely painful. But the scant news that filtered to them day by day seemed ever more alarming. By March 19 Napoleon had reached Paris and Louis XVIII had escaped across the border to Belgium. Although reports were unconfirmed, it was clear that the country might erupt into civil war at any moment; plainly, whatever the dangers to family health, it was foolhardy to remain in France any longer.

Ignoring Masséna's advice, they left Marseilles at the end of March, making a perilous journey through Bonapartist southern France to Nice. "The road from Marseilles here is beautiful," Harriet recorded afterward; "such a profusion of blossoms, fruit, flowers and trees out in the richest foliage—filled with birds singing in the midst of rocks and torrents and mountains, and *banditti,* that it is a much fitter scene for a novel than for a civil war."[38] Her calm front concealed her inner terror. She had heard rumors that Murat, the ex-King of Naples, was threatening the Austrians intent on regaining a grip on Italy, and spent restless nights dreaming of chains and drawbridges and jailers. Despite these anxieties, they arrived safely in Genoa by the end of April. Immediately they set about arranging their passage by sea to England before Barbara's pregnancy became too advanced. But securing berths was difficult in a city bursting at the seams with foreign tourists all with the same intention. Among them was the Princess of Wales, who had been living nearby in some style. Harriet was consumed by embarrassment when she encountered her a few days later:

> The first thing I saw in the room was a short, very fat, elderly woman, with an extremely red face (owing I suppose, to the heat) in a girl's white frock looking dress, but with shoulder, back and neck, quite low (disgustingly so), down to the middle of her stomach, very black hair and eyebrows, which gave her a fierce look, and a wreath of light pink roses on her head. She was dancing and at the end of the dance a pretty little English boy ran up and kissed her. I was staring at her from the oddity of her appearance, when suddenly she nodded and smiled at me, and not recollecting her, I was convinced she was mad, till William pushed me, saying: "do not you see the Princess of Wales nodding to you?"[39]

Days after this mortifying encounter Harriet and her entourage left Genoa. Worried they would never find a boat that could take them, they had decided to travel overland via Milan and Switzerland. They were in the early stages of this journey when news of the bitterly fought Battle of Waterloo, which had taken place on June 18, reached them. Knowing that Frederick was involved in the action, Harriet frantically petitioned every contact she could for further details. In the Swiss town of Schaffhausen news of the worst kind arrived: Frederick had died in the battle. Harriet's agony was barely alleviated the next day when another military official arrived. Sir Robert Lawley told Lord Bessborough that the report of Frederick's death was untrue; he was not dead but had been seriously wounded and now lay clinging to life somewhere in Brussels. According to Harriet, he gave "the most horrible accounts" of Frederick. "Never I believe did human being suffer more with life preserved."[40]

The conflicting reports left Harriet in a ferment of confusion, but it did not take her long to decide on the course of action she would take. Ignoring the considerable danger to her own safety, she separated from the rest of her family and raced alone across Europe to find her son.

TWENTY-SIX

Turmoil

1815 - 1817

WE WERE ON THE LEFT and seeing a large mass of infantry in retreat and in confusion my regiment charged. It entered the mass and at the same time a body of French Lancers charged us on our flank. Nothing could equal the confusion of this melee, as we had succeeded in destroying and putting to flight the infantry. I was anxious to withdraw my regiment, but almost at the same moment I was wounded in both arms, my horse sprung forward and carried me to the rising ground ... where I was knocked off my horse by a blow on the head,"[1] Frederick later wrote of his battlefield experiences. His injuries were horrific: his arms and head were slashed by a lance; then, having fallen to the ground semiconscious, he attempted to stand up, only to be stabbed in the back and collapse again. This last wound penetrated his lungs and, to add to his woes, as he lay helplessly on the ground choking on the blood gushing from his mouth a French foot soldier robbed him. Meanwhile, all around him the French forces were vainly trying to hold the Prussians at bay. At one stage a kindly French officer took time from the battle to revive Frederick by pouring brandy in his mouth; afterward Frederick said he owed his life to this kindness. But when the Prussian cavalry charged the French retreated, leaving Frederick to be badly trampled by the horses. "In general horses will avoid treading upon men but the field was so covered, that they had no spare space for their feet,"[2] he later coolly observed.

After eighteen hours on the ground, during which time he was robbed again—on this occasion by a Prussian—Frederick was discovered by an English soldier who stayed with him until help, in the form of a dragoon from his own regiment, arrived. By then too ill to be transported on horseback, he was heaved onto the back of a wagon and driven a few bone-shattering miles to the Duke of Wellington's quarters at Waterloo, where the duke's physician dressed his wounds. For a week he lay at death's door.

Caro and William Lamb were the first family members to reach Frederick, in early July. They were aghast at his condition: he was still black and blue, covered in lacerations, and unable to speak. William Lamb graphically reported: "The lance had certainly injured the lungs, but that wound . . . is entirely healed . . . his arm and shoulder had been so violently trampled upon that a violent inflammation took place and a large collection of matter formed, which has been let out this morning."[3] Despite Frederick's horrific state, by then the surgeon had declared him out of imminent danger and well enough to be moved to a house in Brussels. Gradually over the following days Frederick recovered sufficiently to speak. His first words to Caro were to ask after Harriet and Caro's son, Augustus.

The Lambs' chief worry was that Harriet might hear "false or imperfect intelligence"[4] and, believing Frederick dead, would not come to see him. They need not have worried. An exhausted Harriet reached Frederick seven days later; having raced across Europe and braved Cossacks, Prussians, and Austrian troops, she had beaten the post by two days. Bessborough and the rest of the family she had left in Switzerland had traveled the route more slowly and would rejoin her a few days later. Meanwhile Harriet was filled with foreboding at Frederick's still feeble condition. "One arm is perfectly useless. Heaven grant it may be restored, but at present it looks terrible. The other . . . is still very sore from the great cuts upon it, the shoulder, the upper part of the arm and below the elbow. The cut on the head is quite well, but it is the wound thro his lungs I mind most,"[5] she told John.

Adding to her concern was the fact that Brussels was far from a pleasant place to stay; the streets were filled with wounded soldiers and anxious relatives, while ghoulish visitors amused themselves by making "large parties and go to the field of battle—and pick up a skull or a grape shot or an old shoe or a letter and bring it home."[6] Nevertheless, Harriet found, there were small reasons to rejoice. Two days after her arrival, Frederick stood for the first time and walked across the room, and there was hope that he might be well enough to return to England within a fortnight. There was promising news too from the wider world: the capture of Napoleon and restoration of Louis XVIII. "What is and what can be done with him?" Harriet wondered anxiously. "We can scarcely give him up to Louis XVIII or the Russians, for we have answered for his life. The Emperor of Austria would not be safe. Russia might quarrel with France or England . . . we cannot keep a prisoner of war when peace is made."[7]

The party returned to England in early August, while Caro and William Lamb traveled on to Paris to witness the extraordinary scenes of British troops streaming down the Champs-Elysées. Frederick was far from mended—movement in his arm was limited, an abscess had developed under his arm, and he was troubled by recurrent feverish bouts that Harriet termed "ague" (probably malaria). Harriet knew that undertaking the journey home while he was still so weak was not without risk, and the now heavily pregnant Barbara was a further cause for unease. In addition, her race across Europe, the anxiety of Frederick's injuries, and the appalling sanitation in Brussels had depleted her own reserves of strength. Nevertheless, she reasoned, staying any longer in such foul conditions would be even more dangerous. "It is not a healthy place," she wrote of Brussels. "I have never been well since I arrived . . . If it should grow hot weather, after all the rain and the smells which already exist in the neighbourhood, [fever] will be almost inevitable."[8] When they finally set off, their journey was painstakingly slow because Frederick's wounds still needed dressing every day, but by mid-August they were safely settled in London, where Harriet directed her attention to nursing him back to health.

By the time Caro and William Lamb returned from Paris in the autumn, Frederick was well enough for Harriet to be drawn once more into the complexities of their marriage. Caro had reconciled herself to Byron's marriage to Lady Melbourne's niece Annabella Milbanke the previous January, but her ceaseless need for attention—especially male attention—had caused William great embarrassment in Paris. Caro, intent on attracting notice, had dressed in a revealing manner and flirted outrageously with several men, including the Duke of Wellington. "No dose of flattery is too strong for him to swallow or her to administer. Poor William hides in one small room, while she assembles lovers and tradespeople in another,"[9] quipped Harryo, who was visiting the French capital at the same time. Fanny Burney also saw Caro and noted that she was "dressed, or rather *not* dressed, so as to excite universal attention and authorise every boldness in staring . . . for she had one shoulder, half her back and all her throat and neck displayed, as if at the call of some statuary for modelling a heathen goddess."[10] Caro's unconventional garb and louche behavior greatly titillated Wellington, who kept up a regular correspondence with her. "Have you had anything to do in the way of cause with the strange conduct of your enemy?" he wrote in reference to Byron. "Between you and I these modern men of genius are sad fellows!"[11]

On her return from Paris Caro retreated to Brocket, where she took to drinking heavily and seemed permanently depressed, wandering the corridors as if in a trance. The Melbournes, anxious for William to revive his political career, began concerted attempts to persuade him to separate and have Caro certified as mad and committed to an asylum. Lady Melbourne enlisted Lavinia Spencer's support in the scheme. To Caro her aunt's treachery was unforgivable. "I will never speak to Lady Spencer again as long as I live were she to kneel for her pardon which she ought to do,"[12] she declared. The breakdown of Byron's marriage and his exile amid rumors of sodomy and incest in April 1816 did nothing to rally Caro's spirits, and the same month she played into the Melbournes' hands by losing her temper with one of her pages and throwing a missile that hit him on the head and drew blood, then panicking and running around screaming, "Oh God, I have murdered the page!"[13] This debacle made Harriet terrified that William might cede to his mother at any moment and have Caro committed.

Conscious that Lavinia was in league with Lady Melbourne, Harriet tried subtly to canvass her brother's support without giving affront. Unusually for her, she acknowledged Caro's guilt. "The consequence cannot change the act and Caroline would be . . . culpable had what she threw hit the table instead of the boy, as she would be had it the most fatal effects that could have followed," she wrote. Nevertheless, Harriet assured George, "temper and not derangement are the cause of Caroline's rash actions." She was, according to Harriet, "perfectly ready to do whatever can be done and is thought best for her with W. Lamb's approbation. I should be sorry to have her separated from him as long as he is willing to remain with her—he still loves her enough to feel pain at the thought of parting with her—but once away and another habit formed I doubt whether he might ever wish to receive her again . . ."[14]

In fact her efforts to save the marriage proved unnecessary. Despite all the provocation Caro had given William, he had no intention of separating from her, especially now that Byron was safely distanced. When Lady Melbourne arrived at Brocket with the separation papers for William to sign, she discovered the couple reconciled, eating breakfast in cozy intimacy.

The threat of separation had receded from Caro's life, but the specter of scandal had not. While living quietly at Brocket she had decided to embark on a literary career and busied herself with writing a novel. *Glenarvon* was a semiautobiographical gothic extravaganza in which thinly disguised members of her family and friends played leading roles. Caro portrayed herself as the feisty Calantha, and Byron as Glenarvon; Mrs. Seymour was supposedly a mixture of Georgiana and Harriet,* and her daughter Sophia was thought to have been inspired by Harryo. More contentious were unflattering characters such as Lady Mandeville, based on Lady Oxford, by whom Caro had felt betrayed during her affair with Byron, and Princess Madagascar, whom she modeled on Harriet's friend Lady Holland.

Caro submitted the final version of her book to John Murray, Byron's publisher, with whom she had a close friendship; but Murray, knowing the book would cause a scandal, turned it down. Undaunted, Caro then approached Henry Colburn: "you will easily see by the style of this book that it is written more from the feelings than the mind,"[15] she wrote in an attempt to sway him in her favor. Colburn, a more courageous publisher than Murray, accepted the book. As the date of publication neared, Caro vacillated between extremes of worry and delight. "It looks beautiful but makes my heart beat,"[16] she exclaimed when she saw advance copies of her book.

Over the following weeks *Glenarvon* became a huge commercial suc-

---

* Opinions vary on the models for many characters. Some readers believed Mrs. Seymour was based on Lady Melbourne; others, that Lady Melbourne appears as Lady Monteith.

cess, the first printing rapidly selling out and orders for more flooding in. Yet among her circle the book drew widespread condemnation rather than the accolades for which she had hoped. "I cannot forgive her for the ridicule that she throws at William by the publishing of all their private secrets," declared Bess's daughter Caroline (who was married to William's brother George). Lady Melbourne claimed she could not even bring herself to finish the book, and her daughter Emily Cowper was equally incensed. "Nothing ever vexed me so much as when I entered to town and found this book upon every table and the subject of general conversation."[17] The reaction among the wider circle of society was equally unfavorable. "This time she has knocked herself up—the Greys, the Jerseys, the Lansdownes and of course the Princess of Madagascar have done with her," wrote Byron's friend Hobhouse. Byron read the book only after Mme. de Staël lent him her copy, and then scathingly dismissed it: "It seems to me that, if the authoress had written the truth, and nothing but the truth—the whole truth the romance would not only have been more romantic, but more entertaining."[18]

Caro was distraught at the damning responses of those she had hoped to impress. "I am on the brink of ruin," she complained; "half my friends cut me, all my acquaintances are offended."[19] Granville had caused her particular distress by threatening to ostracize her from her cousins Harryo and Little G. Caro's response was a revealing letter that gives glimpses of Harriet and Bessborough's anguish as well as her own. In it she claims that she might not have acted as she did if the Melbournes had not tried to have her committed and to force William to separate from her, and turned friends and family against her. "My husband received letters telling him he would be the public ridicule and jest if he supported me—I was *proved* mad. Mr. Moor assured me I was so, and entreated me to persuade my husband of it. I appealed to a few, but my letters were not even answered. I went to Roehampton; Lady Jersey, to the extreme annoyance of my Father, quite turned her back on me and refused to speak to me. I came back to Town and met Lord Holland, who coldly passed me by. Indeed, indeed, Lord Granville, I could not stand it; these people too, had all taken Lord Byron's part... William returned, a dreadful scene passed between me and Lord M[elbourne] and Mama. That night I sent the novel... To write this novel was then my sole comfort . . . do not judge me with severity, for you cannot know half what I have suffered."[20]

Alongside the deepening crisis over Caro another troublesome figure reentered Harriet's life and brought heartache. Sheridan, her erstwhile lover and tormentor for so many years, came to call one day. Harriet was profoundly shocked by his gaunt, frail appearance. "He said in joke that he was dying. I believe he will find it fact. It made me quite melancholy . . ."[21] wrote Harriet afterward. Soon after this, she heard Sheridan had deteriorated and was unable to leave his bed. Most of Sheridan's friends had long ago abandoned him but Harriet could not turn her back on an old friend in such a desperate plight. She called at his lodgings and found him lying in squalor and poverty, while his wife, Hecca, lay gravely ill in the room below, unable to tend him. Harriet did what she could, paying for food, heat, and rent. Yet, she later told Lord Broughton, even as Sheridan struggled for life, his ability to distress her had not diminished. When he asked her how she found him, she told him his eyes "were brilliant still." He grasped her hand hard and told her that he intended to haunt her after his death. Harriet, petrified, asked why, having persecuted her all his life, he was so determined to continue his persecution after death. "Because," said Sheridan, "I am resolved you shall remember me."[22] He then continued to strike such terror in her heart that Harriet could bear no more and fled from the room. He died three days later.

TWENTY-SEVEN

The Last Journey
1821

I N HER LATER YEARS Harriet sometimes claimed that her passion for politics had waned. But the few scrawling letters charting the end of her life do not bear this out; politics were too rooted in her being to wither away. William Lamb, future prime minister, often sought her insight and counsel, as, years earlier, Granville had done. "If you could learn anything about the dissolution for certain, it would be a capital piece of information, and hardly less so if you could learn whether they mean to settle the Civil List before they dissolve . . ."[1] wrote Caro's long-suffering husband, enticing his mother-in-law back to the political fray. As ever, Harriet had useful allies on both sides of the political divide. "Lady Bessborough called on me and rather insinuated she considered *me* as the cause of the Government refusing to come forward for the Whigs. I denied this but, at the same time, asserted that the conduct of the Whigs had been most infamous as they uniformly join the radicals rather than assist a Tory candidate,"[2] recorded the Tory diarist Mrs. Arbuthnot, apropos Harriet's valiant canvassing on William's behalf.

Mrs. Arbuthnot also reveals that Harriet was "a good deal in the confidence of the Whigs" throughout the notorious trial of Queen Caroline. Following the death of George III, the hapless queen had refused an offer of an increased pension provided she were to stay away from Britain and not claim the rights of queen consort. She landed in Dover to public astonishment and delight, proceeding in an open landau to Westminster, where cheering crowds lined the streets. Her husband—now King George IV—was infuriated by her defiance, and a month later Caroline found herself facing a parliamentary Bill of Pains and Penalties for adultery. Harriet said many Whigs knew the queen was guilty as charged but violently opposed the bill, fearing that pursuing it might undermine public confidence in the monarchy. Supporters of the government disagreed vehemently with this view. "All one can say is, if the Whig Lords do not consider the disgusting details they have heard *proof,* the Whig ladies may in future consider themselves very secure against divorces, for it would be impossible to conceive a case in which more proof could be established,"[3] Mrs. Arbuthnot fumed, after a lengthy and no doubt heated discussion with Harriet on the subject.

In fact the Whigs were more divided than Harriet let on. Her own long-standing friendship with the king made her unwilling to join a deputation of Whig ladies, led by Lady Jersey, to call on the queen. But as always she wished to avoid causing ructions, and thus to Mrs. Arbuthnot she nimbly excused herself on the grounds that Lord Bessborough forbade the visit; and since she and Queen Caroline had never been friends, she did not think it necessary to defy him. She begged her friend to treat her views as a matter of confidence, pretending that her chief concern at present was to avoid being "held up as an object for the mob to assault."[4] Eventually the government was forced to abandon the bill owing to dwindling support among both Whigs and Tory factions.

Political differences had never been an obstacle to friendship in Harriet's eyes, and Mrs. Arbuthnot and she were together to witness the opening of the new parliament. This was a far from straightforward feat even for well-connected women, as they had been banished from the chamber since the late eighteenth century and for much of the intervening period could only listen to important debates if they disguised themselves in male dress. Subsequently women were occasionally permitted to sit in a specially designated room high over the chamber with a grill in the center of the floor above the chandelier through which they could peer down at the proceedings. It was from this high and uncomfortable vantage point that Harriet and her friend saw the ceremony pass without incident.

In contrast to the uncertainties of politics, Harriet's domestic life was now a pleasantly settled routine. In the absence of any lovers or overattentive male admirers, a comfortable closeness appears to have developed between her and Bessborough. She was better now at juggling his needs with her own, and he too must have mellowed with maturity. Seemingly contented at last, they entertained frequently and attended numerous glamorous assemblies. Children and grandchildren also took up much time. Modeling herself on her mother, Harriet assisted at the births of her grandchildren and was on hand to dispense practical advice to her daughter-in-law and others in the wider family circle: "Oh, what stories I could tell you of cross births and hard labours! What receipts I could give you for every disorder..."[5] she once wrote.

But still there were clouds in her existence. Caroline's emotional instability and the chronic epilepsy of her son, Augustus, remained an ever-present worry. Despite their huge inheritance, finances were a further vexation, especially when rents from Ireland were interrupted by the ill health of a steward. "I hate troubling you," she wrote to Hart in December 1819, "[but] some years ago the Dss. of Devonshire borrowed a thousand pound of Ld. B...but poor Mr. Walsh's illness seems to have put a stop to all remittances from Ireland...meanwhile a thousand pounds must be paid on Dec. 5."[6] As usual it was Bessborough who had persuaded her to approach his wealthy Cavendish cousins, presumably because he was too embarrassed to do so himself.

Harriet and Bessborough had always relished foreign travel and she was in her sixtieth year when she embarked on what would be her final visit to the Continent. The trip began pleasantly enough. They left London in June together with William and Barbara and their two children, Charles and Henry, and headed for Paris. French society had always adored Harriet and she busily took up with old friends such as Talleyrand and Mme. Récamier, went sightseeing with gusto, and visited the theater and opera, yet still found time to write Granville detailed accounts of all she had witnessed. On one typically exhausting day she walked the Champs-Elysées, watched balloons and firework displays from the Tuileries Gardens, and hosted a large dinner party before going out to supper and playing cards until the small hours.

This carefree but frenetic existence drew to an abrupt halt in early July. Barbara and William decided to return to England for the coronation of George IV, while Harriet took her two grandchildren to Switzerland. She had always loved the mountains in summer and thought the cool mountain air would prove beneficial to the little boys' health. Her expectations were cruelly disappointed when they arrived in Geneva to find the weather stifling and the city seething with tourists. Then, far worse, Henry fell seriously ill with an infectious fever—probably meningitis. After a fortnight he seemed to get better, but Harriet worried that he might suffer a relapse or succumb to further illness in "this great Barracks."[7] In August, soon after Barbara and William had returned, the party thus moved to the quieter alpine resort of St. Martin.

Henry was soon well enough for Harriet to go sightseeing. She and William set out for Chamonix, traveling along the treacherous mountain passes in an open carriage to enjoy the scenery. As the sun set, a violent thunderstorm broke. Harriet was drenched and fearful, but retained her sense of humor. "The woods, rocks, snow and torrents lit up by the lightning at every moment. I had just told William nothing was wanting but *banditti* in this wild place . . . when two men passed us and I saw a third at a little distance who seemed waiting for us, and really thought we were going to complete one of Mrs. Radcliff's novels."[8] As it turned out, the men were not highwaymen but travelers who were lost on the road from Paris.

Such moments of levity were few and far between because soon after this excursion Henry's health again took a turn for the worse and, thinking it unwise to return to England for the winter, the family decided to make their way to the warmer climes of Florence. En route, in Parma, Henry's condition suddenly deteriorated. "I cannot tell you what a scene of misery I am going through, nor how very wretched I feel," Harriet lamented in a letter to Granville. She had spent the last twelve days keeping vigil by Henry's bedside day and night and knew his case was hopeless. "Think of William's beautiful boy, knowing that he cannot recover, and seeing him go on day and night in constant changes for the brilliant flame of fever, his eyes brightly fixed and beautiful, then fading away to the damp paleness of death; then convulsions, and all at once, for half an hour at a time perhaps, every appearance of returning to life and health."[9]

Thanks to the family's eminent connections, Henry was tended by leading doctors. Empress Marie Louise, Napoleon's widow, recommended her physician, who diagnosed hydrocephalus—water on the brain—a condition that may have been congenital or, more probably, given the earlier fever, the result of an infection. Either way the prognosis was grim. "Everything has been tried, but to day they have again repeated what they said at first, that this horrible disorder . . . is incurable, that the finest and strongest children are generally the most liable to it,"[10] Harriet distractedly told Granville. The letter ends abruptly, as if she were called suddenly to Henry's bedside. Her youngest grandchild died two days later.

She never picked up her pen to Granville again. Broken with grief, she and the rest of the party continued on their journey to Florence. Harriet was not only weighed down by melancholy but physically exhausted after spending nights "constantly getting up . . . and going through the open cold galleries to [Henry's] room, sometimes sitting up with him and at others waiting in the passage till the physicians came out of his room."[11] She had never been physically strong and the exertion and emotional strain had eroded what Harryo would later call her "clarity both of mind and body."[12] Unbeknownst to the rest of her family, Harriet was suffering from the beginnings of a serious bowel infection—perhaps cholera or dysentery. But as they crossed the mountains in bitterly cold weather, she gave no outward sign that she was feeling unwell. It was only when the party reached the inn where they were due to spend the night that anyone realized she was suffering from agonizing stomach cramps. The usual remedies were administered but nothing seemed to help, and since the inn was filthy and poorly heated, William—spurred on by the maid Sally—decided Harriet would be warmer and more comfortable if they traveled on to Florence without stopping.

Harriet seemed slightly better when they arrived in the early hours, but it was a short-lived improvement. The next evening she was again stricken by racking pain and the doctors declared her case hopeless. She faced death bravely. Coherent in between bouts of delirium, she was, she said, sorry not for her own sake—she would be thankful to escape the pain—but for the sorrow her death would bring to those she loved. Weak though she was, she sent affectionate messages to her absent children via William, Bessborough, and the ever loyal Sally, all of whom sat in loving vigil at her bedside. At her request a priest arrived to administer last rites; she died not long after on November 11. Sally told Caroline the final moments were "calm, resigned and beautiful."[13]

The following day, numbed by grief, William wrote to Granville, the man who had for so long shared his mother's most intimate thoughts, in the stiff language of one who has yet to come to terms with his shock:

> My dear Lord Granville—I know how you and Harriet will feel the sad intelligence which I have to communicate, and which to you will probably be wholly unexpected; and indeed to me, who never have been absent from my dear, dear Mother from the first moment of her illness, its termination has occurred with a rapidity such that I can hardly feel or understand how great a loss I have experienced . . . To those who knew her as well as you both of you did it is needless to say that she bore her very painful illness with the fortitude and resignation and kind attention for ye feelings of others which she has shown on every occasion throughout her life. She looked forward to her death, which she knew to be inevitable from the first seizure, with ye greatest calmness considering it as a relief from great agony, and only regretting the separation from those she loved, and ye pain which her loss must occasion. Many will feel it deeply . . The present is come upon me with a rapidity which I can scarcely feel or understand and I dare not look forward to ye blank which her loss must cast upon my future existence.[14]

To Caro, who had never been afraid to express her emotions, William felt able to write more openly of the last harrowing hours. "She sometimes, I think, knew me during the night, and stretched out her hand to me and pressed mine and Mrs. Peterson's, and muttered some words which could not be understood . . . as for myself, I dare not look forward . . . the present seems to me more like a hurried dream than reality."[15] Even during Henry's last illness Harriet had been preoccupied by thoughts of Caro. "She makes the joy and torment of my life. I am neither happy with nor without her,"[16] she had confessed to Henry Fox. On her deathbed she had told William to give Caro the pink diamond ring that had been left to her by her mother (Caro's grandmother), Lady Spencer, and "to remember to tell you [Caro] that Dr. Downe (who suffered no deficiency of intellect) suffered most terribly till fourteen or fifteen from epileptic fits and since that period has had no return."[17]

Nor did Harriet forget her adored sister. In her last hours she had asked to be buried beside Georgiana in the Cavendish vault in Derby. Perhaps it was the thought of rejoining the woman she had loved most all her life that gave her such fortitude in her final hours. William made the sad arrangements for the transportation of the bodies of his mother and son across Europe by wagon. Sally was determined to accompany Harriet's coffin throughout the long, slow journey ("Never in ancient story nor fabled romance was there such fidelity as hers,"[18] Caro later wrote of her mother's devoted maid). William would follow a few days behind and then catch up with the cortège en route to France.

And what of Lord Bessborough, meanwhile? According to William, another of Harriet's dying wishes had been that "we should do all we could to contribute to his [Bessborough's] comfort."[19] Whatever their earlier betrayals, tempests, and recriminations, in death only love and loyalty remained.

Bessborough was heartbroken by the suddenness of Harriet's illness and death. He announced his determination to accompany the coffin home with William, but doctors advised that it would be perilous for him to attempt crossing the Alps in winter, and there were also Barbara and little Charles to consider. They could not possibly be left alone in Florence; nor after the recent demise of little Henry could the family bear to contemplate any risk to Charles's health. So, after some protesting, Bessborough agreed to stay behind with them in Florence until the weather improved. There seems little doubt that his grief and shock were genuine, and undoubtedly the trials of travel across Europe in winter were not to be underestimated. Even so, one cannot help feeling a shadow of disappointment at his acquiescence.

A melancholy funeral service was held in Florence before the two coffins were loaded and began their long journey to England. In Paris, a month after Harriet's death, Caroline and William Lamb, together with Frederick, congregated miserably to await the arrival of the wagon bearing her remains. It was delayed at the French border because officials suspected the coffin contained smuggled goods and insisted on opening it.

The world greeted the news of Harriet's sudden death with the varied comment and reaction that the unexpected demise of any colorful celebrity might elicit. "Poor woman," wrote G. A. Ellis, one of Granville's brothers-in-law; "she had some apparent faults, but more hidden virtues." Henry Fox, with whom she had corresponded regularly, expressed kinder sentiments, remembering her as "a warm-hearted person and an excellent mother, who did not deserve such an infliction as Lady Caroline."[20] The Duke of Wellington was also filled with sorrow at the news: "As an acquaintance and friend I feel for her as much as any of those who were attached to her."[21] (He and Harriet had recently been in correspondence over plans to prevent Frederick taking up a post in India.)

Bess, Dowager Duchess of Devonshire, one of Harriet's oldest and most intimate friends, was in Paris when news of Harriet's death reached her. She was inconsolable at the loss of one "who was infinitely dear to me" and it was days before she could begin to recover from the shock. "She is so connected with the recollection of all that was dear to me, that I feel an anxiety as great as if she were indeed my sister."[22] With the duke gone, Harriet's death marked the closing of a chapter. Apart from Bess herself, Harriet represented the final link connecting her to Georgiana's glittering Devonshire House set. That link had now been severed.

Perhaps the most moving tribute to Harriet came from her erstwhile companion at political debates. Mrs. Arbuthnot mourned the passing of her great friend, and the tribute in her journal provides one of the most revealing insights into Harriet's character.

> I do not know when I have been so grieved as at her death. She was much the cleverest and most agreeable woman I have ever known, and to her family she will be a most irreparable loss. She was dotingly fond of her children, who were passionately attached to her. In her youth she had been *très galante,* and in her mature years she retained those charms of mind and manner which in her earlier life, had rendered her irresistibly attractive. She had lived in the intimate society of Fox, Burke and Sheridan, had been the confidante of

many of their most important secrets and had always turned her mind very much to the Whig politics of that day. I used to go with her very often to the House of Commons, and her criticism upon the debate and her recollection of former times were generally more worth listening to than the debate itself. She was the kindest hearted person that ever lived, her purse and her good offices were always at the disposal of anyone in distress, and she used to laugh and say that no one ever got into a scrape without applying to her to help them out. Her errors arose from a false education and the seductive examples of clever but unprincipled men, and were well redeemed by a warmth of heart and a steadiness of friendship that rendered her dear to her family and friends who, I am sure, will long deplore her loss.[23]

Those who had been closest to Harriet were less adept at voicing their grief. Granville was so overwhelmed that for several weeks he withdrew from society and refused to speak to anyone. It fell to Harryo to break the news to Little Harriet and her brother George that the woman they had thought of as a kindly benefactor, but never as their mother, was now dead. "You will feel it my dearest child and so do we as the loss of a most kind and affectionate friend. — I was not myself aware how much I loved her, till she was thus suddenly taken from this world,"[24] Harryo gently consoled Little Harriet.

Of all Harriet's family, it was Caro who felt her mother's death most keenly. Aware of her vulnerability, her brothers — William, in particular, who had always been most understanding — and close friends rallied around, urging her to be strong, if only for her mother's sake. Doctors dosed her with sedatives; Miss Trimmer, governess to the Cavendish children and her grandmother's friend, kept her company; and her cousin Hart[25] offered his sympathy and support. Still Caro struggled, veering between bouts of nervous agitation and calm, desperate to do her duty and attend her mother's funeral, yet uncertain whether she could muster the strength to do so. "I trust I shall be able to do all I ought, but human nature is weak. I am so, and suppose I feel that I cannot do what Miss Trimmer has been suggesting is right — suppose I really cannot, will you promise to forgive me if after all I fail and do not go . . ."[26] she wrote to Hart pathetically on Christmas Day.

Four days later, in what is now Derby Cathedral, Harriet's second funeral took place. Caro and Miss Trimmer, accompanied by Duncannon, William Ponsonby, and William Lamb, had stayed in Derby the previous night in a house belonging to Hart. Despite her apprehension, Caro had been "remarkably calm and determined to attend the ceremony." But as the hour approached, her resolve evaporated. "In the night she became agitated and was so ill in the morning that she gave up being present," recorded Hart. The rest of the family arrived to find that a large crowd had gathered outside the cathedral and "more than one would have chosen within," although Hart conceded that "they all behaved with the greatest respect and quiet."[27] When the service was over, Harriet's coffin was carried to the Cavendish vault to be laid, as she had wished, beside the mortal remains of her beloved Georgiana. Afterward William took Sally down to the vault to pay her last respects. Later that day Caro rallied and declared she too wanted to visit her mother's coffin, but fears over her mental stability persisted and Miss Trimmer and Sally dissuaded her. Immediately afterward, on the orders of Hart, the vault was closed.*

VIEWED THROUGH THE prism of the twenty-first century, what is the appeal and relevance of Harriet—a woman who belonged to a rarified world, who lived two and a half centuries ago? What conclusions should we draw from such a life? On the simplest level, there is much in Harriet's story that strikes a chord today. She inhabited a world of sexual freedom and easy credit, in which the desire for stimulation led to decadence and overconsumption, that has many echoes in the twenty-first century. Like many contemporary high-profile celebrities, Harriet had a taste for the high life and a dissatisfaction with marriage that led her to indulge herself, to gamble recklessly, to spend imprudently, and to embroil herself in extramarital affairs. This was a world that was experiencing rapid change, where the power and invulnerabil-

---

* Sadly, however, Harriet's final resting place was not properly marked. When the coffin plates of the most prominent Cavendish family members were removed years later to be set into the wall of the Cavendish chapel, the simple brass recording Harriet's burial place was found to state erroneously the date of her death as June ? 1793.

ity of the landed aristocracy was fast fading and the burgeoning press were eager for juicy stories of those who should have known better behaving badly.

Much of Harriet's appeal lies, where it always did, in her character. The desire to please was one of the defining strands of her personality, captivating all who came close to her. Even today she is an easy person to like, and her spontaneity effortlessly narrows the historical gap. Harriet's abundant charm contrasts markedly with Bessborough's taciturn character and makes it tempting to cast him as the villain of the piece. But this is to simplify a far more complex and intriguing relationship. Harriet often portrayed Bessborough as a boorish nuisance, and there are collaborative accounts to bear out her early grievances and evidence of his jealousy and bullying nature throughout their marriage. Nevertheless, against this we must remember that it cannot have been easy for a man lacking in social graces to keep his cool when Harriet was in flirtatious full flow. Certainly he was not without kindness; there is much evidence to show that he was a devoted father to his children, and his affectionate letters to Harriet in times of crisis show his fondness for her. In the event, Walpole's skepticism when the engagement was first announced proved extraordinarily prescient: "I should not have selected, for so gentle and very amiable a man, a sister of the empress of fashion, nor a daughter of the goddess of wisdom."[28]

Whatever the reasons for the tensions in the Bessborough marriage, Harriet's marital discontent is not in doubt, and vividly illustrates the limitations of an aristocratic woman's existence in the late eighteenth and early nineteenth centuries. Had she left her husband and married her lover—as she would almost certainly have done today—she would have become the subject of public vilification, lost custody of her children, and been cast out from society. She had no choice but to remain.

In other ways too Harriet's life provides a salutary reminder of female constraint. Born into a life of great privilege, she mingled with the leading thinkers, writers, politicians, and scientists of her age, and today would have probably pursued some sort of profession. Though she was blessed with a brilliant mind and boundless curiosity in the world around her, all intellectual expression—whether literary, scientific, artistic, or musical—was confined to amateur status and her only career option was marriage.

Despite these limitations, Harriet's political influence was widely acknowledged even within her lifetime. She was one of the most influential female members of the Whig cause, and although it is beyond the scope of this book to draw firm conclusions about her ultimate effectiveness, her involvement was undoubtedly an important factor in Fox's 1784 election success and in the Westminster election of 1788. In 1804 she was also instrumental in helping Fox and his followers join Pitt in bringing down Addington, and for the following decade and a half she continued to campaign tirelessly for rapprochement between the Tories and the Whigs. In this sense the ministry of All the Talents represented the final culmination of her hopes.

Harriet's pursuit of her political interests highlights the way in which female political influence waned as the nineteenth century progressed. Despite her political acumen and connections, she was increasingly obliged to feign disinterest or deference. In her youth she unashamedly joined in political debate and assisted Fox and family members in their canvassing. By the end of her life, though, the effectiveness of her political role depended on her willingness to disappear into the shadows. If she transgressed the unwritten line, she laid herself open not merely to censure and mockery, but to a far worse fate— political exclusion.

That we have such insight into her life at all is due to Harriet's fondness for letter-writing. Her correspondents—acquaintances, friends, family, lovers—were numerous, and the letters she wrote them provide fascinating glimpses of her life as a woman in the public eye, as well as the minutiae of the life of a devoted mother. Thus we see her as an unfailingly enthusiastic educator of her children, directing their schooling, nursing them through sickness, and providing advice, sympathy, and practical support when needed. Ingrained from childhood by her own formidable mother with the notion of Christian duty, she also enmeshed herself in a web of wider family connections—siblings, nephews, nieces, cousins, and grandchildren—as well as busying herself with charitable good works and performing the duties expected of the wife of a landowner.

But her most revealing and moving letters were inspired by her great love for Granville, a passion that formed the focus of so much of her life. Her letters to him chart the progress of their affair from its earliest days, through moments of delirious passion and frantic longing, to bitter disappointment and then the tender friendship that characterized the end of her life. There is much poignancy in the unfolding drama. Granville, we discover, on coming to know him, is not the hero of a novel—even if he had film-star good looks. Yet despite being an inconstant lover, his love for Harriet and high regard for her intellect cannot be doubted, and sustained their friendship to the very end.

As she watched soldiers embarking for the Peninsular War, or raced across war-torn Europe, or recovered from the agony of Georgiana's death, or chased Sheridan from her bedroom, or became immersed in the latest political furor, she recorded each event for him, thus lending a particularly eloquent female view on history. With wit and feeling Harriet thus informs and charms us as she once did her lovers, friends, and family. Perhaps Granville realized the importance of his correspondence, since in the final weeks of his life he began to sort and number them in a shaky hand. In this sense he was right—without Harriet's letters, posterity, as well as his life, would have been the poorer.

TWENTY-EIGHT

Harriet's Legacy

FTER MOURNING THEIR MOTHER'S untimely death, Harriet's children returned to pick up the threads of their lives. Her elder sons John, Frederick, and William were perhaps least affected by her unexpected loss.

John took his political career far more seriously than his father had ever done, and in many ways his life represents the realization of hopes that Harriet had harbored yet never fulfilled. Like Bessborough, John detested public speaking, yet he had inherited Harriet's talent for negotiation between different factions, a trait that was to prove invaluable in his work for parliamentary reform and Irish emancipation; "at length nothing could be done without Duncannon,"[1] the politician Grenville wrote in his memoirs.

Duncannon's career flourished in the government of his brother-in-law Lord Melbourne: he was appointed first commissioner of woods and forests—the equivalent of the Department of the Environment—and then home secretary. He was one of the four members of the drafting committee for the Reform Bill of 1832 and, after the Houses of Parliament were destroyed by fire in 1834, oversaw their rebuilding. Also like his mother, John felt an affinity for his Irish estates. Unusually for an ascendancy landlord, he spent long periods living in Ireland, he came to empathize with the cause of his Irish tenants, and although he never abandoned the Whig principles instilled in him from childhood he established a surprising rapport with the Irish liberator Daniel O'Connell. Toward the end of his life he was appointed lord lieutenant of Ireland, and during the famine he struggled to alleviate the sufferings of his tenants and petition Westminster for aid. The father of fourteen children, he was, again like Harriet, devoted to his family.

Frederick inherited Harriet's lack of affectation and easy nature, as well as her haphazard approach to money. His friend the Fourth Lord Holland described him as "one of the simplest, most manly, unaffected men I know, with a very good sterling sense, a sweet temper, and with the manners and experience of a man that has seen much of the world and has profited by what he has seen."[2] Four years after Harriet's death he married Lady Emily Bathurst, by whom he had six children, among them a daughter who was said to be the image of Caro and equally spoiled. He was reputedly so disorganized that he lost the ring on his wedding day and found it in a pantaloon pocket only after a search lasting twenty minutes. Meanwhile, the distinguished military career begun during his mother's lifetime continued apace; he was promoted to major general in command of troops in the Ionian Islands, and a year later became governor of Malta.

Frederick would always attribute the saving of his life at Waterloo to the generosity of the French officer who had given him brandy. According to the politician and writer Captain Gronow, it was while he was living in Malta that he was able to thank him in person for his kindness.

> The Baron de Laussat . . . a gentleman universally respected and beloved by all who knew him . . . had quitted the army [and] travelled in the East for some years, and on his return, when at Malta, was introduced to Sir F. Ponsonby, then a Major-General and Governor of the island. In the course of conversation, the battle of Waterloo was discussed; and on Ponsonby recounting his many narrow escapes, and the kind treatment he had received from the French officer, M. de Laussat said, "was he not in such-and-such a uniform? "He was" said Sir F. "And did he not say so-and-so to you, and was not the cloak of such-and-such a colour?" "I remember it perfectly," was the answer. Several other details were entered into, which I now forget, but which left no doubt upon Ponsonby's mind that he saw before him the man to whom he owed his life.[3]

William's marriage was also to prove a happy and fulfilling one. Having married Barbara, the only child of the wealthy Fifth Earl of

Shaftesbury, William found himself the most affluent of his brothers. He became Baron de Mauley in 1838, and with the title came substantial estates and a fortune to match. His property included Canford Manor, a mansion and estate in Dorset, which he enlarged in the Gothic style using a leading architect, Edward Blore.* His father spent much of his later life at Canford and, having outlived Harriet by twenty-two years, eventually died there at the age of eighty-three.

The story of Caroline, Harriet's adored daughter, is well known. Harriet had always been on hand in her worst crises to offer support and practical assistance when needed. Now she was cast loose with no mother to indulge or protect her, and with Emily, her sister-in-law, working to turn William against her. Caro did not help her own case. Convincing herself of the indifference of her tolerant husband, she chafed against the boundaries of her marriage, embroiling herself in several other illicit liaisons, including one with an aspiring young writer half her age, Bulwer Lytton, whose family home, Knebworth, was next door to Brocket. She spent much time alone with Augustus at Brocket, writing poetry and her third novel, *Ada Reis*—a story in which a girl of violent temper plays center stage.

Gradually Caroline's health worsened; she vacillated between days of lethargy in which she lay in bed unable to do anything but gaze out the window and periods of hyperactivity and exhibitionism that caused embarrassment to all who witnessed them. "Lady Caroline has a predisposition to the high form of insanity which shows itself at certain times, and particularly so when exposed to any excitement, whether mental or physical,"[4] wrote her doctor to William in 1825. Caro's increasingly unpredictable and outrageous behavior made her an outcast from society and eventually caused William to cede to his sister's scheming and agree to a formal separation from her in 1825. Afterward he tried to force her to leave Brocket; then, unable to face her distress, he capitulated and allowed her to return. Caro died in 1828, at the age of forty-one, a pathetic figure, her once sylphlike physique bloated from a disease that at the time was diagnosed as dropsy—possibly cirrhosis of the liver, or cancer.

---

* Later the house was made even bigger by Barry, and in 1923 it became Canford School.

Meanwhile, the Granville marriage continued as happily as it had begun. Even in later life Granville retained the good looks that had first drawn Harriet, while Harryo, "though she did not possess the outward advantages of her husband," was considered his superior in conversational powers and was widely held to have "a high degree [of] the charm of voice and manner which belongs to the Cavendish family."[5] Within the Granvilles' happy household Harriet's two illegitimate children flourished. Little Harriet's childhood friendship with Harryo strengthened as the years passed, and when Granville was made ambassador in The Hague in 1824, just as the question of finding a husband arose, she accompanied the Granvilles on their posting abroad.

In Brussels Little Harriet was schooled in matters of etiquette by a dancing master, as her mother had once been. She was well-mannered and physically attractive to the opposite sex. "All the gentlemen are *à ses pieds,* and one enamoured swain sent her no less than nine pots of flowers,"[6] wrote Harryo, although she knew that Little Harriet's lack of dowry, together with her ambiguous status as Granville's ward, would probably cast a shadow over her matrimonial prospects.

In Holland, however, Little Harriet met and fell in love with George Osborne, son of Lord Godolphin and heir to the Duke of Leeds. "We have had a trying time of it . . . It has been a stronger proof of how much they like each other—she has been crying her eyes out—and he is worn to the bone,"[7] Harryo recorded. Eventually Granville and the Godolphins gave their consent to the marriage and Little Harriet was ecstatic. "I did not think such happiness existed still less did I think it was destined for me," she wrote. Little Harriet was married at the British Embassy in Paris, where Granville became a highly successful ambassador. According to Gronow, "England was never represented more worthily or with greater magnificence"[8] than under Granville and Harryo. The Osbornes settled nearby, taking a house in the Bois de Boulogne, and French society welcomed them with gusto. "Harriet makes her debut in a *oiseau de Paradis gros de Naples* gown, her head dressed by Alexander," wrote Harryo.[9]

Despite its joyous beginning, Little Harriet's married life was destined to be tinged with sorrow. She suffered several miscarriages and it was four years before her first child was born, although she later went on to produce seven more children. A neighbor recalled her as "a refined very delicate looking melancholy person. She was very kind, and once when I had been too naughty to be allowed to accompany my sisters to luncheon . . . she sent for me . . . showered kindnesses upon me and finally presented me with a tiny Dresden figure . . ."[10]

Kindness was not the only trait Little Harriet had inherited from her mother. Both she and her husband were hopeless with money, to such an extent that on more than one occasion indebtedness risked landing them in jail. At such times it was to her brother George that she turned. "I find that he has as usual been living far beyond his means and at this moment has all his last year's bills at Bognor unpaid for the account of £800 without a farthing to pay them with . . . Harriet is not free from blame, but when after all the grief and worry which these repeated involvements have caused her . . . it is not to be wondered at that she should become hopeless and disheartened . . ."[11] her brother George reported to Granville, who always stepped in to help. Little Harriet agonized over the burden she placed upon her guardian, just as her mother had once fretted over asking Georgiana or her brother for help. "I never can be sufficiently grateful to you for the kindness you have again shown me and for the generosity with which you have again relieved our great difficulties. I feel much shame at our having brought these difficulties upon ourselves again,"[12] she wrote two years later, after Granville once more intervened with financial assistance. She died at the relatively early age of fifty-one, in the family home in Gogmagog Hills, Stapleford, Cambridge.

The life of Harriet's youngest child, George Arundel Stewart, remains more mysterious. We can glean that he traveled extensively during his youth, apparently to Asia, since Harryo mentions that he had returned from travels with exotic gifts including Indian turbans, shawls, fans, and a chess set. His personality seems to have been caring and sociable, although he never married. Harryo's children adored him and she was impressed by the ease with which he managed people of very different temperament. "George Stewart . . . does not look like oil on the waves of the sea—is so in fact on the meeting of such very different waters as Rivers and Fullerton. He is so loved by all and I suspect governs all."[13] When the family were disembarking from Ramsgate, Harryo describes him wrapping his coat around one of her children and carrying him along the pier to the inn. He was greatly attached to Granville and in later life became his private secretary. A grandson later recalled: "In appearance he was tall, upright and thin—indeed he might have been called gaunt. He had a pale complexion, dark eyes deeply set in his head, an aquiline nose and a short pointed white beard; not unlike the pictures of Don Quixote. He and my father [Granville] were very fond of each other and travelled together for six months in Spain in 1847."[14] Harriet would not have asked for more.

Notes

Abbreviations

H	Harriet (Countess of Bessborough)
G	Georgiana (Duchess of Devonshire)
LS	Lady Spencer (First Countess Spencer)
GS	George Spencer (Second Earl Spencer)
GLG	Lord Granville Leveson Gower (First Earl Granville)
MP	Mrs. Poyntz
EF	Bess (Lady Elizabeth Foster)
LB	Lord Bessborough
HLG	Harryo (Countess Granville)
HAS	Little Harriet (Harriet Arundel Stewart)
GM	Little G (Georgiana Morpeth)
WL	William Lamb
CL	Caroline (Caro) Lamb
MD	Maria Duncannon

Introduction

1. Bessborough Papers, f. 201, Mrs. Peterson to MD, 1858
2. Ibid.
3. Stone, *Road to Divorce*

One. The Eligible Match

1. Granville, vol. 2 (hereafter GLG2), p. 434, H to GLG, n.d. April 1812
2. British Library (BL), Additional manuscripts (AD) 75691, LS to Thea Cowper, June 27, 1761
3. Bayne-Powell, p. 166
4. Figures based on Spencer, p. 106, though Foreman (p. 4) puts his income even higher, at £36,400 p.a.

5. Bessborough Papers, f. 258
6. Spencer, pp. 177–78
7. Weinreb and Hibbert, p. 830
8. Brewer, p. 257
9. BL, AD75606, LS to H, October 16, 1783
10. Granville, vol. 1 (hereafter GLG1), p. 311
11. Coke, p. 179
12. BL, AD75691, LS to Thea Cowper, December 10, 1754
13. Ibid.
14. BL, AD5691, LS to Thea Cowper, December 20, 1755
15. BL, AD75925, H to GS, n.d.
16. Battiscombe, p. 79; also quoted in Foreman, p. 8
17. Bessborough, *Family Circle,* p. 35, LS to H, n.d. 1780
18. BL, AD75570, LS to Lord Spencer, n.d.
19. Murry, p. 20
20. Spencer, p. 120
21. Bessborough Papers, f. 17; also quoted in Foreman, p. 8
22. GLG1, p. 218, H to GLG
23. BL, AD75606, LS to G, December 21, 1769
24. Ibid.
25. BL, AD75691, LS to Thea Cowper, December 7, 1765; also quoted by
    Foreman, p. 12
26. BL, AD75691, LS to Thea Cowper, November 26, 1766
27. BL, AD75572, MP to LS, January 17, 1768
28. Bessborough Papers, Harriet's Journal, f. 17, November 16, 1776
29. BL, AD75572, MP to LS, February 1769
30. Ibid., n.d. May 1769
31. Ibid., May 9, 1769
32. Coke, p. 179
33. Bessborough Papers, Lady Bessborough's Journal, f. 17, n.d.
34. BL, AD75687, William Jones to LS, March 16, 1770
35. Bessborough Papers, Lady Bessborough's Journal, f. 17, n.d.
36. Ibid.
37. Bessborough, *Family Circle,* p. 24, Journal, December 3, 1772
38. Ibid. p. 23, Journal, November 20, 1772
39. Ibid. p. 22
40. Ibid.
41. Dowden, p. 458
42. Bessborough Papers, Harriet's Journal, f. 17, August 24, 1776
43. Bessborough, *Family Circle,* p. 26, Harriet's Journal
44. Bessborough, *Georgiana,* p. 26, H to G, July 30, 1775
45. BL, Althorp Papers, AD75911, LS to GS, December 9, 1777
46. Delaney, p. 351
47. Wrest Park, Staffordshire and Luton Archive, MS L30/14/333/174
48. Delaney, p. 507
49. Bessborough, *Georgiana,* p. 40, G to LS, November 4, 1778

50. BL, AD75911, LS to GS, February 28, 1778
51. Ibid. March 4, 1778
52. Ibid. March 11, 1778
53. BL, AD75923, G to GS, August 21, 1780
54. Bessborough, *Georgiana,* p. 47, G to LS, June 7, 1780
55. Lane, p. 38
56. BL, Althorp Papers, AD75923, G to GS, August 12, 1780
57. BL, Althorp Papers, AD75911, LS to GS, July 29, 1780
58. Chatsworth Archive, 307, LS to G, July 25, 1780
59. Bessborough, *Georgiana,* p. 48, G to LS, July 21, 1780
60. Bessborough, *Family Circle,* pp. 31–32, H to Miss Shipley, n.d. 1780
61. Foreman, p. 74
62. Ibid., pp. 74–75
63. Bessborough, *Georgiana,* pp. 48–49, G to LS, July 28, 1780
64. Chatsworth Archive, 307, LS to G, July 25, 1780
65. Ibid.
66. BL, AD75606, LS to H, n.d. 1780
67. Delaney, pp. 552–53, Mrs. Delaney to Mrs. Port, August 7, 1780
68. Toynbee, letter to Strafford
69. Bessborough, *Family Circle,* p. 31, H to Miss Shipley, n.d. 1780
70. Ibid.
71. BL, AD75606, LS to H, December 1780

Two. Marriage and Motherhood

1. BL, AD75605, LS to H, December 28, 1780
2. Foster, p. 11
3. BL, AD75606, LS to H, December 28, 1780
4. BL, AD75911, LS to GS, January 5, 1781
5. Ibid.
6. Bessborough, *Georgiana,* p. 50, LS to G, February 14, 1781. Also quoted in Foreman, p. 86
7. Chatsworth Archive, 331, G to LS, February 16, 1781
8. Portland Papers, MS PWG162, Lady Portland to Lord Duncannon, April 1, 1781; transcript in Bessborough Papers; part quoted by Foreman, pp. 87–88
9. Portland Papers, MS PWG163, Lord Duncannon to Lady Portland, April 3, 1781
10. Ibid.
11. Chatsworth Archive, 339, LS to G, April 15, 1781
12. BL, AD75606, LS to H, n.d. 1781
13. BL, AD75911, LS to GS, January 15, 1781
14. Foreman, p. 88
15. BL, AD75911, LS to GS, July 21, 1781
16. Cf. Lyle Massey, *Art Bulletin,* March 2005
17. BL, AD75911, LS to GS, August 8, 1781
18. Bessborough, *Georgiana,* p. 50, G to LS, August 18, 1781

19. BL, AD75911, LS to GS, August 31, 1781
20. Chatsworth Archive, 2014.24, Lady Spencer's Journal, August 31, 1781
21. Bessborough, Georgiana, p. 52, G to LS, September 4, 1781
22. Ibid., September 17, 1781
23. Ibid.
24. Chatsworth Archive, 2014.124, Lady Spencer's Journal, August 31, 1781
25. Chatsworth Archive, 354, LS to G, September 2, 1781
26. BL, AD75911, LS to GS, September 10, 1781
27. Chatsworth Archive, 358, LS to G, September 8, 1781
28. Ibid.
29. BL, AD75617, Mrs. Howe to LS, September 24, 1781
30. Ibid., September 28, 1781
31. BL, AD75606, LS to H, September 24, 1781
32. Ibid., n.d. October 1781
33. Ibid.
34. BL, AD75911, LS to GS, October 9, 1781
35. Ibid.
36. BL, AD75606, LS to H, October 16, 1781
37. Ibid., n.d. October 1781
38. Ibid., December 30, 1781
39. See Foreman for detailed account of Devonshire House politics
40. Bessborough, Georgiana, p. 32, G to LS, August 14, 1777. Also quoted by Foreman, p. 58
41. Lewis debunks the long-vaunted myth that eighteenth-century women were discouraged from participating in politics
42. Lewis, pp. 39–63
43. Bessborough, Georgiana, pp. 53–54, LS to G, June 13, 1782
44. See Foreman, p. 92
45. Walpole, p. 465
46. BL, AD75606, LS to H, August 15, 1782
47. Ibid., August 19, 1782
48. Chatsworth Archive, 419, G to LS, August 27–29, 1782
49. Bessborough, Georgiana, p. 55, G to LS, August 29, 1782
50. BL, AD75606, LS to H, August 31, 1782
51. Bessborough, Georgiana, p. 55, G to LS, August 31, 1782
52. Chapman & Dormer, p. 27
53. Ibid., p. 21
54. Jack Hervey quoted by Chapman & Dormer, p. 24
55. Bessborough, Georgiana, p. 57, LS to G, October 20, 1782
56. Ibid., p. 56, LS to G, October 11, 1782
57. BL, AD75606, LS to H, November 16, 1782
58. Ibid., n.d. November 1782
59. BL, AD75607, LS to H, n.d. November 1782
60. BL, AD75606, G to H, n.d. 1782
61. Ibid., LS to H, November 11, 1782

THREE. BIRTH AND BEREAVEMENT

1. BL, AD75606, LS to H, January 9, 1783
2. Willet Cunnington, p. 91
3. Bessborough, *Georgiana,* p. 61, G to LS, May 8, 1783
4. BL, AD75606, LS to H, May 11, 1783
5. Ibid., May 16, 1783
6. George, p. 61
7. Ashton, p. 71
8. *The Times,* February 14, 1793
9. David, p. 43
10. Kelly, p. 107
11. Ibid.
12. David, p. 40
13. Kelly, p. 108
14. BL, AD75912, LS to GS, July 7, 1783
15. BL, AD75607, LS to H
16. Chatsworth Archive, 520, LS to G, August 30, 1783
17. BL, AD75912, LS to GS, August 30, 1783
18. Chatsworth Archive, 526, Lavinia Spencer to G, September 6, 1783
19. BL, AD75606, LS to H, September 5, 1783
20. Ibid., August 31, 1783
21. Ibid., October 6, 1783
22. Chatsworth Archive, 547, G to EF, October 18, 1783
23. BL, AD75606, LS to H, September 27, 1783
24. Ibid., October 1783
25. BL, AD75909, Journal, November 1, 1783
26. Ibid., Journal of Lady Spencer, November 1788
27. C. Spencer, p. 125
28. Ibid.
29. BL, AD75606, LS to H, November 27, 1783
30. Chatsworth Archive, 561, LS to G, November 6, 1783
31. Ibid., 568, G to EF, December 29, 1783
32. BL, AD75912, LS to LB, October 26, 1784
33. Foreman, p. 131
34. BL, AD75606, LS to H, n.d. December 1783

FOUR. POLITICS AND PLAY

1. BL, AD75607, LS to H, January 11, 1784
2. Ibid., January 29, 1784
3. BL, AD75579, GS to LS, December 16, 1783
4. Kelly, p. 123
5. Bessborough, *Georgiana,* p. 69, G to EF, January 3, 1784
6. BL, AD75607, LS to H, February 13, 1784

7. Cf Lewis, p. 46

8. BL, AD75607, LS to H, February 4, 1784

9. Lewis, p. 47. Also quoted by Foreman, p. 141

10. The following account of Georgiana's and Harriet's electioneering is based on Foreman's detailed account, pp. 136–59

11. Cf Lewis, p. 142

12. *Morning Post,* March 31, 1784, quoted by Foreman, p. 144

13. *Morning Post,* April 8, 1784

14. BL, AD75925, H to GS, April 1, 1784

15. Bessborough, *Georgiana,* p. 80, G to LS, April 1784

16. Ibid., LS to G, April 24, 1784

17. Ibid., G to LS, March–April 1784

18. BL, AD75607, LS to H, April 13, 1784

19. Wraxall, p. 11

20. BL, AD75607, LS to H, May 2, 1784

FIVE. UNGOVERNABLE PASSIONS

1. Bessborough, *Georgiana,* p. 102, EF to G, December 10, 1785

2. BL, AD75607, LS to H, August 26, 1784

3. BL, AD75580, GS to LS, August 2, 1784

4. BL, AD75580, GS to LS, August 2, 1784

5. Ibid., August 1784

6. BL, AD75607, LS to H, August 4, 1784

7. BL, AD75598, Lavinia Spencer to LS, July 18, 1784

8. BL, AD75607, LS to H, August 30, 1784

9. Ibid.

10. Ibid., October 2, 1784

11. BL, AD75581, GS to LS, October 23, 1784

12. Ibid., November 14, 1784

13. BL, AD75607, LS to H, September 20, 1784

14. BL, AD75913, LS to GS, January 31, 1786

15. Melville, p. 42, June 21, 1791

16. G. Leveson Gower, p. 60, HLG to GM, October 6, 1803

17. BL, AD75628, Mrs. Howe to LS, April 8, 1786

18. Bessborough, *Georgiana,* G to LS, October 19, 1786

19. BL, AD75913, LS to GS, February 8, 1786

20. BL, AD75923, G to GS, n.d. 1784

21. GLG, n.d.

22. Arbuthnot, p. 128

23. Weinreb & Hibbert, p. 936

24. Moritz, p. 41

25. Bessborough, *Georgiana,* p. 32, G to LS, August 14, 1777

26. Price, pp. 207–8

27. BL, AD75923, G to GS, November 6, 1784

28. BL, AD75608, LS to H, May 26, 1786

29. Bessborough, *Georgiana,* p. 95, G to LS, February 16, 1785
30. Foreman, p. 180
31. Bessborough, *Georgiana,* p. 92, LS to G, August 26, 1784
32. BL, AD75607, LS to H, May 6, 1785
33. BL, AD75581, GS to LS, March 29, 1785
34. BL, AD75607, LS to H, June 5, 1785
35. Ibid., August 23, 1785
36. Bessborough, *Georgiana,* p. 100, G to EF, September 6, 1785
37. Chatsworth Archive, 2014.155, LS Journal, November 12, 1785
38. Ibid., 679, G to EF, June 1785
39. BL, AD75913, LS to GS, December 13, 1785
40. Ibid., February 7, 1786
41. Bessborough, *Georgiana,* p. 104, LS to G, February 6, 1786
42. Ibid., p. 106, EF to G, February 12, 1786
43. BL, AD75608, LS to H, March 22, 1786
44. Ibid., LS to G, June 27, 1786
45. BL, AD75583, GS to LS, June 19, 1786
46. BL, AD75925, H to GS, n.d.
47. BL, AD75923, G to GS, n.d.
48. BL, AD75583, GS to LS, July 6, 1786. Also quoted in Foreman, p. 81
49. BL, AD75608, LS to H, July 5, 1786
50. BL, AD75628, LS to Mrs. Howe, July 26, 1786
51. *The Times,* July 24, 1784
52. Chatsworth Archive, 751, Lady Salisbury to Lady Melbourne, n.d. July 1786. Also quoted in Foreman, p. 180
53. Chatsworth Archive, 753, Lady Melbourne to G, July 24, 1786
54. BL, AD75583, GS to LS, July 28, 1786
55. BL, AD75608, H to LS, August 2, 1786

Six. Sheridan

1. BL, AD75584, GS to LS, February 5, 1787
2. Ibid.
3. BL, AD75914, LS to GS, February 7, 1787
4. BL, AD75584, GS to LS, February 7, 1787
5. BL, AD75914, LS to GS, February 12, 1787
6. Ibid.
7. *The Times,* March 5, 1787
8. Foreman, chapter 11
9. Manuscripts of His Grace the Duke of Rutland, Historical Manuscripts Commission (1888–1905), p. 395, Daniel Pulteney to the Duke of Rutland, July 3, 1787. Also quoted by Foreman, p. 193
10. NPG Macdonnell, col. 180
11. BL, AD75914, LS to GS, August 3, 1787
12. Mrs. Damer quoted by Foreman, p. 201
13. Foreman, p. 202

14. Bessborough, *Georgiana,* p. 132, LS to Duke of Devonshire, July 22, 1788
15. BL, AD75608, LS to H, July 23, 1788
16. Bessborough, *Georgiana,* G to LS, July 23, 1788
17. Foreman, p. 205
18. Ibid.
19. *The Times,* August 5, 1788
20. BL, AD75585, GS to LS, August 6, 1788
21. Gronow, *Celebrities,* pp. 90–91
22. Kelly
23. Bessborough, *Family Circle,* pp. 47–48, Harriet's Journal, March 26, 1789
24. Kelly, p. 165
25. Ibid.
26. Foreman, p. 238
27. Price, pp. 207–8
28. Sadler, p. 81, Elizabeth Sheridan to Mrs. Canning, January 10 (1791?)
29. Le Fanu, *Betsy Sheridan's Journal,* p. 168, June 14, 1789. Also quoted by Foreman, p. 239
30. "Sheridan has been caught with Lady D. Lord D has commenced a suit in Doctors Commons for a divorce." Hamwood Papers, June 18, 1789
31. BL, AD45548, G to Lady Melbourne, December 29, 1789
32. Foreman, p. 239
33. Sadler, p. 82, Elizabeth Sheridan to Mrs. Canning, n.d.
34. BL, AD75916, LS to GS, January 12, 1790
35. Le Fanu, *Betsy Sheridan's Journal,* March 28, 1790

Seven. The Root of All Evil

1. Chatsworth Archive, 1037, Lady Jersey to G, July 12, 1790
2. *Lady Magazine,* p. 44, January 1790
3. Bessborough, *Family Circle,* p. 54, G to H, n.d. October 1789
4. *Lady Magazine,* p. 314, June 1790
5. *The Times,* January 19, 1791
6. Toynbee, Walpole to Mary Berry, March 5, 1791
7. Foreman, p. 253
8. BL, AD75586, GS to LS, March 3, 1791
9. *The Times,* May 17, 1791
10. Melville, p. 42, June 21, 1791
11. Burney, vol. 1, p. 42
12. BL, AD45548, H to Lady Melbourne, October 24, 1791
13. Bessborough *Family Circle,* p. 180, G to Thomas Coutts, April 29, 1791
14. Chatsworth Archive, 1079.6, G to Thomas Coutts, n.d. March? 1791
15. Bessborough, *Georgiana,* p. 181, G to Thomas Coutts, May 6, 1791
16. Chatsworth Archive, 1603.1, G to Thomas Coutts, September 15, 1801
17. BL, AD75586, GS to LS, n.d. April 1791
18. Burney, p. 35, August 20, 1790
19. BL, AD75638, LS to Mrs. Howe, May 22, 1791

20. Ibid.
21. Ibid., June 3, 1791
22. Ibid., June 11, 1791
23. Ibid.
24. Ibid., June 8, 1791
25. Ibid., June 20, 1791
26. BL, AD75639, LS to Mrs. Howe, July 15, 1791
27. Burney, p. 38, August 20, 1791
28. Also quoted by Foreman, p. 257
29. Burney, p. 38, August 20, 1791
30. BL, AD45548, H to Lady Melbourne, October 24, 1791
31. BL, AD75638, LS to Mrs. Howe, May 26, 1791
32. BL, AD75586, GS to LS, September 4, 1791
33. *The Times,* October 18, 1791
34. Foreman, pp. 260–65
35. BL, AD45548, EF to Lady Melbourne, n.d. 1791
36. Ibid., H to Lady Melbourne, October 11, 1791
37. BL, AD45911, G to Lady Melbourne, October 15, 1791
38. BL, AD75639, LS to Mrs. Howe, October 21, 1791
39. BL, AD45548, H to Lady Melbourne, October 24, 1791
40. Foreman, p. 263
41. BL, AD45548, H to Lady Melbourne, n.d. October 1791

Eight. A Test of Loyalty

1. BL, AD45548, H to Lady Melbourne, n.d. October 1791
2. BL, AD75639, LS to Mrs. Howe, October 24, 1791
3. BL, AD45548, H to Lady Melbourne, n.d. October 1791
4. Bessborough, *Georgiana,* p. 63, Lord Duncannon to H, October 21, 1791
5. Ibid.
6. BL, AD75925, H to GS, n.d. November 1791
7. BL, AD75639, LS to Mrs. Howe, November 16, 1791
8. Bessborough, *Family Circle,* H to her sons, November 20, 1791
9. BL, AD45548, H to Lady Melbourne, December 11, 1791
10. Ibid.
11. Bessborough, *Georgiana,* p. 64, H to John Ponsonby, December 3, 1791
12. BL, AD75639, LS to Mrs. Howe, November 26, 1791
13. Bessborough, *Georgiana,* p. 68, Duncannon to LB, February 11, 1792
14. BL, AD45548, G to Lady Melbourne, December 17, 1791
15. Chatsworth Archive, 1115, Georgiana's will, January 27, 1792
16. Foreman, chapter 16
17. Bessborough, *Georgiana,* p. 65, H to John Ponsonby, January 3, 1792
18. Bessborough, *Georgiana,* p. 66, H to her sons, January 13, 1792
19. Bessborough Papers, Duncannon to LB, February 11, 1792
20. Ibid., March 9, 1792
21. BL, AD75640, LS to Mrs. Howe, February 7, 1792

22. BL, AD45548, H to Lady Melbourne, February 11, 1792
23. BL, AD75641, LS to Mrs. Howe, June 1, 1792
24. Bessborough, *Georgiana*, p. 67, H to an unknown correspondent, January 29, 1792
25. Sichel, p. 435, Sheridan to G and H, May 3, 1792
26. Ibid., p. 439, Sheridan to H, August 27, 1792
27. Price, p. 239, n.d. March 1792
28. BL, AD51723, H to Lady Holland, August 2, 1793
29. BL, AD75640, LS to Mrs. Howe, n.d. February 1792
30. BL, AD75641, LS to Mrs. Howe, July 7, 1792
31. BL, AD45548, H to Lady Melbourne, February 11, 1792
32. Ibid., March 11, 1792
33. Bessborough Papers, f. 20, LB to Lord Duncannon, December 6, 1791
34. BL, AD45911, H to Lady Melbourne, February 28, 1742
35. BL, AD75916, LS to GS, n.d. 1792
36. Ibid.
37. Bessborough Papers, f. 20, LB to Lord Duncannon, April 30, 1791
38. BL, AD45911, H to Lady Melbourne, March 29, 1792
39. BL, AD75916, LS to GS, n.d. 1792
40. Ibid., n.d.
41. BL, AD45911, H to Lady Melbourne, February 28, 1792
42. Chatsworth Archive, 1124, Duke of Devonshire to LS, April 3, 1792
43. Bessborough Papers, f. 16, Duncannon to LB, May 11, 1792
44. BL, AD45911, H to Lady Melbourne, n.d. 1792. Also quoted by Foreman, pp. 272–73

NINE. UNEXPECTED DEPARTURES

1. BL, AD51723, H to Lady Webster, n.d. 1792
2. BL, AD75641, LS to Mrs. Howe, June 1, 1792
3. BL, Holland Papers, AD51723, H to Lady Webster, n.d. 1792
4. Ibid.
5. BL, AD75641, LS to Mrs. Howe, July 7, 1792
6. BL, Holland Papers, AD51723, H to Lady Webster, n.d. 1792
7. Duvall, p. 55, January 11, 1793
8. BL, AD74641, LS to Mrs. Howe, June 24, 1792
9. Ibid., July 17, 1792
10. Ibid., July 27, 1792
11. Bessborough, *Georgiana*, p. 194, Lady Sutherland to G, August 31, 1792
12. BL, Holland Papers, AD51723, H to Lady Webster, n.d. 1792
13. BL, AD51723, H to Lady Webster, October 3, 1792
14. BL, AD75641, LS to Mrs. Howe, September 26, 1792
15. Ibid.
16. Ibid., October 6, 1792
17. Bessborough Papers, f. 18, H to her sons, n.d. December 1792
18. BL, AD51723, H to Lady Webster, n.d.

19. Ibid., January 9, 1793
20. Bessborough, *Georgiana,* p. 76, Lord Duncannon to H, December 10, 1792
21. Bessborough, *Family Circle,* Lord Duncannon to H, December 18, 1792
22. BL, AD75642, LS to Mrs. Howe, February 14, 1793
23. Ibid., February 21, 1793
24. Ibid., April 5, 1793
25. Bessborough, *Family Circle,* LB to H, April 12, 1793
26. Chatsworth Archive, 1152.2, Thomas Coutts to G, March 26, 1793
27. BL, AD76642, LS to Mrs. Howe, April 18, 1793
28. Bessborough Papers, f. 19, LB to H, April 29, 1793
29. Bessborough, *Family Circle,* LB to H, May 10, 1793
30. Bessborough, *Georgiana,* p. 86, LB to H, May 14, 1793
31. Ibid.
32. Ibid., p. 87, LB to H, May 25, 1793
33. Bessborough Papers, f. 19, LB to H, May 28, 1793
34. Chatsworth Archive, 1152.2, G to Thomas Coutts, April 10, 1793
35. Ibid., 1142.1, Thomas Coutts to G, November 30, 1792
36. Sheffield Archives, WWM f.115−108, H to Lord Fitzwilliam, June 19, 1793
37. Bessborough, *Family Circle,* LB to H, May 28, 1793
38. Bessborough, *Georgiana,* p. 92, LB to H, June 17, 1793
39. Bessborough, *Family Circle,* LB to H, July 5, 1793
40. Ibid.
41. Bessborough, *Georgiana,* p. 98, LB to H, July 21, 1793
42. BL, AD75916, LS to GS, June 15, 1793
43. BL, AD51723, H to Lady Webster, August 2, 1793
44. Chatsworth Archive, 1181, LS to G, September 19, 1793
45. Ibid., 1174, LS to Miss Trimmer, September 4, 1793
46. BL, AD75643, LS to Mrs. Howe, November 26, 1793
47. Hudson, p. 189
48. Bessborough Papers, f.17, H to John and Frederick, n.d. December 1793
49. Bessborough, *Family Circle,* H to her sons, n.d. 1793

Ten. The Meeting

1. Gronow, *Recollections,* p. 131
2. GLG1, p. 3, Lady Gower to GLG, n.d. 1781
3. Ibid., p. 11, Lady Stafford to GLG, August 18, 1788
4. Ibid., p. 5, Lady Gower to GLG, February 19, 1785
5. Ibid., p. 14, Lady Stafford to GLG, February 12, 1789
6. Ibid., Lady Stafford to GLG, February 14, 1792
7. Holland, vol. 1, p. 116, February 3, 1794
8. GLG1, p. 32, Lady Sutherland to Lady Stafford, n.d. February 1790
9. Ibid., p. 52, Lady Stafford to GLG, August 29, 1792
10. Holland, vol. 1, p. 121, June 10, 1794
11. BL, Holland Papers, AD51731, Henry Holland to Caroline Fox, January 24, 1794
12. GLG1, p. 82, Lady Stafford to GLG, February 16, 1794

13. Ibid., p. 86, GLG to Lady Stafford, February 22, 1794
14. Holland, vol. 1, p. 121, June 10, 1794
15. Ibid., p. 122, June 10, 1794
16. BL, Holland Papers, AD51731, Lord Holland to Caroline Fox
17. BL, AD75643, LS to Mrs. Howe, February 25, 1794
18. BL, AD75925, H to GS, n.d., rec'd. February 1794
19. BL, AD51723, H to Lady Webster, February 7, 1794
20. GLG1, p. 87, Lady Stafford to GLG, April 1, 1794
21. Ibid., p. 84, GLG to Lady Stafford, January 30, 1794
22. Holland, vol. 1, p. 117, February 3, 1794
23. Ibid., p. 125, n.d. May 1794
24. Ibid., p. 124, n.d. May 1794
25. GLG1, p. 88, H to GLG, May 9, 1794
26. Ibid., p. 91, H to GLG, June 1, 1794
27. Ibid., p. 90, Lady Stafford to GLG, May 14, 1794
28. Ibid., p. 92, Lady Stafford to GLG, July 18, 1794
29. Ibid., p. 94, Lady Stafford to GLG, July 22, 1794

Eleven. Friendship

1. Bessborough, *Georgiana,* p. 105, H to her sons, May 12, 1794
2. Chatsworth Archive, 1253, LS to G, n.d. 1794
3. GLG1, p. 98, H to GLG, n.d.
4. Ibid., p. 102, H to GLG, n.d. November 1794?
5. Ibid., p. 110, H to GLG, n.d. January 1795
6. Ibid., p. 112, H to GLG, n.d. April 1795
7. Lewis, p. 148
8. GLG1, p. 102, H to GLG, n.d. November? 1794
9. Ibid., p. 108, H to GLG, January 15, 1795
10. Annual Register, p. 148, 1795
11. GLG1, p. 102, H to GLG, n.d. November? 1794
12. Ibid., p. 107, H to GLG, n.d. December? 1794
13. Ibid., p. 114, H to GLG, n.d. July? 1795
14. Ibid., p. 114, H to GLG, August 20, 1795
15. Ibid., p. 113, Lady Stafford to GLG, May? 5, 1795
16. Ibid., p. 119, Lady Stafford to GLG, January? 18, 1796
17. Ibid., p. 124, n.d. June? 1796
18. Ibid., pp. 124–25, July 2, 1796
19. Ibid., p. 123, n.d. July? 1796
20. Ibid., p. 126, H to GLG, n.d. 1796
21. Public Record Office, 30/23/6/2
22. Smith, *Collected Letters,* pp. 242–43, Charlotte Smith to Thomas Cadell, November 20, 1796
23. Smith, *Elegiac Sonnets,* vol. 2, facing p. 29
24. GLG1, p. 129, GLG to Lady Stafford, October 12, 1796
25. Ibid., p. 130, GLG to Lady Stafford, October 23, 1796

26. Ibid., p. 131, H to GLG, October 1796
27. Ibid., p. 133, H to GLG, n.d.
28. Ibid., p. 132, GLG to H, n.d.
29. Ibid., p. 136, GLG to H, November 12, 1796
30. Ibid., p. 134, H to GLG, n.d.

Twelve. The Start of the Affair

1. Kelly, p. 217
2. GLG1, p. 146, Lady Stafford to GLG, n.d.
3. Ibid., p. 147, H to GLG, n.d.
4. Ibid., p. 218, H to GLG, n.d.
5. Ibid.
6. Ibid., p. 157, Lady Stafford to GLG, June 26, 1797
7. Ibid., p. 158, GLG to Lady Stafford, June 30, 1797
8. Ibid., p. 128, H to GLG, n.d. October? 1797
9. Ibid., p. 148, H to GLG, n.d.
10. Ibid., p. 160, H to GLG, July 1797
11. Ibid., p. 162, H to GLG, July 9, 1797
12. Ibid., p. 163, H to GLG, n.d. 1797
13. Ibid., p. 161, H to GLG, n.d. July 1797
14. Ibid., p. 167, Lord Malmesbury to Lord Greville, August 6, 1797
15. Ibid., p. 172, Lady Stafford to GLG, September 16, 1797
16. Ibid.
17. Ibid., p. 175, H to GLG, n.d.
18. Ibid., p. 217, H to GLG, n.d. August 1798
19. Ibid., p. 177, H to GLG, October 1797
20. Ibid., p. 178, H to GLG, n.d. November?
21. Ibid., p. 180, H to GLG, n.d. November? 1797
22. Ibid., p. 183, GLG to Lady Stafford, November 25, 1797
23. Ibid., p. 184, Lady Stafford to GLG, December 9, 1797
24. Ibid., p. 185, H to GLG, n.d. December 1797
25. Ibid., p. 200, H to GLG, February 4, 1798
26. Ibid., p. 196, H to GLG, February 19, 1798
27. Ibid., p. 198, H to GLG, n.d. February 1798
28. Ibid., p. 200, February 4, 1798
29. Ibid., p. 208, H to GLG, n.d. 1798
30. Ibid., p. 202, GLG to H, January 27, 1798
31. Ibid., p. 203, GLG to H, January 27, 1798
32. Ibid., p. 209, H to GLG, n.d. May? 1798

Thirteen. Extravagance and Ruin

1. Bessborough Papers, f. 271, LS to H, March 22, 1798
2. GLG1, p. 223, H to GLG, n.d. September? 1798
3. Garlick and MacIntyre, p. 749, January 15–17, 1797

4. Chatsworth Archive, 1374.1, G to Thomas Coutts, October 19, 1796
5. Bessborough Papers, f. 260, William Shane to LB, July 27, 1798
6. GLG1, p. 234, H to GLG, n.d. December 1798
7. PRO, 30/23?6/2, Lady Anne Hatton to GLG, n.d. 1796
8. GLG1, p. 224, H to GLG, n.d. September 1798
9. Ibid., p. 241, H to GLG, February 27, 1799
10. Ibid., p. 211, H to GLG, July 26, 1798
11. PRO, 30/23/6/2, Elizabeth Monck to GLG, n.d. 1796
12. Ibid., 30/29/6/2, Lady Anne Hatton to GLG, n.d. 1796
13. Ibid., 30/29/6/2 (32), Lady Anne Hatton to GLG, n.d.
14. GLG1, p. 225, H to GLG, n.d. October 1798
15. Ibid., p. 226, H to GLG, n.d. 1799
16. Ibid., p. 260, H to GLG, n.d. summer 1799
17. Bessborough Papers, f. 271, LS to H, June 12, 1799
18. Ibid., November 13, 1799
19. GLG1, p. 274, H to GLG, n.d. November 1799
20. Ibid., p. 288, H to GLG, n.d. October 1800
21. Holland Papers, 51723, LB to Lord Holland, n.d. February 1800?
22. BL, AD75924, G to GS, n.d. January 1800
23. Ibid.
24. GLG1, p. 239, H to GLG, n.d. 1799
25. Ibid., p. 243, H to GLG, n.d. March 1799
26. Ibid., p. 242, Sheridan to H, n.d. March 1799
27. Ibid., p. 216, H to GLG, n.d. August 1798
28. Ibid., p. 248, H to GLG, n.d. 1799
29. Ibid., p. 250, H to GLG, n.d. 1799

FOURTEEN. THE SECRET CHILD

1. Bessborough Papers, f. 271, LS to H, n.d. January 1800
2. BL, Holland Papers, 51723, H to Lord Holland, January 1800
3. Chatsworth Archive, 1560, LS to G, January 7, 1801
4. Bessborough Papers, f. 271, LS to H, April 30, 1800
5. GLG1, pp. 280–81, H to GLG, n.d. 1800
6. Murray, *High Society,* p. 248
7. PRO, 30/29/17/3, H to HAS, August? 1813
8. Ibid., 30/29/17/3, HLG to HAS, December 2, 1821
9. Ibid., 30/29/6/2, Lady Anne Hatton to GLG, n.d.
10. Ibid., 30/29/6/2 (32), Lady Anne Hatton to GLG, n.d.
11. Chatsworth Archive, 1522, G to LS, September 9, 1800
12. GLG1, p. 284, H to GLG, September 15, 1800
13. Chapman & Dormer, p. 146
14. GLG1, p. 284, H to GLG, September 15, 1800
15. Ibid., p. 283, G to GLG, September 16, 1800
16. Ibid., p. 277, H to GLG, n.d. November/December? 1800
17. Ibid., p. 287, H to GLG, n.d. November/December 1800

FIFTEEN. PEACE AND LOVE

1. Hague, p. 468
2. *Parliamentary History,* vol. XXXV, pp. 962–63, quoted in Hague, p. 478
3. GLGI, p. 289, GLG to Lady Stafford, February 7, 1801
4. Ibid., p. 290, Lady Stafford to GLG, February 8, 1801
5. Ibid., p. 302, H to GLG, April 8, 1801
6. Ibid., p. 311, H to GLG, n.d. November 1801
7. Ibid., p. 305, H to GLG, n.d. autumn 1801
8. Ibid., p. 307, GLG to Lady Stafford, November 5, 1801
9. Ibid., p. 317, H to GLG, n.d. January 1802
10. Ibid., p. 321, H to GLG, n.d. January 1802
11. Ibid., pp. 311–12, Lady Stafford to GLG, November 30, 1801
12. Ibid., p. 317, H to GLG, n.d. January 1802
13. Ibid., n.d. 1802
14. Ibid., p. 324, H to GLG, n.d. January 1802
15. Ibid., p. 322, H to GLG, n.d. January 1802
16. Ibid., p. 329, H to GLG, n.d. 1802
17. Ibid., p. 330, H to GLG, n.d. February 1802
18. Ibid., p. 334, H to GLG, n.d. postmark March 26, 1802
19. Ibid., p. 351, H to GLG, August 23, 1802
20. Dormer Archive, f. 199, EF's Journal, July 19, 1802
21. GLGI, p. 350, H to GLG, August 23, 1802
22. Ibid., p. 351, H to GLG, August 23, 1802
23. Ibid., p. 352, H to GLG, n.d. August 1802
24. Ibid., p. 347, H to GLG, n.d. August 1802
25. Ibid., p. 344, H to GLG, n.d. 1802
26. Ibid., p. 349, H to GLG, n.d. August 1802
27. Ibid., p. 351, H to GLG, August 23, 1802
28. G. Leveson Gower, p. 23, HLG to GM, n.d. August 1802
29. GLG, p. 366, H to GLG, n.d. October 1802
30. G. Leveson Gower, p. 34, HLG to GM, September 19, 1802
31. Howell Thomas, p. 66
32. GLGI, p. 365, H to GLG, n.d. 1802
33. Ibid., p. 366, H to GLG, n.d. October 1802

SIXTEEN. PARIS

1. GLGI, p. 358, H to GLG, September 20, 1802
2. Bessborough Papers, f. 272, LS to H, November 1, 1802
3. Ibid., December 29, 1802
4. Ibid., December 23, 1802
5. Bessborough Papers, f. 273, LS to H, January 17, 1803
6. Ibid., January 24, 1803
7. G. Leveson Gower, p. 51, HLG to GM, n.d. February 1803
8. GLGI, p. 376, H to GLG, December 15, 1802

9. Bessborough Papers, f. 272, LS to H, November 12, 1802
10. Ibid., f. 18, H to GLG, December 19, 1802
11. GLGI, p. 400, H to GLG, January 18, 1803
12. Ibid., p. 381, H to GLG, December 23, 1802
13. Ibid., p. 385, H to GLG, December 24, 1802
14. Ibid., p. 382, H to GLG, December 23, 1802
15. Ibid., p. 385
16. Ibid., p. 377, H to GLG, December 15, 1802
17. Ibid., p. 379, H to GLG, December 17, 1802
18. Ibid., p. 376, H to GLG, December 15, 1802
19. Ibid., p. 378
20. Ibid., p. 390, H to GLG, January 5, 1803
21. Ibid., p. 390, H to GLG, January 5, 1803
22. Ibid., p. 396, H to GLG, January 10, 1803
23. Ibid., p. 400, H to GLG, January 16, 1803
24. Ibid., p. 407, H to GLG, January 25, 1803
25. G. Leveson Gower, p. 45, HLG to GM, January 20, 1803
26. Ibid., p. 47, HLG to GM, January 25, 1803
27. Ibid., p. 49, HLG to GM, January 30, 1803
28. GLGI, p. 389, H to GLG, January 4, 1803
29. G. Leveson Gower, p. 51, HLG to GM, n.d. February 1803
30. GLGI, p. 396, H to GLG, January 10, 1803
31. Ibid., p. 411, H to GLG, February 15, 1803
32. Ibid., p. 393, H to GLG, January 6, 1803
33. Ibid., p. 413, H to GLG, February 23, 1803
34. Ibid., p. 414, H to GLG, n.d. 1803

Seventeen. Intrigues

1. GLGI, p. 415, Lady Stafford to GLG, n.d. March? 1803
2. Ibid.
3. Ibid., p. 417, H to GLG, n.d. 1803
4. Ibid., p. 420, GLG to Lady Stafford, March 29, 1803
5. Ibid., p. 416, Lady Stafford to GLG, March 23, 1803
6. PRO, 30/29/4/11, f. 54, H to Lady Stafford, n.d. 1803?
7. GLGI, p. 424, H to Lady Stafford, June 13, 1803
8. PRO, 30/29/4/11, f. 58, H to Lady Stafford, July 27, 1803
9. GLGI, p. 425, Lady Stafford to GLG, June 18, 1803
10. Ibid., p. 420, GLG to Lady Stafford, March 29, 1803
11. Ibid., p. 422, Charles Grey to G, n.d. 1803
12. Ibid., p. 437, H to GLG, October 17, 1803
13. Ibid., p. 427, H to GLG, August 17, 1803
14. Ibid., p. 433, H to GLG, n.d. September 1803
15. Ibid., p. 440, GLG to H, December 28, 1803
16. Ibid., p. 440, H to GLG, December 28, 1803

17. Ibid., p. 441, H to GLG, n.d. 1803/1804
18. Ibid., p. 442, H to GLG, n.d. 1803/1804
19. Dormer Archive, f. 539, EF's Journal, January 1804
20. Ibid., f. 540, H to EF, February 15, 1804
21. Ibid., f. 722, EF's Journal, May 6, 1804
22. Ibid., f. 724, EF's Journal, May 7, 1804

EIGHTEEN. SEPARATION

1. Chatsworth Archive, 1786, EF to G, October 28, 1804
2. GLG1, p. 458, H to GLG, n.d. July 1804
3. Dormer Archive, f. 783, EF's Journal, June 10, 1804
4. GLG, p. 461, H to GLG, n.d. August? 1804
5. Bessborough Papers, f. 273, LS to H, July 22, 1804
6. GLG, p. 462, H to GLG, n.d. September 1804
7. G. Leveson Gower, p. 96, HLG to GM, August 18, 1804
8. GLG1, p. 462, H to GLG, n.d. September/October? 1804
9. Ibid.
10. Ibid.
11. Ibid., p. 463, GLG to H, October 5, 1804
12. Ibid., p. 472, H to GLG, November 5, 1804
13. Ibid., p. 500, GLG to H, November 14, 1804
14. Ibid., p. 487, H to GLG, December 2, 1804
15. Ibid., p. 466, GLG to H, October 11, 1804
16. Ibid., p. 466, H to GLG, October 11, 1804
17. Ibid., p. 467, H to GLG, October 22, 1804
18. Chatsworth Archive, 1785.1, EF to G, October 22, 1804
19. BL, AD51723, H to Lady Holland, November 4, 1804
20. Chatsworth Archive, 1786, EF to G, October 28, 1804
21. Ibid., 1787, EF to G, November 1, 1804
22. Bessborough Papers, f. 273, LS to H, November 5, 1804
23. GLG, p. 475, H to GLG, n.d. Nov 1804
24. Bessborough Papers, f. 273, LS to H, November 22, 1804
25. GLG1, p. 472, H to GLG, November 5, 1804
26. Ibid., p. 484, H to GLG, November 27, 1804
27. Ibid., p. 486, GLG to H, November 8, 1804
28. Ibid., p. 490, GLG to H, November 12, 1804
29. Ibid., p. 487, H to GLG, December 2, 1804
30. GLG2, p. 62, Correspondence of Sarah, Lady Lyttelton
31. GLG1, p. 499, GLG to H, November 14, 1804
32. Ibid., p. 506, GLG to H, November 30, 1804
33. Ibid., p. 509, H to GLG, December 29, 1804
34. Ibid., p. 492, H to GLG, December 6, 1804
35. Ibid., p. 491, H to GLG, December 5, 1804
36. Ibid., pp. 495–96, H to GLG, November 10, 1804

Nineteen. Defamation and Disturbance

1. GLG2, p. 3, H to GLG, January 3, 1805
2. Gronow, *Celebrities,* p. 95
3. GLG2, p. 48, GLG to H, February 28, 1805
4. Ibid., pp. 7–8, H to GLG, January 22, 1805
5. Ibid., p. 34, H to GLG, March 1, 1805
6. Ibid., p. 93, H to GLG, July 13, 1805
7. Ibid., p. 15, H to GLG, February 9, 1805
8. Ibid.
9. Ibid., p. 74, H to GLG, May 19, 1805
10. Ibid., p. 76, H to GLG, June 7, 1805
11. Ibid., p. 101, GLG to H, July 10, 1805
12. Ibid., p. 107, H to GLG, August 21, 1805
13. Ibid., p. 25, H to GLG, February 24, 1805
14. Ibid., p. 38, H to GLG, January 9, 1805
15. Ibid., p. 71, H to GLG, n.d. May 1805
16. Ibid., pp. 71–72, GLG to H, April 20–24, 1805
17. Bessborough, *Family Circle,* p. 129, WL to CL, May 2, 1805
18. GLG2, p. 67, H to GLG, May 1, 1805
19. Ibid., p. 81, H to GLG, June 8, 1805
20. Ibid., p. 68, H to GLG, May 8, 1805
21. Chatsworth Archive, 1804, G to LS, May 4, 1804
22. Bessborough Papers, f. 274, LS to H, May 6, 1805
23. Bessborough, *Family Circle,* Duncannon to CL, May 13, 1805
24. Ibid., p. 130, WL to CL
25. GLG2, p. 81, H to GLG, June 12, 1805
26. Ibid., p. 73, H to GLG, May 16, 1805
27. Ibid., pp. 75–76, H to GLG, June 7, 1805
28. Bessborough, *Family Circle,* p. 133, H to CL, n.d. 1805
29. Bessborough Papers, f. 18, H to CL, n.d. June 1805
30. GLG, p. 79, H to GLG, n.d. June 1805
31. GLG2, p. 80, H to GLG, June 10, 1805
32. Ibid., p. 92, H to GLG, July 10, 1805
33. Ibid., p. 99, GLG to H, July 4, 1805
34. Ibid., p. 100, GLG to H, July 4, 1805
35. Ibid., p. 106, H to GLG, 1805
36. Ibid., pp. 130–31, GLG to H, October 4, 1805
37. Ibid., p. 114, H to GLG, September 21, 1805
38. Ibid.
39. Bessborough, *Family Circle,* p. 138, LB to Duncannon, September 21, 1805
40. GLG2, p. 114, H to GLG, September 21, 1805
41. Ibid., p. 117, H to GLG, September 27, 1805
42. G. Leveson Gower, p. 128, HLG to GM, November 10, 1805
43. GLG2, p. 129, H to GLG, November 5, 1805
44. Ibid., p. 132, H to GLG, November 6, 1805

45. Ibid., p. 134, H to GLG, November 10, 1805
46. Ibid., p. 140, George Canning to H, December 3, 1805
47. Ibid., p. 148, GLG to H, November 23, 1805
48. Ibid., p. 151, GLG to H, December 6, 1805

TWENTY. HEARTBREAK

1. G. Leveson Gower, p. 136, HLG to GM, December 18, 1805
2. GLG2, p. 155, H to GLG, January 9, 1806
3. Ibid., p. 157, H to GLG, January 12, 1806
4. Ibid., p. 158, H to GLG, January 14, 1806
5. Ibid., p. 160, H to GLG, January 20, 1806
6. Ibid., p. 161, H to GLG, January 21, 1806
7. Hague, p. 578
8. Ibid., p. 576
9. GLG2, p. 163, H to GLG, January 23, 1806
10. Ibid., p. 177, H to GLG, February 5, 1806
11. Ibid., p. 180, H to GLG, February 22, 1806
12. Bessborough Papers, f. 274, LS to H, March 14, 1806
13. GLG2, p. 184, H to GLG, March 22, 1806
14. Ibid., p. 185, H to GLG, March 23, 1806
15. Foreman, pp. 388–89
16. GLG2, p. 185, H to GLG, n.d. March 1806
17. Ibid.
18. Ibid., p. 186, H to GLG, April 11, 1806
19. Ibid., p. 186, H to GLG, April 15, 1806
20. Ibid., p. 187, H to GLG, April 20, 1806
21. Ibid., p. 188
22. Ibid., p. 188, H to GLG, April 22, 1806
23. Wraxall, p. 8
24. GLG2, p. 199, GLG to H, April 25, 1806
25. Ibid., p. 200, GLG to H, April 27, 1806
26. Ibid., p. 205, H to GLG, June 27, 1806
27. Quoted by David, p. 253
28. Ibid.
29. GLG2, p. 206, H to GLG, June 29, 1806
30. Ibid., p. 217, H to GLG, October 10, 1806
31. G. Leveson Gower, p. 154, HLG to GM, July 21, 1806
32. Ibid., p. 159, HLG to GM, November 12, 1806
33. Ibid., p. 167, HLG to GM, November 20, 1806
34. Ibid.
35. Ibid.

TWENTY-ONE. THE RIVALS

1. G. Leveson Gower, p. 170, HLG to GM, November 22, 1806
2. Ibid., p. 174, HLG to GM, November 27, 1806

3. Ibid., p. 78, HLG to GM, December 1, 1806

4. Ibid., p. 191, HLG to GM, n.d. March 1807

5. GLG2, p. 242, H to GLG, February 14, 1807

6. Ibid., p. 241, H to GLG, February 14, 1807

7. Ibid., p. 247, Harrowby to GLG, April 3, 1807

8. Ibid., p. 302, H to GLG, October 29, 1807

9. Ibid., p. 253, H to GLG, June 13, 1807

10. Ibid., p. 276, H to GLG, August 28, 1807

11. Ibid., p. 259, H to GLG, June 29, 1807

12. G. Leveson Gower, p. 185, HLG to GM, n.d. March 1807

13. Ibid., p. 190, HLG to GM, n.d. March 1807

14. Ibid., p. 231, HLG to GM, November 1, 1807

15. Royal Archives, Geo.ADD.MSS 3/67, by kind permission of HM The Queen

16. GLG2, p. 292, H to GLG, October 4, 1807

17. Ibid., p. 318, H to GLG, n.d. March or May 1808

18. G. Leveson Gower, p. 189, HLG to GM, n.d. March 1807

19. Ibid., pp. 251–52, HLG to GM, November 19, 1807

20. Ibid., pp. 273–74, HLG to GM, December 21, 1807

Twenty-Two. Harryo

1. GLG2, p. 319, H to GLG, August 16, 1808

2. Ibid., p. 320, H to GLG, August 22, 1808

3. Ibid., p. 330, H to GLG, September 27, 1808

4. Ibid., p. 340, H to GLG, October 20, 1808

5. Gronow, *Recollections,* p. 131

6. G. Leveson Gower, p. 329, HLG to Miss Trimmer, October 8, 1809

7. Ibid., p 326, HLG to Hart, September 12, 1809

8. GLG2, p. 346, GLG to H, n.d. September? 1809

9. Bessborough, *Family Circle,* p. 194, Hart to CL, October 11, 1809

10. Ibid., p. 192, CL to Hart, October 11, 1809

11. GLG2, p. 346, H to GLG, n.d. September? 1809

12. G. Leveson Gower, pp. 329–30, HLG to Hart, October 14, 1809

13. Ibid., pp. 328–29, HLG to Miss Trimmer, October 8, 1809

14. GLG2, p. 347, H to GLG, n.d. September 1809

15. G. Leveson Gower, p. 331, HLG to Miss Trimmer, n.d. October 1809

16. Ibid., p. 332, HLG to Miss Trimmer, n.d. October 1809

17. GLG2, p. 348, GLG to H, November 14, 1809

18. Ibid., p. 348, H to GLG, n.d. November 1809

19. Ibid., pp. 348–49, GLG to H, November 17, 1809

20. G. Leveson Gower, p. 335, HLG to Hart, November 16, 1809

21. Chatsworth Archive, 1963, Hart to LS, November 24, 1809

22. Dormer Archive, EF to Augustus Clifford, December 19, 1809

23. Ibid., n.d. December 1809

24. Chatsworth Archive, 1965, CL to Hart, December 27, 1809

25. GLG2, p. 350, GLG to H, December 27, 1809

Twenty-Three. New Perspectives

1. GLG2, pp. 349–50, H to GLG, n.d. 1809–10
2. Ibid., p. 352, H to GLG, January 9, 1810
3. Ibid., p. 352, H to GLG, n.d. January? 1810
4. Ibid., p. 368, H to GLG, September 21, 1810
5. Ibid., p. 360, August 28, 1810
6. Ibid.
7. Askwith, p. 70
8. F. Leveson Gower, p. 2, HLG to Hart
9. Askwith, pp. 69–70
10. Chatsworth Archive, 1991, CL to Hart, October 28, 1810
11. BL, AD75925, H to GS, February 24, 1810
12. Bessborough Papers, f. 277, LS to H, March 6, 1810
13. Douglass, p. 91
14. Ibid., p. 92
15. Bessborough, *Family Circle*, p. 215, LS to H, June 12, 1811
16. Ibid., p. 214, H to GLG, n.d. March 1811
17. GLG2, p. 389, H to GLG, n.d. August 1811
18. Ibid., p. 390
19. Ibid., p. 434, n.d. April 1812
20. Ibid., p. 379, H to GLG, n.d. 1811
21. p. 424, H to GLG, December 21, 1811
22. Ibid., p. 388, H to GLG, n.d. July 1811
23. Ibid., p. 434, note by H, n.d. April 1812

Twenty-Four. Love Is Made of Brittle Stuff

1. Douglass, p. 103
2. Ibid.
3. Dormer Archive, EF's Journal, March/April 1812
4. Douglass, p. 102
5. Eisler, p. 335
6. Blyth, p. 93
7. Bessborough, *Family Circle*, p. 222, LS to H, May 9, 1812
8. F. Leveson Gower, p. 34, HLG to Hart, May 10, 1812
9. Chatsworth Archive, Sixth Duke, 62, HLG to Hart, May 12, 1812
10. Dormer Archive, EF's Journal, March 5, 1811
11. GLG2, p. 443, H to GLG, n.d. 1812
12. Ibid., August 7, 1812
13. *See* Lewis, for a detailed explanation of the multiple causes of the change
14. GLG2, p. 444, GLG to H, August 8, 1812
15. Ibid., p. 447, H to GLG, August 12, 1812
16. Ibid., pp. 447–48, H to GLG, n.d. August 12?, 1812
17. Ibid., p. 448, H to GLG, n.d. August 1812
18. Blyth, pp. 128–29

19. GLG2, p. 448, H to GLG, n.d. August 1812
20. Ibid., p. 449, H to GLG, n.d. August 13?, 1812
21. Ibid., pp. 452–53, CL to LB, n.d.
22. Ibid., p. 452, Frederick Ponsonby to H, p.m. August 21, 1812
23. PRO, 30/29/6/8, H to GLG, n.d. August 1812
24. GLG2, p. 456, H to GLG, n.d. September 1812
25. Ibid., pp. 456–57, H to GLG, September 17, 1812
26. Ibid.
27. Cecil, p. 168
28. Douglass, p. 133
29. Askwith, p. 80
30. PRO, 30/29/6/8, GLG to H
31. Ibid., 30/29/6/8/17, HS to H
32. F. Leveson Gower, p. 40, September 11, 1812
33. PRO, 30/29/6/8, f. 1459, H to GLG
34. Ibid., 30/29/6/8/17
35. Ibid.

TWENTY-FIVE. LADY BLARNEY

1. Marchand, vol. 2, p. 259, Byron to Lady Melbourne, December 21, 1812
2. Marchand, vol. 3, p. 16, Byron to Lady Melbourne, January 22, 1813
3. Ibid., Byron to Lady Melbourne, March 18, 1813
4. Ibid., pp. 40–41, Byron to Lady Melbourne, April 19, 1813
5. Douglass, p. 152
6. Cecil, p. 176
7. Marchand, vol. 3, p. 87, Byron to Lady Melbourne, n.d. August 1813
8. GLG2, p. 499, H to GLG, September 6, 1814
9. Ibid., p. 469, H to GLG, n.d. July 1813
10. BL, AD75925, H to GS, June 23, 1813
11. GLG2, p. 474, H to GLG, August 31, 1813
12. BL, AD75925, H to GS, July 1, 1813
13. Bessborough Papers, Frederick to H, July 19, 1813
14. GLG1, p. 380, H to GLG, December 19, 1802
15. Gronow, *Celebrities,* p. 61
16. Douglass, p. 154
17. GLG2, p. 478, H to GLG, September 29, 1813
18. Ibid., p. 477–78, H to GLG, n.d. 1813
19. Ibid.
20. BL, AD75608, H to LS, December 21, 1813
21. Bessborough Papers, f. 278, LS to H, December 22, 1813
22. Ibid., f. 293, Lavinia to H, December 10, 1813
23. Ibid., December 12, 1813
24. BL, AD75608, H to LS, January 7, 1814
25. Bessborough Papers, f. 278, LS to H, January 16, 1814
26. Ibid., n.d. March 1814

27. Ibid., f. 293, anon, n.d.
28. GLG2, p. 502, H to GLG, n.d. October 1814
29. Ibid., p. 503, H to GLG, November 1, 1814
30. BL, AD75925, H to GS, January 21, 1815
31. GLG2, p. 517, H to GLG, December 29, 1814
32. Ibid., p. 518, H to GLG, January 4, 1815
33. Ibid., February 23, 1815
34. Ibid., February 23, 1815
35. Ibid., p. 520, H to GLG, March 24, 1815
36. Ibid., p. 525, H to GLG, March 8, 1815
37. Ibid., p. 531, H to EF, April 22, 1815
38. Ibid., p. 530, H to GLG, April 6, 1815
39. Ibid., p. 535, H to GLG, May 12, 1815
40. Ibid., July 13, 1815

Twenty-Six. Turmoil

1. Bessborough, *Family Circle,* p. 242, FP to H, n.d.
2. Ibid., p. 243
3. Bessborough Papers, f. 182, WL to Duncannon, July 2, 1815
4. Ibid.
5. Bessborough, *Family Circle,* p. 248, H to Duncannon, July 18, 1815
6. BL, AD45546, ff. 85–6, CL to Lady Melbourne, n.d. July 1815
7. Bessborough, *Family Circle,* p. 250, H to Lady Duncannon, July 20, 1815
8. Ibid., p. 254, H to Lady Duncannon, August 2, 1815
9. Douglass, p. 173
10. Blyth, pp. 172–73
11. Bessborough, *Family Circle,* Duke of Wellington to CL, April 19, 1816
12. BL, AD45546, f. 90, CL to Lady Melbourne, n.d. April/May 1816
13. Douglass, p. 180
14. BL, AD75925, H to GS, April 10, 1816
15. Douglass, pp. 182–83
16. Ibid., p. 184
17. BL, AD45548, f. 141, Emily Cowper to Lady Melbourne, n.d.
18. Marchand, vol. 5, p. 131, Byron to Thomas Moore, November 17, 1816
19. BL, AD45546, f. 91, CL to Lady Melbourne, n.d. 1816
20. GLG2, pp. 542–43, CL to GLG, n.d. 1816
21. Bessborough, *Family Circle,* p. 256, H to William Ponsonby, November 20, 1815
22. Broughton, p. 102

Twenty-Seven. The Last Journey

1. Broughton, p. 260
2. Arbuthnot, p. 10, March 14, 1820
3. Ibid., p. 35, August 31, 1820
4. Ibid.

5. GLG2, p. 434, H to GLG, n.d.

6. Bessborough, *Family Circle,* pp. 259–60, H to Hart, December 2, 1819

7. GLG2, p. 549, H to GLG, August 5, 1821

8. Ibid., p. 550, H to GLG, August 26, 1821

9. Ibid., p. 553, H to GLG, November 2, 1821

10. Ibid.

11. Bessborough, *Family Circle,* p. 267, WP to CL, November 12, 1821

12. PRO, 30/29/17/3, HLG to HAS, December 2, 1821

13. Bessborough, *Family Circle,* p. 271, Mrs. Peterson to CL, November 23, 1821

14. GLG2, pp. 554–55, WP to GLG, November 12, 1821

15. Chatsworth Archive, Sixth Duke, 559, WP to CL, November 12, 1821

16. Journal of Henry Edward Fox, p. 88, December 6, 1821

17. Chatsworth Archive, Sixth Duke, 559, WP to CL, November 12, 1821

18. Bessborough, *Family Circle,* p. 272

19. Ibid.

20. Ilchester, *The Journal of the Hon. Henry Edward Fox,* p. 88

21. Bessborough, *Family Circle,* p. 272, Wellington to Duncannon, December 4, 1821

22. Dormer Archive, EF's Journal, December 3, 1821

23. Arbuthnot, pp. 128–29, December 1, 1821

24. PRO, 30/29/17/3, HLG to HAS, December 2, 1821

25. As previously noted, he was now Sixth Duke of Devonshire, but the family continued to know him by his old soubriquet

26. Bessborough, *Family Circle,* p. 274, CL to Duke of Devonshire, December 25, 1821

27. Chatsworth Archive, 586, Duke of Devonshire to EF, December 30, 1821

28. Walpole, *The Last Journals*

Twenty-Eight. Harriet's Legacy

1. Howell-Thomas, p. 1

2. Ponsonby, p. 123

3. Gronow, *Recollections,* pp. 38–39

4. Blyth, p. 214

5. Gronow, *Recollections,* p. 130

6. Askwith, p. 139

7. Ibid., p. 140

8. Gronow, *Recollections and Anecdotes,* pp. 269–70

9. Askwith, pp. 140–41

10. Ibid., p. 141

11. PRO, 30/29/6/12, GS to GLG, January 22, 1836

12. Ibid., HAS to GLG, August 29, 1838

13. Askwith, p. 173

14. G. Leveson Gower, p. xii

BIBLIOGRAPHY

ORIGINAL SOURCES

Althorp Papers
Bessborough Papers
Canning Papers
Chatsworth Archive
Dormer Archive
Granville Papers
Hervey Papers
Holland Papers
Melbourne Papers
Osborne Papers
Portland Papers
Royal Archives, Windsor
Sheffield Archives
Staffordshire and Luton Archive

PUBLISHED SOURCES

Arbuthnot, Mrs., *The Journal of Mrs. Arbuthnot,* ed. F. Bamford, 1950
Ashton, J., *The History of Gambling in England,* 1898
Askwith, Betty E., *Piety and Wit: A Biography of Harriet, Countess Granville,* 1982
Aspinall, A., ed., *Correspondence of George, Prince of Wales,* 1964
Battiscombe, Georgina, *The Spencers of Althorp,* 1984
Bayne-Powell, R., *The English Child in the Eighteenth Century,* 1939
Bell, G. H., ed., *The Hamwood Papers,* 1930
Berry, Mary, *Extracts of Journals and Correspondence,* 1865
Bessborough, Earl of, ed., *Georgiana: Extracts from the Correspondence of,* 1955; *Lady Bessborough and Her Family Circle* (with A. Aspinall), 1940
Bessborough, Earl of, and Clive Aslet, *Enchanted Forest: The Story of Stansted in Sussex,* 1984

Blyth, Henry, *Caro the Fatal Passion: The Life of Lady Caroline Lamb,* 1972

Brewer, John, *The Pleasures of the Imagination: English Culture in the Eighteenth Century,* 1997

Broughton, John Cam Hobhouse, *Recollections of a Long Life,* 1911

Burney, Frances, *The Journals and Letters,* ed. Joyce Hemlow, 1980

Butler, Lady E., *The Hamwood Papers,* 1930

Calder-Marshall, Arthur, *The Two Duchesses,* 1978

Cecil, D., *The Young Melbourne,* 1939

Chapman, Caroline, and Jane Dormer, *Elizabeth & Georgiana,* 2002

Clarke, John, *George III: The Life and Times,* 1972

Coke, Lady Mary, *Letters and Journals,* 1970

Courtais, Georgine de, *Women's Headdress and Hairstyles,* 1973

Creevey, T., *Creevey,* ed. John Gore, 1948

Croly, Revd. George, *George IV: The Personal History,* 1841

D'Arblay, Madame, *Diary and Letters,* ed. C. Barrett, 1905

David, Saul, *Prince of Pleasure,* 1998

Davis, I. M., *The Harlot and the Statesman: The Story of Elizabeth Armistead and Charles James Fox,* 1986

Delaney, Mrs., *Autobiography and Correspondence,* 1862

Derry, John W., *Charles James Fox,* 1972; *Charles, Earl Grey,* 1992

Dolan, Brian, *Ladies of the Grand Tour,* 2001

Douglass, Paul, *Lady Caroline Lamb,* 2004

Dowden, Wilfred S., ed., *The Journal of Thomas Moore,* 1984

Duvall, Edmund, "An Unwritten English Chapter in the History of Swiss Botany" (pamphlet), 1793

Eisler, Benita, *Byron,* 1999

Fawcett, Trevor, *Voices of Eighteenth-Century Bath,* 1995, *Bath Entertain'd,* 1998

Fletcher, Lorainne, *Charlotte Smith: A Critical Biography,* 1998

Foreman, Amanda, *Georgiana, Duchess of Devonshire,* 1998

Foster, Vere, *The Two Duchesses,* 1898

Fraser, Flora, *The Unruly Queen,* 1996

Garlick, K., and A. MacIntyre, eds., *The Diary of Joseph Farington,* 1978 – 98

George, Dorothy M., *Hogarth to Cruikshank: Social Change in Graphic Satire,* 1967

Gerhold, Dorian, *Putney and Roehampton Past,* 1994

Granville, Countess Castalia, ed., *Lord Granville Leveson Gower: Private Correspondence 1781–1821* (two vols), 1916

Gronow, Captain R. H., *Recollections and Anecdotes,* 1863; *Celebrities of London and Paris,* 1865

Hague, William, *William Pitt the Younger,* 2004

Hartcup, A., *Love and Marriage in the Great Country Houses,* 1984

Haslip, Joan, *Lady Hester Stanhope,* 1934

Hibbert, Christopher, *George III,* 1998; *George IV,* 1973

Hickman, Katie, *Courtesans,* 2003

Hill, Georgiana, *History of English Dress,* vol. 2, 1893

Hodge, Jane Aiken, *Passion and Principle,* 1996

Holland, Lady E., *Journal*, 1909

Howell-Thomas, Dorothy, *Duncannon*, 1992

Hudson, Roger, ed., *The Grand Tour*, 1993

Huish, Robert, *Memoirs of George IV*, 1830

Ilchester, Earl of, ed., *The Journal of the Hon. Henry Edward Fox*, 1923; *The Home of the Hollands*, 1937

Kelly, Linda, *Richard Brinsley Sheridan*, 1997

Lane, Maggie, *A City of Palaces: Bath Through the Eyes of Fanny Burney*, 1999

LeFanu, William, ed., *Betsy Sheridan's Journal*, 1960

Leveson Gower, F., ed., *Letters of Harriet, Countess Granville 1810–1845*, 1894

Leveson Gower, Sir George, *Harry-O: The Letters of Lady Harriet Cavendish*, 1940

Leveson Gower, Iris, *The Face Without a Frown*, 1944

Lewis, Judith, S., *Sacred to Female Patriotism: Gender, Class and Politics in Late Georgian Britain*, 2003

Marchand, L. A., ed., *Byron's Letters and Journals*, 1974

Mayne, Ethel, *A Regency Chapter: Lady Bessborough and Her Friendships*, 1939

McCreery, Cindy, *The Satirical Gaze: Prints of Women in Late Eighteenth-Century England*, 2004

Melbourne, Viscount, *Memoirs*, 1878

Melville, Lewis, ed., *The Berry Papers*, 1914

Mickhail, E. H., ed., *Sheridan Interviews and Recollections*, 1989

Milward, Richard, *Wimbledon Past*, 1998

Moritz, Carl Philip, *Journeys of a German in England in 1782*, 1965; *Travels in England in 1782*, 1924

Murray, Venetia, *High Society in the Regency Period*, 1998

Perkin, J., *Women and Marriage in Nineteenth-Century England*, 1989

Ponsonby, Major-General Sir John, *The Ponsonby Family*, 1929

Porter, Roy, *Bodies Politic*, 2001; *Patients and Practitioners*, 1985

Powell, David, *Charles James Fox, Man of the People*, 1989

Price, Cecil, ed., *The Letters of Richard Brinsley Sheridan*, 1966

Priestley, J. B., *The Prince of Pleasure*, 1969

Sadler, M.T.H., *The Political Career of Richard Brinsley Sheridan*, 1912

Sichel, Walter, *Sheridan*, 1909

Smith, Charlotte, *Collected Letters*, ed. Judith Phillips Stanton, 2003; *Elegiac Sonnets and Other Poems*, 1797

Smith, J. T., *Nollekens and His Times*, 1949

Spencer, Charles, *The Spencer Family*, 1999

Spencer, H. R., *The History of British Midwifery from 1650–1800*, 1927

Stone, Lawrence, *Road to Divorce*, 1990

Stuart, Dorothy Margaret, *Dearest Bess: The Life and Times of Lady Elizabeth Foster*, 1955

Thomson, S., *Health Resorts of Britain*, 1860

Tillyard, Stella, *Aristocrats*, 1994

Tomalin, Claire, *Mrs. Jordan's Profession*, 1994

Toynbee, Paget, ed., *The Letters of Horace Walpole: Fourth Earl of Orford*, 1967

Turner, E. S., *Taking the Cure*, 1967

Vickery, A., *The Gentleman's Daughter,* 2003
Walpole, H., *The Last Journals,* 1910
Weinreb, Ben, and Christopher Hibbert, *The London Encyclopedia,* 1983
Willett Cunnington, P., *The History of Underclothes,* 1951; *Handbook of English Costume in the Eighteenth Century* (with C. Willet Cunnington), 1972
Wraxall, Sir N., *Posthumous Memoirs,* 1836

ILLUSTRATION CREDITS

FRONTISPIECE (PAGE XX): HARRIET'S BOOKPLATE
BY GIOVANNI BATTISTA CIPRIANI.

FIRST COLOR INSERT

Portrait of Harriet with her two sons, John and Frederick, by John Hoppner: Stansted Park Foundation, Rowlands Castle, Hampshire.

Portrait of Margaret Georgiana, Countess Spencer, and her daughter Lady Georgiana, afterward Duchess of Devonshire, by Sir Joshua Reynolds, 1759: private collection/Peter Willi/The Bridgeman Art Library. Portrait of George John Spencer, Viscount Althorp, later Second Earl Spencer, by Sir Joshua Reynolds, c. 1778: private collection © Philip Mould Historical Portraits Ltd., London/The Bridgeman Art Library. Design for a monument to John, First Earl Spencer, by Giovanni Battista Cipriani, 1783: Sotheby's Picture Library. Postcard of Althorp House: © Popperfoto/Alamy. Marlborough House, Wimbledon: © Wimbledon Society Museum. The Great Room at Spencer House, London: © Massimo Listri/CORBIS. View of Spencer House from Green Park: © Corporation of London.

The Duchess of Devonshire and her Sister, the Countess of Bessborough by Thomas Rowlandson: © Yale Center for British Art, Paul Mellon Collection/The Bridgeman Art Library. *A Gaming Table at Devonshire House* by Thomas Rowlandson, 1791: Sotheby's Picture Library. *Vauxhall Gardens* from Ackermann's "Microcosm of London" by Thomas Rowlandson, 1809: Victoria & Albert Museum, London/The Bridgeman Art Library.

Parkstead House, Roehampton: © Roger Ford/fotoLibra. Portrait of William Ponsonby in Turkish dress, studio of Liotard: Sotheby's Picture Library. Portrait of Frederick, Viscount Duncannon, by a follower of Sir Joshua Reynolds: Christie's Images. Miniature of Lady Caroline Lamb as a two-year-old child by Richard Cosway, 1787: photo Bonhams. Portraits of Lady Georgiana Cavendish and Lady Henrietta Cavendish by Elizabeth Royal: © The Devonshire Collection, Chatsworth, reproduced by Permission of the Chatsworth Settlement Trustees. *The Two Duchesses of Devonshire* by John Downman: © NTPL/Christopher Hurst. Portrait of Lavinia, Countess Spencer, and her eldest son, Lord Althorp, by Sir Joshua Reynolds: courtesy of the Huntington Library, Art Collections and Botanical Gardens, San Marino, California.

The Westminster Election of 1788 by Robert Dighton: © Museum of London. Portrait of Richard Brinsley Sheridan by John Hoppner: Hermitage, St. Petersburg, Russia/ RIA Novosti/The Bridgeman Art Library. *The Gower Children* by George Romney: © Abbot Hall Art Gallery, Kendal, Cumbria/The Bridgeman Art Library.

SECOND COLOR INSERT

Portrait of Lord Granville Leveson Gower, later First Earl Granville, by Sir Thomas Lawrence, c. 1804–6: © Yale Center for British Art, Paul Mellon Collection/The Bridgeman Art Library.

The Chairing of Fox: Stansted Park Foundation, Rowlands Castle, Hampshire. *Charles James Fox Addressing the House of Commons During the Pitt Ministry* by Anton Hickel: Houses of Parliament, Westminster, London, UK/The Bridgeman Art Library. Portrait of William Pitt the Younger by John Hoppner: © South African National Gallery, Cape Town, South Africa/The Bridgeman Art Library. Portrait of George IV by Sir Thomas Lawrence, c. 1814: National Portrait Gallery, London.

View of the great eruption of Vesuvius from the mole of Naples in the night of October 20, 1767, plate 6 from *Campi Phlegraei: Observations on the Volcanoes of the Two Sicilies* by Sir William Hamilton, 1776: © Lambeth Palace Library, London/The Bridgeman Art Library. *La Place des Victoires, Paris* by Thomas Rowlandson, c. 1789: © Yale Center for British Art, Paul Mellon Collection/The Bridgeman Art Library. "The King's Bath," plate 7 from *The Comforts of Bath* engraved by Thomas Rowlandson, 1798: © Victoria Art Gallery, Bath and North East Somerset Council/The Bridgeman Art Library. Early twentieth-century photo of Bessborough House, County Kilkenny. Seaside resort with pier and bathing machines, possibly Margate: British Library, London/The Bridgeman Art Library.

Portrait of Lady Georgiana Spencer by Thomas Gainsborough: © The Devonshire Collection, Chatsworth, reproduced by permission of the Chatsworth Settlement Trustees. Frederick, Third Earl of Bessborough, by John Russell: Stansted Park Foundation, Rowlands Castle, Hampshire. Portrait of Harriet by Angelica Kauffmann, 1793: Stansted Park Foundation, Rowlands Castle, Hampshire. Portrait of Sir Frederick Ponsonby by T. Heaphy, 1813–14: National Portrait Gallery, London. Portrait of Lady Caroline Lamb by Sir Thomas Lawrence, c. 1813: © Bristol City Museum and Art Gallery/The Bridgeman Art Library. Portrait of Lord Byron by Théodore Gericault: Musée Fabre, Montpellier/Giraudon/The Bridgeman Art Library. Portrait of the Hon. William Lamb, Second Viscount Melbourne, by Sir Thomas Lawrence: Sotheby's Picture Library.

Portrait of Granville Leveson Gower and his family by Thomas Phillips: private collection/© Bonhams, London/The Bridgeman Art Library.

Acknowledgments

My interest in Harriet was first sparked when I read Amanda Foreman's inspirational biography of Georgiana, Duchess of Devonshire, which is an important source for many sections in this book. There was much overlap in the two sisters' lives and Amanda Foreman's exhaustive research into Georgiana's life greatly helped my research by leading me to source material with little effort and by explaining the complexities of the sisters' lives. Without her groundbreaking work my own task would have been far more time consuming, and I am grateful for her interest and encouragement from the earliest days of this project. I am also grateful to Lord Bessborough for allowing me access to his family's archive, and to the Hon. Jane Glennie, who not only allowed me access to the Dormer Archive and to read Bess's journals and letters relating to Harriet, but who also kindly read and made comments on the manuscript. Thank you also to: Andrew Peppitt, archivist at Chatsworth, who was similarly generous with help and advice, and who read the manuscript and made several useful suggestions; Peter Wilkinson, archivist at Chichester Records Office, who traveled to and fro with the necessary Bessborough folders; John Cunningham, cataloger of the library at Stansted House, who spent a morning taking me through Lord Bessborough's collection of prints and watercolors; and Tracey Earl, archivist at Coutts, who painstakingly copied out records of Harriet's bank accounts. For encouragement, advice, and expert help I am grateful to readers Stephen Pratt, Julian Fellowes, and Caroline Chapman, and also to Lucy Butler; John Pile; Pamela Clark, registrar of the Royal Archive Windsor; Laura Klein, archivist at the

Bieneke Library Yale; Graham Snell, Secretary of Brooks's; and the information service at the House of Commons. My thanks also to my editorial coordinator, Vivien Garrett, and to Kate Samano, who polished the text valiantly, and to the unfailingly helpful staff at the London Library, the British Library Manuscripts Collection, the Public Records Office at Kew and Chichester, the National Portrait Gallery Archive, the British Musuem Print Room, and the London Archives. I owe a large debt of gratitude to the Earl and Countess Granville, who tried their best to help me locate the missing letters Harriet wrote to Granville—it was disappointing not to find the letters in the safe-deposit box, but thank you for letting me look. Last, but most important, words cannot express my gratitude for the unfailing support and enthusiasm of my agent, Christopher Little, and my publisher, Sally Gaminara, at Transworld.

For the American edition, I thank my editor, Allison McCabe, and the team at Crown.

INDEX

ABOUT THE AUTHOR

JANET GLEESON studied English and art history at Notting-
ham University. She is the author of *The Arcanum*, a #1 *Sunday
Times* bestseller in the U.K., and *The Moneymaker*, which was
published in the United States as *The Millionaire*. She lives in
Dorset with her husband, three children, and two dogs.